Revision Symbols

ab	Abbreviations	
ad	Adjec...	
agr	Sub...	34a–c
amb	Amb...	
ap	Apo...	
awk	Awk...	
cap	Capi...	89
con	Concreteness	7a
cs	Comma Splice	56d
cx	Unnecessary Comma	9a, 75f
d	Diction	93–95
di	Dangling Infinitive	41a
dial	Dialect	91
dp	Dangling Participle	53a
frag	Sentence Fragment	60
fv	Feature Violation	15a
gl	Glossary of Usage	96
inc	Incomplete Comparison	56a
ital	Italics	87
j	Jargon	93b
log	Logic	97a–c
m	Mechanics and Manuscript Form	70–73
mm	Misplaced Modifier	44c
neg	Double Negative	23a
plan	Planning and Writing the Paper	100–104
pv	Point of View	65
red	Redundancy	6a, 46a
ref	Pronoun Reference	8a, 31–33
sp	Spelling and Hyphenation	Consult your dictionary
sub	Subordination	51b, 52a
t	Tense and Mode	17–20
var	Variety	57–59
w	Wordiness	94e
[ ]	Brackets	84
○	Colon	77
⊙	Comma	75
—	Dash	82
!	Exclamation Point	80
∧	Omission of Necessary Word(s)	
¶	Paragraph	103a
No ¶	No Paragraph	
//	Parallelism	54–55
( )	Parentheses	83
○	Period	78
?	Question Mark	79
⊙	Quotation Marks	85
⊙	Semicolon	76

D0142904

HANDBOOK OF CONTEMPORARY ENGLISH

Handbook
of
Contemporary
English

WALTER E. MEYERS
North Carolina State University

HARCOURT BRACE JOVANOVICH, INC.
New York   Chicago   San Francisco   Atlanta

ISBN: 0-15-530848-3

Library of Congress Catalog Card Number: 73-15038

Printed in the United States of America

The author and publisher are grateful to the copyright holders for permission to reprint material on the following pages:

133: I.P.C. Newspapers, Ltd., and Publishers-Hall Syndicate
384: © King Features Syndicate 1973
385: Copyright, 1973, Universal Press Syndicate
414: From *Webster's New Collegiate Dictionary* © 1973 by G. & C. Merriam Co., Publishers of the Merriam-Webster Dictionaries
416: From *Webster's Third New International Dictionary* © 1971 by G. & C. Merriam Co., Publishers of the Merriam-Webster Dictionaries
417: From *The Oxford English Dictionary*, The Clarendon Press, Oxford

Preface

The most important assumption this handbook makes is that students have a natural interest in language, an interest that can be increased if language is approached as a continent to be explored, not a back yard of mistakes to be weeded out. It also assumes that language can always yield new insights and that new facts about it can always be discovered. In the last twenty years, the work of the transformational-generative theorists has brought about an unprecedented reawakening of interest in grammar, and it is their approach that has been adapted for the grammar section of this handbook. This approach includes many of the virtues of traditional grammar—nouns are called nouns, verbs are called verbs—while avoiding the difficulties and ambiguities inherent in a system that has remained static for hundreds of years.

Using the Handbook This handbook is designed for two kinds of freshman composition classes. For the class in which a detailed study of grammar is included, the handbook provides a simplified but systematic transformational grammar. For the class in which the grammar section is needed only for reference, the handbook will serve as a rhetoric and a guide for the correction of student papers. For both these classes, the intent throughout the handbook is to provide help for specific writing problems. Its aim—like the aim of the freshman composition course—is not to produce linguists, but to produce student writing that is clear, well organized, and concise.

The Grammar and Composition The mechanical details of the transformational system—the phrase structure rules and the few transformations explicitly stated—are included not as exercises in rote memorization, but as guides to the formation of grammatical constructions and the variety of ways in which students can re-arrange the parts of sentences. The emphasis is always on what the transformations can do, not on *how* they do it.

Many students will be unfamiliar with transformational grammar, so the instructor who wishes to use the grammar of this handbook only for reference should be sure that the class is thoroughly familiar with the introduction (pages 4 to 22) by discussing the material and working through the exercises with the students. The class should then be readily able to use the grammar itself for reference. Cross-references have been generously supplied in the text as reminders of particular terms and procedures.

The forty-five Applications in the grammar deal with specific com-position problems; they are distinguished from the more general sections by their letter suffixes—8*a*, 32*b*, and so on. Although the endpapers provide a list of symbols for those instructors who wish to use them, the simplest way to mark papers for revision is to use the number and letter of the relevant Application, each of which is relatively short and direct. Section 9a, for example, discusses the placement of commas within a noun phrase; any student who needs more help than that Application provides can then turn to Section 9, which deals in more detail with the structure of adjectives within the noun phrase.

The Rhetoric and Composition   The rhetoric opens with an analy-sis of the act of communication—who is the writer? who is the audience? what is the message? what is the purpose of the mes-sage? This analysis is designed to help students write what they want to write in the way they want to write it by showing them how intimately such topics as logical thinking and stylistic considerations are related in the writing process. Throughout the rhetoric, as well as the grammar, the examples and exercises draw on the work of contemporary writers to show how the language is actually being used in our own day and our own culture.

Usage and Dialect   The sources for the usage comments, listed on pages 385 and 386, are the most comprehensive and recent studies available. These sources are cited within each entry in the Glossary of Usage, and no attempt is made to ignore any legitimate division of usage. Many of the comments deal with correcting what might be called the ''folklore'' of usage. Similarly, the sources for the information in the dialect sections—which include an objective discussion of some aspects of Black English—are cited within each section.

Sample Papers   The handbook contains two sample papers that illustrate each of the two systems of documentation discussed. One paper is in accordance with the system of *The MLA Style Sheet;* the other shows the "name and year" system of the natural and social sciences. Students are thus given the opportunity to familiarize themselves with the system used in their own major disciplines.

Instructor's Manual   An Instructor's Manual is available for this handbook. It contains suggestions for using the handbook; a rationale for the adaptation of transformational grammar to composition; a summary of the grammar, explaining and exemplifying all the phrase structure rules and transformations contained in the text; answers to all the exercises in which a specific solution is called for; and suggestions for further reading.

Acknowledgments   My debt to transformational theorists is apparent on every page. I accept full responsibility for any deficiencies in my adaptation of their ideas, of course, and I am happy to share any praise with those colleagues who have contributed to the improvement of the manuscript at its various stages; among them are Boyd Davis (University of North Carolina at Charlotte), Robert M. Gorrell (University of Nevada at Reno), Richard H. Hendrickson (California State College at Sonoma), Roderick A. Jacobs (University of California at San Diego), Charlton G. Laird (University of Nevada at Reno), Horace T. McDonald (Northern Virginia Community College), Jean G. Pival (University of Kentucky), and Stanley Schatt (University of Houston). Special thanks are due to James A. Kilby and Deborah W. Siegfried, who consented to test the book in their freshman composition classes at North Carolina State University, and to Brenda Jones, a former student at North Carolina State, for her help with the research sections. I am grateful to the many congenial and knowledgeable people at Harcourt Brace Jovanovich who have provided as much help and encouragement as I am capable of receiving; they include Natalie Bowen, Ronald Campbell, Geri Davis, Susan Joseph, and Eben W. Ludlow. Like guardian angels, they have protected me time and again from my own excesses.

Finally, to my wife, Julia Reed Meyers, and to my children go my deepest thanks for contributing generously of their share of me to the preparation of this book.

WALTER E. MEYERS

Contents

Preface

A Grammar of English

An Introduction to Transformational Grammar

Nouns and Noun Phrases

Subordination

Conjunctions and Compounds

Sentence Variety

A Practical Rhetoric

About Communication

Addresser: The Writer

CONTENTS

Addressee: The Reader

Channel: The Mechanics

Channel: Punctuation

Code: The Language

Context: The Background and Research

A Grammar of English

An Introduction
to
Transformational
Grammar

STRUCTURE IN LANGUAGE

To form an analogy of the way language works, think back to the time when your grade-school teachers first showed you how to do something like this:

$$\begin{array}{r} 15 \\ +37 \\ \hline 52 \end{array}$$

Before you could work a problem in addition, you had to learn some very basic items and processes: you learned first of all a small set of elements: 0, 1, 2, 3, 4, 5, 6, 7, 8, 9; you also learned that the value of these elements depended in part on their positions: a number appearing in a given column counted ten times the value of the same number in the next column to the right. We might call this relationship the ''structure'' of numbers. Perhaps you inferred the relationship from the names of the columns (the units column, the tens column, the hundreds column, and so on), but the principle was the same for *any* two adjacent columns. You learned a few rules for adding the numbers in the basic set—for example, $3 + 4 = 7$. Further, you learned what to do with more complicated totals that added up to more than nine: you ''carried'' a digit to the next column on the left. What you learned was, in fact, a simple grammar of addition.

You learned a finite set of basic elements. You learned that when these elements appeared in a line (for example, 1,577,368), their ordering was important—that the line had internal structure. And you learned a finite set of rules for producing or interpreting these structures. Yet from the set of elements and the set of rules, you gained the ability to work *any* problem of addition. In other words, the system of addition (the elements and the rules for combining them) ''generates'' answers to an infinite number of problems. ''Generate'' here means something like ''have the capability of producing.'' The system derives infinite results from finite means.

Now this sounds very much like what happens when we use language. Although we have a finite number of words, and our minds are obviously finite, every day we produce without effort sentences we have neither spoken nor heard before. If we can produce and understand a theoretically infinite number of sentences, then we are getting infinite results from finite means. What we can aim at in writing a grammar, then, is the production of a set of instructions. These instructions will tell us how the elements of language go together, in the same way that the rules of addition tell us how numbers go together. We would like our set of instructions to generate all the grammatical sentences of English and none of the ungrammatical ones. We can judge how well the grammar works by examining the sentences it produces, and deciding whether adult, native speakers would judge the results to be normal English sentences.

But if language and addition are similar in some respects, they are certainly different in others. To begin with, although we can completely describe what is necessary for addition, we cannot completely describe what is necessary to produce all English sentences. There is no complete grammar of any natural language. How humans produce and understand sentences is in many respects unknown, and most of what is known is controversial. What follows, then, is just a theory about English, a theory to be used only so long as it explains the facts we observe: a theory to be modified or replaced by a better one when we better understand those facts.

LEVELS IN LANGUAGE

We talked about the relation between the columns in the system of addition as the structure of a string of digits. In our decimal system, there is just one way to write the number *three hundred forty-seven* in figures: you cannot write it 743, or 374, or 437; you have to write it 347. In other words, the order of the elements makes a difference. In this sense, language has structure, too. Sentences are put together only in certain ways. Take this sentence, for example:

His aunts are expert in cellular biology.

How do we know what this sentence means? It cannot be that we know the meaning of each individual word, add them all up, and get the meaning of the sentence—if that explanation were sufficient, we could put the words together in any order and the sentence would mean the same thing. But if we rearrange the words, say, alphabetically, we certainly do not have a sentence:

*Are aunts biology cellular expert his in.[1]

Sentences have structure: the words must be ordered in specific ways if the sentence is to qualify as English and grammatical.

Notice too that there are connections among the words of the sentence. Suppose we add an *s* to one of the words—the meaning of the sentence as a whole changes slightly, but the sentence is still grammatically acceptable:

His aunts are experts in cellular biology.

The order of the words and the connections among some of those words are part of what we know about the structure of sentences.

Consider the number 347 again. We know, because of the positions of the figures, that this symbol stands for three hundreds, four tens, and seven units; the positions are part of the information we use to interpret the symbol. Now suppose we say that *his aunts* and *cellular biology* are both noun phrases. One of the connections we spoke of a few sentences above is, of course, number agreement between subject and verb. We know that the verb *are* is plural, agreeing with the noun phrase *his aunts* rather than with the noun phrase *cellular biology*. We know that *his aunts* is the subject, rather than *cellular biology*, because it is the first noun phrase in the sentence, and we know that in sentences like this, the subject noun phrase comes first. In other words, the position of the noun phrase is part of the information we use to interpret this sentence, and that position is part of the structure.

But notice that some sentences mean more than they seem to say:

His aunts are expert in cellular biology.

---

[1]The asterisk (*) before a sentence in this book marks that sentence as ungrammatical. Many of the sentences so marked will be grossly deviant (like the one above), and would be rejected by any speaker of English; others would be ungrammatical only in some dialects of English. The question of what is or is not "grammatical" requires too much space to be handled in a footnote; for a more extensive discussion, see the part titled "Code: The Language."

We can pretty well account for our understanding of this sentence just by examining what is printed on the page—the words and their relationships. What about sentences like the following, though?

1a   Close the door.
2a   Only the brave deserve the fair.
3a   Tormenting Billy pleased Claggart.

The words actually present do not fully account for the way we understand these sentences. Don't we rather interpret them as meaning something like this?

1b   (You will) close the door.
2b   Only the brave (ones) deserve the fair (ones).
3b   (Claggart's) tormenting Billy pleased Claggart.

Note that *Close the door,* representing the kind of sentence traditionally called "imperative," has no subject as it appears on the page. We need then to explain just how it is that we all do in fact interpret it as if *you* were understood. Do we have any evidence that, at some stage in the production of this sentence, the word *you* was present, and later on was removed?

To start with, we might note how sentences with a reflexive pronoun behave:

I outsmarted myself.
You outsmarted yourself.
She outsmarted herself.
We outsmarted ourselves.
They outsmarted themselves.

We begin by pointing out the obvious: in each sentence, there is a certain agreement between the subject and the reflexive pronoun; if the subject is first person, so is the reflexive pronoun; if the subject is second person, so is the reflexive pronoun; and so on. But the only reflexive pronoun we can add to our ostensibly "subjectless" sentences is *yourself,* the second person pronoun:

Close the door yourself.
Improve yourself.
Familiarize yourself with these codes.

7

Here then is evidence that at some level of analysis, *you* must be postulated as the subject of imperative sentences.

Another argument involves what are called "tag-questions." Tag-questions are the structures to the right of the commas in the following sentences:

> I should get up now, shouldn't I?
> He will do whatever he's told, won't he?
> You can lend me five dollars, can't you?

Notice that the subject of the sentence and the auxiliary (*should, will, can*) are repeated in the tag-question. But the tag-questions that appear with our imperatives are

> Close the door, won't you? (or will you?)
> Improve yourself, won't you?

Both the reflexive pronouns and the tag-questions show that the subject of imperative sentences can only have been *you* at some stage in their derivation.

As a second example, reconsider the sentence

> Only the brave deserve the fair.

How do we know that some word like *ones* occurred at some step in the derivation of this sentence? Remember that our grammar should explain the form of the sentence and account for the way we understand it. One strong argument in favor of saying that *only the brave* derives from *only the brave ones* is the form of the verb in the sentence: *deserve*. Compare these two sentences:

> Those men deserve something better.
> That man deserves something better.

The first has the plural subject *those men,* with the verb in the form *deserve.* The second, with the singular *that man,* has the verb form *deserves.* But observe that in the sentence *Only the brave deserve the fair,* the verb form is the same as that of the first sentence above—plural. If we limit our attention to the words as they appear, to the surface structure, there is no way to explain why the verb has the plural form. So we make this hypothesis: at an early stage in the production of this sentence, it had the form *Only the brave ones*. . . . At a subsequent stage, the verb form *deserve* was chosen to agree with the plural subject *ones*. The sentence would then have had the form it had in 2b:

> **Only the brave ones deserve the fair ones.**

At a still later stage, words like *ones* may be removed in some cases, giving us 2a, the surface structure of the sentence.

As a final example of the difference between surface structure and deep structure, consider this sentence:

> **Claggart tormented Billy.**

If someone asked, "Who tormented Billy?" your answer would be "Claggart." If you were then asked how you knew this, you might answer that *Claggart* is the subject of the verb *tormented*. But let us repeat sentence 3a:

> **Tormenting Billy pleased Claggart.**

Now if you were asked, "Who tormented Billy?" your answer would again be "Claggart," but this time, what would you reply to the question "How do you know?" In the surface structure of sentence 3a, the way the sentence reads on the page, the gerund *tormenting* has no subject. In a traditional grammatical system, it might be impossible for us to assert that gerunds *can* have subjects. But suppose we say that on a deeper level, one more closely expressive of the meaning of the sentence, sentence 3a is made of two constructions, one inside (or "embedded in") the other:

> **[Claggart tormented Billy] pleased Claggart.**

To reach the surface structure of the sentence (3a), two changes take place, among others. The first change converts the structure to something like

> **Claggart's tormenting Billy pleased Claggart.**

And the second deletes the first word, giving us the sentence as it stands.

The sentence as it is written or spoken is organized by the "surface structure." It seems that we understand surface structures because we know two things: we know all the meaningful elements as they are organized by the "deep structure" (even though all the elements may not appear on the surface), and we know the changes necessary to convert the deep structure to the surface structure. The exact nature of deep structure is a matter of controversy among language investigators. At the deepest level, it may turn out that the organization of language is unlike anything in this book. If that is the case, the grammar that this book assumes is simply that of an intermediate level. But since important insights are yielded, our analysis will have value no matter how "deep" our deep structure is.

THE PHRASE STRUCTURE RULES

Think of a grammar as a machine for producing sentences; a sentence begins in a part of the machine, the base, that consists of a short list of rules, called "phrase structure rules." The base produces the deep structure of the sentence. From this deep structure we derive the meaning of the sentence. A second part of the machine, the "transformational component," then acts on the deep structures produced by the base. The transformational component is also a list of rules, but much longer than the base list. As each rule, or "transformation," is applied to a deep structure, an intermediate structure results. When the last transformation has been applied, we have the surface structure. The sound of the sentence is determined by the surface structure. Notice that we get from the meaning of the sentence to its form by means of the transformations. Transformations can therefore be regarded as devices for connecting form and meaning, the devices through which we interpret the sentences we see and hear.

The base, it was said, consists of a small number of rules. The form and number of these rules are the subject of much theoretical controversy at the present, but the following rules will serve as examples:

1   Sentence → Noun Phrase + Verb Phrase
2   Verb Phrase → Auxiliary + Main Verb
3   Main Verb → Verb + (Noun Phrase) + (Preposition + Noun Phrase)
4   Auxiliary → Tense + (Modal)
5   Noun Phrase → (Determiner) + Noun

There are only two unfamiliar elements in the rules: the arrows may be read as "consists of"—that is, rule 1 may be read, "A sentence consists of a noun phrase and a verb phrase." The other element used with a special meaning is the parenthesis. Parentheses enclose optional elements that can be selected or omitted at will; rule 5, therefore, could be read, "A noun phrase consists of a determiner plus a noun, or just a noun alone."

More often, the rules are written in an abbreviated form, like this:

1 $S \rightarrow NP + VP$
2 $VP \rightarrow AUX + MV$
3 $MV \rightarrow V + (NP) + (PREP + NP)$
4 $AUX \rightarrow T + (MODAL)$
5 $NP \rightarrow (DET) + N$

The production of a sentence begins with rule 1, and each of the successive rules is applied as many times as necessary. Starting with rule 1 and putting the symbol S at the top of the diagram, we show that this sentence-to-be is composed of two parts, a noun phrase and a verb phrase, like this:

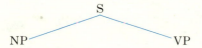

Rule 2 specifies that a verb phrase has two parts, an auxiliary and a main verb. We therefore expand our diagram to show this development:

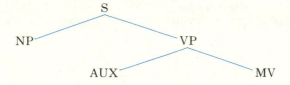

We are developing structures, structures that by the choice of their different options will describe the relationship of the parts of English sentences to one another. Of course, we do not have a sentence yet, and will not until we have finished with the phrase structure rules and have attached words to our structure. To show how the choices built into the phrase structure rules affect what we end up with,

11

look at rule 3. It states that the main verb will consist of a verb followed by one or two optional noun phrases. If the second noun phrase is selected, it will be preceded by a preposition. Suppose we skip the second noun phrase and use rule 3 to rewrite the main verb as a verb and one noun phrase:

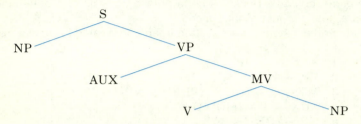

Rule 4 rewrites the auxiliary as a tense indicator and an optional modal (for example, *may, must, can, shall, will*). If we select the modal, we will have a structure that looks like this:

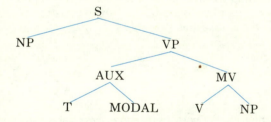

Finally, rule 5 rewrites the noun phrase as an optional determiner (for example, *the, a, this*) and a noun. Note that rule 5 will apply twice to our structure, once to the noun phrase produced by rule 1, and once to the noun phrase produced by rule 3. Suppose we omit the determiner in the first noun phrase, and select it for the second:

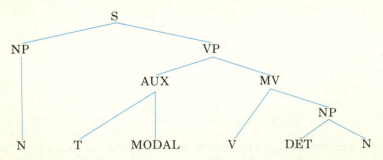

Words will be attached to each of the final symbols except tense, which will be either PAST-& or PRESENT-&.[2] The whole diagram might look like this, then:

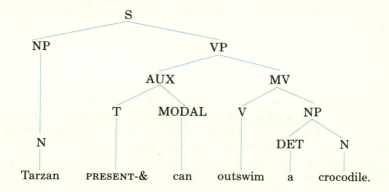

The ampersand (&) after PAST or PRESENT indicates that the tense marker is to be joined to the next element to the right. In the example above, for instance, if a modal had not been chosen, PRESENT-& would be next to *outswim*. Combining PRESENT-& and *outswim* would give us *outswims* in the surface structure. Had we chosen PAST-& as tense, joining that tense marker to *outswim* would, of course, give us *outswam*.

Because the rules of the base are limited, the deep structures they produce are very simple. Variety and complexity will be introduced to the surface structures of sentences by transformations.

TRANSFORMATIONS

We do some surprising things when we interpret sentences. Although we may never have seen this sentence before

    1a   There are footprints in the lunar dust now.

we realize immediately that it is synonymous with this sentence:

    1b   Footprints are in the lunar dust now.

---

[2] If you are wondering about "future tense," see Section 17.

How can we account for our perception that the two sentences have the same meaning? The theory of transformational grammar argues that sentences with the same meaning have the same deep structure. If this is true, then the two sentences above have the same structure at some level of understanding. But the surface structures of the two obviously differ. We can, though, describe the relationship between the structures, and see if we can precisely define the difference.

Sentence 1b has a noun phrase consisting of the single noun *footprints* as its subject; the verb is a form of *be;* a group of words, *in the lunar dust,* tells us the location of the subject; and finally, the word *now* describes the time. We have first to decide whether the sentence needs all these parts to be grammatical, or whether some of them may be there optionally. We can test the necessity of each part by omitting it from the sentence and seeing what we get:

1c * Are in the lunar dust now. (subject noun phrase omitted)

1d * Footprints in the lunar dust now. (*be* omitted)

1e * Footprints are now. (specification of place omitted)

1f Footprints are in the lunar dust. (specification of time omitted)

It is clear from our test that this kind of sentence must have a subject noun phrase, some form of the verb *be,* and a phrase specifying place to be grammatical. On the other hand, sentence 1f—grammatical even though *now* has been removed—shows us that a specification of time might be there or might not: it is not needed for the sentence to be grammatical. We can therefore abstract the structure of the sentence like this:

Footprints	are	in the lunar dust	now.
NP	be	place	X

The symbol *be* will stand for any form of the verb *be; X* in the formula is a variable ranging over any structure that occurs to the right of *place.* Now if we abstract the structure of sentence 1a in the same way, we get

There	are	footprints	in the lunar dust	now.
	be	NP	place	X

If we now contrast the different structures, we get

NP   be   place   (X)   =   There   be   NP   place   (X)

The description of the syntax of the two sentences that we have analyzed does more than tell the difference between the two; we now have a guideline for converting one structure into the other. We have, in fact, isolated a transformation. As a base for our operation, we take sentence 1b since, with a few modifications, we could produce it with our phrase structure rules. We then perform the changes indicated by the transformation, and we have produced, not just a new sentence, but a new *kind* of sentence, because the rule will hold good for all sentences that meet the structural requirements on the left-hand side of the description. Instead of the equals sign, it is customary to show a double arrow pointing from the base structure to the new structure produced:

Half a million men   are   in Cuba   with wives.   ⇒
          NP   be   place   X

There   are   half a million men   in Cuba   with wives.
          be   NP   place   X

ARTHUR KOPIT

A veil   was   upon you,   Pocahontas, bride.   ⇒
  NP   be   place   X

There   was   a veil   upon you,   Pocahontas, bride.
          be   NP   place   X

HART CRANE

This transformation (for the sake of a name, we might call it the THERE transformation) is optional: we can perform the indicated changes or not, as we please. Other transformations will be obligatory: they must be performed or an ungrammatical sentence will result.

The THERE transformation illustrates two of the general functions served by transformations. It adds an element (*there*) to the structure, and it moves the subject noun phrase to the right of the verb.

15

Transformations will add elements, delete (remove) them, or rearrange them.

The IMPERATIVE transformation serves as an example of a transformation that deletes an element; it also illustrates another fact about transformations in general: some of them have very specific restrictions. The IMPERATIVE transformation changes structures like 2a to structures like 2b:

2a   You PRESENT-& will close the door. ⟹
2b   Close the door.

In the transformation just illustrated, the word *you* (the subject noun phrase), the tense marker PRESENT-&, and the modal *will* were deleted. Obviously, for the transformation to be able to work at all, the original structure must first of all have the three elements that are subsequently deleted. The transformation has a fourth restriction: the verb of the sentence must be marked •action (this last restriction is explained in Section 16).

Finally, as an example of a transformation that rearranges the old elements of the structure and adds some new ones, consider the PASSIVE transformation. The following two sentences are synonymous, and we therefore derive them from the same deep structure:

3a   Gus will play a madrigal.
3b   A madrigal will be played by Gus.

The structure underlying 3a is converted to that of 3b by the PASSIVE transformation. We can perform this change on any sentence containing a transitive verb (see Section 12) marked •action. Suppose 3a to have a deep structure like this:

Gus PRESENT-& will play a madrigal.

If we want the transformation to operate on any structure similar to 3a, we will have to formulate the transformation in general terms, identifying the parts of structures involved rather than particular words. *Gus* could be identified as a noun phrase, but since there are two noun phrases involved in this change, we will have to distinguish them somehow. Consequently, the left one, *Gus,* will be marked NP'. and the right noun phrase, *a madrigal,* will be marked NP''. PRESENT-& and *will* both derive from the auxiliary; we can distinguish them both by AUX. V marked •action specifies the kind

16

of verb needed. Now we can describe the change involved with this formula:

NP′   AUX   V   NP″ (X) $\Rightarrow$
                   • action

NP″   AUX   be   EN-&   V   by   NP′ (X)
                              • action

(Remember, X is a variable covering any structure that may occur in its position.)

Notice that the transformation inserts *be,* EN-& (for "past participle"), and *by;* notice also that the two noun phrases have changed position. If we label the deep structure of sentence 3a with the formula, we get

Gus   PRESENT-& will   play   a madrigal.
                                       $\Rightarrow$
NP′   AUX   V   NP″
                      • action

A madrigal   PRESENT-& will   be   EN-&   play   by Gus.
     NP″   AUX   V   NP′
                            • action

When we connect the tense to the modal, and the past participle marker (EN-&) to the verb, we get

A madrigal   PRESENT-& will   be   EN-& play   by   Gus.

A madrigal   will   be   played   by   Gus.

This transformation, too, is optional. Note that the subject noun phrase of the active voice sentence, 3a, is found in a *by*-phrase, called the "agentive phrase," in the passive counterpart, 3b.

When the agentive phrase contains an indefinite noun phrase (*somebody, someone, anybody, anyone*), the whole agentive phrase can be removed by a transformation called AGENTIVE DELETION. By means of this transformation, sentence 4b can be produced from 4a:

4a   A madrigal will be played by someone.
4b   A madrigal will be played.

EMBEDDED SENTENCES

In some sentences, certain constructions that seem themselves to be much like sentences occur in places where we know noun phrases can occur. Some of these "embedded sentences" occupy the place of the subject of the larger sentence (or "outer" sentence), a place where the phrase structure rules produce a noun phrase:

1a

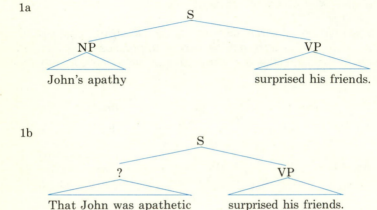

1b

Where structure 1a has a noun phrase, *John's apathy,* structure 1b has the more complex group of words *that John was apathetic.* Similarly, something like a sentence may also occur where a direct object noun phrase may appear. Compare the groups of words that follow the verb *believed* in structures 2a and 2b:

2a

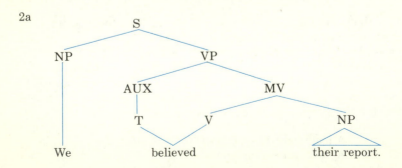

2b

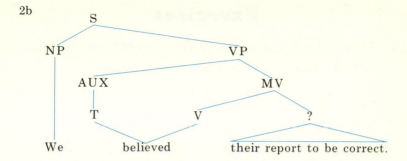

Finally, as in 3a and 3b, a more complex group sometimes occurs following a preposition, a third position in which a noun phrase can appear:

3a

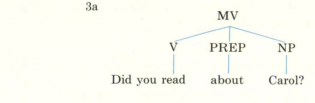

3b

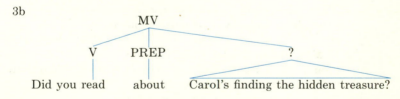

The three groups of words that appear in the positions of noun phrases in structures 1b, 2b, and 3b are these:

> that John was apathetic
> their report to be correct
> Carol's finding the hidden treasure

All three of these groups can be produced from deep structure sentences by using the appropriate transformations, and they appear in outer sentences in places where a noun phrase can occur. The production of these embedded sentences is discussed in detail in Section 36.

Exercises

1. *Fred* is the surface structure subject of the following sentence:

> 1   Fred began to write a letter late last night.

But consider what the sentence means. Is it accurate to say that Fred was *beginning* last night? Compare sentence 1 with 2:

> 2   The writing of the letter began late last night.

Now answer the question of what began last night. Compare sentences 3 and 4:

> 3   The lecture began at 9:00.
> 4   The lecture began to get boring.

The surface structure of both sentences has *the lecture* as the subject. But what is the deep structure subject in each sentence? Consider what *began* in each sentence.

2. What elements are absent from but "understood" in the following sentences? (These elements would be present in deep structure, to account for the way we understand each sentence.)

> 1   Jane takes piano lessons because she wants to.
> 2   The plane is expected to arrive at noon.
>   (Hint: What is the ''subject'' of *arrive?* Who expects the plane?)
> 3   Sid ordered milk, and Sally rum.
> 4   Harry and Barbara went to Vienna in September and October, respectively.
> 5   George hates Martha, and vice versa.

3. Examine the following sentences; remember that the sentences marked * are ungrammatical:

> 1   There are three players on the field.
> 2   There is a player on the field.
> 3 * There is three players on the field.
> 4 * There are a player on the field.

Is the word *there* a surface structure subject in these sentences? How can you tell?

4. Transformational grammars that produce a limited number of sentences are easy to make. Here is one that produces just one sentence.

Phrase Structure Rules	Lexicon
1 S → NP + VP	DET → the
2 NP → DET + N	N → leaves
3 VP → V	V → sprouted

Produce a tree diagram according to the phrase structure rules. Then substitute a word from the lexicon for each symbol at the bottom of the tree.

5. Here is a somewhat larger grammar that still produces only one sentence. What is it?

Phrase Structure Rules	Lexicon
1 S → NP_1 + VP	ADJ → castle
2 VP → V + PLACE	DET → the
3 PLACE → PREP + NP_2	N_1 → splendor
4 NP_1 → DET + N_1	N_2 → walls
5 NP_2 → ADJ + N_2	PREP → on
	V → falls

6. Modify the grammar of exercise 5 so that it will produce a sentence with the following meaning: *Nothing but splendor falls on castle walls.* You are allowed to add this item to the lexicon: MOD → *only,* but no other words may be added. The desired meaning can be produced by inserting MOD in the proper place in the phrase structure rules.

7. By inserting MOD in a different place in the phrase structure rules of exercise 5, make a grammar that will produce the sentence having the meaning *The only way splendor gets on castle walls is to fall there.*

8. By inserting MOD in a still different place in the phrase structure rules of exercise 5, make the grammar produce a sentence having the meaning *You find splendor nowhere else but on castle walls.*

9. Here is a still larger grammar, one that will produce a considerable number of sentences. Draw diagrams and produce four or five

sentences. Remember that elements enclosed in parentheses are optional; you can add them or not, just as you prefer. For each element, choose one word from those available in the lexicon.

Phrase Structure Rules

S → NP + VP
NP → (DET) + N
VP → AUX + MV
AUX → MODAL

$$MV \rightarrow \left\{ \begin{array}{l} V_i \\ V_t + NP \end{array} \right\}$$

Lexicon

DET → the, a
N → Mary, Gus, grammarian, masseuse, doctor, pilot, Major E. A. Montouth
MODAL → can, may, should, will
V_i → disappear, get lost, perform, stumble, triumph
V_t → consult, disturb, hire, suspect, wrestle

Braces enclose alternatives: in rewriting MV, you may select either the top line, V_i (an intransitive verb), or the bottom line, V_t (a transitive verb) + NP, but you must pick one or the other.

Nouns and Noun Phrases

SECTIONS **1-7**

1 TOPICS AND COMMENTS

If we try to discover what most sentences have in common, in a very general way, we might find that they include something we want to talk about. Suppose we call this something "the topic." It might be something tangible like a house or something abstract like the idea of honor. It might be an action like singing, something neither strictly concrete nor abstract. In any case, the normal procedure is to establish the topic and make some comment about it.

In the most general sense, even in minimally complicated sentences like *Birds sing,* there are two different parts to the sentence: the first establishes the topic—in this case, *birds;* and the second makes some comment about the topic—in this case, that birds *sing.* Many sentences, even lengthy ones, lend themselves easily to a two-part division into topic and comment. Consider this example:

> 1   A lingering shred of light caught the stone near me.
>
> MARY STEWART

The topic of the sentence, of course, is the group of words *a lingering shred of light;* the comment, *caught the stone near me.*

But there is no reason to stop here. If it seems correct to say that the phrase *caught the stone near me* tells us something about the phrase *a lingering shred of light,* why not say that the word *lingering* tells us something about the phrase *shred of light,* or that the words *of light* tell us something about *shred?* Dividing each group of words into topics and comments as far as we can, we end up with a structure like the one on the opposite page.

A more familiar term for the process of applying a comment to a topic is "modification." Modification seems to be one of the most basic concepts in language, and like basic concepts in other fields of study, it is extremely difficult to define. It is neither very precise nor very helpful to say that a modifier "tells us something" about the word or words it modifies, but we have this assurance: if we did not somehow understand modification, we would find it impossible to speak at all, to form even the simplest sentence. We must already possess an intuitive grasp of this process of forming larger and larger topics by modifying them with comments.

A comment may restrict or limit the topic in some way: it may tell us that we are dealing with the whole topic or only part of it. For example, suppose the topic is *cows.* Nouns (such as *cows*) often

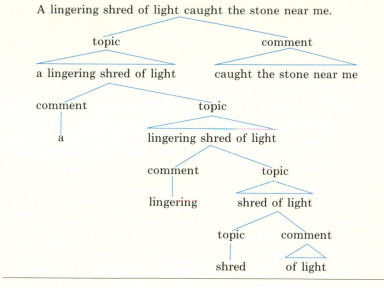

express topics. When we master a language, one of the things we learn is how to modify nouns to produce noun phrases. The most commonly used modifiers in English are the determiners, a relatively small group of words, including *a, the, some,* and *all,* among others (see Section 8). We use them so often it seldom occurs to us to examine closely what the different determiners tell us about the topics they modify.

In many cases, the precision of determiners seems surprising; they sometimes behave almost like elements in logic or mathematics. Take the musical mnemonic *All cows eat grass.* If we say that the topic of the subject noun phrase is *cows,* and the modifier (or comment) is *all,* the noun phrase *all cows* can have its meaning expressed very neatly in the terminology of set theory as ''every member of the set of cows.'' Or suppose the noun phrase had been *both cows.* Here, the topic *cows* is modified somewhat differently: we assert again that we are speaking of every member of the set, but we are also asserting that in this case the set consists of precisely two members. Or again, *some cows* restricts the topic to some unspecified portion of the set, just as *most cows* restricts the topic to an unspecified majority of the set.

But the determiners provide us with very large and very simple restrictions that may be made of the topic. There are no determiners for color, or place, or many specific concepts. For modifications of this kind, we may have recourse to adjectives: *a purple cow*—that is, the topic *cow,* modified in such a way as to specify any single cow, so long as it is purple in color.

Modification, then, boils down to the different ways that the grammar provides us with for talking about the things we wish to discuss. Determiners and adjectives provide us with two means of modification, but there are still richer methods available. A large part of the grammar of English is concerned with the higher levels of modification, making whole sentences into topics or modifiers. In a sentence like 2, the words enclosed in brackets are a modifier of the noun phrase *some final guest:*

> 2 Probably it was some final guest [who had been away at the ends of the earth and didn't know that the party was over].
>
> F. SCOTT FITZGERALD

Exercise

Divide the sentences below into two parts, the first part consisting of the topic (what the sentence is about), and the second part consisting of the comment made about the topic:

1 The rumor spread.
2 The rumor that the chancellor reads cereal boxes spread.
3 Sex on campus will be discussed by the Young Dionysians tonight.
4 All that grammar stuff leaves me cold.
5 *The Wife of Bath's Tale* was not written by D. H. Lawrence.
6 Your next few papers had better be A's.
7 The first three students in line get free tickets.
8 Each of the repairmen is due for a raise.
9 Just a few more good students are all we really need.

2   NOUN PHRASE STRUCTURE

In English, topics are expressed by noun phrases, grammatical units built around a noun. But the deep structure of a noun phrase may differ from its surface structure. For example, in a sentence like

1   Only the brave deserve the fair.

the subject is the noun phrase *only the brave;* in the surface structure, the noun phrase contains no noun: it has a prearticle, *only*
(see Section 8); an article, *the;* and an adjective, *brave.* To account
for number agreement, though, we say that the noun phrase in deep
structure was ''only the brave *ones,*'' where the noun *ones* appears.

In the system of grammar we are adapting here, a noun phrase
will always have a noun, at least in deep structure. The noun phrase
will consist of this noun together with the modifiers, if any, that
precede and follow it. A noun phrase may contain smaller noun
phrases:

2   The defection of Arran marked the first turning-point
in the life of Mary Queen of Scots.

ANTONIA FRASER

In sentence 2, *Mary Queen of Scots* is a noun phrase, part of the
larger noun phrase *the life of Mary Queen of Scots.* The latter is,
in turn, part of the still larger noun phrase *the first turning-point in
the life of Mary Queen of Scots.*

Exercises

1. Only a few school grammars still present the old definition of a
noun as "the name of a person, place, or thing." More often, definitions are arrived at by considering the form of the words in question, or their function. For example, we might define nouns as those
words that have certain different forms in the plural. For most
English nouns, this different form (in writing) would be the original
form plus -*s* or -*es.* This definition would tell us that *chair,* say,
is a noun because it has the plural form *chairs.* What different
endings for the plural would have to be specified? Make sure your
definition will cover words like *alumnus, child, die* (the little cube
with spots on it), *foot, index, ox, phenomenon, seraph, tooth,* and
woman.

2. Obviously, the words listed in the last sentence of exercise 1 are
all exceptions: they do not follow the general rules for forming
plurals in modern English. But there are two separate reasons why

these words are exceptions. By referring to your dictionary, find out what separates words like *child, foot, ox,* and *tooth* from words like *alumnus, index, phenomenon,* and *seraph.* The answer lies in the histories of the words. Can you add a few more words to each group?

3. We can also define nouns as those words that will form acceptable sentences when inserted in "sentence frames." Sentence frames look like this:

> 1 The _____ was lying on the ground.
> 2 John suddenly thought of a _____ .

Sentence frames can be used to define any part of speech by testing the function of words in sentences. Can you think of any words that you would like to call nouns, but that do not fit in sentence frames 1 and 2? Can you compose a sentence frame that will test your words?

3 SYNTACTIC FEATURES

A fact of language used by dictionary-makers is the "sharing" of part of their meanings by large groups of words. If we ask what the words *father, mother, sister, brother, daughter, son, aunt,* and *uncle* have in common, we note that they all share the idea of "family relationship." To go further, *father, brother, son,* and *uncle* have in common their denotation of "male," while *mother, sister, daughter,* and *aunt* denote "female." We can group nouns, then, in terms of the elements of meaning that they have in common. But although such an exercise may be an interesting diversion, does it advance our understanding of grammar? The words we are here concerned with are those having elements of meaning with some relevance to the grammar of English—hence, "syntactic" features of meaning.

For example, we need to distinguish between nouns that refer to human beings and those that do not. This is certainly of grammatical importance: if the noun refers to a human, it in turn will be referred to by the relative pronouns *who, whom, whose,* or *that;* a nonhuman noun by *which* or *that.* We can consider then that all nouns referring to humans will function in the grammar as if they had the label "human" attached to them. Sections 4, 5, and 6 detail the syntactic features we will need.

Exercise

There is an element of meaning common to the words in each of the groups below. Identify the element of meaning for each group:

1. education
   honesty
   New York State
   Einstein's theory of relativity
   September 25
   deep structure
   Euclid's theorems
   friendship

2. log
   carcass
   rock
   Jupiter (the planet)
   Ford Mustang
   Hoover Dam
   corpse
   pencil
   napkin
   peanut butter
   Mount Etna

3. Emily Dickinson
   cow
   vixen
   actress
   Joan of Arc

4. 82nd Airborne Division
   committee
   swarm
   Daughters of the
       American Revolution
   flock
   fleet

5. Captain Ahab
   Julius Caesar
   salesman
   priest
   Isis
   Cordelia
   lawyer
   Happy
   Sneezy
   Bashful
   Grumpy
   Dopey
   Sleepy
   Doc

4 COUNT NOUNS AND MASS NOUNS

One of the syntactic features we will need to distinguish for any noun is whether the noun is singular or plural in form, not meaning. For example, a noun like *scissors* is plural in form (note the ending of the word) even though it may mean only one cutting implement. On the other hand, nouns like *committee* or *government*, although they are plural in meaning—obviously implying more than one individual—are singular in form.

29

For the sake of exposition, we can show information like the number of a noun, when that information is relevant, by marking it below the noun in question:

envelope	child	vertebra
•singular	•singular	•singular
envelopes	children	vertebrae
•plural	•plural	•plural

Nouns subject to this distinction between singular and plural forms are sometimes called "count nouns," that is, they can be counted:

1   one envelope, two envelopes, three envelopes . . .

and they can be preceded in a grammatical sentence by a number

2   I have three children and thirty-three vertebrae.

But there is another large class of nouns that cannot be marked either singular or plural, and that cannot be counted or preceded by a number. Nouns in this class are called "mass nouns." Mass nouns refer to substances usually thought of as an indivisible whole or an uncountable aggregate, rather than as composed of parts that can be discriminated. If I tear an envelope in half, I do not have two envelopes; but if I split a block of ice in half, I have two blocks of ice. Like *envelope*, *bean* is a count noun; like *ice*, *rice* is a mass noun. Note how the two words behave in identical sentences:

3   I have a collection of 38,000 beans.
                            •plural

4 * I have a collection of 38,000 rices.
                            •mass

We are not talking about physical reality here—certainly beans or fleas or pebbles are no more "countable" than is rice or sand or gravel—but English treats the words for them as if they were. Mass nouns will be marked as such by a syntactic feature:

| air | blood | butter | rain | spaghetti |
| •mass | •mass | •mass | •mass | •mass |

Many words can be used both as mass nouns and as count nouns. For instance, *glass* is usually analyzed as a mass noun but indicates something made from glass when used as a count noun:

5   We plan on lining the side of the building with glass.

    •mass

6   Gus broke my new set of water glasses.

    •plural (count)

Or, the mass noun is converted to a count noun meaning a special kind, variety, or brand of the substance:

7   Paper won't be strong enough for that use.
    •mass

8   Two of the papers are treated for fire-resistance.
    • plural

The switch can operate in the other direction, too: from what is usually a count noun to a mass noun. In this context, the mass noun has a meaning something like "the substance of which the count noun is composed."[1]

9   Ev eats an apple   a day.
    •singular

10   These tarts are filled with apple.

    •mass

4a   Application

VERB AGREEMENT

Agreement in number between subject and verb is partially dependent on the mass–count distinction. You may sometimes need to check your own writing for subject–verb number agreement. In difficult cases, first test whether the noun in question is a count

[1] This analysis of the mass–count distinction follows H. A. Gleason, *Linguistics and English Grammar.* New York: Holt, Rinehart and Winston, 1965. Pp. 136–37.

noun or a mass noun. Consider, for example, *committee* and *mathematics*. The first can be grammatically preceded by a number, marking it as a count noun (note sentence 1). On the other hand, the deformity of sentence 2 marks *mathematics* as a mass noun:

> 1   The chancellor appointed Jones to three committees.
> 2 * This week we had three mathematics.

As a second test, try placing *much* before the word in question. If the result is acceptable (as sentence 4 is), the noun is a mass noun. If the result is unacceptable (like sentence 3), the noun is a count noun:

> 3 * Has Jones been appointed to much committees?
> 4   I don't know much mathematics.

Once you have determined whether the noun is mass or count, follow this guide: with count nouns, verb agreement follows form—if a count noun as subject has a plural ending, the verb is also plural. Thus we say

> 5   The scissors are on the table.

even if we mean only one pair. Despite their plural meanings, count nouns like *crew* or *committee* take a singular or plural verb depending on their form:

> 6   The crew has not been selected yet.
> 7   The crews have not been selected yet.
> 8   A committee was appointed to study the question.
> 9   Two committees were appointed to study the question.

Mass nouns as subjects consistently take a singular verb, regardless of form, whenever the word is in fact used in the mass sense; whether the noun appears to have a plural ending or not, the verb is singular:

> 10   Education is the largest single expense in my budget.
> 11   Mathematics is my easiest subject.

Exercises

1. Some words, although not among those commonly called pronouns, are used to substitute for or refer to other words. We may take it for granted that such words have features like those of the words they refer to. On the basis of the sentences below, draw up feature specifications for *stuff* and *thing*. Tell what evidence you used to reach your decision:

   1 Would you like some pomegranate wine? No thanks, I never touch the stuff.
   2 Would you like some pomegranates? No thanks, I never touch the things.
   3 Would you like some gravel? Give me a bucketful of the stuff.
   4 Would you like some pebbles? Give me a bucketful of the things.

2. If we assume sentence 1 below to be grammatical, what does the sentence tell us about the features of the word *data?*

   1 The data are too few to be conclusive.

   If we assume sentence 2 below to be grammatical, what does the sentence tell us about the features of the word *data?*

   2 The data is insufficient to be conclusive.

   If both 1 and 2 are grammatical, what conclusion can we draw about the features of the word *data?*

5 OTHER SYNTACTIC FEATURES

In the same way that we abstracted number features, we can determine other features of nouns needed for the explanation of English sentences.

One feature puts nouns like *honesty, patience, self-control,* and *victory* into one group, and nouns like *buckle, fountain, ink,* and *mixture* into another. Members of the first group all refer to things not perceptible to the senses, and carry the feature •abstract, while the second group has its members marked •concrete. Many, but not all, of the abstract nouns carry the number feature •mass:

> 1 Honesty ranks high among the virtues.
> •mass
> •abstract

But others behave like count nouns:

> 2 The rumors are flying today.
> •plural
> •abstract

Concrete nouns are further divided: nouns like *cloud, magazine, tree,* and *truck* are used differently from nouns like *alligator, lecturer, salmon,* and *salesman.* This distinction depends on whether or not the thing referred to can move of its own volition. The group that moves carries the feature •animate; nouns referring to things that cannot move at will carry the feature •inanimate.

Certain parts of the grammar require us to set nouns like *partridge, bee,* and *reindeer* apart from ones like *teacher, girl,* and *manager.* This distinction marks nouns as •nonhuman or •human.

There are interconnections among these last three sets of features. If a noun is marked •human, it need not be also marked •animate and •concrete, since these concepts are implied by that of •human. That is to say, there are no inanimate or abstract humans (in a grammatical sense, that is). Similarly, any noun marked •animate is already implicitly specified as •concrete.

The features •abstract, •inanimate, and •nonhuman share a similar relationship. A noun marked •abstract need not also be marked •inanimate or •nonhuman, since abstractions like *beauty* are necessarily inanimate and nonhuman. The same reasoning allows us to say that nouns marked •inanimate need not be marked •nonhuman, since inanimate nouns cannot refer to human beings, all of whom are animate.

An additional set of features we need to distinguish for nouns is not involved in the classification above. These are the syntactic features for gender. In English, nouns that refer to a male are marked •masculine; those that refer to a female, •feminine; and, with a few exceptions, those referring to things without sex are marked •neuter. Whether a noun is marked •masculine, •feminine, or •neuter will guide the selection of the pronoun *he, she,* or *it* to refer to or replace the noun.

Exercises

1. The following book review appeared in *Time* (15 September 1967):

> Back in 1940, Dutch-born psychiatrist Renatus Hartogs suffered a traumatic experience on a Long Island highway. Unable to fix a flat tire, he summoned a garage mechanic, who failed also. "I can't get this . . . wheel off!" the fellow cried. Dr. Hartogs was astounded. As he recalls: "The idea of a wheel engaging in sexual intercourse perplexed me."
>
> Then a revelation hit Dr. Hartogs: English is virtually without gender—it is, in fact, suspiciously without sex. Dr. Hartogs was educated in Germany, where a girl (*das Mädchen*) is neuter, spring (*der Frühling*) is masculine, and a door (*die Tür*) is feminine (apparently the doctor cannot bear to hear one slammed). As he sees it, a language in which only *he* and *she* are sexed must be up to no good. In English, what is the sex of a bicycle, an eggplant, a subway? None. And what does this engender? According to Dr. Hartogs and Hans Fantel, a "professional writer" who has tried to guide the psychiatrist through sexless English, Americans turn "grammatical lack of gender into a linguistic sex orgy" as a reaction against—guess what? "The Puritan tradition."

   Distinguish between sex and gender (note the three examples given in the review), and discuss whether it is true that only *he* and *she* are marked for gender in English.

2. Discuss the following excerpt, deciding which of the correspondents you agree with. Base your consideration on the features of the words involved:

> Dear Ann Landers: Usually you're on the ball. But you blew it when you agreed with "Service Oriented" that a male nurse should be called by another name, something less feminine. Do you believe a female physician should be called something other than "doctor" because she is a woman? Why then should a male nurse be called something other than a nurse? Think about it, Ann.
>
> APPLETON READER
>
> Dear Ap: I have thought about it, and the advice stands. The word "nurse" is also a synonym for "breast-feed." This double-

meaning noun-verb gives "nurse" a strong feminine flavor. I hope someone comes up with a better name for men who want to work in the field of patient care.

 GENERAL AND SPECIAL FEATURES

In many cases, language seems designed to allow us to proceed even when we have only fragmentary knowledge of the situation under discussion. The system of features is one of those cases. In English, every noun with the feature •human must be marked for gender, but what do we do if we are unaware of the sex of the person referred to by the noun? The answer is that, in English, we often speak as if the person referred to were male unless we have specific information to the contrary. For example, if someone asks, ''Do you know what the demonstrator outside the building is doing?'' We might answer something like, ''No, what is *he* doing?'' although we have no evidence about the sex of the demonstrator. For some sets of features, one of the features has general application; the other (or others) are used only when we know that the general one does not apply. When we hear a new inanimate noun, for instance, we tend to assume that it is a count noun rather than a mass noun; here •count would be the general feature, •mass the special one. This assumption is at the heart of this old joke:

> "Don't you think William has poise?"
> "I don't know—what's a poi?"

For our purposes, the features we need to distinguish are

1 mass   or   count

                                                     singular   plural

2 human   or   nonhuman
3 animate   or   inanimate
4 concrete   or   abstract
5 masculine   or   feminine   or   neuter

Some examples of nouns marked for syntactic features are listed below:

aunt	Charlemagne	dice	driver	peace
•singular	•singular	•plural	•singular	•mass
•human	•human	•inanimate	•human	•abstract
•feminine	•masculine	•concrete	•masculine	

plastic	snow	team	tigresses	wreath
•mass	•mass	•singular	•plural	•singular
•inanimate	•inanimate	•human	•nonhuman	•inanimate
•concrete	•concrete	•neuter	•animate	•concrete
			•feminine	

6a   Application

REDUNDANCY

A system of features has been proposed by J. J. Katz and J. A. Fodor in their work "The Structure of a Semantic Theory"[1] as the basis for defining words. They use as an example the word *bachelor* in its various senses, with each of the meanings symbolized by a different path on a tree like this:

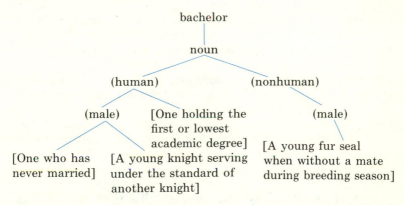

If we take, for example, the left line at each branching, we would arrive at the complete definition "human—male—who has never married." The system proposed here illustrates clearly the concept of word meanings made up of features that each contribute an element to the whole. There must be at least two kinds of features,

[1] *Language,* 39 (1963).

syntactic and semantic. The syntactic features, outlined in Sections 4, 5, and 6, contribute those elements of meaning that function as part of the grammar, guiding the selection of pronouns, matching verb features, and so on. Any syntactic feature is shared by large numbers of words—note the generality of ideas like •human, •animate, •masculine, and so on. Semantic features, on the other hand, may be shared by only a relative handful of words: think how few English words there are that contain as part of their meaning the idea of "blood relative." Semantic features are not sharply distinguished from syntactic features. We can say only that semantic features do not affect the form of other words in the sentence, as syntactic features do.

The writing problem called "redundancy" arises when two words used close together repeat a syntactic or semantic feature. In the tree above, one of the semantic features of one definition of *bachelor* contained the concept "unmarried." Now consider a phrase like *the unmarried bachelor;* in the definition just referred to, the phrase is redundant—unnecessarily repetitive—because the word *bachelor* includes the idea "unmarried," and that idea need not be repeated. *Single bachelor* would be just as bad, for the same reason.

Redundancy may be a flaw of the sentence, rather than of just a phrase. In such a case, syntactic or semantic features may be repeated in a verb, rather than in an adjective or a noun. For example, the problem with a sentence like *She killed him dead* lies in the combination of the verb and the word *dead: kill* means something like "cause someone to die," so the word *dead* is unnecessary.

It should be noted that redundancy is often objectionable only when the two words causing it occur within a relatively short stretch. Many handbooks object to the construction *the reason . . . is because,* on the ground of redundancy: a strong argument can be made that the word *reason* has the feature •cause as part of its meaning; so has the word *because.* But the repetition in the construction is most apparent when the two words are close together. Many reputable writers have used the construction, often when a considerable number of words intervene between *reason* and *because,* as if we needed to be reminded of the feature •cause after the space of several words. Compare the clear redundancy of sentence 1 with sentence 2, which seems unobjectionable:

1 The reason for haste is because we lack time.
2 The reason the new Leedsians will keep their appointment with Samarra, as Miss McCarthy sees it, is

because they have traded every traditional ethic and
set of values for a half digested belief.

ALICE S. MORRIS

Redundancy is simple to correct; check the dictionary entries for
the words in question. It may be possible to substitute a word for
one of the words containing the repeated feature, or to omit one
of the words entirely.

Exercises

1. List the features for the following nouns. Avoid redundancy:

circuit-breaker   oil   raccoon
cotton   pajamas   relaxation
exercise   power   Winston Churchill
minute

2. If we add the syntactic features •proper and •common, we can
prevent sentences like 1 from occurring:

1 * I saw a movie with the Clark Gable last night.

How then can we make sure that sentences like 2 will be allowed?

2   He's the Clark Gable of our neighborhood.

For a hint of the answer, look at exercise 3.

3. Look up *generic* in the dictionary and decide whether we need such
a feature. Consider sentences like 1 and 2 before deciding:

1   The alligator is an American reptile.
2   Our center fielder doesn't cover the ground like a Willie
    Mays.

4. In terms of features, what change has occurred in the use of these
words? (Your dictionary will give you the answers.)

boycott   dry ice   ping pong
calico   escalator   raglan sleeve
cellophane   kerosene   sandwich
celluloid   linoleum   shredded wheat

39

7 PRO-FORMS

Obviously, some nouns have more general meanings than others. For example, the word *mother* refers to persons in a certain group. *Woman* refers to persons in a certain group too, but a larger group. Every person who can be referred to by *mother* can also be referred to by *woman,* but it does not work the other way around—every mother is a woman, but not every woman is a mother. *Woman* is thus more general in its meaning than *mother.* Notice something else, too: the more general a noun, the less information it gives us. We learn more from *beagle* than from *dog;* more from *dog* than from *animal;* and more from *animal* than from *creature.*

We can think of relatively specific words like *beagle* as being made up of many features, many units of meaning, often very specialized ones. But semantic features like these are extremely limited in their application—for example, English does not have one pronoun to refer to beagles and another to refer to cocker spaniels. On the other hand, syntactic features like mass–count, human–nonhuman, and so on, are found in large classes of words.

In the first part of this text, the production of sentences was analyzed as beginning with something like a syntactic skeleton, a diagram of the grammatical relationships existing between different parts of the sentence. At a subsequent stage in the production of a sentence, words were added to the diagram. But suppose that, in the production of a sentence, we might simply attach syntactic features instead of words to that diagram. We might then end up with derivations like this:

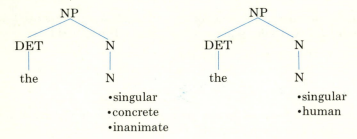

If symbols like N •singular, •concrete, and •inanimate turn out to be words in the surface structure, we would expect those words to be very general indeed, since they would offer us almost no information except for the few syntactic features listed. Most transformational grammars account for extremely general nouns like *thing* or *one* by deriving them from what are called "pro-forms," symbols like N together with certain syntactic features. We give the following derivations for these two words:

$$N \rightarrow \text{thing} \qquad N \rightarrow \text{things}$$
•singular •plural
•concrete •concrete
•inanimate •inanimate

$$N \rightarrow \text{one} \qquad N \rightarrow \text{ones}$$
•singular •plural
•human •human

Now if we look at nouns like *hour, second, day, week,* and so on, their element of meaning is the indication of a unit of time. Similarly, words like *city, town, field, Pennsylvania,* have the idea of "place" in common. Let us add, then, the features •time and •place to those that can be listed beneath an occurrence of N. Pro-forms with these features will appear in surface structures simply as:

$$N \rightarrow \text{time} \qquad N \rightarrow \text{place}$$
•time •place

Many transformations allow for the deletion of pro-forms, probably because they contribute very little to the meaning of a sentence: a sentence like "This is *the place* where I was born" tells us no more than *This is where I was born.*

7a   Application

SPECIFIC WORDS

Words like *thing* and *one* are sometimes unavoidable in writing, but often some way exists to substitute for them a word that will carry more information. Suppose you wanted to write a transition from one section of your essay to the next, and you produced something like this:

The next thing to be considered is . . .

Depending on what you meant here, a number of more specific words might replace *thing:* did you mean *argument,* or *evidence,* or *problem?* Since each of these words would provide additional meaning at no greater length, one of them would be an improvement. Much the same advice applies for other words as well: if you can substitute *beagle* for *dog,* or *dog* for *animal,* or *animal* for *creature,* do so: the more specific the word, the more information it carries. Substituting the specific word for the general will certainly save your reader's time, and perhaps some guessing at exactly what you mean by *thing.*

Exercises

1. The pro-forms of Section 7 were described as very general words, consisting of only a few features, that function like nouns. Consider now whether there might be words which can, as pro-forms, function like other units of syntax. We are used to the idea of pronouns, but are there such things as pro-*verbs,* pro-*adjectives,* and so on? Each of the words in color in the sentences below substitutes for some construction in the first half of the sentence. Identify the words that have been substituted for, and tell how the emphasized word is functioning in the sentence.

   1 Tony eats mashed potatoes with his fingers, but Sam never does.
   2 You can operate the machine yourself if you do so carefully.
   3 The sheriff is looking for a tall, dark stranger; have you seen any such man?
   4 Christina Rossetti was eccentric, and so was her brother.

2. This exercise asks you to test the statement of Section 7 that *thing* has the feature •concrete. In the following excerpt from the New York Times News Service, the word *something* occurs twice. The married couple quoted appear to be in agreement with the text about the feature specification of *thing.* Do you think the people they refer to would agree that *something* must always carry the feature •concrete?

NOUNS AND NOUN PHRASES **7a**

The thing I find amusing is there are people our age with two or three children, struggling along, and they tell us we are missing something. Meanwhile we ride in a new car, own our own lakefront home, spend our summers on our boat, go away every weekend, and spend every Christmas holiday skiing in Europe. And they tell us we are missing something.

Modifiers

SECTIONS **8·11**

8 DETERMINERS

We can distinguish three main classes of modifiers preceding a noun within a noun phrase. Words in the first class are called "determiners." (See Sections 9 and 10 for adjectives and noun-modifiers in the noun phrase.)

Consider a sentence like this:

1 Your next few papers had better be A's.

The first three words in the noun phrase *your next few papers* illustrate three subclasses of determiners: articles, ordinals, and cardinals. We can establish the three kinds by a process of substitution. Suppose we say that a word may be replaced by another of the same part of speech without any *grammatical* difficulties. There may be a resulting problem in meaning: the sentence may become ludicrous or contradictory or illogical, but there should be no grammatical problem. Thus, given a sentence like

2a How does your car run these days?

if we substitute *walk* for *run* on the theory that they are both verbs, the result is a strange-sounding sentence:

2b How does your car walk these days?

But this is not ungrammatical in the same way it would be if, in order to test whether these two words are the same part of speech, we substitute *walk* for *your:*

2c * How does walk car run these days?

If we analyze *your next few papers* in this way, we would very soon find that, although thousands of words could be substituted for the noun *papers,* only a handful can be substituted for *your,* or *next,* or *few.* We can replace *your* with *the, these, those, her,* and so on; for *next,* we can substitute *first, second* (and so on), *last,* or *final;* and for the word *few,* we can use such words as *one, two, three* (and so on), *several,* or *many.* Giving each list a name, we can arrange a tabular form:

your	next	few
ARTICLES	ORDINALS	CARDINALS
a, an	first	one
the	second	two
any	third (etc.)	three (etc.)
each	next	several
either	last	many
every	final	etc.
enough	etc.	
much		
neither		
no		
some		
etc.		

Articles also include what are traditionally called "demonstratives": *this, that, these, those;* and the possessive pronouns: *her, his, its, my, our, their,* and *your.*

Members of a small group of words can precede some of the articles; they are the "prearticles," and include *all, both, half, double, only,* and *just.*

The determiner system in a noun phrase is relatively rigid and highly ordered. The words appear in a fixed order: article, ordinal, cardinal. Note too that only one word from each subclass may occur in a phrase.

8a   Application

BROAD REFERENCE

Deleting the headnoun of a noun phrase can sometimes cause trouble, especially if the determiner in the noun phrase is a demonstrative: *this, that, these, those.* The demonstratives "point" to something. In fact, in one of their uses, they are often accompanied by a gesture. If I, pointing at an apple, remark, "This is red," my statement could be interpreted on a deeper level as "This apple is red." Since you have learned to look in the direction of a pointing finger, the word *apple* is redundant in the sentence—you have the thing referred to in front of you, and the reference is unmistakable. Therefore, *apple* can be deleted from what I say with no loss of essential information. But in an essay, your reader obviously cannot follow your finger to the words on the page that you would like his attention drawn to. The reference must be clear and unambiguous; the deleted headnoun must be ''recoverable''—the reader must be able to discover it. Consider what must be the deleted headnoun following *these* in example 1a:

> 1a The hellenization of the Christian faith's speculation has produced certain parallel inadequacies in Catholic philosophical thought. The most obvious of these is not directly relevant to the question of theism and, therefore, will be but mentioned here.
>
> **LESLIE DEWART**

Of course, the deleted headnoun is *inadequacies*. We might investigate just how this term is recoverable: to begin with, *these* has the feature •plural; of the noun phrases in the preceding sentence—*hellenization, the Christian faith's speculation, certain parallel inadequacies,* and *Catholic philosophical thought*—only one, *certain parallel inadequacies,* also has the feature •plural. Of the possible things being pointed to, only one matches the demonstrative in number.

Broad reference with a demonstrative occurs when the demonstrative could be pointing to several noun phrases, or even to none. If we change 1a only slightly, making another noun phrase also plural, we destroy the unique reference of the demonstrative:

> 1b The hellenization of the Christian faith's speculation has produced certain parallel inadequacies in Catholic philosophical writings. The most obvious of these is not directly relevant to the question of theism and, therefore, will be but mentioned here.

Now we cannot tell if *these* is intended to point to *inadequacies* or *writings,* since both are plural. But even with the wording of 1b, the difficulty can be overcome if the headnoun is not deleted:

> 1c The hellenization of the Christian faith's speculation has produced certain parallel inadequacies in Catholic

philosophical writings. The most obvious of these inadequacies is not directly relevant to the question of
theism and, therefore, will be but mentioned here.

If you have to repair an uncertain reference of a demonstrative,
the example above shows two methods of correction: either word the
preceding material so that only the intended noun phrase matches
the demonstrative in number (as in 1a), or restore the deleted headnoun (as in 1c).

Exercises

1. Section 8 claims that only one word from each subclass of the
   determiners may appear in a phrase and that determiners do not
   vary from their fixed order. Do the two sentences below prove that
   statement to be false?

   1 Sal was the fifth second baseman the team tried this year.
   2 The team faced several important third down situations.

2. Note that although our grammar will generate a phrase like *all
   the gold,* it will not generate *all of the gold.* Several transformational grammars attempt to solve the problem by establishing
   a class of words called "quantifiers." Quantifiers are two-word units
   like *all of, both of, some of,* and *each of.* This approach probably
   raises more problems than it solves, since quantifiers modify nouns.
   Thus, in a phrase like *all of the boys, all of* is a quantifier, *the*
   is an article, and *boys* is the headnoun of the phrase. Why would
   the quantifier approach run into problems in verb agreement in
   a sentence like

   Each of the boys is over six feet tall.

   Another approach to the question claims that a phrase like *all of
   the boys* starts in deep structure as *all boys of the boys,* with the
   first occurrence of *boys* later deleted. In this system, what would
   be the deep structure of the subject noun phrase in the sentence
   above? Does this approach solve the problem of verb agreement
   in the sentence?

9 ADJECTIVES IN THE NOUN PHRASE

The phrase structure rules in the introduction made no provision for including adjectives in noun phrases, although they frequently occur there, following determiners, and preceding noun-modifiers.

> Allen lighted a straight-grain pipe and exhaled the sweet smooth smoke of an expensive mixture.
>
> JOHN P. MARQUAND

In this sentence we have three noun phrases containing adjectives: the first is *a straight-grain pipe,* and the second, *the sweet smooth smoke of an expensive mixture,* includes the third, *an expensive mixture.* Note that in each case, the adjectives (*expensive,* for example) come between the last element of the determiner and the headnoun. Note too that, as *sweet smooth* shows, adjectives are not bound by the restriction that determiners are subject to, that allows us to select only one word from each subclass of articles, cardinals, and ordinals. We can pile up as many adjectives before a headnoun as considerations of style will allow.

Exactly how adjectives get into noun phrases is a subject for discussion, but their position in the surface structure of noun phrases is easy to describe: most often they follow the last element (if any) of the determiner. There are two classes of exceptions to this statement. One handful of items results from the fact that in French, an adjective may follow the noun it modifies. Our language contains a few phrases modeled on the French structure: *battle royal, court martial, inspector general.* In phrases like these, the plural would presumably be formed by pluralizing the headnoun, thus *courts martial.* So un-English is this construction, however, that we probably do not think of this or similar phrases as nouns-plus-adjectives when we first see them. They seem to us simply to be compound nouns. Thus we find plurals like *court martials.* This is no sign of ignorance —just the reduction of a piece of imported grammar to the English patterns we know well and use constantly.

The other exception to the normal placement of adjectives in noun phrases occurs with a small group of nouns—*something, someone,* etc.—derived from the determiner *some* and one of the noun pro-forms. Note that with these forms, a modifying adjective cannot precede the headnoun—it must follow it: *something strange, somebody special, somewhere convenient.*

9a   Application

PLACING COMMAS

The only punctuation problem likely to arise in the noun phrase involves commas—unnecessary ones or missing ones. The rule for comma placement in a noun phrase is simple: place a comma only between adjectives. In this noun phrase, for example

Just	a	few	good	diligent	students
PREARTICLE	ARTICLE	CARDINAL	ADJ	ADJ	N

good and *diligent* are the only words we have called adjectives, and therefore a comma may be placed between them. There are two quick, reliable tests to tell whether the advice above applies. First, if the order of two or more consecutive words in a noun phrase can be interchanged without making the result sound strange or ungrammatical, the words are adjectives, and a comma may be placed between them. Second, if *and* can be inserted between two or more words in the noun phrase without making the result sound strange or ungrammatical, the words are again adjectives, and a comma may be placed between them.

Exercises

1. Are adjectives themselves divisible into smaller classes that have specific orderings? For example, have you ever heard of an *old little lady?* From the adjectives below, construct several multiword noun phrases (supply your own noun); then try reversing the order of adjacent adjectives in the phrases, and see whether the results sound acceptable to you. Then substitute other adjectives for those in your phrases, until you have classified them all:

big	green	old
blue	huge	orange
brown	Italian	red
elderly	large	small
English	mature	tiny
French	new	young
German		

2. Is there any difference between the situation in which you might speak of a *green plastic pot,* and the one in which you would speak of a *plastic green pot?* Try pronouncing the second phrase with extra emphasis on *plastic.* Is the notion of contrasting one thing with another relevant here?

10 NOUNS AS MODIFIERS

Nouns themselves are the last class of modifiers to appear before the headnoun in a noun phrase. They occur immediately before the nouns they modify, and are extremely frequent in some styles of writing. One article from the Associated Press showed the following combinations of noun-modifiers and headnouns in a single paragraph: *college students, day care centers* (two noun-modifiers here), *Bible reading, drug addicts, mountain history, voter registration.*

To say that one noun modifies the other does not shed much light on constructions like these. Specifically, these pairs of nouns derive from greatly different sources, sources that become clearer when we examine the logical or deep structure relations between the two nouns. Phrases like *Bible reading* and *voter registration* contain noun-modifiers (*Bible* and *voter*) that are related to their headnouns (*reading* and *registration*) in the same way that a direct object noun phrase is related to a verb. A transformational grammar would derive the surface structure forms like this (the double arrow indicates a transformation):

> someone reads the Bible $\Rightarrow$ reading of the Bible $\Rightarrow$ Bible reading
>
> someone registers voters $\Rightarrow$ registration of voters $\Rightarrow$ voter registration

Where these phrases have what we might call "direct object" noun-modifiers, other noun-modifiers are related to their headnouns by a relationship of purpose. Thus we might derive *day care centers* from something like "centers *for* the care of someone by day." Compare *research center,* which would presumably come from "center *for* research," or *movie theater* from "theater *for* movies."

Still other combinations of headnouns and noun-modifiers have a relation that we might call one of place. *College students* could be derived from ''students *at* college.'' Compare *hospital patients* or *San Francisco Bay.*

In effect, these numerous transformations obscure the relations in deep structure between the words that become noun-modifiers and headnouns in surface structure.

10a Application

AMBIGUITY

Many noun-modifier and headnoun constructions cause us no problem, perhaps because of their familiarity. We know from experience that *college student* means someone who studies *at* a college rather than someone who studies colleges. When we encounter new noun-modifier and headnoun constructions, we interpret them more or less on the best guess we can make. Suppose we read that someone is *a phlogiston student;* the phrase could be interpreted in two ways: parallel to *a Harvard student*—someone who studies at Harvard—or parallel to *a history student*—someone who studies history. The only clue to the meaning intended here is that *phlogiston* begins with a lower-case letter and place-names usually begin with a capital letter.

In other cases, we have no hint of the derivation of the construction. Consider a phrase like *University Study Committee.* Is this a committee that studies universities or a committee that studies something *at* a university? We cannot resolve the ambiguity of the phrase; we have no grounds on which to judge the meaning intended.

If you have written an ambiguous construction consisting of noun-modifier and headnoun, try to straighten out the phrase and make your intent plain by deciding on the derivation of the phrase and rewording accordingly. The examples above may help in parallel cases, but often a simple paraphrase is enough to solve the problem.

Exercise

What are the sources of the following noun-pair combinations?

Harvard University	gift edition
family reunion	newspaper boy
cocktail party	delivery boy
birthday party	gold watch
bachelor party	wristwatch
Conservation Council	pocket watch
pollution control	assassination attempt
reference file	bird dog
smokestack	bird feeder
rooftop	birdbrain

11 CHANGING NOUN PHRASES TO DETERMINERS

The determiner system in a noun phrase is relatively rigid and highly ordered. The different kinds of words occur in fixed order, and allow only one member of each subclass to appear in a given noun phrase. Notice what a hash it makes of a sentence if we select two articles:

1 * The a rumor spread.

Or if we switch the positions of, say, an article and a cardinal:

2 * Just few a more good students are all we really need.

One construction brings flexibility to the determiner system—that of changing a whole noun phrase to a determiner.

This change results from a series of transformations, producing what in traditional grammars is called the possessive case of a noun. Here we modify the traditional approach in two ways. First, we adopt the term "genitive" rather than "possessive," to avoid the narrow connotations of "possession" that the traditional term implies. Second, and more important, we will maintain that the whole noun phrase is transformed to a determiner, not just a noun.

First, the transformed noun phrase becomes a determiner as far as its function in the sentence is concerned. We have established that *the* is a determiner; note that *John's*, the transformed noun phrase in sentence 4a, occupies the same position that *the* has in sentence 3:

3   Both **the** circus wagons were found in the service elevator.

4a Both **John's** circus wagons were found in the service elevator.

It was also established that two determiners from the same subclass in the same noun phrase made the noun phrase ungrammatical. Note that we have the same result if we try to include both *the* and *John's* in the same noun phrase:

4b * Both **the John's** circus wagons

Functionally, the result of what we might call the GENITIVE transformation is a determiner.

Now what we need to show is that the GENITIVE transformation adds (in written English) an apostrophe or *'s* to a noun phrase rather than to a noun. Our strongest evidence comes from a noun phrase in which the headnoun is modified by a preposition and a smaller noun phrase. One such would be *the Wife of Bath;* here we have the noun phrase *Bath*. With the preposition *of,* the two words form a prepositional phrase in the surface structure. The prepositional phrase *of Bath* modifies the headnoun *Wife*. The larger noun phrase is all four words, *the Wife of Bath*. Now when the *'s* is added by the GENITIVE transformation, it comes after the last word in the phrase, not after the headnoun: "The Wife of Bath*'s* Tale." From this point of view, a form like *John's* also had *'s* added to the end of the noun phrase, but the noun phrase had only one word to start with, *John*. When the *'s* of the genitive is added to a noun phrase that has words following the headnoun, the resulting construction is called a "group genitive" in traditional texts.

11a   Application

THE GROUP GENITIVE

When *'s* is added to a noun phrase with words following the headnoun (the group genitive construction), as in *The Wife of Bath's Tale,* a stylistic effect occurs which is not always appropriate. In most cases, the group genitive adds a strongly conversational tone to the context. We are all familiar with sentences like *The man across the street's dog bit me*. At least, we are all familiar with them in speech; their occurrence in writing is much rarer when speech is not being imitated or suggested. Avoid the group genitive construction unless you want an extremely informal style or are writing dialogue.

An exception to this general tone of informality is found when the *'s* is added to short noun phrases that we are used to seeing and understanding as a unit—such as *the King of England, the Knights of Columbus,* or *Mutual of Omaha*. Although noun phrases like these fall within the group genitive classification, they form the genitive by simply adding *'s* after the last word in the group:

> the King of England's abdication
> the Knights of Columbus' meeting hall
> Mutual of Omaha's *Wild Kingdom*

11b Application

GENITIVES AND AMBIGUITY

Genitive constructions can be ambiguous if they occur with adjectives inside a noun phrase. Something like *the dull boy's knife* illustrates the ambiguity possible—here, we do not know what is modifying what. The phrase has two possible interpretations. First, we might have the noun phrase *boy* changed to a determiner by the GENITIVE transformation. If the resulting determiner modifies the noun *knife,* we would have a structure like this:

INTERPRETATION A

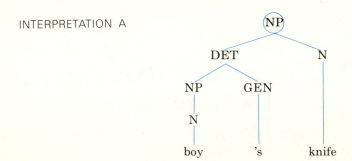

Now, if we have the adjective *dull* modifying the circled noun phrase, we are talking about a dull knife. On the other hand, if we start out with *boy* modified by *dull,* the noun phrase turned into a determiner has a structure like this:

INTERPRETATION B

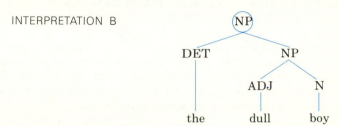

When we have this construction changed to a determiner (the circled noun phrase, the whole structure, has *'s* added to it), then we mean a knife belonging to the dull boy. Some other examples of the same kind of ambiguity, all cited by Norman C. Stageberg, are *a blond artist's model, a clever reporter's story,* and *a plain man's necktie.*[1]

If you run into a similar ambiguity in your own writing, your meaning can be clarified in many cases by substituting a different genitive construction: instead of NP + *'s,* use the construction *of* + NP. Thus Interpretation B would become ''the knife *of* the dull boy.'' Similarly, for the other examples we would have ''a model *of* a blond artist,'' ''a story *of* a clever reporter,'' and ''a necktie *of* a plain man.'' A second method of correction moves the adjective as close as possible to the headnoun. Thus, for Interpretation A, we could change the phrase to *the boy's dull knife.* Revising the other phrases this way would yield *an artist's blond model, a reporter's clever story,* and *a man's plain necktie.*

Exercises

1. As Section 11 shows, we can turn a noun phrase into a determiner (*John* becomes *John's*) and then use the construction to modify another noun phrase—for example, *John's wife.* If we go through the same process again, we can make this larger noun phrase into a determiner and use it to modify still another noun phrase. *John's*

---

[1] ''Some Structural Ambiguities,'' *A Linguistics Reader,* ed. Graham Wilson. New York: Harper & Row. 1967. P. 78.

wife's house. Obviously, this kind of construction can quickly become clumsy: *John's wife's uncle's lawyer's friend's dog's right front paw.* How many of these transformed determiners in a row do you feel comfortable with? Write a few phrases that are unquestionably clumsy, and revise them by using *of* + NP; for example, *John's wife's house* to *the house of John's wife.*

2. Read an extended section of prose—from a newspaper, for example, or a chapter in a novel—and see how many instances you can find of two consecutive genitive constructions (like *John's wife's house*). Listen for the construction in conversation for a time. Does it seem to you more common in speech than in writing?

Verbs
and
Verb
Phrases

12 TRANSITIVES AND INTRANSITIVES

We can classify verbs by the number and kinds of noun phrases that occur in the sentence with them. If we start our analysis of verbs with the simplest constructions we can find, we will begin with sentences having just one noun phrase:

> 1 The twig snapped.

A sentence like 1 shows that, in the surface structure at least, the verb phrase may consist of a single word. For the sake of exposition, let us separate the tense from the verb:

> The twig PAST-& snap.

The verb appears in this group of words as the last element in the verb phrase. Words that can grammatically occur in this position are traditionally called ''intransitive verbs.'' This class includes such verbs as *disappear, look,* and *sing.* But many sentences are like the next example:

> 2 The accountant balanced the books.

In 2, a noun phrase occurs on both sides of the verb, *the accountant* to the left and *the books* to the right. The noun phrase to the right of this and similar verbs is traditionally called the ''direct object,'' and verbs taking direct objects are termed ''transitive verbs.'' This large group of verbs has many subclasses, each of which behaves differently in sentences.

TRANSITIVE

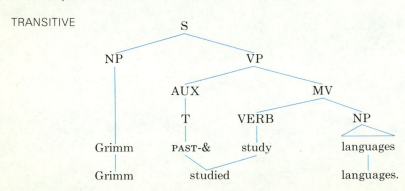

60

A transitive verb, then, is one that appears in a grammatical sentence with a direct object noun phrase to the right of the verb; an intransitive verb is one that appears in a grammatical sentence without an object noun phrase.

INTRANSITIVE

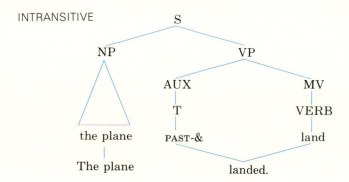

Exercises

1. Some verbs are transitive in some sentences and intransitive in others:

Group A

1a	John grew a beard.	1b	John's beard grew.
2a	John baked a cake.	2b	John's cake baked.
3a	John sounded his horn.	3b	John's horn sounded.
4a	John crashed his car into a tree.	4b	John's car crashed into a tree.

Group B

1a	Liz ran a mile.	1b	Liz ran.
2a	Liz sang a song.	2b	Liz sang.
3a	Liz read a story.	3b	Liz read.
4a	Liz danced a polka.	4b	Liz danced.

In what way are the sentences in Group A different from those in Group B?

2. In the sentences of exercise 1, could the "b" sentences of either group be produced by deleting something from the "a" sentences of the group? What would you lose as far as the meaning of the sentence is concerned?

3. Write five sentences with verbs that can be used only transitively, and five with verbs that can be used only intransitively.

13 VERB FEATURES

The grammar as we have developed it will satisfactorily account for sentences like 1 and 2:

> 1 Ann hesitated.
> 2 Charlie maintains a private taxi fleet.

Unfortunately, nothing we have said so far tells us *which* verbs can be followed by noun phrases and which cannot. In other words, how can we rule out sentences like 3 and 4?

> 3 * Ann hesitated the private taxi fleet.
> 4 * Charlie maintains.

When we examine many such cases, we find that we can use the same apparatus of features established for nouns to exclude non-sentences like 3 and 4.

On the basis of its occurrences in sentences, we would classify *vanish* as an intransitive verb:

> 5 The rabbit vanished.

We can specify that *vanish* is intransitive by marking a feature beneath the word's entry in the hypothetical dictionary (called "the lexicon") that will form part of the grammar. The feature would look like this:

> vanish
> •NP __

The line in the feature specification indicates the place of the verb in a sentence; since nothing follows the line, we can conclude that *vanish* may occur in sentences when a noun phrase does not follow the verb. Transitive verbs can be handled in the same way. For a verb like *maintain,* we would have a feature specification like •NP ___ NP, showing that the verb occurs with a noun phrase (the subject) to the left, and a noun phrase (the direct object) to the right.

Features like these are sometimes called "selectional features." Using them, we can predict that a sentence will be ungrammatical if the selectional feature of the verb does not match the structure of the sentence in which the verb occurs. Thus, we would account for the ungrammaticality of ** Charlie maintains* by the mismatch of the structure and the selectional feature of the verb: the feature shows that a noun phrase is required to the right of the verb, a noun phrase that is lacking in the sentence itself:

> * Charlie   maintains.
> NP   •NP ___ NP

Similarly, ** Ann hesitated the private taxi fleet* will have its ungrammaticality explained by the grammar: here a noun phrase, *the private taxi fleet,* occurs to the right of the verb, but the verb's selectional feature makes no provision for a noun phrase in that position:

> * Ann   hesitated   the   private taxi fleet.
> NP   •NP ___   NP

14   INDIRECT OBJECTS AND DOUBLE OBJECTS

As we develop the feature specifications of verbs, we are also sub-classifying verbs: we have already used features to divide verbs into transitives and intransitives. We can establish further divisions by noting sentences like these:

> 1a   The signers pledged their lives to each other.
> 1b   The signers pledged each other their lives.
> 2a   Jim tossed a long pass to Frank.
> 2b   Jim tossed Frank a long pass.

3a   The senator asked several questions of the secretary.
3b   The senator asked the secretary several questions.
4a   Someone made a birthday cake for you.
4b   Someone made you a birthday cake.
5a   Mrs. Brown bought another slide rule for her son.
5b   Mrs. Brown bought her son another slide rule.

Letting PREP stand for preposition, we have roughly the following structure in each of the ''a'' sentences:

Jim	tossed	a long pass	to	Frank.
NP	VERB	NP	PREP	NP

In each of the ''b'' sentences, the preposition has disappeared and the two final noun phrases have switched places. The two sentences in each pair are obviously the same in meaning; our grammar can explain their synonymy by deriving one structure from the other by a transformation.

The first point to be noted about all these sentences is that two noun phrases follow the verb, hence the term ''double object verbs.'' In each case, we will consider the sentence with the preposition as the more basic form. This preposition can be specified in the verb's selectional feature. Thus, for the verbs of sentences 1a, 3a, and 4a, for instance, we would have the following selectional features:

pledge
•NP __ NP (to NP)

ask
•NP __ NP (of NP)

make
•NP __ NP (for NP)

Some verbs, these three among them, that take a double object will carry another feature, •indirect object. This feature shows that the INDIRECT OBJECT transformation can apply; it switches the position of the two noun phrases following the verb and deletes the preposition. Thus, if the optional INDIRECT OBJECT transformation is applied to 6a, we get 6b:

6a   Bill lent his guitar to Judy.
6b   Bill lent Judy his guitar.

On the other hand, there are double object verbs like *base* that do not carry the feature •indirect object. Through the omission of the feature, our grammar describes the fact that there are no sentences like 7b in English, though there are ones like 7a:

7a   The governor based his decision on our report.
7b * The governor based our report his decision.

Since •indirect object is not a feature of *base,* the transformation cannot be applied to a sentence with this verb.

Most of the verbs carrying the feature •indirect object will have as a preposition either *to* or *for*—for example

> mail
> •NP __ NP (to NP)
> •indirect object

8a   The garage mailed the final bill to Dorothy.

and after the INDIRECT OBJECT transformation

8b   The garage mailed Dorothy the final bill.

> buy
> •NP __ NP (for NP)
> •indirect object

9a   The rajah bought several elephants for his friends.

and after the INDIRECT OBJECT transformation

9b   The rajah bought his friends several elephants.

14a   Application

VERBS WITH IDIOMATIC PREPOSITIONS

Note that certain verbs have prepositions closely associated with them. *Put,* for example, requires the preposition *to* in one of its meanings:

1   The prosecutor put several questions to the witness.

while *ask* requires that we use *of,* not *to:*

> 2 The prosecutor asked several questions of the witness.

Toss, like most verbs that express the idea of throwing, requires *at,* even if the verb is not meant in a literal sense:

> 3 The prosecutor tossed several questions at the witness.

But verbs like *demand, desire, require,* and so on, usually take *from:*

> 4 The prosecutor demanded an answer from the witness.

Although difficult for a foreign student, this tie between verb and preposition seldom presents much difficulty to a native speaker of English. There are, however, cases where the writer uses the wrong preposition, perhaps because he is unfamiliar with the particular verb involved, or because he is using a familiar verb in a sense new to him. If you have this problem, your dictionary can be of help. In some entries, sentences will illustrate the preposition associated with the verb; for example, *Webster's New Collegiate* (eighth edition) includes this phrase in its entry for *imbue:* "a man *imbued* with a strong sense of duty." The phrase informally provides the information that *with* is the preposition used with *imbue.*

Exercises

1. We accounted for sentences like *She sent him a letter* by deriving them from constructions like *She sent a letter to him* by the IN-DIRECT OBJECT transformation. There are a number of other constructions, though, where two noun phrases follow the verb in the surface structure:

> 1 They named their baby Fred.
> 2 We elected him vice-president.
> 3 That job will take you three hours.

Can these sentences be productions of the INDIRECT OBJECT transformation?

2. Note the difference between sentences 1 and 2 below; 2 is representative of some dialects of British English:

    1 They thought him to be a fool.
    2 They thought him a fool.

Do these two sentences suggest any possible sources for the two noun phrases in sentence 2 of exercise 1? Consider whether sentence 2 above might be produced by deleting something from 1.

3. What verbs can you put in the place of *take* in sentence 3 of exercise 1? What element of meaning do these verbs have in common? What phrases can you substitute for *three hours* in the same sentence? What do these phrases have in common? In sentence 1 below, the phrase *for three hours* is traditionally labeled an adverbial of time:

    1 The meeting lasted for three hours.

Can noun phrases act as adverbials in surface structures with certain verbs, even without a preposition like *for?* What would you call the phrase *a mile* in sentence 2 below?

    2 She walked a mile.

15   SELECTIONAL FEATURES OF VERBS

So far our grammar has made some elementary distinctions among verbs, but in the terms of that grammar we cannot yet explain what is wrong with sentences like 1:

    1 * The left turn was appointed to the Highway Commission.

Actually, we have not yet taken full advantage of selectional features. A verb like *scheme,* for instance, characteristically occurs with a subject that indicates a human or some group of humans. Thus we say

    2 Al schemed.
    3 The committee schemed.

but not

4 * The phonograph record schemed.
5 * The history of Rome schemed.

Since we have an elaborate system for marking the syntactic features of nouns, we can use that same system to evaluate the various restrictions between verbs and nouns with varying features.

Looking at intransitive verbs to begin with, we might note which syntactic features occur with the subject noun phrases of typical verbs. *Vanish,* for example, occurs with subjects marked •concrete. *Quarrel* is even more selective: its subjects are characteristically marked •human. Recall that we have the symbol NP occurring in the selectional features of verbs: for example, *vanish* has a feature •NP ___ , showing that the verb is intransitive. If a particular verb has certain restrictions on its subject noun phrases, we can mark those restrictions beneath the NP symbol in the selectional feature of that verb (note that with *weep,* we have to make an exception for *willows!*):

vanish   wander   weep
•NP(concrete) __ •NP(animate) __ •NP(human) __

Adding these markings further subclassifies the intransitive verbs. Now we can predict that a sentence in which these additional specifications are violated will be at least strange-sounding, if not ungrammatical:

6 * the meadow   wandered.
      NP   •NP(animate) __
      •inanimate

7 * the carrot   wept.
      NP   •NP(human) __
      •inanimate

If we extend this marking procedure to the other classes, we have a simple yet rather sophisticated system for categorizing verbs. In the list below, sample verbs and their feature specifications are given, followed by sentences showing the ''agreement'' of the selectional features of the verbs with the syntactic features of the associated noun phrases (the list is not intended to exhaust the possible combinations of features):

INTRANSITIVES

> glitter
> •NP(concrete) __

8   My teeth   glitter   because I brush
>   •concrete   •NP(concrete) __
> them with salt.

> bleed
> •NP(animate) __

9   The boxer   bled from a cut near his eye.
>   •human   •NP(animate) __

Remember that the feature •human implies •animate.

TRANSITIVES

> lack
> •NP(any) __ NP(any)   ("any" stands for any feature
>   listed)

10   This chair   lacks   elegance.
>   •concrete   •NP(any) __ NP(any)   •abstract

> admit
> •NP(human) __ NP(abstract)

11   The suspect   admitted   his guilt.
>   •human   •NP(human) __ NP(abstract)   •abstract

DOUBLE OBJECT

> teach
> •NP(human) __ NP(abstract) to NP(human)

| 12 | Mr. Chips
•human | taught
•NP(human) —— NP(abstract) to NP(human) |
| | Latin
•abstract | to my father.
•human |

The specifications on the chart above are intended for illustration, not for reference. Some of them may be incorrect in some respects; in fact, the whole system of marking nouns and verbs with specifications in this way is subject to revision or rejection—as any theory is—as new research indicates. The system has been covered in this much detail for two reasons: first, imperfect though it may be, it shows the great complexity between constructions within a sentence; and second, it illustrates one of the current concerns of research in the cloudy region of language between what is clearly syntax and what is clearly semantics.

15a   Application

FEATURE VIOLATIONS

A host of relations tie together the words of a sentence; most of these ties we handle effortlessly through long practice. Some verbs, for example, take human subjects only; some take abstract subjects only; some permit a variety of features in their subjects or objects. These relationships are among the first things we learn when we study a foreign language. A simple illustration is the two German verbs, *essen* and *fressen,* that would both be translated into English as *to eat.* But every elementary German text carries the information that *essen* is used with human subjects, *fressen* with subjects denoting animals. Just as we have to learn these distinctions for a verb in German, so too must we learn the restrictions on a new verb in English.

Yet there is a great increase in the vocabulary of students during their college years. Many of these words they learn from only a handful of contexts, perhaps not enough to fully determine the feature specifications of the words. The possibility of misunderstanding a word is closely connected with the possibility of misusing it. As an example, consider the following sentence from a student paper:

1 * Caliban knows what terrible wrath he can occur.

This student misunderstood the feature specification of the verb *occur. Occur* requires a subject bearing the feature •abstract, or perhaps even the feature •event. The word he was after was *incur,* a verb that requires a subject with at least the feature •concrete. A similar problem faced the student who wrote this sentence:

2a * Her position is one of importance, but her values of social standing question her sincerity.

The trouble lies in the connection of the subject noun phrase *her values of social standing,* marked •abstract, and the verb *question,* which usually requires a subject marked •human. Note the difference in the sentence if we add such a noun phrase:

2b   Her position is one of importance, but her values of social standing make us question her sincerity.

If your paper is marked for a feature violation, you have two things to do. First, you need to correct the sentence. The questionable word was probably unfamiliar to you to begin with. If you can, replace the word with one better known to you. Second, you need to increase your knowledge of the restrictions on the original word by consulting your dictionary. You may find there, perhaps in an example sentence, perhaps in a statement about usage, the information you need to figure out the feature specifications of the word. Remember that the unabridged dictionaries offer many example sentences.

Exercises

1. Explain, in terms of features of verbs and nouns, what is wrong with the following sentences:

1 * She originates her idea from records of the past.
2 * The real nature of a pilgrimage is reminded of the reader by these actions.
3 * Salaried occupations such as computer programmers, teachers, and clerical workers require additional training.

4 * It was about two Western robbers which did everything wrong.

5 * Henry drifted the smoke rings from his mouth.

2. The system of syntactic features, like other parts of language, seems to be based on assumptions we make about the nature of the world. A sentence like *The rock shuddered at his touch* seems strange because the verb *shudder* requires a subject marked •animate, and we do not consider rocks to be animate. But suppose the sentence occurred in a science fiction story about a world inhabited by sentient (and sensitive) rocks. The sentence then would not be out of place. Since our beliefs about the nature of the universe were temporarily suspended, our requirements for the language that described that universe would be altered. Consider the following sentence:

1   The boy dispersed.

Describe what is bizarre about sentence 1, and decide if the same thing is still "wrong" with sentence 2:

2   The boy who had been changed by magic into a swarm of bees dispersed.

3. Consult a standard work such as Cleanth Brooks and Robert Penn Warren's *Understanding Poetry,* and examine the definition and examples of "metaphor" found there. See how many of the examples you can describe in terms of deviations from the normal feature relations among words.

4. What "feature violation" (as far as everyday language is concerned) is consistently used in the following stanza from Thomas Gray's "Hymn to Adversity":

Wisdom in sable garb arrayed,
Immersed in rapturous thought profound,
And Melancholy, silent maid
With leaden eye, that loves the ground,
Still on thy solemn steps attend:
Warm Charity, the general Friend,
With Justice to herself severe,
And Pity, dropping soft the sadly-pleasing tear.

16   ACTION AND STATE VERBS

Besides selectional features, verbs may have syntactic features of their own. One useful distinction sets apart verbs marked •action from verbs marked •state. To put the matter very roughly, some verbs describe what a person does, what actions he performs. One such verb is *interview:*

1   We interview job applicants twice a year.

Interview would carry the feature •action. Verbs like this refer to activities usually thought of as under someone's conscious control or direction: you can tell someone to start performing the action described by such a verb. A personnel manager might tell his assistant

2   Interview some more applicants.

Action verbs can be modified by a construction telling us the manner in which the action is performed (called a "manner adverbial"). Thus, our personnel manager might say

3   Interview these applicants carefully.

where *carefully* is a manner adverbial. Finally, if the action described by these verbs is directed by a person's will, the action can hardly be performed if the person is in no condition to exercise his will. It would not make much sense to order the assistant thus:

4 * Next time you're unconscious, interview some more applicants.

Verbs marked •state, on the other hand, have to do more with conditions that a person is in than with things he does. *Resemble* is a verb marked •state. Although we could say of someone

5   Dan resembles Rudolph Valentino.

it would hardly occur to us to say to Dan

6 * Resemble Rudolph Valentino.

He might reasonably reply, ''I couldn't if I wanted to.'' If the verb describes a state not under one's control, a person cannot be ordered or commanded to be in that state. Again, since state verbs are not thought of as under a person's control, they are not modified by manner adverbials—after all, if you cannot do it at all, you can hardly do it in a certain way. Note that an ungrammatical sentence results if we attach the manner adverbial of sentence 3 to a new sentence with a state verb:

7 * Dan resembles Rudolph Valentino carefully.

State verbs describe conditions: if you are in the condition, you are in it, whether you want to be or not. Thus, as is not the case with action verbs, we can say

8 Even when he's unconscious, Dan resembles Rudolph Valentino.

Briefly then, you perform an action, but you are in a state. Some verbs marked •state are *have, doubt, inherit, know, lack,* and *resemble.* Some verbs marked •action are *render, inhale, join,* and *go.*

Exercises

1. The strangeness of the sentences below provides the primary evidence for dividing verbs into two classes, marked •action and •state.

    1 * Laurel is resembling Greta Garbo.
    2 * Resemble Greta Garbo.
    3 * If you want to inherit Howard Hughes' fortune, you'll have to do it now.
    4 * I ordered Chuck to doubt Walter Cronkite.
    5 * Chuck doubted Walter Cronkite enthusiastically.

    Section 16 suggests reasons why some of these sound odd; why do the other sentences seem strange?

2. Given the following evidence, what conclusions can you draw about the features of adjectives?

1   Bill sells insurance.
    Bill is selling
    insurance.
    Sell insurance!
2   Bill skates.
    Bill is skating.
    Skate!
3   Mary knows Serbo-
    Croatian.
    * Mary is knowing Serbo-
    Croatian.
    * Know Serbo-Croatian!
4   Mary has five dollars.
    * Mary is having five
    dollars.
    * Have five dollars!

5   Bill is kind.
    Bill is being kind.
    Be kind!
6   Bill is quiet.
    Bill is being quiet.
    Be quiet!
7   Mary is pregnant.
    * Mary is being
    pregnant.
    * Be pregnant!

8   Mary is tall.
    * Mary is being tall.
    * Be tall!

17   THE AUXILIARY: TENSE AND MODALS

The verb phrase (in traditional terms, the complete predicate) may consist of any of a large number of different constructions, but under examination, patterns begin to emerge from the profusion. Our analysis up to this point would lead us to identify everything to the right of the line in the sentences below as the verb phrases of the sentences:

1a   The people / speak.
2a   That man / borrowed my adjusting wrench.
3a   A grammarian / told the class a political allegory.

These, like all English sentences, can undergo several changes in the form of the verb phrase and still remain grammatical. First, we can add one of a group of words called "modals" (*can, may, must, shall, will*):

1b   The people / may speak.
2b   That man / will borrow my adjusting wrench.
3b   A grammarian / can tell the class a political allegory.

75

Next, we can vary the tense:

> 1c The people / spoke.
> 2c That man / borrows my adjusting wrench.
> 3c A grammarian / tells the class a political allegory.

The first change, that of adding a modal, is optional: certainly a sentence need not have one of these words to be grammatical. The other change, that of tense, illustrates a necessary part of the sentence: the vast majority of English sentences have at least one verb inflected for either past or present tense.

This does *not* mean, obviously, that every English sentence indicates either past or present time. Although tense is involved in showing the time of the action of the sentence, at least three other devices are also involved: modals, aspect, and time adverbials. To illustrate the difference between tense and time, note the difference in meaning of state and action verbs: a state verb in the present tense does indicate a state continuing through the present moment, but an action verb in the present tense does not indicate an action occurring now; rather it denotes an action that occurs habitually:

> 4 John needs a lot of help. (state)
> 5 John leaves on the 9:15 train every morning. (action)

There is a close fit between past tense and states or actions in the past:

> 6 John needed a lot of help. (state)
> 7 John left on the 9:15 train. (action)

Future actions can be shown with the modals *shall* or *will:*

> 8 John will leave on the 9:15 train.

Note, though, that future time can be shown with a present tense verb and our third device, an adverbial indicating some future time:

> 9 John leaves on the 9:15 train tomorrow.

Sentences 4 through 9 above can be analyzed by setting up our phrase structure rules so that an indicator of tense, either past or present, appears as the first element in the auxiliary. Suppose we symbolize these elements as PAST-& and PRESENT-& (the ampersands to the right show that these elements are joined to whatever stands to their right in the sentence). In some instances, these elements will occur immediately before the main verb. Thus sentence 4, for example, is derived from something like this:

John PRESENT-& need a lot of help.

A later rule will convert PRESENT-& and *need* to *needs*. Similarly, sentence 7 would be derived from

John PAST-& leave on the 9:15 train.

and again, PAST-& and *leave* would be rewritten as *left*.

The second element in the auxiliary, a modal, will occur between the tense and the main verb. Thus, by combining PAST-& with *can, may, must, shall,* or *will,* we will produce *could, might, must* (same form), *should,* and *would,* respectively. There is a real advantage to analyzing this second group of modals as containing the past tense; look at sentences 10 and 11, noting the tense of the verbs in each one:

10   John needs all the help he gets.   (both PRESENT)
11   John needed all the help he got.   (both PAST)

Now note that if the first verb is PAST, and the second PRESENT, the sentence is ungrammatical:

12   * John needed all the help he gets.

If we try inserting a modal in the second part of sentences like 10 and 11, we will find that the modal *can* (analyzed as PRESENT-& and *can*) will fit in sentence 10, and that *could* (analyzed as PAST-& and *can*) will fit in 11:

10a   John needs all the help he can get.
11a   John needed all the help he could get.

So far we have analyzed very simple time relations with a two-tense system and the modals. But these two parts of the auxiliary are sufficient for only a limited range of sentences. The next three sections cover ways in which the auxiliary may be expanded by transformations to cover more complex situations.

Exercises

1. Using one sentence as a base, we can produce twelve different variations by changing the tense and inserting or omitting modals. Write the twelve possible variations of the sentence below (remembering that elements in parentheses are optional:

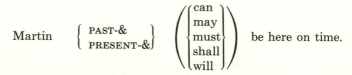

Martin { PAST-& / PRESENT-& } ({ can / may / must / shall / will }) be here on time.

2. Some other elements can be classified as modals in English. Some speakers use *need* and *dare* as modals, as 1 and 2 show:

> 1   You need trouble us no longer, Mr. Fotheringill.
> 2   I dare not speak to Natalie that way.

What other words or two-word combinations are used as modals? Test your answers in 3:

> 3   Martin _____ be here on time.

3. The phrase structure rules place the tense marker in the sentence in what may appear to be an unnecessarily confusing position. What parts of the verbs in 1 and 2 below tell you that the sentences are present or past tense?

> 1   Sandy looks tired.   2   Sandy looked tired.

Obviously, the *-s* of *looks* and *-ed* of *looked* are the parts we associate with present and past tense. But these parts come after the verb in speech and to the right of it in writing. Why then does the rule for auxiliaries place tense to the left of the verb or modal? For the answer, examine the following sentences. We associate one word in each sentence with past tense. Which word is that, and what common position do all these words occupy?

> 3   Sandy wrote a letter.
> 4   Sandy did not write a letter.
> 5   Sandy could not write a letter.
> 6   Sandy had written a letter.
> 7   Sandy was writing a letter.

8   Sandy had been writing a letter.
9   Sandy could have been writing a letter.
10   The letter was written by Sandy.

18   PROGRESSIVE ASPECT

''Aspect,'' as it is usually explained, has to do with the duration or completeness of what the verb denotes. The first aspect we need to distinguish, the ''progressive,'' can be illustrated by comparing the ''a'' versions of the sentences below with the simpler ''b'' versions, which contain only a tense marker before the main verb:

1a   Art was writing a book.
1b   Art wrote a book.
2a   Barbara is writing a book.
2b   Barbara writes a book.
3a   Chet will be writing a book.
3b   Chet will write a book.

(Sentences 3a and 3b, of course, also have a modal, *will*.) The ''a'' sentences seem to stress the idea of an ongoing activity. They state that the action had, or has, or will have, duration through time. The ''b'' sentences, on the other hand, give no indication of whether the action ''progresses'' or not. Suppose we imagine some action that can only occur instantaneously, one where a continuance of the action is impossible. If we put this action into a sentence, we can test our theory of progression in verb forms like those of 1, 2, and 3. Sentence 4 will serve our purpose:

4a   Kate fell in love with Jack the instant she saw him.

But if we try a progressive form in this sentence, we end up with something very odd:

4b * Kate was falling in love with Jack the instant she saw him.

The oddity arises from a contradiction in the sentence between the progressive form, which implies that the action extended over a period of time, and the words *the instant she saw him,* which state that the action took place all at once.

To account for the form of the progressive aspect, we begin by noting that sentences 1a, 2a, and 3a all have some form of the verb *be,* plus *-ing* attached to the main verb. How can we account for these forms or give instructions for producing them? We have already said that the auxiliary precedes the main verb, and consists of a sign of tense (PAST-& or PRESENT-&) and an optional modal. If we let T stand for tense, we can describe the ordering of these elements like this:

$$AUX \rightarrow T \quad (MODAL)$$

Now suppose that a sentence that will end up with the progressive aspect can have that fact marked in its derivation. We might theorize that the auxiliary, at its most basic level, will have something like progressive as an optional element following the modal. Later, the PROGRESSIVE transformation will replace this marker with the two elements *be* and ING-&:

The derivation of sentences 1a, 2a, and 3a would therefore be

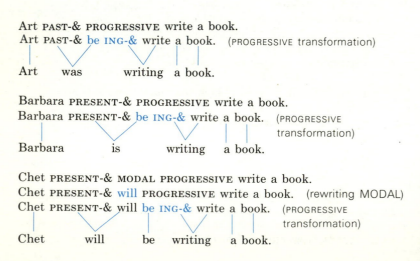

Art PAST-& PROGRESSIVE write a book.
Art PAST-& be ING-& write a book.   (PROGRESSIVE transformation)

Art   was   writing a book.

Barbara PRESENT-& PROGRESSIVE write a book.
Barbara PRESENT-& be ING-& write a book.   (PROGRESSIVE transformation)

Barbara   is   writing   a book.

Chet PRESENT-& MODAL PROGRESSIVE write a book.
Chet PRESENT-& will PROGRESSIVE write a book.   (rewriting MODAL)
Chet PRESENT-& will be ING-& write a book.   (PROGRESSIVE transformation)

Chet   will   be   writing   a book.

There is one restriction on the PROGRESSIVE transformation: the verb in the sentence must have the feature •action. Put another way, verbs marked •state do not undergo the PROGRESSIVE transformation. We need this restriction to account for the ungrammaticality of sentences like 5:

5 * Dan is resembling Rudolph Valentino.

Sentence 5 is grammatically redundant. It was pointed out in Section 17 that state verbs in themselves imply duration through time—they do not need the PROGRESSIVE transformation to show a continuing state.

Exercise

Test the definition of the progressive aspect given in the text by composing some sentences like 1:

1   Kate fell in love with Jack the instant she saw him.

The sentences should express some action that occurs instantaneously. Then rewrite the verb of the sentence in the progressive aspect. For example, suppose we start with a sentence like this:

2a Clark Kent turned into Superman in the twinkling of an eye.

We would analyze 2a as

Clark Kent PAST-& turn into Superman in the twinkling of an eye.

To put 2a into the progressive aspect, we need to insert *be* ING-& following the tense, since we have no modal in this sentence. We would therefore have

Clark Kent PAST-& be ING-& turn into Superman in the twinkling of an eye.

Joining PAST-& and *be* gives us *was;* joining ING-& and *turn* gives us *turning*. The result is the rather strange-sounding 2b:

2b Clark Kent was turning into Superman in the twinkling of an eye.

If the progressive aspect expresses duration in time, then your sentences should also sound odd, since the aspect of the verb will be contradicting the part of the sentence that states that the action occurred instantaneously (*in the twinkling of an eye,* in 2b).

19 PERFECT ASPECT

Compare sentences 1a, 2a, and 3a, traditionally said to have "perfect aspect," with the simpler 1b, 2b, and 3b:

1a Dave had written a book.
1b Dave wrote a book.
2a Elizabeth has written a book.
2b Elizabeth writes a book.
3a Fred will have written a book.
3b Fred will write a book.

The difference in meaning within each pair of sentences is difficult to express precisely. One grammarian suggests that the perfect aspect contributes the idea of "later relevance" to the sentence. That is, 1a, 2a, and 3a all imply an action that can be described as completed, but the relevance of that completed action comes at a time later than the time of the completion itself. Note that 2a, for example, states that Elizabeth has finished writing a book, and the fact of that completion is relevant or important at the moment the sentence is spoken. The sentence might occur in a dialogue like this:

Q: Do you know anyone who might want to enter this writing contest?
A: Elizabeth has written a book—I'll ask her.

But the relevance of the completed action in 1a was in the past, though later than the time of completion:

Q: I see the deadline has passed for this writing contest. Did anyone enter it?
A: Dave had written a book before the deadline. Maybe he entered.

Finally, 3a suggests that the time of relevance will come after the completion of some future action:

> Q: You have to enter this writing contest by next February. Do you know anyone who might want to try?
>
> A: Fred will have written a book by then—I'll ask him.

The PERFECT transformation operates in much the same manner as the PROGRESSIVE transformation. It produces sentences like 1a, 2a, and 3a by replacing PERFECT in the auxiliary with two elements immediately after the tense, or after the modal if there is one. The two elements are *have* and EN-&, which stands for the notion of past participle. Joined to a verb, EN-& produces the form traditionally called the past participle (both *-en* forms like *written* and *-ed* forms like *walked*). We can produce sentences 1a, 2a, and 3a with derivations like this:

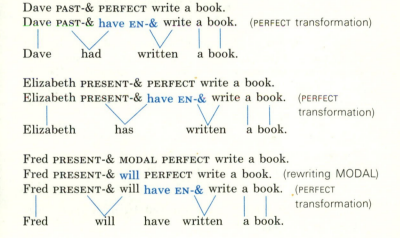

Dave PAST-& PERFECT write a book.
Dave PAST-& have EN-& write a book.   (PERFECT transformation)

Dave   had   written   a book.

Elizabeth PRESENT-& PERFECT write a book.
Elizabeth PRESENT-& have EN-& write a book.   (PERFECT transformation)

Elizabeth   has   written   a book.

Fred PRESENT-& MODAL PERFECT write a book.
Fred PRESENT-& will PERFECT write a book.   (rewriting MODAL)
Fred PRESENT-& will have EN-& write a book.   (PERFECT transformation)

Fred   will   have   written   a book.

Exercise

There should be two distinct times expressed in a sentence (or sequence of sentences) having a verb in the perfect aspect: the time of the action of the verb in the perfect aspect, and a later time at which that action is relevant. Distinguish these two times in the following passages (the verb in perfect aspect is in color; the first one is worked out for you):

> 1 She had three of the girls in Nerve Clinic over her place one night, for bridge and supper, and stuck the casserole into the oven with the frozen raspberry tarts and wondered an hour later why they weren't warm, when all the time she hadn't thought to turn the oven on.
>
> SYLVIA PLATH

Answer: The first time, that of *hadn't thought,* is the time when the woman forgets to turn on the oven. This action becomes relevant *an hour later* when she is wondering why her supper has not cooked. The verb expressing the time of relevance is *wondered.*

> 2 In the middle of the table were the flowers, stuck in a tall glass, red and yellow plastic roses he had bought at the dime-store, bold and glittering under the naked light.
>
> ROBERT PENN WARREN

> 3 What was needed was a vernacular corresponding to the creatively messy New York environment to ventilate the concentrated Surrealist imagery of poems like "Hatred," "Easter," and "Second Avenue." Though a conversational tone had existed in his poetry from the beginning, it had often seemed a borrowed one.
>
> JOHN ASHBERY

> 4 The Peace Corps represents the largest group of Americans who have ever tried to live abroad "up country."
>
> SARGENT SHRIVER

> 5 Still, Mr. Wolfe does know a great deal. He has not only been there; he has looked too.
>
> RICHARD HOGGART

20 PERFECT AND PROGRESSIVE ASPECTS TOGETHER

All the elements preceding the main verb, which taken together make up the auxiliary, are strictly ordered like this:

AUX → T + (MODAL) + (PERFECT) + (PROGRESSIVE)

Note that the last three elements are optional, and that perfect elements come before progressive. If we select both perfect and progressive, we produce some relatively complex sequences. For example, suppose that in the derivation of a sentence where PAST-& has been selected, we include both aspects. At some stage, the sentence would have a form like this:

Grace PAST-& PERFECT PROGRESSIVE write a book.

The PERFECT transformation replaces the PERFECT marker with *have* and EN-&.

Grace PAST-& have EN-& PROGRESSIVE write a book.

Next, the PROGRESSIVE transformation replaces the PROGRESSIVE marker with *be* and ING-&.

Grace PAST-& have EN-& be ING-& write a book.

PAST-& and *have* will give us *had;* EN-& and *be* will give us *been;* and ING-& and *write* will give us *writing.* The final form of the sentence would then be

1 Grace had been writing a book.

Sentences 2 and 3 provide two more examples. In 2, the development of tense has been PRESENT-&:

2 Hank has been writing a book.
   Hank PRESENT-& PERFECT PROGRESSIVE write a book.
   Hank PRESENT-& have EN-& PROGRESSIVE write a book.
   (PERFECT transformation)

Hank PRESENT-& have EN-& be ING-& write a book.

Hank   has   been   writing   a book.
   (PROGRESSIVE transformation)

And in 3, a modal is added:

3 Isabel will have been writing a book.

Isabel PRESENT-& MODAL PERFECT PROGRESSIVE write a book.
Isabel PRESENT-& will PERFECT PROGRESSIVE write a book.
Isabel PRESENT-& will have EN-& PROGRESSIVE write a book.

(PERFECT transformation)

Isabel PRESENT-& will have EN-& be ING-& write a book.

Isabel   will   have   been   writing   a book.

(PROGRESSIVE transformation)

20a   Application

PRINCIPAL PARTS

Sections 18, 19, and 20 show a transformational way of accounting for the different forms of English verbs, traditionally called the "principal parts," together with some generalizations about their meanings. All of these verbs will have a base form, traditionally called the "infinitive." As a native speaker, you learned in your first few years that the great majority of verbs formed the past tense by adding a certain set of sounds at the end of the word. In writing, the form is even simpler to express—most verbs are like *walk:*

> PAST-& + walk → walked

Some few verbs, the so-called irregular verbs, show past tense with a vowel change. Most of these occur frequently and present no problem:

> PAST-& + sing → sang

All English verbs are completely regular in their method of combining with ING-& to produce the progressive form, or "present participle"; for example, with *find:* ING-& and *find* → *finding.* Similarly, most verbs combine with EN-& to produce a past participle that is indistinguishable from the simple past tense in form: EN-& and *walk* → *walked;* PAST-& and *walk* → *walked.* A few verbs, though (again, the so-called irregular verbs), have special forms for combining with EN-&: for example, EN-& and *sing* → *sung.*

The irregular verbs are actually survivals of an older stage of the language when many more verbs formed the past tense and past participle by internal vowel change rather than by suffixation. With the passage of time, dozens of these verbs have become regular. Most of them are listed below. Note that there are alternate forms for some of the entries: this reflects a division of usage. Where an item has several entries, the number following the past tense or past participle form notes the number of occurrences of that form in the Brown Corpus (see Section 66), but the best practice in any instance of divided usage is to follow the example of respected speakers and writers in your area.

Consult your dictionary for the principal parts of other (mostly obsolete) irregular verbs.

	With: PAST-&	EN-&
abide	abode 4	abode
	abided 0	abided
arise	arose	arisen
awake	awoke	awoke 9
	awaked	awakened 4
		awaked 0
		awoken 0
bear	bore	borne
beat	beat	beat 68
		beaten 15
become	became	become
begin	began	begun
bend	bent	bent
bet	bet	bet
bid (make an offer)	bid	bid
bid (command)	bid	bid
	bade 1	bidden 0
bind	bound	bound
bite	bit	bitten
bleed	bled	bled
blow	blew	blown
break	broke	broken
breed	bred	bred
bring	brought	brought
build	built	built
burn	burned	burned 40
	burnt	burnt 6
burst	burst	burst
buy	bought	bought

	With: PAST-&	EN-&
cast	cast	cast
catch	caught	caught
chide	chided	chided 1
	chid	chid 0
		chidden 0
choose	chose	chosen
cleave	cleft	cleft 2
	cleaved	cleaved 1
	clove 1	
cling	clung	clung
clothe	clad	clad 7
	clothed	clothed 5
come	came	come
cost	cost	cost
creep	crept	crept
cut	cut	cut
deal	dealt	dealt
dig	dug	dug
dive	dived	dived 5
	dove	dove 4
do	did	done
draw	drew	drawn
dream	dreamed	dreamed 19
	dreamt	dreamt 1
drink	drank	drunk
drive	drove	driven
dwell	dwelt	dwelt 1
	dwelled	dwelled 0
eat	ate	eaten
fall	fell	fallen
feed	fed	fed
feel	felt	felt
fight	fought	fought
find	found	found
fit	fit	fit 75
	fitted	fitted 20
flee	fled	fled
fling	flung	flung
fly	flew	flown
forbid	forbad 1	forbidden
	forbade 1	

With:	PAST-&	EN-&
forget	forgot	forgotten
freeze	froze	frozen
get	got	got
		gotten
give	gave	given
go	went	gone
grind	ground	ground
grow	grew	grown
hang	hanged (executed)	hanged
	hung (suspended)	hung
hear	heard	heard
hide	hid	hidden
hit	hit	hit
hold	held	held
hurt	hurt	hurt
keep	kept	kept
kneel	knelt	knelt 8
	kneeled	kneeled 2
knit	knit	knit 10
	knitted	knitted 8
know	knew	known
lay	laid	laid
lead	led	led
leap	leaped	leaped 20
	leapt	leapt 2
leave	left	left
lend	lent	lent
let	let	let
lie (recline)	lay	lain
lie (tell a lie)	lied	lied
light	lighted	lighted 29
	lit	lit 17
lose	lost	lost
make	made	made
mean	meant	meant
meet	met	met
pay	paid	paid
put	put	put
raise	raised	raised
rid	rid	rid 19
	ridded	ridded 0

	With: PAST-&	EN-&
ride	rode	ridden
ring	rang	rung
rise	rose	risen
run	ran	run
say	said	said
see	saw	seen
seek	sought	sought
sell	sold	sold
send	sent	sent
set	set	set
shake	shook	shaken
shed	shed	shed
shine	shone	shone 5
	shined	shined 0
shoot	shot	shot
show	showed	shown 166
		showed 141
shrink	shrank	shrunken 1
		shrunk 0
shut	shut	shut
sing	sang	sung
sink	sank	sunk
sit	sat	sat
sleep	slept	slept
slide	slid	slid
sling	slung	slung
speak	spoke	spoken
speed	sped	sped 9
	speeded	speeded 3
spell	spelled	spelled 6
	spelt	spelt 0
spend	spent	spent
spin	spun	spun
spread	spread	spread
spring	sprang 13	sprung
	sprung 8	
stand	stood	stood
steal	stole	stolen
stick	stuck	stuck
sting	stung	stung

	With: PAST-&	EN-&
stink	stank	stunk
	stunk	
stride	strode	stridden
strike	struck	struck 59
		stricken 6
string	strung	strung
strive	strove 4	striven 1
	strived	strived 0
swear	swore	sworn
swell	swelled	swelled 3
		swollen 12
swim	swam	swum
swing	swung	swung
take	took	taken
teach	taught	taught
tear	tore	torn
tell	told	told
think	thought	thought
thrive	thrived	thrived 5
	throve 0	thriven 0
throw	threw	thrown
thrust	thrust	thrust
tread	trod	trodden
		trod
wake	woke	woke 14
	waked	waked 2
		wakened 1
		woken
wear	wore	worn
weave	wove	woven
wed	wedded	wedded 4
	wed	wed 2
weep	wept	wept
wet	wet	wet 53
	wetted	wetted 0
win	won	won
wind	wound	wound
wring	wrung	wrung
write	wrote	written

Exercises

1. Revise the sentences below according to the indicated transformations. Where two transformations are listed, show how the sentence would read after both have operated on it. For some transformations you may need to consult pages 13 to 17.

   1 Our company is sending you another mongoose. (Use PASSIVE transformation.)

   2 Someone keeps close watch on George. (Use PROGRESSIVE and PERFECT transformations.)

   3 The sheriff became nervous. (Use PROGRESSIVE transformation.)

   4 I extend my heartiest congratulations to you. (Use PROGRESSIVE and INDIRECT OBJECT transformations.)

   5 A tavern is in the town. (Use THERE transformation.)

   6 You will throw out that bum. (Use IMPERATIVE transformation.)

2. List all the transformations you can for each of the following sentences. Some have undergone more than one.

   1 There are some new items on the menu today.

   2 Buntline was seen lurking near the library.

   3 Our professor is sleeping again.

   4 Send me another mongoose.

   5 Gary had been seen at the burlesque show last Tuesday.

   6 The flu is going around.

Adverbials

SECTIONS **21-26**

21   **ADVERBIALS**

The word "adverb" is to grammar what the word "democracy" is to politics: we have to find out who is using it before we know what it means. Looking at traditional grammars often adds to the confusion—there we find that "adverb" is the name given to members of a large group of words, some of which modify verbs; some of which modify adjectives; some of which modify gerunds, infinitives, and participles; and some of which modify whole phrases, clauses, or even sentences. In short, adverbs are words that modify anything! A definition like this is too loose to capture any fact of language. Our procedure will be to isolate and identify the subgroups of words covered by this one term. We will try to sort them out according to the jobs they do in sentences, the changes they undergo in form, the positions in which they occur, and the relationships they express.

We began this grammar with the simple observation that a sentence can be divided into a noun phrase and a verb phrase. These parts themselves turned out to be complex, especially the verb phrase. Within it, there were smaller parts that functioned differently: the auxiliary, the main verb, and so on. Before we say that any modifiers are connected to the verb phrase, we should consider whether the parts of the verb phrase may not have modifiers of different kinds.

For example, look at *hardly, competently,* and *obviously.* Since all three end in *-ly,* they meet the simple criterion sometimes used to identify adverbs. But the three words cannot be substituted for one another in sentences. While all three can appear immediately after a modal, as in

> 1a   Roy can hardly make a desk out of two old crates.
> 2a   Roy can competently make a desk out of two old crates.
> 3a   Roy can obviously make a desk out of two old crates.

if we shift all three to the end of the sentence, only 2b seems natural. 1b is surely ungrammatical, and 3b sounds odd and strained:

> 1b * Roy can make a desk out of two old crates hardly.
> 2b   Roy can make a desk out of two old crates competently.
> 3b ? Roy can make a desk out of two old crates obviously.

Again, if we shift all three to the front of the sentence, only example 3c is now possible:

1c *Hardly Roy can make a desk out of two old crates.
2c *Competently Roy can make a desk out of two old crates.
3c Obviously Roy can make a desk out of two old crates.

Despite the formal similarity of the three words caused by their endings, they function differently—they modify different elements in the structure of the sentences. As these examples suggest, some modifiers are closely connected to the auxiliary (for instance, *hardly* in 1a), some apparently to the verb phrase itself (for instance, *competently* in 2b), and some to the sentence as a whole (for instance, *obviously* in 3c). Sections 22 to 26 cover in more detail the various words and structures that act as modifiers of these different levels.

Exercises

1. A traditional handbook of English lists the following words as examples of adverbs: *slowly, very, almost, too, sometimes, soon.* Write sentences containing each of these words. Then try substituting the words, one by one, for each of the others. Do they all interchange? Is it helpful to label all these words as adverbs?

2. Using the sentences you wrote for exercise 1, try moving the adverbs to different positions in the sentences. Which are moveable? Do any change the meaning of the sentences when they are moved?

22 PARTICLES

One part of speech traditionally considered to be made up of adverbs is not composed of adverbs at all, but rather separable parts of the verb. These are the ''particles.'' Examine the word *over* in the following sentences:

1a The grammarian thought over his mistake.
2a My guests stayed over the weekend.
3a Somebody continually watches over me.
4   Sarah turned over in her sleep.

To call all these occurrences of *over* the same part of speech grossly distorts their functions in the sentences. Even to divide them into prepositions and adverbs is not sufficient.

In sentence 1a, what we have is not an intransitive verb followed by a prepositional phrase (*over his mistake*), but a simple case of a transitive verb followed by a direct object noun phrase. The verb happens, though, to consist of two words, *think over*, and it would be entered in the lexicon in this form. The second of these two words can be shifted to the other side of the object noun phrase:

1b The grammarian thought his mistake over.

We can provide for this usage by calling the second word a particle, and giving the combination *think over* the feature specification •particle. An optional transformation, PARTICLE MOVEMENT, will allow the particle to be moved to the right of the direct object noun phrase. Compare the sentences below, all with verb-and-particle combinations:

5a Our committee kicked off the campaign with a mass meeting.
5b Our committee kicked the campaign off with a mass meeting.
6a Can we break down his resistance?
6b Can we break his resistance down?
7a The new administration takes over the office in January.
7b The new administration takes the office over in January.

PARTICLE MOVEMENT is usually, but not always, obligatory if the object noun phrase is a pronoun:

8a * To check the muffler we'll have to jack up it.

8b   To check the muffler we'll have to jack it up.

Now consider sentences like 2a and 3a. Obviously, *over* is not a particle in these sentences: it cannot be moved to the right of the next noun phrase:

2b * My guests stayed the weekend over.
3b * Somebody continually watches me over.

We might be inclined to think that these sentences have a structure like this:

My guests	stayed	over	the weekend.
NP	AUX + V	PREP	NP

This answer presents us with some difficulties, though. Note that the passive of sentence 2a is ungrammatical:

2c * The weekend was stayed over by my guests.

Yet the passive of sentence 3a sounds unobjectionable:

3c   I am continually watched over by somebody.

The problem is to set up the grammar so that sentences like 3a can have passives, but not sentences like 2a. The answer adopted here goes like this: we will analyze combinations like *watch over* as two-word verbs, like the verb-and-particle combinations illustrated. The entry in the lexicon will list the two words as a unit. But the feature specification for the unit will not carry the feature •particle, so the PARTICLE MOVEMENT transformation cannot apply to sentences with these two-word verbs. If *watch over* is listed as a unit, then *me* in sentence 3a will be the direct object noun phrase, and the PASSIVE transformation can be applied to produce 3c. On the other hand, *over the weekend* in sentence 2a will be an adverbial developed as a prepositional phrase. Since the PASSIVE transformation cannot reach into a prepositional phrase to pull out a noun phrase, passives like 2c will not be produced.

Finally, *over* in sentence 4 will be developed in a very simple way as an adverb.

Exercises

1. Which of the emphasized words below are particles?

   1. The hunter brought down a hot air balloon.
   2. Keelboats were brought down the Mississippi to New Orleans.
   3. The repairman looked up the elevator shaft.
   4. Mary Ann looked up "dolt" in the dictionary.
   5. Senator Flick pushed through a bill to make the ant the state insect.
   6. The soldiers pushed through the barricade.
   7. Alice ran up a large bill in Pittsburgh.
   8. Alice ran up a large hill in Pittsburgh.
   9. The lion-tamer turned on the radio.
   10. The lion turned on the lion-tamer.

2. It is usually claimed that particles cannot be moved across an embedded sentence. If the word *over* in 1 is moved to the end of the sentence, how does the result sound to you?

   1. Marge brought over her friend who paints still lifes.

   Does this same restriction apply to long noun phrases? Can you move *over* to the end of sentence 2?

   2. Jean brought over two long loaves of French bread, a pound of unsalted butter, and a large Camembert cheese.

   If you feel that the movement restriction applies to long noun phrases too, try to determine just how long the noun phrase must be for an awkward sentence to result.

23 PREVERBS

The "preverbs," words like *almost, always, barely, frequently, never,* and so on, offer little difficulty in their use. The name for the group is suggested by their frequent occurrence just before the tense. But the group is defined by the set of transformations applicable to it, rather than by any one of the positions in which words from the set may occur. These transformations shift the words to different positions within the sentence. Preverbs can be developed within the phrase structure rules by including an additional, optional category in the auxiliary:

$$AUX \rightarrow (PREVERB) + T + (MODAL)$$

The new version of the rule will generate sentences like

1   She frequently disagrees with her professors.

The preverb is thus generated as the first element in the auxiliary, but this single position will not alone be sufficient to classify a word as a preverb. These words occur in at least two other places in sentences, and the three positions taken together identify a particular word as a preverb. Our first transformation, PREVERB RIGHT SHIFT, moves the preverb to the right, over certain other words, relating a sentence like 2a to 2b:

2a   The 10:15 always is late.
2b   The 10:15 is always late.

The transformation shifts the preverb to the right of any modal:

3a   I usually can be found in my office at that time.
3b   I can usually be found in my office at that time.

This transformation also shifts the preverb to the right of *have* (inserted by the PERFECT transformation):

4a   I rarely have met anyone like him.
4b   I have rarely met anyone like him.

Finally, the PREVERB RIGHT SHIFT transformation shifts the preverb to the right of *be* from any source, transformational or not:

5a   The champion barely is holding his serve.
5b   The champion is barely holding his serve.
6a   Dr. Johnson seldom was contradicted.
6b   Dr. Johnson was seldom contradicted.
7a   The committee often was indecisive.
7b   The committee was often indecisive.
8a   Her opinions frequently are a cause of trouble.
8b   Her opinions are frequently a cause of trouble.

This transformation (and the one to follow) must obviously take place very late in the generation of a sentence, since it has to follow all the transformations that insert *be* or *have*.

From each of the "a" examples above we can derive a second variation, by means of the PREVERB LEFT SHIFT transformation. However, there are two subclasses of preverbs, and this transformation produces two different results, depending on which kind of preverb is being moved.

In the first subclass (for convenience, we can call them "positive" preverbs) are words like *always, frequently, often,* and *usually*. With positive preverbs, the PREVERB LEFT SHIFT transformation moves only the preverb to the left of the sentence, producing

> 3c   Usually I can be found in my office at that time.
> 7c   Often the committee was indecisive.
> 8c   Frequently her opinions are a cause of trouble.

The second subclass, the "negative" preverbs (so called because they are felt to contribute an element of negation to the sentences in which they occur), includes words like *barely, hardly, never, rarely,* and *seldom*. With negative preverbs, the PREVERB LEFT SHIFT transformation moves the preverb, together with the tense, any modal, and *have* or *be*, to the left of the subject noun phrase, yielding

> 4c   Rarely have I met anyone like him.
> 5c   Barely is the champion holding his serve.
> 6c   Seldom was Dr. Johnson contradicted.

23a   Application

DOUBLE NEGATIVE

If a sentence already containing *not* has a negative preverb (*barely, hardly,* etc.), we have a so-called double negative:

> I can't hardly find the part I need.

Although common in earlier writings, the double negative was vigorously (if mistakenly) attacked by grammarians, beginning in the eighteenth century. Their efforts were successful for the most part, and the double negative, of which sentence 1 is only one kind, has largely disappeared from edited written English. The double negative still survives, of course, in speech and in the reflex of speech in writing, dialogue: the construction provides an easy way of characterizing the speaker as extremely casual, or provincial, or lacking formal education. The section on usage has more information on these variations.

Exercises

1. You may have noted that all the preverbs qualify the action of the verb in a particular way. What element of meaning do the preverbs share?

2. Find ten sentences containing preverbs in works by ten different authors. Where in the sentences do the preverbs occur? Then find ten sentences with preverbs by a single author. Do you find any characteristic placement? Be sure to note the source of each example sentence.

3. Arrange the preverbs in order from most positive to most negative, and try them one by one in a sentence with a negative verb. Which preverbs give you a so-called double negative?

24   THE DO-INSERTION TRANSFORMATION

The PREVERB LEFT SHIFT transformation (Section 23) has one un-expected result: when a negative preverb occurs in a sentence with-out a modal, *have,* or *be,* the transformation can still take place, but then only the preverb and the tense will be moved to the left of the sentence. Thus, from 1a we would derive 1b by PREVERB LEFT SHIFT:

1a   Zola never PAST-& yield to those who would silence him.

1b * Never PAST-& Zola yield to those who would silence him.

As 1b stands, it is no sentence at all. We have no rule that allows us to join the tense to a noun phrase. An obligatory transformation, though, will specify that *do* is inserted to the right of a tense marker whenever it is separated from a modal, *have, be,* or a verb. Applying the DO-INSERTION transformation to 1b gives us

> 1c   Never PAST-& do Zola yield to those who would silence him.

Joining PAST-& and *do* gives us

> 1d   Never did Zola yield to those who would silence him.

We can be doubly sure we are correct here in general, if not in detail, since DO-INSERTION is also required following a transformation that produces a question.

Exercises

1. Section 24 points out that DO-INSERTION is needed for questions as well as for PREVERB LEFT SHIFT. Compare question and statement forms of the same sentence (1 and 2 illustrate a typical pair):

    1   The band will be here at sunrise.
    2   Will the band be here at sunrise?

    Based on your examination of a number of pairs, tell briefly how a QUESTION transformation would operate to turn statements into questions. The problem will be easier if you start with sentences containing modals; then try some without modals. Note how the DO-INSERTION transformation fills the need with this second group of sentences very nicely.

2. Which transformation would have to operate first in the production of sentences, QUESTION or DO-INSERTION? Why?

25   TIME AND PLACE ADVERBIALS

Adverbial constructions are an extremely varied lot, so much so that perhaps the variety is an indication that there is something faulty in our analysis. But adverbials are themselves so diverse—and their study within a transformational framework so recent—that a more consistent analysis is difficult, if not impossible. Moreover, the analysis here is only a partial one. Many constructions that seem to modify the verb phrase will resist classification as one of the types we will distinguish. But many frequently used adverbials can be analyzed in the manner presented here, and that fact makes the next few sections useful in the absence of a more comprehensive treatment.

Two easily spotted adverbials specify the time and place of the action indicated by the verb:

1   Chaucer may have met Petrarch in Italy in 1373.
                                     •place   •time

For the moment, we will need to distinguish two kinds of time and place adverbials.

Single-word time and place modifiers, and these only, we will call adverbs:

2   My computer is being rewired tonight.
                                   •time

3   I saw a two-dollar bill nearby.
                             •place

Time or place can also be shown by a construction consisting of a preposition followed by a noun phrase, if the noun phrase has a headnoun carrying the feature •time or •place:

4   Meet me at seven o'clock.
             •time

5   Meet me on the corner.
             •place

Whether a single-word adverb or a prepositional phrase serving as an adverbial, time and place modifiers can be isolated and identified through the use of questions beginning with *when* and *where*. Suppose we are to identify the time adverbial in a sentence like 6a:

6a   Hemingway's last book was published in 1964.

All we need to do is rephrase the sentence in question form beginning with *when:*

>   6b   When was Hemingway's last book published?

The answer, *in 1964,* identifies the time adverbial of the original sentence. In the same way, place adverbials can be identified by a related question beginning with *where:*

>   7a   Several small children were playing under the crab-apple tree.
>   7b   Where were several small children playing?

The answer to question 7b, *under the crabapple tree,* identifies the place adverbial.

The prepositions used with time and place adverbials differ, as the examples above show, and would have to be specified for individual nouns. Note, for example, that we signal time with the preposition *in* for years or months, *on* for days of the week, and *at* for the hours of the day:

>   8   Our club meets at 6:30 on the first Saturday in September.

Similarly, prepositions used with place adverbials differ: we use *in* for countries, regions of the country, states, and cities; we say a building is located *on* a certain street, and *at* a particular address:

>   9   Bud lives at 313 Tabor Street.
>   10   The old Market House stood on Diamond Street.
>   11   First prize is a two-week vacation in West Bradford, Illinois.

The easiest way to mark these usages in a formal grammar might be to include them in a feature of a particular noun in its lexicon entry. Thus, for a noun like *Chicago,* one of its features would be •place: *in.*

Exercises

1. If time and place adverbials can be identified by asking *when* and *where,* what kinds of adverbials are identified by asking *how* and *why?*

2. How many single-word adverbs of time and place can you list?

3. The text states that prepositions have to be specified for individual nouns. Now consider whether other factors besides the noun influence which preposition is used. Which sentence do you prefer, 1 or 2?

> 1 Robert lives in San Francisco.
> 2 Robert lives at San Francisco.

Which do you prefer, 3 or 4? ·

> 3 Our plane landed at San Francisco.
> 4 Our plane landed in San Francisco.

Do 5 and 6 mean the same thing?

> 5 Gerda stopped at San Francisco.
> 6 Gerda stopped in San Francisco.

Can you account for the use of different prepositions with the same noun?

26   MANNER ADVERBIALS

"Manner adverbials" derive their name from the relationship they bear to the rest of the verb phrase: they describe the manner or way in which the action of the verb occurs. Manner adverbials in a sentence appear as answers to related questions beginning with the pronoun *how*. We can find the manner adverbial in a sentence like 1a

> 1a   Cecelia defused the bomb competently.

by means of the related question beginning with *how* in 1b:

> 1b   How did Cecelia defuse the bomb?

The answer, *competently,* is the manner adverbial of 1a.

Single-word manner adverbials, of which there are thousands, are illustrated by the words in color in the example sentences below:

> 2a   The motor coughed and sputtered disturbingly.

3a   Ishmael *eagerly* signed aboard Ahab's ship.
4a   Gauguin left for Tahiti *impulsively*.

The most obvious thing about the manner adverbials in these sentences is their form—all three end in *-ly*. Nearly as obvious is what would happen if the *-ly* were omitted: we would have three words that can be used as adjectives—*disturbing, eager,* and *impulsive.* If we derive the adverbials from the adjective forms, we would build into our grammar the relationship between the two forms. At the same time, we can formalize our idea that these adverbials tell us something about *how* the action of the verb takes place: we can postulate that manner adverbials are derived from prepositional phrases made up of pro-forms. Just as the pro-forms for time and place were symbolized by •time and •place, so we can adopt •manner to stand for a pro-form of a manner adverbial. Suppose we start, then, with a form like this:

4b   Gauguin left for Tahiti *in an impulsive manner*.

Now we need a transformation to show the relation that exists between the phrase *in an impulsive manner* and the word *impulsively.* We can call this the ADVERBIAL transformation; it will change 4b to 4a:

4a   Gauguin left for Tahiti *impulsively*.

Similarly, the other example sentences would have, as underlying forms

2b   The motor coughed and sputtered *in a disturbing manner*.
3b   Ishmael signed aboard Ahab's ship *in an eager manner*.

26a   Application

ADJECTIVE AND ADVERB FORM

Although the ADVERBIAL transformation changes a phrase like *in an impulsive manner* to *impulsively,* it is a little misleading to think that the transformation mechanically adds *-ly* to an adjective and thereby changes it to an adverb. Natural languages are not that neat or orderly. Usually adverbial forms end in -ly, but there are a handful of words that have an adverb form identical to the adjective form—fast, for instance. With this particular word, we would have to maintain that the ADVERBIAL transformation changes 1a to 1b without affecting the form of fast at all:

> 1a Sally habitually drives in a fast manner.
> 1b Sally habitually drives fast.

Some other words that, like fast, do not change in form from adjective to adverb are quick, hard, and slow. Note that two of these, quick and slow, have a second adverb form that follows the regular pattern: quickly and slowly. But these few examples lead us to a further complication: note that in sentences up to this point, a manner adverbial can be moved to a position between the noun phrase and the verb phrase. This stylistic transformation changes the examples of Section 26 to

> 2c The motor disturbingly coughed and sputtered.
> 3c Ishmael eagerly signed aboard Ahab's ship.
> 4c Gauguin impulsively left for Tahiti.

But with fast we cannot make this change. If we try, we get something like this:

> 1c * Sally fast habitually drives.

Words like quick, hard, slow, and fast retain their peculiar form from an older stage of the English language; they are survivals (or fossils, if you like) from a time when adverb formation was different from what it is now.

One final caution: words like friendly, likely, and lovely are adjectives despite the -ly. From our point of view, they are simply adjectives that coincidentally have the same ending as adverbs.

Exercises

1. A sentence like 1 below is superficially similar to those in Section 26:

> 1 The train to Scranton will be delayed slightly.

But it presents some problems for our analysis. Obviously, we cannot say that 1 derives from 2:

> 2 * The train to Scranton will be delayed in a slight manner.

Note that we would not ask, "How will the train to Scranton be delayed?" and expect to get the answer "Slightly." What question would you ask to identify the adverbial we find in 1? Can you suggest a source for adverbials like *slightly,* and the ones in 3, 4, and 5?

> 3   Gus is highly musical.
> 4   Some of the travelers were greatly inconvenienced.
> 5   The disruption disappointed the stationmaster intensely.

2. Is sentence 1 odd in the same way or for the same reason that phrase 2 is odd?

> 1   The clam acted tactfully.
> 2   the tactful clam

If the two constructions are odd for the same reason, how does the ADVERBIAL transformation keep the grammar from having to say the same thing twice, as far as feature restrictions are concerned?

Pronouns

SECTIONS **27-33**

27 PRONOUNS

Grammarians argue about how pronouns should be handled in a transformational grammar. There is a certain amount of difficulty in the material itself, but a larger cause of the disagreement is the greater task that transformationalists accept. They want their grammars to embody a theory explaining how pronouns refer to antecedents. For example, consider this sentence:

> 1 The later Heidegger is far more the historical prophet, *his* tone is more sweeping and apocalyptic, and the themes of *his* thought are the total historical perspectives of Western civilization.
>
> WILLIAM BARRETT

In example 1, the two occurrences of *his* both refer to *Heidegger*. In traditional terms, *Heidegger* would be called the antecedent of *his*. But how do we know that? Some transformational grammars claim that pronouns do not occur in deep structure; if the same noun phrase occurs two (or more) times in the deep structure of a sentence, the first occurrence of that noun phrase (the antecedent) causes the second occurrence to be replaced in the surface structure by a pronoun. Example 2a shows a sentence at a level of derivation where the noun phrases are both still present in full form:

> 2a But in 1960 and 1961 for the first time *the idea* was joined with the power and the desire to implement *the idea*.

Note the repetition of *the idea*. Such noun phrases are called "equivalent" noun phrases. A transformation called EQUIVALENT NOUN PHRASE REPLACEMENT changes 2a to 2b:

> 2b But in 1960 and 1961 for the first time *the idea* was joined with the power and the desire to implement *it*.
>
> SARGENT SHRIVER

Another difficulty of a transformational approach arises from a rigid insistence that the conditions for pronoun replacement be based on examination of single sentences. The conditions for the change from example 2a to 2b are easily described: the equivalent noun phrase to the right is replaced by a pronoun. But a sentence like 3 complicates matters:

> 3 Since returning from his world tour last year, Bruce has been arrested seven times in all.
>
> ALBERT GOLDMAN

When we try to describe the conditions for replacement here, the descriptions quickly become very complex; as the descriptions increase in complexity, so do the rules that try to account for these descriptions. But for theme-writing purposes at least, we can disregard the grammarian's restriction: there is no such thing as a one-sentence theme, so our equivalent noun phrases can appear in sequences of sentences. The next eight sections discuss pronouns in more detail.

Exercise

Your elementary grammars probably claimed that a pronoun might substitute for a noun. This simple explanation need no longer be accepted unquestioningly, though, since it is easily shown to be misleading, if not false. Consider this sentence:

> The leafy green plant was on the windowsill, but someone moved it.

What does *it* substitute for? Test your answer by replacing *it* with the word or words you believe the pronoun replaces. If the resulting sentence is grammatical (although a little redundant), your answer is correct. Do pronouns like *it* replace nouns?

28 PERSON

We will begin with what are traditionally called the "personal pronouns," those words that show the grammatical features of "person," "number," "gender," and "case." The personal pronouns are a catalogue of some grammatical features that have become obsolete elsewhere in the language. Hence, for many of these features there are no easy comparisons we can make. An examination of each of the features in turn, though, will give us some understanding of general processes that contribute to the transfer of information in other languages besides our own.

Some of the personal pronouns refer to the addresser—the person speaking or writing: these are the "first person" pronouns. Some refer to the addressee—the one spoken or written to: these are called "second person." Still others refer to some other person or thing—that is, to anyone or anything except the addresser or addressee: these are the "third person" pronouns. First and third person pronouns have different forms for singular and plural, and even the second person has a singular form, *thou,* which is rarely used:

	Singular	Plural
First person	I	we
Second person	you	you
Third person	he, she, it	they

At one time, verbs in English had distinct forms, too, depending on the person of their subject noun phrases: one ending was used with a first person subject, another ending was used with a second person subject, and so on. In the table below, the left column shows how the form of the verb *sing* changed according to the person of its subject (the language illustrated, usually called Old English, was in use about A.D. 1000). Some obsolete letters in the Old English examples have been replaced by the customary modern English equivalents. The middle column shows what the regular developments of the Old English forms would have been. These are probably familiar to you from liturgical language or older literary works. The column on the right shows the usual forms for current English: note that *sing* has a change in form—*sings*—only in the third person singular:

First person	ic singe	I sing	I sing
Second person	thū singest	thou singest	you sing
Third person	hē, hēo,	he, she,	he, she,
	hit singeth	it singeth	it sings

Exercises

1. Language is systematic, and the first table above lists part of that system, the subject noun phrase forms of the personal pronouns

common to all speakers of English. There are, however, several forms in use by large numbers of speakers; two of the most frequently heard are spelled *you-all* (or *y'all*) and *you'ns.* Persons who use one of these forms do not use the other. If you have used or do use one of these forms, can you determine where it fits in the table? After you have located the form in the table, consider whether speakers of English who use this form are trying to fill a gap in the table and thus make the personal pronouns more systematic. Would forms like *y'all* and *you'ns,* or other forms doing the same job, be almost predictable? Are any obsolete pronoun forms relevant to this discussion?

2. In D. H. Lawrence's *Sons and Lovers,* a young man suggests to his girlfriend that she might enjoy visiting a coal mine to see how it is operated. Then he changes his mind:

> "Shouldn't ter like it?" he asked tenderly. " 'Appen not, it 'ud dirty thee."

We are then told about the young woman:

> She had never been "thee'd" and "thou'd" before.

Would you suspect that at this time (late nineteenth century), in this particular dialect, there was some special significance in a young man's addressing an unrelated young woman as *thou?*

3. Would it be easy or difficult to translate *She had never been "thee'd" and "thou'd" before* into French or German?

29 GENDER

Among third person pronouns, there are limitations on what noun phrases each can replace: the singular forms *he, she,* and *it* are selected on the basis of whether the noun phrase being replaced has the feature •masculine, •feminine, or •neuter. For human nouns, •masculine appears to be the general feature, •feminine the special one: that is, unless a human noun is specifically marked •feminine, the noun phrase of which it is the headnoun is replaced by *he, his,* or *him.* Sentences like the following illustrate this convention:

One hundred years later, the Negro is still languished

in the corners of American society, and finds himself an exile in his own land.

MARTIN LUTHER KING, JR.

Although the noun phrase *the Negro* is not specifically marked for gender, it is replaced by the pronouns *himself* and *his,* both having the feature •masculine. (See Section 6 for more information on the distinction.)

Exercises

1. In the preview issue of *Ms.* magazine (Spring 1972), Kate Miller and Casey Swift wrote an article entitled "De-Sexing the English Language," in which they argue that the use of *he* as a generic pronoun inflicts psychic damage on women. The authors cite examples such as the following as objectionable, since both males and females are referred to:

   1 You take each child where you find him.
   2 The next time you meet a handicapped person, don't make up your mind about him in advance.

   Miller and Swift approvingly quote a woman college president who says that

   this habit of language . . . implies that personality is really a male attribute, and that women are human subspecies. . . . It would be a miracle if a girl-baby, learning to use the symbols of our tongue, could escape some wound to her self-respect: whereas a boy-baby's ego is bolstered by the pattern of our language.

   Two currently used methods of avoiding the problem meet with disapproval from the authors. The first of these is to use both pronouns: "And as for every citizen who pays taxes, I say that *he or she* deserves an accounting!" The authors dismiss this solution as "often awkward." The second solution is found in another example quoted by Miller and Swift: "Anybody can join the Glee Club as long as *they* can carry a tune." They describe this use of *they* as unacceptable, "at least to grammarians." A similar sentence is noted as being "in blatant defiance of every teacher of freshman English." They conclude that "there is no way in English to solve problems like these with felicity and grace," and they propose a new set of singular pronouns of common gender:

	SINGULAR		PLURAL
	Distinct gender	*Common gender*	
Nominative	he, she	tey	they
Possessive	his, her(s)	ter(s)	their(s)
Objective	him, her	tem	them

Are any of the new common gender forms already in use in any dialect of English? (See exercise 2, Section 28.) Would this present an obstacle to their adoption?

2. Consult a few up-to-date freshman handbooks to test Miller and Swift's opinion of sentences like "Anybody can join the Glee Club as long as *they* can carry a tune."

3. Has English ever had a common gender singular pronoun? What happened to it? (See Thomas Pyles, *The Origins and Development of the English Language,* 2nd ed. New York: Harcourt Brace Jovanovich, 1971. P. 171.)

4. How do the following sentences relate to the Miller and Swift article?

   1 "Somebody called you while you were out."
   "What did they want?"

   2 "What a nice baby! What's its name?"

30 CASE

Modern English relies heavily on the order of the words in a sentence (at least in surface structure) to convey essential grammatical information. In a sentence like

John saw Mary.

we understand from the word order that John did the seeing, and Mary was seen. If we call the notion of subject or object a "grammatical function," an examination of several languages shows us that word order is not the only way in which grammatical functions can be expressed. Suppose we make up a language: in this imaginary tongue, the subject noun phrase always has the word *subject* tacked onto its end; the object noun phrase always has the word *object* attached to it. Our example sentence, written in the new language, looks like this:

> Johnsubject saw Maryobject.

We no longer need to preserve word order, since the information that it carried can be signaled by our two new suffixes. Therefore, all the following sentences are synonymous with the first two versions in our new language:

> Johnsubject Maryobject saw.
> Maryobject Johnsubject saw.
> Maryobject saw Johnsubject.
> Saw Maryobject Johnsubject.
> Saw Johnsubject Maryobject.

In every one of the examples, John does the seeing, Mary is seen. Our new language has free word order; the words can come in any sequence whatever and no information about their grammatical functions is lost.

Our tags, *-subject* and *-object,* are examples of case markers. A "case marker" is a change in the form of a word that shows the grammatical function of that word in the sentence. At one time English nouns had several case markers, but with the passage of time only one of these has survived: that which appears in written English as *'s,* for genitive case, as in "the *man's* hat."

English pronouns, on the other hand, have retained almost all their different forms for showing grammatical function: they have one form for use as the subject noun phrase (called, traditionally, "nominative" case):

I have some thoughts on this matter.	(first person singular)
We have some thoughts on this matter.	(first person plural)
You seem troubled today.	(second person singular and plural)
He (or she, or it) can be found at home.	(third person singular)
They can be found at home.	(third person plural)

116

A second form, "objective" case, is used when the pronoun occupies the object position or follows a preposition:

Robert Graves fascinates me. Sam gave the schedule to me.	(first person singular)
Robert Graves fascinates us. Sam gave the schedule to us.	(first person plural)
The club elected her (or him) president. Jones lives on the floor above him (or her).	(third person singular)
The club elected them officers. Jones lives on the floor above them.	(third person plural)

Note that there is no special objective form for either *you* or *it:*

The committee elected you secretary.
I collected it on my last field trip.

A third form, called "genitive" or "possessive" case, results when the pronoun is changed to a determiner:

Have you seen my new house?	(first person singular)
Have you seen our new house?	(first person plural)
This is your fall schedule.	(second person singular and plural)
Walter established his theory. Wendy established her theory. Even grammar has its uses.	(third person singular)
The guests took their seats.	(third person plural)

Finally, the pronouns have special forms when used following *be*, sometimes called the "predicate adjective" forms:

The fault is mine.	(first person singular)
The fault is ours.	(first person plural)
A great opportunity is yours.	(second person singular and plural)
The ticket is hers (or his, or its).	(third person singular)
The tickets are theirs.	(third person plural)

117

All the different forms of the personal pronouns are summarized in the following table:

SINGULAR

	Subject noun phrase (nominative)	*Object noun phrase* (objective)	*Determiner* (genitive)	*Following* be (predicate adjective)
First person	I	me	my	mine
Second person	you	you	your	yours
Third person	he	him	his	his
	she	her	her	hers
	it	it	its	its

PLURAL

First person	we	us	our	ours
Second person	(same as singular forms)			
Third person	they	them	their	theirs

30a   Application

CASE AND COMPOUND FORMS

Ironically, some of the problems writers have with case forms of pronouns are the result of instruction in grammar. Somewhere along the line, a pupil writes something like this:

> 1 * Billy and me went to the circus.

The teacher so effectively purges him of the flaw that he never again uses *me* in a compound form, and ends up writing sentences like this:

2 * Dad took Billy and I to the circus.

For compound noun phrases, remember that there is absolutely no difference in edited English between the pronoun form that would appear in a grammatical position by itself, and the form that appears in that position as part of a compound. Thus, since you would use *me* in a sentence like 3a, you should also use *me* in a compound in that position, as in 3b:

3a   The infirmary gave me an excuse.
3b   The infirmary gave Tom and me excuses.

Similarly, for the subject position we would have

4a   Tom and I were given excuses by the infirmary.

since the pronoun form / would be used if it were not part of a compound:

4b   I was given an excuse by the infirmary.

30b   Application

CASE IN EMBEDDED SENTENCES

Notice the different pronouns used in two sentences below that are otherwise very similar:

1a   I know he is trustworthy.
1b   I know him to be trustworthy.

Sentence 1a shows a straightforward use of the THAT transformation, followed by THAT DELETION (see Section 36 for information on embedded sentences); 1b starts from the same deep structure:

I know [he PRESENT-& be trustworthy].

but here the FOR . . . TO transformation has been used to embed the sentence:

1c   * I know [for he to be trustworthy].

Following a preposition, the objective form of the pronoun is needed. Hence, *he* becomes *him:*

> 1d   I know [for him to be trustworthy].

The only problem with this solution is that we have called *for* introduced by the FOR . . . TO transformation an embedder. Note, though, that we have sentences like 2:

> 2   It is desirable for him to be here on time.

In sentence 2, we have evidence that *for* is an embedder with respect to the sentence it introduces, and at the same time a preposition with respect to the noun phrase immediately following it. This accounts for the form of 1d. *Know* is one of the verbs for which FOR DELETION is obligatory, giving us the final form of the sentence (1b).

Here is a quick test to decide which form of the pronoun to use: if the pronoun in question is followed by a verb in the so-called infinitive form (that is, preceded by *to*), the pronoun should be objective:

> 3a   Al expected them to win the Series.

If *that* can be inserted before the pronoun in question, the pronoun will have the nominative form:

> 3b   Al expected (that) they would win the Series.

Exercises

1. Find out as much as you can about the reasons for and persistence of the Quakers' use of the pronoun *thee*. Which of the following sentences represents normal seventeenth-century English and which might have been spoken by a nineteenth-century Quaker?

> 1   Thou art old, Father William.
> 2   Thee is old, Father William.

2. Theoretically, the different case forms of pronouns provide us with grammatical information that only word order gives us for nouns.

Pronouns should therefore be more moveable than noun phrases, since the information will not be lost by moving the pronoun from its place in the sentence. Write two sentences, differing only in that one has a pronoun where the other has a noun phrase. Move the pronoun and noun phrase to different positions in the sentence, testing whether one has more freedom of placement than the other.

3. Revise the sentence *John saw he.*

31   THE REFLEXIVE TRANSFORMATION

In the analysis adopted in this text, third person pronouns replace an equivalent noun phrase. Two transformations accomplish this result fairly well. The first of these, the transformation that produces reflexive pronouns, operates within simple sentences—that is, sentences that contain no embedded sentences. (See Section 32 for EQUIVALENT NOUN PHRASE REPLACEMENT, the other pronoun transformation.) When equivalent noun phrases (Section 27) appear in a simple sentence, the noun phrase to the right is replaced by the appropriate reflexive pronoun. Thus, from the deeper structure in 1a below, we derive 1b by the REFLEXIVE transformation (assuming that both instances of Tony refer to the same person):

1a Tony cut Tony while shaving.
1b Tony cut himself while shaving.

The REFLEXIVE transformation is obligatory, and it operates before the various deletions that occur in embedded sentences.

31a   Application

REFLEXIVE PRONOUNS

A grammarian does not expect to find a thoroughgoing consistency in natural languages—their history is too chancy for that. The reflexive pronouns teach this lesson effectively. The reflexives look very much like forms of personal pronouns plus *self* or *selves*. In the case of *herself, myself, yourself, yourselves,* and *ourselves*, the pronoun form seems to be the genitive case: *her, my, your,* etc. We can add *itself* to the list if we think of it as *its* and *self.* But two other reflexives, *himself* and *themselves,* seem to use the objective form of the personal pronouns—*him* and *them.* Why these two reflexives should have forms like the objective, and all the rest like the genitive, is hard to say. No only that: if we were to be completely consistent and use the genitive pronoun forms for the last two, we would have *hisself* and *theirselves*—two forms that, while heard, enjoy definitely less status in society than *himself* and *themselves.*

Exercise

We have seen how the REFLEXIVE transformation changes sentences like 1a to 1b

    1a   John outsmarted John.
    1b   John outsmarted himself.

and how the IMPERATIVE transformation changes sentences like 2a to 2b:

    2a   You will open the door.
    2b   Open the door.

Now suppose that we have a sentence like 3, where both IMPERATIVE and REFLEXIVE have operated:

    3   Educate yourself.

In what order must the IMPERATIVE and REFLEXIVE transformations apply to produce a sentence like 3? Is it first IMPERATIVE, then RE-FLEXIVE, or vice versa? Explain your answer.

32 PRONOUNS AND REFERENCE

Traditional grammars view the "pronoun" as a word that refers to or replaces a noun. This statement needs some modification, though. In a sentence like 1, we can think of the word *one* as replacing a second occurrence of *theologian* in deep structure:

    1   As a critical theologian, Barth ranks with Kierke-
        gaard; as a constructive one, with Aquinas and Calvin.

                                  JOHN UPDIKE

We can call this process EQUIVALENT NOUN REPLACEMENT (see Section 27). But the third person pronouns must replace a noun phrase, not just a noun. In a sentence like

> 2a Harvey misplaced his new celluloid collar, and can't find it anywhere.

it replaces a repetition of the phrase *his new celluloid collar*. If the pronoun replaced only the noun *collar,* we should be able to insert *it* in the place of that word alone, but we cannot:

> 2b * Harvey misplaced his new celluloid collar, and can't find his new celluloid it anywhere.

Clearly, a third person personal pronoun must replace a noun phrase. We can call this process EQUIVALENT NOUN PHRASE REPLACEMENT. In the great majority of cases, the EQUIVALENT NOUN PHRASE REPLACEMENT transformation substitutes a pronoun for the equivalent noun phrase to the right (a process called ''right pronominalization''). From 3a, therefore, we would derive 3b:

> 3a The fox squirrel had been a relatively common animal in the town; after the spraying the fox squirrel was gone.
>
> 3b The fox squirrel had been a relatively common animal in the town; after the spraying it was gone.
>
> RACHEL CARSON

Usually, right pronominalization means that the closest applicable noun phrase preceding the pronoun is its antecedent. For example:

> 4 To those new states whom we welcome to the ranks of the free, we pledge our word that one form of colonial control shall not have passed away merely to be replaced by a far more iron tyranny. We shall not always expect to find them supporting our view.
>
> JOHN F. KENNEDY

Them in the example above has among its features •third person and •plural. Although many noun phrases intervene between *them* and its antecedent, we are not in doubt that the pronoun refers to *those new states;* all the other noun phrases between *those new states* and the pronoun are disqualified, either because they have the feature •singular (*one form, colonial control,* and *a far more iron tyranny*), or because they have the feature •first person (*we*).

Under certain complex conditions, the equivalent noun phrase to the left may be replaced by a pronoun (''left pronominalization'')—for example:

> 5a   Six months after his death, John F. Kennedy is certain to take his place in American lore as one of those sure-sell heroes out of whose face or words or monuments a souvenir dealer can turn a steady buck.
>
> TOM WICKER

Presumably, this sentence derives from

> 5b   Six months after John F. Kennedy's death, John F. Kennedy, is certain. . . .

and it therefore illustrates left pronominalization. In a sequence of sentences, though, we can usually disregard the possibility that the left equivalent noun phrase will be replaced by a pronoun.

32a   Application

AMBIGUOUS REFERENCE

The strategies we use in interpreting the reference of pronouns sometimes fail us—we cannot tell what the antecedent of a particular pronoun is. But when this happens, the fault is invariably the writer's, not the reader's. We need to consider, therefore, the most frequent problems in pronoun reference. Sometimes it is possible for any one of several noun phrases to be mistaken for the antecedent of a pronoun:

> 1   The student assault upon the attempt of Berkeley deans to control their tiny strip of land at Bancroft and Telegraph Avenues marshalled support from students and faculty on a scale unprecedented at American universities.
>
> MICHAEL VINCENT MILLER

Here the problem involves the antecedent of *their: to control their tiny strip of land at Bancroft and Telegraph Avenues* is all that remains of an embedded sentence. That embedded sentence has had its subject noun phrase deleted, and we do not know which of the following constructions sentence 1 should be derived from:

> for the students to control the students' tiny strip of land
>
> for Berkeley deans to control Berkeley deans' tiny strip of land

As 1 stands, the closest noun phrase preceding *their* is *Berkeley deans,* making it appear to be the antecedent. We know from news of the affair that the students controlled that strip of land, but we cannot always depend on the reader's knowledge of the context of a sentence to get us out of difficulty. In the terminology of transformational grammar, the deleted subject noun phrase is ''unrecoverable.'' Make sure, then, that your deletions have not obscured the relationship between a pronoun and its antecedent.

A similar ambiguous reference occurs in the first sentence of an essay by Jimmy Breslin:

2　The wife of a new neighbor from up on the corner came down and walked up to my wife and started acting nice, which must have exhausted her.

Who is exhausted, Breslin's wife or the neighbor's wife? The rest of the essay makes the answer abundantly clear, but the readers have to tolerate Breslin's ambiguities in the hope of being repaid by his humor: he makes no pretense of clear thinking and logical argument in this essay. But even in humorous writing, forcing a reader to puzzle over a pronoun reference wins no audiences.

32b　Application

REMOTE ANTECEDENT

In comprehending speech or writing, our problem is the reverse of that of composition: instead of replacing noun phrases with pronouns, we decide what noun phrases have been replaced. It may be that when we read, we retain certain information for a short time; perhaps when we see a noun phrase like *the tall man,* part of what we remember is the feature specification of the noun phrase, which in this case would be:

the tall man
- •singular
- •human
- •masculine
- •third person

Suppose then that the phrase occurs in a sentence like this:

> Although the tall man had been missing for several months, sought after by the CIA and his faithful dog Scout, it was not until Sheila DeVere joined the search that he was located.

Matching the features of *he* (•singular, •human, •masculine, •third person) with those of the noun phrases preceding the pronoun, we find that only *the tall man* matches the features of *he,* and we select *the tall man* as the antecedent.

Although we remember the content of what we read for an extended time, we apparently retain the exact wording for a very short time. Thus, if the antecedent is too far removed from the pronoun replacing the equivalent noun phrase, comprehension becomes difficult. It is hard to say exactly how far is too far; certainly, the more noun phrases that intervene between the antecedent and the pronoun, the heavier the load on our memory. Keeping the antecedent and the pronoun close together avoids the problem.

The repetition of parallel structures offers a second way to aid comprehension, even if the pronoun is far removed from the antecedent, as the following example shows:

> For it can be shown—I intend to show—that with all the harmonious belonging and all the tidying up of background conditions that you please, our abundant society is at present simply deficient in many of the most elementary objective opportunities and worthwhile goals that could make growing up possible. It is lacking in enough man's work. It is lacking in honest public speech, and people are not taken seriously. It

is lacking in the opportunity to be useful. It thwarts aptitude and creates stupidity. It corrupts ingenuous patriotism. It corrupts the fine arts. It shackles science. It dampens animal ardor. It discourages the religious convictions of Justification and Vocation and it dims the sense that there is a Creation. It has no Honor. It has no Community.

PAUL GOODMAN

Here, the *it* in *It has no Community* is ten sentences away from its antecedent noun phrase *our abundant society*. But that noun phrase is the subject of its sentence. The next sentence has *it,* referring to that noun phrase, *our abundant society,* as the subject; so does the second sentence; so does the third sentence, and so on. By easy stages, then, the memory of *our abundant society* is carried through an extraordinary distance for a pronoun reference.

Every so often we find a pronoun, not with a remote antecedent, but with no antecedent at all. Remember that the reader must have some indication of which noun phrase the pronoun has replaced; he knows only what is on the paper, not what is in your mind.

32c Application

BROAD REFERENCE

We have asserted so far that third person pronouns replace equivalent noun phrases. But we find pronoun references in examples like the following, which appear to contradict that claim:

1a In fact one feels that some of those who responded least to this deep humaneness of the Pope were men close to him in Rome. It is a shameful but nevertheless understandable fact.

THOMAS MERTON

2 In recognizing the justice of the Negro's demands there are many temptations to sentimentality. One such temptation is to assume that it is all a matter of feeling—that we must consult our feelings in order to do justice.

ROBERT PENN WARREN

What structures has *it* replaced in the sentences above? There seem to be references to whole sentences involved here. In 1a, our intuition suggests that the antecedent of *it* is *some of those who responded least to this deep humaneness of the Pope were men close to him in Rome.* In 2, *it* seems to refer to *recognizing the justice of the Negro's demands.* In both these cases, though, the difficulty is more apparent than real: we can still say that the pronoun replaces an equivalent noun phrase. Note that both of the antecedents are not independent sentences, but embedded sentences. Sentence 1a, for example, has the following structure, in part:

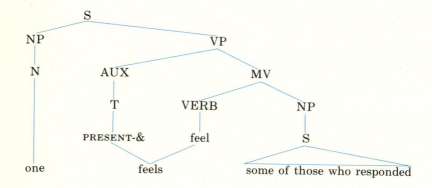

Since we can expand any noun phrase to an embedded sentence, a pronoun can refer to a whole embedded sentence.

"Broad reference" is the term sometimes given to the problem that arises when a pronoun refers to an independent sentence, rather than to an embedded sentence. Compare the clarity of example 1a with 1b, where the outer sentence of the antecedent has been removed:

> 1b Some of those who responded least to this deep humaneness of the Pope were men close to him in Rome. It is a shameful but nevertheless understandable fact.

Our first impulse on reading the pronoun *it* in 1b is to seek the antecedent among the noun phrases of the first sentence, but we won't find it there—*it* refers to the first sentence as a whole, not to any part of it.

Before you can refer to a sentence as a whole, you must establish that you are talking about that sentence as a whole. The next example clarifies this distinction:

> 3a Betsy bought a Picasso. It seemed unbelievable.

In the first sentence of 3a, the topic—the focus of our remark—might be Betsy, or the painting she bought, or the action of her buying the painting. In a single sentence, the lack of specific focus usually does not disturb us much; we depend on the statements that follow to narrow down the topic if there is need to be more specific. But when a sentence with a pronoun follows, such as the second sentence in 3a, the reference of that pronoun can give us trouble: as the example stands, the word *it* seems to refer to the noun phrase *a Picasso*. But we do not mean that Betsy bought an unbelievable painting; we mean that the action seems somehow unbelievable. Embedding the first sentence can make it clearer that we are talking about the whole sentence, not just one of its noun phrases. Suppose we revise 3a to

> 3b I heard that Betsy bought a Picasso. It seems unbelievable.

Now we have established the embedded sentence in its entirety as the thing we are talking about; we have made it possible for the entire embedded sentence to be referred to by a subsequent pronoun, with little danger that the reader will take the pronoun to refer to only part of the sentence.

33 INDEFINITE PRONOUNS

There are a few commonly used pronoun constructions where the pronoun refers to nothing. The first of these conventional usages is the so-called indefinite construction.

As we saw in the section on the functions of transformations, the PASSIVE transformation together with AGENTIVE DELETION makes it possible for a writer to describe an action without reference to the actor. We say, or write, something like this

> 1a Chris is said to be uxorious.

and do not commit ourselves to identifying the speaker. A sentence with an indefinite *they* as the subject noun phrase can be viewed as an active voice counterpart of 1a, asserting the action of the sentence without specifying the performer of the action:

1b   **They** say Chris is uxorious.

Here, *they* has no antecedent; it does not replace an equivalent noun phrase. If it had an antecedent, it would not be indefinite; we would know who *they* are:

1c   The Wilsons talk about Chris a lot. **They** say he is uxorious.

The second person pronoun, *you,* also has several conventional uses in modern English. Often the word is used to address the reader directly, as do many of the sentences in this book. The word *you,* however, can have general application: in such sentences, the word *anyone* can replace it, since the writer asserts that what he says holds true for every person who performs the indicated action:

2   The higher **you** go in the scale, the less and less true it is that "So careful of the type she seems, so careless of the single life."

JOSEPH WOOD KRUTCH

Roughly synonymous with the indefinite *you* is the use of *one* to express a universal application. Like *you, one* does not replace an equivalent noun phrase: it is the surface structure equivalent of a general pro-form, with the noun having the feature •human:

3   **One** might replace both movies and the Tin Lizzie, but the presence of Edison and Ford was as undeniable as that of Pike's Peak.

GERALD W. JOHNSON

33a   Application

ONE, YOU, WE, AND IT

It is sometimes claimed that there is a stylistic difference between a sentence with the indefinite *one* and the same sentence with the indefinite *you*. Thus, 1a would be considered more "formal" than 1b, and 1b more "colloquial" than 1a:

> 1a One can find examples everywhere.
> 1b You can find examples everywhere.

Actually, the practice of respected writers varies: sometimes they consistently use *one*, sometimes they use *you*, sometimes they use both. In an essay by Howard Nemerov in *The American Scholar*, certainly a storehouse of formal writing, we find a general statement with *one*:

> 2   The computer, which one would have thought should be on the side of rational constructiveness, turns up not on that side at all but on the other, the side of Plato.

On the next page of the same article, Nemerov writes

> 3   You can't argue with people who feel this way.

Even more strikingly, in an essay by Anthony Burgess in the same publication, one of the sentences reads

> 4   Like many others of my class, I believed that to go to a university was an honor and that one must pay for the honor with hard work.

In the very next paragraph, we find

> 5   If you didn't like the course, it was implied by the hierarchy, you could get out.

There are two guidelines to follow in the question of *one* versus *you*: a sequence of sentences using *one* has had a stiff sound for decades.[1] At the other extreme, a string of indefinite *you*'s tends to make the writing sound like imitation Hemingway:

> 6   You don't walk into airplanes any more; they inject you into them. The airplane is mainlining people. You

[1] In 1953, Dora Jean Ashe observed that students thought *one* lent an archaic sound to the sentence in which it appeared. See her "One Can Use an Indefinite 'You' Occasionally, Can't You?" *College English*, 14, No. 4 (January 1953). Pp. 216–19.

> walk through this tube—the same air-conditioning
> and Muzak that is in the terminal—you never know
> you're on a plane.
>
> JEAN SHEPHERD

If the essay is of any length, this tough pose quickly becomes tiring. For the occasional use, however, do not be afraid of the indefinite *you*.

The word *we* is sometimes used indefinitely. The sentence below is from a paragraph that draws a number of comparisons between animal qualities and those qualities valued by human beings. The sentence mentions Aldous Huxley's novel, but despite the use of the word *we*, it is not presupposed that the reader is familiar with the book. Rather, *we* is indefinite here, meaning anyone who might read the book:

> 7   In Aldous Huxley's *Brave New World,* we see a world
> designed by those who would model human beings
> after the social ants.
>
> S. I. HAYAKAWA

Finally, there are certain verbs, sometimes called ''impersonal'' verbs, that take an indefinite *it* as their subject. This *it* replaces no equivalent noun phrase; the word may have something in common with the *it* introduced by the EXTRAPOSITION transformation (see Section 38), merely filling the subject position. Impersonal constructions are limited in number; for some reason, the most common ones have to do with the weather:

> 8   It had snowed for two days, thawed a little, then froze,
> and the five guests left in the house had skated on
> the lake.
>
> CATHERINE COOKSON

Exercises

1. Mark all the pronouns in the following passages. Identify the antecedents of the pronouns that have them. Note any instances of indefinite or impersonal pronouns.

1   A jeep was parked on a cracked asphalt street somewhere in the mestizo quarter. A man sat in it, holding a cane across his lap. It was past midnight.

DAVID ELY

2   That was the end on that November morning of silent worship in the Grove Meeting House. Eliza was not sure whether it was not also the end of worship, silent or spoken. In any case, she herself did not recover the First Day calm she had anticipated all week until nearly nightfall. Now in her rocking chair, soothed by the rhythm of its gentle up-and-down, by gathering darkness, by the fire's rosy diligence she was beginning to recover what she had lost in that morning's contention at Meeting. And it was just then that the third of the bad things "that go by threes" occurred.

JESSAMYN WEST

3   Alexander gazed into the black peak of the rafters. "No one can equal the gifts of the gods, one can only try to know them. But it's good to be clear of debt to men."

MARY RENAULT

4   The first significant discovery we shall make as we racket along our female road to freedom is that men are not free, and they will seek to make this an argument why nobody should be free. We can only reply that slaves enslave their masters.

GERMAINE GREER

2. What difficulty are Andy and Flo having?

ANDY CAPP

Agreement

SECTIONS **34-35**

34 SUBJECT–VERB AGREEMENT

Agreement in number between subject and verb is one of the most rigorously applied conventions in written edited English. When we look at the question within the framework of transformational grammar, we find it easier to describe what occurs by saying that the subject noun phrase, rather than just a noun, agrees with the verb. Since every noun will be marked •singular or •plural, we need to consider how the noun phrase is marked for number depending on the nouns it contains.

In all cases but those resulting from conjunction, a noun phrase is singular if its headnoun is singular, and plural if its headnoun is plural. Sentences like those below, where the subject noun phrase contains just one noun, usually present no problem:

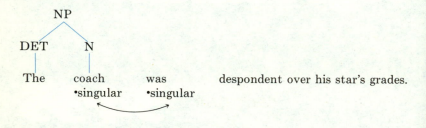

The coach was despondent over his star's grades.

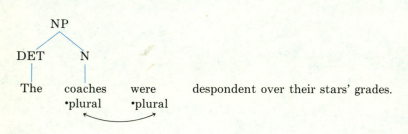

The coaches were despondent over their stars' grades.

Of course, noun phrases can contain more than one noun, with the headnoun modified by structures that contain other nouns. The next few sentences show examples of these "complex" noun phrases; note that in each case, the verb still agrees with the headnoun, not with a noun in a modifier:

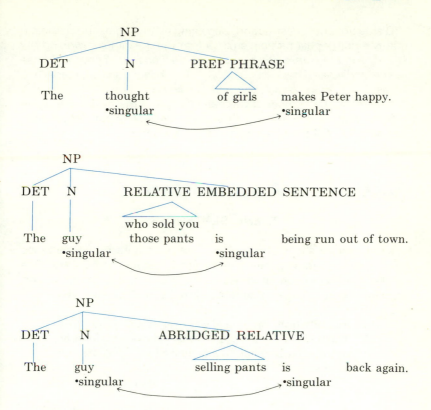

34a Application

INTERVENING NOUN

In determining the headnoun of the subject noun phrase, disregard any constructions introduced by prepositions—for example, *of success* in *our chances of success,* or *with them* in *the woman with them.* This would leave *chances* and *woman* as the remaining nouns, the headnouns of the phrases.

Disregard any constructions introduced by *who, which,* or *that*— for example, *who introduced them* in *the man who introduced them,* or *that you asked* in *the question that you asked.* Thus, the headnouns of these phrases would be *man* and *question.*

Disregard any construction beginning with a present participle (ING-& form) or past participle (EN-& form)—for example, *running the elections* in *the committee running the elections,* or *deprived of hope* in *the candidates deprived of hope.* The headnouns in these two phrases are, then, *committee* and *candidates.*

Determine the number of the headnoun, and make the verb agree in form with that headnoun. If you are unclear about determining the number of a particular headnoun, see Section 4a.

34b   Application

THERE SENTENCES

A few transformations allow the subject noun phrase of a sentence to be shifted from its position immediately before the auxiliary. One of the most common of these is the THERE transformation. This transformation changes a sentence like 1a into one like 1b:

> 1a   A family from Brookfield was over on the other street.
> 1b   There was a family from Brookfield over on the other street, who had apparently moved at the same time we had.
>
> **JOYCE CAROL OATES**

Notice what has happened here: the transformation has shifted the subject noun phrase, *a family from Brookfield,* to a position between the verb and the place adverbial. At the same time, the transformation has inserted *there* in the former position of the headnoun. But note too that the verb still agrees with *a family from Brookfield.* Sentences beginning *there is* or *there are* are especially productive of agreement errors, but are easily corrected. All we need to do is (mentally, at least) reverse the transformation. Suppose we have

> 2a * There is certain strong points in this argument.

The transformation introduced *there;* to reverse the operation we delete *there:*

> is certain strong points in this argument

The noun phrase *certain strong points* has been moved to its position from the front of the sentence, so we return it to that spot:

certain strong points   is in this argument
•plural   •singular

Now the conflict between *points*, marked •plural, and *is*, marked •singular, can be clearly seen, and can be easily corrected by changing *is* to *are:*

    2b   There are certain strong points in this argument.

34c   **Application**

COMPOUND SUBJECTS

If the subject noun phrase is a complex one, containing within it two or more noun phrases as the result of conjunction, the procedure for number agreement is somewhat different. When the conjunction joining the noun phrases is *and,* the subject noun phrase is considered plural, whatever number features the individual nouns may have, and the verb will accordingly be plural:

    1   Ben and I were traveling last month.
    2   My brothers and I were traveling last month.
    3   My brothers and sisters were traveling last month.

When the conjunction is *or,* the verb will agree with the number feature of the noun phrase closest to it:

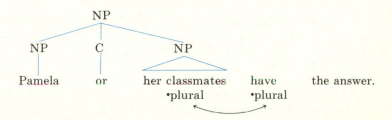

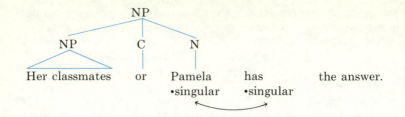

35 AGREEMENT AND WORD ORDER

In discussing subject–verb number agreement, it is sometimes help-ful to think of sentences as if they were puzzles. In a sentence we have an indication of an event, together with a description of who or what takes part in that event. A sentence like *John studied* pre-sents no problems: there is only one noun phrase, *John,* to associate with the act of studying. But in a sentence with two noun phrases, we have a different situation:

1   John sees the spiders.

Here two noun phrases, *John* and *the spiders,* are involved somehow in the act of seeing. Consider how it is that we decide which one does the seeing, and which one is seen. Note that *John* is singular, that *the spiders* is plural, and, finally, that the verb form, *sees,* is singular (compare ''the birds *see* the spiders''). Now suppose we know that, in this particular language, the verb has the same number as (or ''agrees in number with'') the noun phrase that is the subject. This knowledge allows us to select the subject noun phrase from among the noun phrases in the sentence. In example 1, therefore, it is John who does the seeing, not the spiders.

Now consider a sentence in the past tense:

2   John saw the spiders.

Note that past tense verbs in English show no number difference: ''John *saw* the spiders''; ''The birds *saw* the spiders.'' Here we rely exclusively on word order: in sentences like 2, the noun phrase preceding the verb is the subject. In fact, word order is so predomi-nantly the signal of grammatical relations in English that agreement by means of an ending, such as *-s* on *sees* in 1, is decidedly secondary in importance. In some dialects of English, in fact, the -*s* is dispensed with, and we have

    3   John see the spiders.

But as English comes to rely more and more on word order, we pay a price in a loss of flexibility in the forms of sentences. If we reverse the order of the noun phrases in 2, for instance, we have an entirely different meaning:

    4   The spiders saw John.

Of course, not all languages rely on word order, just as not all languages rely on a change in the forms of the words; but all languages have some means of indicating which noun phrase is performing the action, which noun phrase is the recipient of the action, and so on. In other words, there is always some form of agreement among the parts of a sentence; the puzzle of what role each noun phrase plays in the sentence can usually be solved. In the exercises that follow, you are asked to find how each of several languages signals certain grammatical relationships.

Exercises

1. Each of the Latin sentences below is translated at the right. By examining the change (or lack of change) in the sentences, together with the changes in the translations, answer the following questions: Is word order in Latin fixed or free? Does the verb agree in number with a noun phrase in the sentence? If your answer to the second question is yes, which noun phrase does it agree with? If your answer is no, how does Latin signal which noun phrase is the subject and which is the object?

1	Augustus frisbum iecit.	Gus threw the frisbee.
2	Iohannes frisbum iecit.	John threw the frisbee.
3	Frisbum Iohannes iecit.	John threw the frisbee.
4	Iecit Iohannes frisbum.	John threw the frisbee.
5	Barbarus frisbum iecit.	The barbarian threw the frisbee.
6	Barbarus frisbos iecit.	The barbarian threw the frisbees.
7	Barbari frisbum iecerunt.	The barbarians threw the frisbee.

2. By examining the change (or lack of change) in the Russian sentences below, together with the changes in the translations, answer the following questions: Does the verb agree in number with a noun phrase in the sentence? If your answer is yes, which noun phrase does it agree with? If your answer is no, how does Russian signal which noun phrase is the subject and which is the object?

1	Ivan brosil frisbiy.	John threw the frisbee.
2	Avgust brosil frisbiy.	Gus threw the frisbee.
3	Komissar brosil frisbiy.	The commissar threw the frisbee.
4	Komissar brosil frisbii.	The commissar threw the frisbees.
5	Komissary brosili frisbiy.	The commissars threw the frisbee.

3. By examining the change (or lack of change) in the Hawaiian sentences below, together with the changes in the translations, answer the following questions: What is the word order in these Hawaiian sentences? How does Hawaiian show number? Does the verb agree in number with a noun phrase in the sentence? If your answer is yes, which noun phrase does it agree with? If your answer is no, how does Hawaiian signal which noun phrase is the subject and which is the object?

1	Ua noi 'o Keoni i ka wa'a.	John requested the canoe.
2	Ua noi 'o Keoni i ka palikapi.	John requested the frisbee.
3	Ua nou 'o Keoni i ka palikapi.	John threw the frisbee.
4	Ua nou 'o Kuk i ka palikapi.	Gus threw the frisbee.
5	Ua nou ka wahine i ka palikapi.	The woman threw the frisbee.
6	Ua nou ka wahine i na palikapi.	The woman threw the frisbees.
7	Ua nou na wahine i ka palikapi.	The women threw the frisbee.

4. By examining the change (or lack of change) in the Urdu sentences below, together with the changes in the translations, answer the following questions: What is the word order in these Urdu sentences? Does the verb agree in number with a noun phrase in the sentence? If your answer is yes, which noun phrase does it agree

with? If your answer is no, how does Urdu signal which noun phrase
is the subject and which is the object?

1	Jon ne frisbi phengki.	John threw the frisbee.
2	Ghus ne frisbi phengki.	Gus threw the frisbee.
3	Raja ne frisbi phengki.	The raja threw the frisbee.
4	Rajaong ne frisbi phengki.	The rajas threw the frisbee.
5	Raja ne frisbiang phengking.	The raja threw the frisbees.

Embedded Sentences

SECTIONS **36-45**

36 SENTENCES AS TOPICS

In Section 1, we saw how a sentence could be successively divided into smaller and smaller combinations of topics (that is, the thing spoken of) and comments (the qualifications or modifications made of the topics). The three transformations in this section—the THAT, the FOR . . . TO, and the NOMINAL transformations—make it possible to use whole sentences in syntactic positions where noun phrases occur. We can think of the function of these transformations as turning sentences into topics. We must have some ways of forming complex topics, since often we want to talk about complex things—not just about Hamlet, nor just about revenge, but about the fact that Hamlet sought revenge.

We can provide for the construction or generation of complex groups of words by modifying our rule analyzing noun phrases to read something like this:

$$NP \rightarrow \begin{Bmatrix} (DET) + N \\ S \end{Bmatrix}$$

Now we have two ways of rewriting the symbol NP: if we choose the top line in the braces, we can rewrite NP as an optional DET and N, just as we could before; but if we choose the bottom line, we can rewrite NP as S, and go back through the phrase structure rules again. We might have a structure beginning like this, for instance:

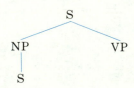

The lower S will itself be developed by the phrase structure rules. We will then have a sentence (the embedded sentence) "inside" the larger (outer) sentence, as in the diagram on page 147.

But there must be some differences between outer sentences and embedded sentences: example 1 below is grammatical if punctuated as a separate sentence, but it cannot alone serve as the subject of a larger sentence, as example 2a shows:

1   Hamlet seeks revenge.
2a *Hamlet seeks revenge unnerves the king.

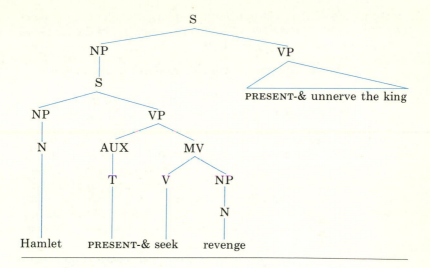

We can make 2a grammatical, though, simply by putting the word *that* first:

2b   **That** Hamlet seeks revenge unnerves the king.

Forms like *that* are inserted by transformations that convert lower sentences in deep structure into constructions that can function like noun phrases. These forms—we can call them "embedders"—are inserted by the following transformations:

The THAT transformation places *that* to the left of the embedded sentence, changing a structure like 3a to 3b:

3a   [John PAST-& be apathetic] surprised his friends. ⇒
3b   [**That** John PAST-& be apathetic] surprised his friends.
3c   That John was apathetic surprised his friends.

The FOR . . . TO transformation adds *for* and *to,* one on either side of the subject noun phrase of the sentence to be embedded. The second of these elements, *to,* replaces the tense of the embedded sentence:

4a   [John PAST-& be apathetic] surprised his friends. ⇒
4b   [**For** John to **be** apathetic] surprised his friends.
4c   For John to be apathetic surprised his friends.

Note that the FOR . . . TO transformation has a restriction: it cannot be used if a modal has been selected in the auxiliary of the sentence or the result will be ungrammatical:

> 5a [Hamlet PRESENT-& will seek revenge] unnerved the king. ⟹
> 5b [For Hamlet to will seek revenge] unnerved the king.
> 5c * For Hamlet to will seek revenge unnerved the king.

Since *to* replaces either development of the tense, in the examples that follow T (for tense) will be used instead of PAST-& or PRESENT-&.

The third embedding transformation, the NOMINAL transformation, places a pair of elements after the subject noun phrase of the sentence to be embedded. The first of these, &-'s, the sign of the genitive, converts (for example) *Hamlet* to *Hamlet's;* the second, NOM-&, may take different forms depending on the particular verb, but it replaces the tense just as *to* does. NOM-& is short for "nominal form," and it describes the relationship between verb-and-noun pairs like *believe* and *belief, choose* and *choice, defend* and *defense,* and so on. The NOMINAL transformation accounts for the differences between the "a" and "b" forms of the sentences below:

> 6a [Sol T choose hearts for trumps] was a ghastly mistake. ⟹
> 6b [Sol &-'s NOM-& choose of hearts for trumps] was a ghastly mistake.
> 6c Sol's choice of hearts for trumps was a ghastly mistake.
>
> 7a [Ney T receive the orders] was never proven. ⟹
> 7b [Ney &-s NOM-& receive of the orders] was never proven.
> 7c Ney's receipt of the orders was never proven.

Note that with these developments of NOM-&, *of* is inserted before the object noun phrase, if there is one.

Some verbs have no special nominal form—that is, the noun form of the word is identical to the verb form:

> 8a [The platoon T patrol this area] will be discontinued. ⟹
> 8b [The platoon &-'s NOM-& patrol of this area] will be discontinued.
> 8c The platoon's patrol of this area will be discontinued.

Other verbs, including all those that end in -ate, have a related nominal form with a suffix:

9a   [The barometer T indicate a storm] worried the captain. ⟹

9b   [The barometer &-'s NOM-& indicate of a storm] worried the captain.

9c   The barometer's indication of a storm worried the captain.

Verbs having identical nominal forms or nominal forms with suffixes like -tion are limited in number; a development of NOM-& with greater generality is ING-&:

10a   [John T be apathetic] surprised his friends. ⟹

10b   [John &-'s ING-& be apathetic] surprised his friends.

10c   John's being apathetic surprised his friends.

Note that when ING-& is the development of the NOMINAL transformation, of is not inserted. In the examples to follow, ING-& will be used as the usual development of the transformation.

In summary, the simple change of the phrase structure rule rewriting NP has done two things. First, it has achieved the goal set in the introduction—to allow our grammar to produce an infinite number of sentence structures from a limited number of phrase structure rules. An initial S is rewritten as NP and VP when we start to generate a sentence, and that NP can now be rewritten as S. We apply the phrase structure rules again to this second S (as in the diagram on page 150), rewriting it as NP and VP. This second NP can again be rewritten as S, and the process can be repeated as many times as we like.

Second, the change in the NP rule allows our grammar to describe the countless English sentences that have structures very much like sentences embedded within them. We outlined three transformations that allow embedded sentences to function as often very complex topics. As a later section will show, not all three transformations can always be applied to a particular embedded sentence, but a sentence like 11a below illustrates the choice we often have of several ways of developing an embedded sentence:

11a   [The rabbit T vanish] mystified the audience.

11b   [That the rabbit T vanish] mystified the audience.
        (THAT transformation)

11c   That the rabbit vanished mystified the audience.

11a   [The rabbit T vanish] mystified the audience.
11d   [For the rabbit to vanish] mystified the audience.
      (FOR . . . TO transformation)
11e   For the rabbit to vanish mystified the audience.

11a   [The rabbit T vanish] mystified the audience.
11f   [The rabbit &-'s ING-& vanish] mystified the audience.
      (NOMINAL transformation)
11g   The rabbit's vanishing mystified the audience.

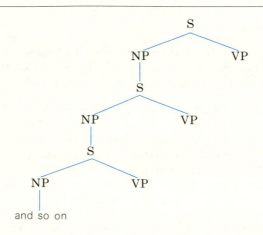

and so on

Exercise

Underline the embedded sentences in the sentences below. In each case, tell which embedding transformation has been used, and write the embedded sentence as it would appear before being transformed.

1   Locke thinks that men have a right to rebel against unjust laws, but, like Aquinas, he also advocates caution.

   MORTIMER ADLER

2   Henri Frankfort's . . . exposition of the role of kingship in early civilizations provides a clue to the utopian nature of the city.

   LEWIS MUMFORD

3 On the side bunk . . . is a bucket or sealskin basin for ice to thaw in for drinking water.

PETER FREUCHEN

4 Watts, and the history of this place and these times, makes it impossible for the cop to come on any different, or for you to hate him any less.

THOMAS PYNCHON

5 Armstrong knew he was being told that the future for him was not too bright.

MICHAEL SINCLAIR

37 SENTENCES WITHIN SENTENCES

Since the symbol NP can be rewritten as S, an embedded sentence may occur in any place within a sentence where a noun phrase can occur. Noun phrases can occur in the subject position, as in

1 Hamlet unnerved the king.

Therefore, embedded sentences can also occur in the subject position:

2 That Hamlet sought revenge unnerved the king.

Here the subject of the outer sentence is the whole embedded sentence *that Hamlet sought revenge.*

Similarly, since noun phrases can occur in the object position—that is, following a transitive verb, as in

3 We believed the report.

—embedded sentences can appear in the object position (*the report* in example 3):

4 We believed that no one wrote a better report.

The particular embedding transformation used does not affect the position in which the embedded sentence can be developed. Example 4, for instance, shows the use of the THAT transformation, but sentences generated in the object position can undergo the FOR . . . TO transformation (the embedded sentence is in brackets):

> I intended [the test PAST-& be short].
> 5   I intended for the test to be short.

Similarly, a sentence embedded in the object position may undergo the NOMINAL transformation:

> I dreaded Monday morning T come.
> I dreaded Monday morning &-'s ING-& come. (NOMINAL
>   transformation)
>
> 6   I dreaded Monday morning's coming.

Exercise

In some prose selections of your choice, locate sentences with embedded sentences in the subject position, in the object position, and following a preposition. Find nine sentences in all that illustrate each of the three embedding transformations in each position. If, after a reasonable search, you cannot find some of the ones you need, make up sentences of your own to fit the requirements.

38   THE EXTRAPOSITION TRANSFORMATION

Consider sentences 1a and 1b; it is obvious that they are closely related, since they have the same meaning and are nearly the same in structure:

> 1a   That Michelangelo preferred sculpting meant little to Pope Julius.
> 1b   It meant little to Pope Julius that Michelangelo preferred sculpting.

If we could derive these two sentences from the same deep structure, we could account for the synonymy of the sentences and simplify our grammar at the same time. The EXTRAPOSITION transformation does just this. It begins when we have a structure with an embedded sentence in the subject position:

2a [That you believe me] is important to me.

In EXTRAPOSITION, the embedded sentence is moved to the right of the outer sentence; the word *it* is inserted in the place where the embedded sentence was, yielding

2b It is important to me that you believe me.

EXTRAPOSITION of embedded sentences in the subject position works equally well if the sentences have been embedded by the FOR . . . TO transformation. From

3a [For the gun to sound then] startled Gene.

we can derive by this transformation

3b It startled Gene for the gun to sound then.

There are some unexpected effects, though, with the application of EXTRAPOSITION to sentences embedded by the NOMINAL transformation. The extraposed sentence must be separated from the outer sentence by a comma, reflecting the unusual intonation the sentence has when spoken:

4a [Amy's departure for New York] pleased everybody.
4b It pleased everybody, Amy's departure for New York.

Both the intonation in speech and the punctuation in writing make the extraposed NOMINAL sentence appear to be an afterthought, almost parenthetical.

The EXTRAPOSITION transformation gives us a way of analyzing sentences beginning with a pronoun (*it*) that appears to lack an antecedent (see Section 34 for similar cases of pronouns that refer to nothing). But what can we do with an apparently related sentence like 5a?

5a It seems [that Morris is late again].

Certainly, *that Morris is late again* looks like a sentence embedded by the THAT transformation. The embedded sentence comes at the right of the outer sentence, where EXTRAPOSITION would place it. The sentence even begins with an *it* that seems to refer to nothing. The trouble with saying that EXTRAPOSITION has occurred in 5a is that we have an ungrammatical underlying sentence; we would have to maintain that 5a comes from 5b:

> 5b *[That Morris is late again] seems.

The solution to the problem lies in our treatment of the verb *seem*. If we add an adjective to 5b, the difficulty disappears:

> 5c [That Morris is late again] seems unlikely.

In most cases, EXTRAPOSITION is an optional transformation; with verbs like *seem, appear,* and *happen,* the transformation is optional if an adjective occurs following the verb in question. If, however, such a verb is the last word in the outer sentence, then EXTRAPOSITION is obligatory: it must occur to prevent surface structures like 5b from appearing. We will maintain then that 5b is a deeper structure of 5a, but for verbs like *seem,* when they are the last words in the sentence, EXTRAPOSITION is obligatory.

38a Application

FRONT-HEAVY SENTENCES

No matter how long or involved a sentence may be, it can still be embedded in a noun phrase position in an outer sentence, although sometimes the results are unfortunate. Readers of English, unlike readers of German, are used to having the verb of the sentence relatively near the beginning. A sentence strikes us as awkward if the verb follows an extremely long subject. Here is one such sentence:

> 1a [That our own offenses should seem to us so much
>   less heinous than the offenses of others] is curious.

There is even a name for this particular rhetorical flaw—''front-heaviness.'' Of course, a front-heavy sentence is not always caused by having an embedded sentence in the subject position—a long string of prepositional phrases following the subject's headnoun has the same effect:

> 2　The growing enthusiasm on the part of many teachers of English for giving careful attention to linguistic matters is noteworthy for several reasons.
>
> PETER S. ROSENBAUM

However, when front-heaviness *is* caused by an embedded sentence, extraposing that sentence remedies the situation. Note how example 1a is improved by EXTRAPOSITION (giving us the form in which the sentence was actually written):

> 1b　It is curious that our own offenses should seem to us so much less heinous than the offenses of others.
>
> W. SOMERSET MAUGHAM

38b　**Application**

CONCISENESS—DELETING *THAT*

In examples 1a and 2a below, we have sentences embedded by the THAT transformation occurring at the right of the sentences. The embedded sentence in 1a comes from a structure embedded in the object position; the embedded sentence in 2a has been shifted there by EXTRAPOSITION:

> 1a　We thought [that no one wrote a better report].
> 2a　It seemed unlikely [that Morris would be late again].

Note that we can grammatically remove the word *that* from these sentences:

> 1b　We thought [no one wrote a better report].
> 2b　It seemed unlikely [Morris would be late again].

We can call this transformation THAT DELETION. On the other hand, *that* cannot be removed when it precedes a sentence embedded in the subject position:

> 3a　[That Shirley's play flopped] surprised her friends.
> 3b　*[Shirley's play flopped] surprised her friends.

Unlike some of the restrictions we encounter, this one seems straightforward: the great majority of English sentences have the first noun phrase as their subject. When the sentence has an embedded construction as its subject, though, we need some signal to tell us that the first noun phrase is *not* the subject of the outer sentence. Hence, *that* functions as such a signal: it tells us the upcoming noun phrase is the subject of an embedded sentence, not the subject of the outer sentence. But when the embedded sentence follows the verb, we need no such signal—we have already passed the subject and verb of the outer sentence. As far as style is concerned, the principle of economy tells us that we should prefer sentence 4b to 4a, since 4b says the same thing with one less word:

4a Roland hoped that Charlemagne would arrive.
4b Roland hoped Charlemagne would arrive.
(THAT DELETION)

But this principle cannot be applied unthinkingly. Compare 4a and 4b with 5a and 5b:

5a Roland suspected that Ganelon was a traitor.
5b Roland suspected Ganelon was a traitor.
(THAT DELETION)

There are good reasons why 5a is the preferable sentence. Note the verb in sentences 4a and 4b: *hope* is a verb that cannot have a single human noun as its object, as 4c shows:

4c * Roland hoped Charlemagne.

But the verb of 5a and 5b, *suspect,* can have as its object either an embedded sentence or a single human noun, as in 5c:

5c Roland suspected Ganelon.

When we read a sentence, we are interpreting grammatical signals at an incredible rate of speed, and we may be misled by ambiguous signals. Reading 5b, we are in doubt for an instant whether *Ganelon* is the direct object of *suspected* or the subject of its own embedded sentence. Hence, with verbs like *suspect* that can lead to confusion, we need the *that* to signal the boundary between the outer and the embedded sentence.

We are gaining some insight into the use of the word *that* to mark the beginning of a separate grammatical structure. In 2b, where THAT DELETION is perfectly possible, the embedded sentence was extraposed across the verb *seemed* and the adjective *unlikely*. But suppose EXTRAPOSITION had moved the embedded sentence across a noun phrase in the object position of the outer sentence—for example, the word *Jerry* in 6a:

6a [That the philologist was dishonest] surprised Jerry.

EXTRAPOSITION will move the embedded sentence to the end, giving us 6b:

6b It surprised Jerry [that the philologist was dishonest].

Notice that we cannot remove the word *that* here:

6c * It surprised Jerry the philologist was dishonest.

Again, the source of the restriction appears obvious. THAT DELETION in 6c puts two unconnected noun phrases, *Jerry* and *the philologist,* next to each other. The possibility is very strong that, on first reading, we might take these words to be related, such as *Einstein the scientist* or *Picasso the painter.* Again the word *that* serves as a necessary signal of the boundary between grammatically unrelated words.

Exercises

1. Rewrite the following sentences, using the EXTRAPOSITION transformation:

    1 For someone to like Andy is impossible.
    2 For Sadie to sell apples is troublesome.
    3 For you to say that is easy.

2. Compare the sentences in exercise 1, after EXTRAPOSITION, with the following:

    1 Andy is impossible for someone to like.
    2 Apples are troublesome for Sadie to sell.
    3 That is easy for you to say.

What has been done to the extraposed sentences to produce the new forms of the sentences found in this exercise? There are restrictions involved in this change (note the set below). Where are these restrictions located?

> 4a For someone to like Andy is stupid.
> 4b It is stupid for someone to like Andy.
>   (EXTRAPOSITION)
> 4c *Andy is stupid for someone to like.

3. See if you can use some form of EXTRAPOSITION to improve the sentence below. The form of the transformation will not be identical to that learned in Section 38, but some material will need to be shifted to the right of the sentence.

> Also, for that matter, ballets away from their own choreographer, or alternatively from a continually performing tradition backed up by a rehearsal schedule far less demanding than is the case during a rushed and packed New York season when the company is dancing eight performances a week, do deteriorate with every company.
>
> CLIVE BARNES

4. Can some construction that is already at the end of the sentence be moved to the end of the sentence? It hardly seems logical even to ask. But consider, in the abstract, what happens when EXTRAPOSITION occurs. We have two elements, an embedded sentence (S) and anything else (X). The S moves to the right of the structure, and *it* occupies the former position of the embedded sentence. We could express this in a formula as:

$$
\begin{array}{ccccc}
\text{S} & \text{X} & & \text{it} & \text{X} & \text{S} \\
1 & 2 & \Rightarrow & 1 & 2 & 3
\end{array}
$$

The numbers below the elements serve to mark their relative positions before and after the change. Now suppose that the position indicated by X is empty; this would be the same as saying that the embedded sentence came at the end of the construction. Following the formula above, show the result of EXTRAPOSITION on this sentence:

> I foresaw [that he would get into trouble].

39 EQUIVALENT NOUN PHRASE DELETION

Now that we have outlined the mechanics of embedding sentences in the subject and object positions, we have an opportunity to examine another feature of English grammar, one that applies when a noun phrase in the embedded sentence is the same as a noun phrase in the outer sentence. The two noun phrases are then said to be "equivalent" and usually one of them must be either deleted or replaced by a pronoun. Suppose we have the following derivation:

1a Washington intended [Washington T cross the Delaware at night].

1b Washington intended [for Washington to cross the Delaware at night]. (FOR . . . TO transformation)

The equivalent noun phrases here are, of course, *Washington* and *Washington*. The one to the right must be deleted, giving us

1c Washington intended [for to cross the Delaware at night].

The form of sentence 1c would have been perfectly acceptable four or five hundred years ago, as sentences from older literature illustrate:

2 Himself he learned for to harp.

ANONYMOUS, *Sir Orfeo,* early fourteenth century

3 Then Merlin went to the Archbishop of Canterbury and counselled him for to send for all the lords of the realm.

THOMAS MALORY, late fifteenth century

But between that day and this, a rule we may call FOR DELETION has been added to the language. This rule requires that the embedder *for* be deleted when the embedded sentence is in the object position (there are only a handful of exceptions to this rule—sentence 5 in Section 37 illustrates one, and even that sentence could have the *for* removed without difficulty). When FOR DELETION is applied to sentence 1c, we get

1d Washington intended to cross the Delaware at night.

This seemingly complicated derivation—the removal first of the equivalent noun phrase, and then of the embedder *for*—has the advantage of accounting for our understanding of *Washington* as the subject of *cross* in 1d.

If the subject of an embedded sentence were deleted when that subject was not equivalent to a noun phrase in the outer sentence, the sentence would take on a meaning different from the one desired. If we delete the subject of the embedded sentence in

> 4a Tom Sawyer wanted [for his friends to paint the fence].

we get (assuming FOR DELETION has also occurred)

> 4b Tom Sawyer wanted to paint the fence.

which is quite another thing. Note too that the noun phrase that will be deleted is located in the embedded sentence, even if the embedded sentence is in the subject position:

> 5a [Claggart T torment Billy] pleased Claggart.
> 5b [Claggart &-'s ING-& torment Billy] pleased Claggart. (NOMINAL transformation)
> 5c [ING-& torment Billy] pleased Claggart. (EQUIVALENT NOUN PHRASE DELETION)
> 5d Tormenting Billy pleased Claggart.

Exercise

Diagram the following sentence as it would appear in deep structure before any embedding or deletion transformations:

> John decided to try to quit taking so much time off.

40 EMBEDDED SENTENCES FOLLOWING PREPOSITIONS

In the section on two-word verbs (Section 22), we saw that some prepositions have to be included in the feature specification of the verb in the lexicon. We had analyses, for example, like

watch over	base
•NP__NP	•NP__NP on NP

Watch over, we said, was simply a transitive verb, listed in the lexicon as a unit. *Base,* on the other hand, is a verb that takes a double object; the second object is preceded by the preposition *on.* We want to see what happens when embedded sentences follow verbs of these two kinds. We can first consider two-word verbs:

1a   Tristan longed for Iseult.

We do seem to have a grammatical passive for this sentence:

1b   Iseult was longed for by Tristan.

If we take the passive sentence as evidence that we have a transitive verb, we would have to list *long for* in the lexicon as a two-word verb. Let us assume that this analysis is correct, and see if we can embed a sentence in the direct object position following *long for:*

Tristan longed for [Iseult T arrive].
Tristan longed for [Iseult &-'s NOM-& arrive]. (NOMINAL
transformation)
2   Tristan longed for Iseult's arrival.

Similarly, with the FOR . . . TO transformation:

Tristan longed for [Iseult T arrive].
Tristan longed for [for Iseult to arrive].[1]
(FOR . . . TO transformation)
3   Tristan longed for Iseult to arrive.
(FOR DELETION)

[1] If this stage in the derivation seems rather peculiar because of the double *for*'s, it should be noted that history is on the side of the derivation. We do in fact find just such sentences in English written before FOR DELETION became obligatory. Note the following, from Thomas Malory, writing in the fifteenth century.

And this lord, Sir Ector, let him be sent for for to come and speak with you.

But notice what happens when the embedded sentence and the outer sentence have equivalent noun phrases:

> Odysseus longed for [Odysseus T be home].
> Odysseus longed for [for Odysseus to be home].
> (FOR . . . TO transformation)
> Odysseus longed for [Odysseus to be home].
> (FOR DELETION)

At this point, if we delete the equivalent noun phrase in the embedded sentence, we get

> 4a * Odysseus longed for to be home.
> (EQUIVALENT NOUN PHRASE DELETION)

We do, however, have a clearly related grammatical sentence:

> 4b Odysseus longed to be home.

We need to formulate another deletion rule to explain why and under what conditions *for* is removed from sentences like 4a to produce ones like 4b. As we will see when we examine double object verbs, the words deleted are always prepositions specified in the lexicon (as in the case of *long for*) as the second part of a two-word verb. We can say, then, that a preposition (not a particle, not an adverb) must be deleted when it stands directly before one of the embedders. Thus, in 4a, *for* stands immediately before the embedder *to*, and must be removed, giving us 4b.

Now suppose we have a double object verb like *assure*, which would have the feature specification •NP __ NP of NP. Since we can rewrite NP as S, we could have an embedded sentence developed in the position of the noun phrase following *of:*

> 5a Queen Elizabeth assured Essex of [Essex would be comfortable].
> 5b Queen Elizabeth assured Essex of [that Essex would be comfortable]. (THAT transformation)

Since *that* in 5b is an embedder, the preposition *of* must be deleted, since it stands immediately before *that:*

5c   Queen Elizabeth assured Essex [that Essex would be comfortable]. (PREP DELETION)

The second of the equivalent noun phrases in 5c is replaced by the appropriate pronoun, giving us

5d   Queen Elizabeth assured Essex that he would be comfortable.

With the other embedding transformations used with double object verbs, we have derivations like these:

Baldwin had warned Richard about [Richard T be careful].

Baldwin had warned Richard about [for Richard to be careful]. (FOR . . . TO transformation)

Baldwin had warned Richard [for Richard to be careful]. (PREP DELETION)

Baldwin had warned Richard [for to be careful]. (EQUIVALENT NOUN PHRASE DELETION)

6   Baldwin had warned Richard to be careful. (FOR DELETION)

With the NOMINAL transformation, we get

Philip bribed the emperor into [the emperor T increase the ransom].

Philip bribed the emperor into [the emperor &-'S NOM-& increase the ransom]. (NOMINAL transformation)

Note that when the NOMINAL transformation is used to embed, PREP DELETION will never apply: since the embedders &-'s and NOM-& are not at the left of the sentence to be embedded, a preposition can never be immediately before them:

7   Philip bribed the emperor into increasing the ransom. (EQUIVALENT NOUN PHRASE DELETION)

Exercise

What prepositions would be listed for the following verbs?

acquire	discover	paint
assign	expect	participate
collate	forget	receive
cross	give	rely
disclose	inure	suspect

Test your answers by using them in sentences. Thus, with a verb like *tell* we would associate the preposition *to,* as in sentences like 1:

1   John told a story to the horrified guests.

Some verbs may need to have more than one preposition listed, since they may precede more than one preposition and noun phrase construction, as in 2 and 3:

2   Mary bought a lampshade from Al.
3   Mary bought a lampshade for Ben.

41   EMBEDDED SENTENCES AND VERB FEATURES

When we produce an embedded sentence, we follow restrictions more specific than any that have so far been discussed. If we look closely, we find that we can embed sentences only when the outer sentence contains certain verbs. In short, embedding will not work with just any verb. In a sentence like

1a   Trees shed leaves.

we have a noun phrase, *leaves,* in the object position, but we cannot embed a sentence in its place by any of the three transformations:

1b * Trees shed that leaves fall.   (THAT transformation)
1c * Trees shed for leaves to fall.   (FOR . . . TO transformation)
1d * Trees shed leaves' falling.   (NOMINAL transformation)

The verbs used in the outer sentences of some previous examples illustrate the restrictions on embedding. Notice that those verbs fall into two classes. In the first class are verbs like *surprise, astonish,* and *please,* which have embedded sentences as their subjects. They are all verbs that will accept as subject a noun marked with the feature •abstract:

2   His sincerity surprised me.
        •abstract

3   The verdict astonished the friends of the defendant.
        •abstract

4   Thoughts of home pleased Odysseus.
    •abstract

The second class includes such verbs as *doubt, learn,* and *suspect,* all of which take an embedded sentence as their object. Note that these verbs will also accept an abstract noun phrase as their object:

5   I doubt his sincerity.
            •abstract

6   The friends of the defendant quickly learned the verdict.
    •abstract

7   Circe suspected Odysseus' motives.
                •abstract

The restriction may be stated like this: in general, an embedded sentence can occur in a context in which a noun phrase marked •abstract can appear. The embedded sentence may occur as the subject of any verb that will take an abstract noun phrase as its subject. An embedded sentence may appear as the object of any verb that will accept an abstract noun phrase as its object, but in this case there are further restrictions between the verb of the outer sentence and the transformation used to embed. Take a verb like *know,* for instance: it will take, as its object, a sentence that has been embedded by the THAT transformation:

8a   I know that John is honest.

Or it will take, with FOR DELETION, an object sentence embedded by the FOR . . . TO transformation:

8b   I know John to be honest.

But it will not take an object sentence embedded by the NOMINAL transformation:

8c * I know John's being honest.[1]

Similarly, with a verb like *admit,* we can have an object sentence embedded by the THAT transformation or the NOMINAL transformation, but not by the FOR . . . TO transformation:

9   The witness admits that he perjured himself. (THAT transformation)
10   The witness admits his perjuring himself. (NOMINAL transformation)
11 * The witness admits for him to perjure himself. (FOR . . . TO transformation)

The nature of these restrictions appears to be extremely complex, and is hardly well enough understood to permit general statements to be made.

41a   Application

DANGLING INFINITIVES

Handbooks of grammar invariably have a section on what is called the "dangling infinitive"—the remains of a sentence embedded by the FOR . . . TO transformation, where both equivalent noun phrases —the one in the embedded sentence and the one in the outer sentence—have been deleted. Here is a typical example:

1a   To compete successfully, discipline is required.

We have no mention of *who* requires discipline—the sentence has no agentive phrase (by NP). The sentence seems to express something like a general statement, since our first impulse is to supply a noun like *anyone* to replace the missing agentive phrase:

1b   To compete successfully, discipline is required by anyone.

[1] Sentence 8c is, of course, grammatical if we assume the interpretation *I know that John is being honest,* an interpretation not intended here.

Thus we suppose the writer of the sentence to be making a general statement, applicable in every circumstance.

But suppose the writer did not intend a general application. Far worse, suppose he intended just the opposite. Sentence 1a might occur in an essay maintaining that the kind of discipline which a coach exercises over the members of a team could be superfluous or harmful when the manager of a company tries it. A principle that the writer intended to apply only to athletes has become a universal statement expressing the reverse of his meaning. The following sentences illustrate how this misleading statement might come about:

1c Athletes require discipline for [athletes T compete successfully].

1d Athletes require discipline for [for athletes to compete successfully]. (FOR . . . TO transformation)

The problem begins when the outer sentence, through the PASSIVE transformation, is changed to the passive voice. Now we have

1e Discipline is required by athletes for [for athletes to compete successfully].

1f Discipline is required by athletes for [athletes to compete successfully]. (FOR DELETION)

Grammatical sentences would have resulted either if a pronoun had been substituted for the second equivalent noun phrase at this point, as in 1g:

1g Discipline is required by athletes for them to compete successfully.

or if both *for* and the equivalent noun phrase had been deleted from 1f:

1h Discipline is required by athletes for [to compete successfully]. (EQUIVALENT NOUN PHRASE DELETION)

1i Discipline is required by athletes to compete successfully. (PREP DELETION)

Problems arise, though, because *two* kinds of noun phrase deletions are possible in a structure like 1f: of course, EQUIVALENT NOUN

PHRASE DELETION is possible, as example 1h shows, but, as the discussion of the PASSIVE transformation on page 16 shows, the agentive phrase of a passive sentence may be deleted. Now, the outer sentence of 1f is in the passive voice. If we delete the agentive phrase in that sentence, after the equivalent noun phrase in the embedded sentence has been removed, we have something like this:

> 1j   Discipline is required by athletes [to compete successfully]. (after EQUIVALENT NOUN PHRASE and FOR DELETIONS)
>
> 1k   Discipline is required to compete successfully.
> (AGENTIVE DELETION)

Since people have a natural desire to make sense out of language, they supply for themselves some very general noun like *anyone*—for instance, "Discipline is required for *anyone* to compete successfully"—and thus give the sentence its undesired general meaning. A stylistic transformation, shifting what is left of the embedded sentence to the front of the outer sentence, gives us the classic dangling infinitive:

> To compete successfully, discipline is required.

This whole problem of dangling infinitives can be avoided by exercising care in the use of passive voice sentences. If a paper is returned to you with a dangling infinitive marked, try the simple expedient of putting the outer sentence back in the active voice. For example, suppose you had written

> 2a   To find the trail, a map must be used.

(Note here that, for an instant, it sounds as if the map will have to find the trail.) Putting the outer sentence back into the active voice will straighten out the difficulty:

> 2b   To find the trail, you (or one) must use a map.

Exercises

1. What embedding transformations are possible in the object noun phrase position following these verbs?

allege	foresee	prefer
consider	guarantee	presume
deny	justify	remember
expect	loathe	verify

2. Find example sentences of your own that show each of the three embedding transformations. Remember to list the source of each sentence.

42 SENTENCES AS COMMENTS

The sections on the embedding transformations discussed ways of turning whole sentences into topics; in reference to the syntax, we said that these embedded sentences occupy the positions of noun phrases in the outer sentences, and in fact behave syntactically as if they were noun phrases. The embedding transformations allow us to form complex topics. But sometimes we wish to express complicated comments about these topics. We may need to modify a topic by an often intricate comment. In a sentence like 1, we can say that the modifier *green* gives us a comment about the topic *her scarf:*

1 Her scarf was green.

But notice how much more detailed the comment about the shade of the scarf is in example 2:

2 Her scarf was a green that reminded me of the shade of the leaves outside.

In the next few sections, we will discuss the ways in which English can turn sentences into comments, just as we previously discussed the ways sentences could be turned into topics.

Two of the embedded sentence transformations discussed in Section 36 can serve us here. In example 3, the THAT transformation turns the sentence it embeds into a modifier of the noun phrase *the hint:*

3 The hint [that Phil was a misogynist] alarmed his friends.

Similarly, when preceded by *of,* the NOMINAL transformation can make a modifier of an embedded sentence, as example 4 shows:

> 4 The mere hint [of Phil's being a misogynist] was enough to alarm his friends.

The nouns that can be modified in this way are limited. Examples of other nouns that might occur in the position of *hint* are *idea, fact, news, statement,* and *disclosure.* Notice that all these nouns are abstract and all refer in some way to a linguistic structure containing information.

43 RELATIVE CONSTRUCTIONS

We have seen so far some transformations that, in general, do two things. First, the embedding transformations provide us with a way to get sentences into positions that can be occupied by noun phrases, thereby turning the sentences into topics. Second, two of those transformations enable us to turn whole sentences into comments and allow them to modify a small group of nouns like *rumor* and *fact.* English has other means of modifying any noun by a sentence, not just this handful. One way is ''relativization,'' the means by which we produce what are traditionally called ''relative clauses.''

English has two constructions that are similar in that they share many of the same transformations. Traditionally called ''nonrestrictive'' and ''restrictive'' relative clauses, these constructions must be carefully distinguished. In the examples below, the relative clause is in color, and the kind of clause is indicated:

> 1 I wrote a novel, which sold poorly. (nonrestrictive relative clause)
> 2 I wrote a novel which sold poorly. (restrictive relative clause)

Now let us suppose that we have two authors, Steinwell and Orbeck. Steinwell wrote just one novel, which, although it had critical acclaim, sold only thirty-six copies. Orbeck, on the other hand, has written two dozen novels, all of them best-sellers but the first. Steinwell could truthfully say sentence 1, and Orbeck, sentence 2. Now, if we drop the clauses from both sentences, they become simply

> 3 I wrote a novel.

Steinwell could truthfully affirm this sentence, but Orbeck would be misleading (at least) if he said it, since our ordinary interpretation of sentence 3 would be "I wrote just one novel." In other words, the meaning of example 2 is changed in a significant way when the "restrictive" clause is deleted, whereas sentence 1 does not have its meaning significantly changed if the "nonrestrictive" clause is dropped. For those of you who have had an introduction to logic, it may help to say that nonrestrictive relatives, when added to sentences, preserve the truth conditions of those sentences, while restrictive relatives do not.

In summary, a restrictive clause gives us information that we need to know to identify the subject. Look at the two restrictive clauses in sentence 4:

> 4 A brief comment must be made about the "conservative" theorists who argue that American educators suffer from hubris, and that they should stop even trying to do tasks which can only be handled by the family, by employers, by churches, or by other social institutions.
>
> **CHRISTOPHER JENCKS**

Does it matter that the sentence contains the words *who argue that American educators suffer from hubris?* Yes, indeed—note what Jencks is talking about: he is not going to comment about *all "conservative theorists"*; he will make a comment only about *some* theorists—those *who argue that American educators suffer from hubris.* Similarly, those theorists are not saying that American educators should stop trying to do *all* tasks, only *some* tasks—those particular tasks specified by the second restrictive. If we dropped these two restrictives from the sentence, its meaning would be drastically changed.

A nonrestrictive clause, by contrast, gives us information that is in a sense "extra." The topic is sufficiently identified without the nonrestrictive, and if the nonrestrictive is removed, the meaning of the sentence is not changed; in sentence 5, the nonrestrictive clause is emphasized:

> 5 The first person to be buried in the new Potter's Field on the island was an orphan named Louisa Van Slyke, who died in Charity Hospital in 1869.
>
> **WILLIAM STYRON**

The topic, *Louisa Van Slyke,* is already identified; even if the non-restrictive clause is removed, we would still be talking about this particular person.

Exercise

Under ordinary circumstances it sounds extremely odd to have a proper noun modified by a restrictive clause:

> 1 * John Wilkes Booth who shot Lincoln was an actor.

Note too how odd sentences seem when they contain a proper noun modified by either a definite or an indefinite determiner:

> 2 * This is the John Wilkes Booth.
> 3 * This is a John Wilkes Booth.

Now consider what job a restrictive clause usually does; look at sentence 4:

> 4 The man got on the bus.

How many men are there? And which one of them got on the bus? We have no way of telling from sentence 4. But suppose we add a restrictive clause, as in 5:

> 5 The man who had one blue eye and one brown eye got on the bus.

We are still dealing with the same class, *men,* but this time we have some information about which member of the class is meant—that particular man with one blue eye and one brown eye. We can think of proper nouns as being classes that have only one member: that is, there is only one Sherlock Holmes; only one Mount Everest; only one Orlando, Florida, and so on. And if a class has only one member, obviously that class cannot be divided any further. Therefore it makes no sense to modify proper nouns by constructions like a restrictive clause (which separates one member from the class), a definite determiner (which specifies some particular member of the class), or an indefinite determiner (which refers to any individual member of the class). How then would you account for the fact that sentence 6 does not sound ungrammatical, despite its having a proper noun modified by both a definite determiner and a restrictive clause?

> 6 The John Wilkes Booth whom I knew was a much shorter man.

44   RESTRICTIVE RELATIVES

The restrictive relative clause can be produced from a simple structure formed by the phrase structure rules, a fact that makes the process look like a special kind of embedding. We will therefore dispense with the term ''clause,'' and call the structure a ''restrictive embedded sentence.'' We can call the transformation that does this job the RESTRICTIVE EMBEDDING transformation. It operates on one of the same structures as the THAT transformation, the structure produced by rewriting NP as NP and S:

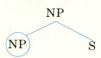

It is necessary only that the embedded sentence have a noun phrase, in any position, equivalent to the circled noun phrase above, which occurs in the outer sentence.

As examples of the process, we will examine the derivations of these sentences:

1a   The man who had red hair got on the bus.
2a   The man whom we saw got on the bus.
3a   The man whom we depended on got on the bus.

These sentences all illustrate the procedure with noun phrases that are the subjects of the outer sentences, but the procedure is the same no matter what the position of the noun phrase in the outer sentence. Sentences 1b, 2b, and 3b show the form of our sentences just before RESTRICTIVE EMBEDDING OCCURS:

1b   The man [the man had red hair] got on the bus.
2b   The man [we saw the man] got on the bus.
3b   The man [we depended on the man] got on the bus.

First, the equivalent noun phrase in the embedded sentence is replaced by the appropriate relative pronoun: (1) noun phrases with the feature •human are replaced by *who* when they are subjects of embedded sentences, and by *whom* when they are objects or when they follow prepositions; (2) noun phrases with the feature •nonhuman are replaced in any position by *which;* (3) noun phrases with either feature may be optionally replaced in any position by *that*. Replacing the equivalent noun phrase in the embedded sentence by a relative pronoun gives

1c   The man [who had red hair] got on the bus.

or

1d   The man [that had red hair] got on the bus.

2c   The man [we saw whom] got on the bus.

or

2d   The man [we saw that] got on the bus.

3c   The man [we depended on whom] got on the bus.

or

3d   The man [we depended on that] got on the bus.

Next, the relative pronoun is moved to the left of the embedded sentence if it is not already there. Obviously, only groups 2 and 3 will be affected:

2e   The man [whom we saw] got on the bus.
2f   The man [that we saw] got on the bus.

3e   The man [whom we depended on] got on the bus.
3f   The man [that we depended on] got on the bus.

If the embedded sentence has its equivalent noun phrase following a preposition, we have an additional option in this second step: either the relative pronoun alone may be moved to the left (as in the development of 3e and 3f), or both the preposition and *whom* or *which* may be moved (*that* cannot be moved with the preposition). This option would give us the following development of 3c:

3g   The man [on whom we depended] got on the bus.

There is one more illustration of RESTRICTIVE EMBEDDING that remains to be shown, a use of the transformation that requires a special relative pronoun. Suppose we have a structure like this:

4a   The man [we met the man's sister] got on the bus.

One of the noun phrases in the outer sentence is *the man*. Although the phrase *the man's* in the embedded sentence has the function of a determiner, it is a transformed noun phrase (see Section 11).

Even if a noun phrase has been changed to a determiner, the RE-STRICTIVE EMBEDDING transformation can still operate if the noun phrase in question has the feature •human. The two steps in this case are shown in examples 4b and 4c:

4b   The man [we met whose sister] got on the bus.
4c   The man [whose sister we met] got on the bus.

The reason for the limitation to noun phrases with the feature •human is not complex: the relative pronouns *who* and *which* take their forms according to the human—nonhuman distinction. The relative pronoun with the feature •human has a special determiner form, *whose;* the relative pronoun marked •nonhuman does not have this special form.

44a   **Application**

CONCISENESS—RELATIVE PRONOUN DELETION

In relative embedded sentences where the equivalent noun phrase is *not* the subject, a further transformation is possible. If the equivalent noun phrase is an object or follows a preposition, it may be replaced by a relative pronoun and moved to the left of the embedded sentence. Samples of these constructions are

1a   The man [whom we saw] got on the bus.
2a   The man [whom we depended on] got on the bus.

In cases like these, the relative pronoun may be deleted (RELATIVE PRONOUN DELETION), and by the principle of economy should be deleted:

1b   The man [we saw] got on the bus.
2b   The man [we depended on] got on the bus.

44b   **Application**

LEVELS OF FORMALITY

Note that there are a number of forms, all of them grammatical, in which the restrictive embedded sentence may finally appear. Here

175

is an especially obvious place where style can be manipulated, since the choices are few in number, and clear in the tone they convey. The three forms of example 1 below can be arranged in an order of formality, from sentences appropriate to a relaxed, informal essay to those appropriate to the most formal style of writing. We can thus begin with 1a:

> 1a   The man we depended on was known to us all.

1a has the most general applicability of all the variations. It would call attention to itself neither in an informal essay nor in a formal one. 1b is a little incongruous, though:

> 1b   The man whom we depended on was known to us all.

In this formulation, we have two elements going in different directions: other things being equal, grammatical constructions not frequently used in speech lend a formal tone to writing. The word *whom* alone gives a feeling of formality. But leaving the preposition behind when the relative pronoun is moved to the left of the sentence (''whom we depended *on*'') sounds much less formal than bringing the preposition to the left *along with* the relative pronoun (''*on* whom we depended''). Thus, 1b is a construction to be avoided—not because it is ungrammatical, but because it is contradictory as far as formality is concerned: *whom* suggests formality, *depended on* suggests informality.

Finally, 1c is the most formal of all. It suggests planning and study rather than spontaneity:

> 1c   The man on whom we depended was known to us all.

Beginning writers should avoid constructions like 1c until they have learned to sustain a formal tone throughout an essay. Section 90 has more complete information on the different levels of formality mentioned here.

44c   Application

MISPLACED MODIFIERS

In Section 38, the EXTRAPOSITION transformation was discussed. This transformation moved an embedded sentence in the subject position to the end of the outer sentence and inserted *it* in the vacated position:

1a   [That he might establish his point by actual demonstration] occurred to Isherwood.

1b   It occurred to Isherwood that he might establish his point by actual demonstration. (EXTRAPOSITION)

ELTING A. MORISON

In Section 42, we saw that these embedding transformations could be used to turn a sentence into a modifier of one of a small group of nouns:

2a   The idea [that she could double her money] appealed to Nina.

When the embedded sentence is not itself a topic but is a modifier of one of the abstract nouns—*idea, fact, rumor,* and so on—EXTRAPOSITION is still possible. Moving the embedded sentence in 2a to the end gives us

2b   The idea appealed to Nina [that she could double her money].

Note that when the extraposed sentence already modifies a noun phrase (in this case, *the idea*), the word *it* is not inserted in the sentence's former place.

Similarly, relative embedded sentences can be extraposed. The embedded sentence is moved to the right of the outer sentence in the normal way:

3a   The woman [who had a green hat] disappeared.

3b   The woman disappeared [who had a green hat].
     (EXTRAPOSITION)

There is a restriction on the use of EXTRAPOSITION with relative embedded sentences, though. Remember that the relative embedded sentence is a modifier of the equivalent noun phrase in the outer sentence. In 4a below, obviously, the embedded sentence *who had a green hat* modifies *the woman:*

4a   The woman [who had a green hat] started her car.

Note that there is another noun phrase, *her car,* at the right of 4a. If we move the relative sentence to the right, we end up with 4b, where the relative embedded sentence appears to modify the noun phrase *her car:*

> 4b * The woman started her car [who had a green hat].

4b illustrates one type of "misplaced modifier." Keep a relative embedded sentence next to its equivalent noun phrase if EXTRAPOSITION would move the embedded structure over another noun phrase.

Exercises

1. Analyze the following passage by showing where RESTRICTIVE EMBEDDING has occurred and where RELATIVE PRONOUN DELETION has occurred.

> It was the woman his finest motives had needed to make them valid; the woman who not only gave to him, but to whom he could give; the woman of memory, of desire, of youth, of restlessness, of completion.
>
> HARLAN ELLISON

2. The following classified advertisement is ambiguous. What two meanings could it have?

> Widow lady in rural area, Nash County, wants female companion with car to live in.

To see how the ambiguity can be analyzed, perform the indicated transformations on the structures below:

> 1   wants female companion with car [female companion T live in]

Perform the following transformations, in the order given, on the embedded sentence: FOR . . . TO transformation, EQUIVALENT NOUN PHRASE DELETION, FOR DELETION.

> 2   female companion with car [female companion T live in car]

Perform the following transformations, in the order given, on the embedded sentence: FOR . . . TO transformation, EQUIVALENT NOUN PHRASE DELETION, FOR DELETION, RESTRICTIVE EMBEDDING (move

only the relative pronoun; leave the preposition behind), RELA-
TIVE PRONOUN DELETION.

The results of 1 and 2 should be identical when you finish.

3. Rewrite the advertisement in exercise 2 to remove the ambiguity.

45 APPOSITIVE (NONRESTRICTIVE) RELATIVES

Section 44 discussed the formation of one type of relative construction, the restrictive embedded sentence. Now we can examine
the other relative construction, the nonrestrictive embedded sentence, or, as we shall call it, the "appositive embedded sentence."
   In Section 43, we talked about appositive (nonrestrictive) embedded sentences as if their information is not essential to the meaning
of the outer sentences in which they are located. Compare the three
examples below as stylistic variations of essentially the same information:

1a   Mergenthaler will be the relief pitcher, and Mergen-
      thaler has a devastating curve.
1b   Mergenthaler (and Mergenthaler has a devastating
      curve) will be the relief pitcher.
1c   Mergenthaler, who has a devastating curve, will be the
      relief pitcher.

The restrictive relative gives us necessary information about the noun
phrase it modifies; it is closely connected to that noun phrase;
hence, it is developed from the same source as that noun phrase.
But an appositive relative gives us information that does not restrict
the noun phrase it modifies. As example 1a shows, this information
could just as well be in a separate half of the sentence. For this
reason (and also because an understanding of the following transformations can aid you when you revise your papers), we will analyze
an appositive embedded sentence as if it had developed from an
entirely separate sentence.
   The transformation that produces appositives (APPOSITIVE EMBED-
DING transformation) can be an effective way of avoiding a succession
of short, repetitive sentences. Again, the only condition is that the

sentences have equivalent noun phrases in some position. For example, consider the following:

> 2a   Vaughn must certainly have known ap Gwilym's poems. He belonged to a very ancient Welsh family, and he was educated in England.

The first noun phrase is the single word *Vaughn*. (We remember from Section 32 that the two occurrences of *he* in the rest of the example each replaced a deep structure occurrence of *Vaughn*. The condition is met: we have equivalent noun phrases in all three sentences, which we can separate for convenience as follows:

> 2b   Vaughn must certainly have known ap Gwilym's poems.
> 2c   Vaughn belonged to a very ancient Welsh family.
> 2d   Vaughn was educated in England.

To combine them, we need to decide which part to make the outer sentence and which ones to transform to appositive sentences. Since the appositives in a sense interrupt the statement of the outer sentence, the shorter parts (2c and 2d) will cause the least interruption. Example 2b will be the outer sentence, then, and the appositives will immediately follow the equivalent noun phrase in that sentence.

First, we will change the equivalent noun phrases in the appositive structures to the appropriate relative pronoun (see Section 44). This is the same procedure we would use for a restrictive embedded sentence, except that the word *that* cannot be used as a relative pronoun with appositives. Since *Vaughn* has the syntactic feature •human, and is a subject noun phrase, the pronoun *who* is selected.

Second, if the relative pronoun is not already at the left of the sentence to be embedded, we move it there. Thus:

> who belonged to a very ancient Welsh family
> who was educated in England

Finally, we insert the appositive relative sentences immediately after the noun phrase in the outer sentence:

> 2e   Vaughn, who belonged to a very ancient Welsh family and who was educated in England, must certainly have known ap Gwilym's poems.

DYLAN THOMAS

These three steps comprise the APPOSITIVE EMBEDDING transformation. Note that the first two steps are the same as those for the RESTRICTIVE EMBEDDING transformation.

The next example illustrates the transformation when it is used with a noun phrase with the feature •nonhuman:

> 3a There is the first part of the Shakespearean, or pseudo-Shakespearean, trilogy of Henry VI. Joan is one of the leading characters in the Shakespearean trilogy.

Here the equivalent noun phrases are the two occurrences of *the Shakespearean trilogy*. First, we change the equivalent noun phrase of the shorter sentence to the appropriate relative pronoun:

> 3b Joan is one of the leading characters in which

Second, we move the pronoun (or the pronoun and any preceding preposition, if you prefer) to the left of the structure:

> 3c in which Joan is one of the leading characters

Third, we insert the appositive sentence immediately after the equivalent noun phrase in the outer sentence:

> 3d There is the first part of the Shakespearean, or pseudo-Shakespearean, trilogy of Henry VI, in which Joan is one of the leading characters.
>
> G. B. SHAW

Finally, remember that one of the equivalent noun phrases can be in determiner form. This use is illustrated by the next example:

> 4a It had been rebuilt by Duke Henry of Lancaster, the father of John's first wife, Blanche. Blanche's virtues are memorialized in Chaucer's "Book of the Duchess."

Here the process will be the same as in examples 2 and 3, except that we select the relative pronoun *whose* to replace, in the embedded sentence, the determiner form of the equivalent noun phrase. Inserting the appositive in place, we derive

4b   It had been rebuilt by Duke Henry of Lancaster, the father of John's first wife, Blanche, whose virtues are memorialized in Chaucer's "Book of the Duchess."

D. W. ROBERTSON, JR.

45a   Application

CONCISENESS—WH-BE DELETION

The alert and retentive student may have noticed that up to this point we have made no mention of some very common structures that modify a noun phrase—those structures traditionally called "participial phrases," and many prepositional phrases. Actually, we have no need to mention them separately, since they can be produced by shortening relative embedded sentences by the transformation to be discussed now, WH-BE DELETION (WH stands for *who, whom, which,* or *that*).

WH-BE DELETION is optional when the equivalent noun phrase of the embedded sentence is in the subject position. The transformation applies to structures like these:

1a   The woman [who was wearing a green hat] got on the bus.
2a   The men [who were elected to office] won by a slim margin.
3a   The boy and girl [who were in the sports car] were known to us all.

All three examples have some form of the verb *be* in the embedded sentence. The word comes from a variety of sources: in 1a, the PROGRESSIVE transformation (Section 18) inserted *be;* in 2a, the PASSIVE transformation (page 16) introduced *be* to the structure; in 3a, however, *be* was present from the very beginning, introduced as a verb in deep structure. Regardless of the source of *be,* when an embedded relative has a relative pronoun as its subject noun phrase, and some form of *be* as its verb, WH-BE DELETION optionally removes the pronoun, the tense, and *be,* giving us

1b   The woman [wearing a green hat] got on the bus.
2b   The men [elected to office] won by a slim margin.
3b   The boy and girl [in the sports car] were known to us all.

The only structure of this general form where WH-BE DELETION cannot take place is that which has the form NP *be* NP (the ''predicate nominative'' of traditional grammar). As sentences 4a and 4b show, WH-BE DELETION in this case gives an ungrammatical result:

4a   Jones [who is our leader] is a problem-solver.
4b * Jones our leader is a problem-solver.

WH-BE DELETION will work with appositive embedded sentences in the same way that it applied to restrictive embedded sentences. Suppose we have two sentences like those in 5a:

5a   The three of them stood abreast, fielding the grounders and lobbing the ball out about forty feet to Ernie Banks. Banks was the Chicago shortstop.

The APPOSITIVE EMBEDDING transformation changes this to

5b   The three of them stood abreast, fielding the grounders and lobbing the ball out about forty feet to Ernie Banks, who was the Chicago shortstop.

WH-BE DELETION removes the relative pronoun and the form of *be*, giving us

5c   The three of them stood abreast, fielding the grounders and lobbing the ball out about forty feet to Ernie Banks, the Chicago shortstop.

GEORGE PLIMPTON

Structures like *the Chicago shortstop*—all that remains of an appositive embedded sentence after WH-BE DELETION—are traditionally called ''appositives''; hence the name of the first transformation necessary to produce them.

45b   Application

PUNCTUATING RELATIVES

As many examples throughout these sections have shown, punctuation is often the only indication the reader has of whether you intend a certain embedded sentence to be restrictive or appositive. You as the writer know what you intend. The problem is to make that intention clear to the reader. Whether the problem arises in composition or revision, there are two fairly accurate tests that can be applied. First, read the sentence aloud, listening to your reading of the embedded sentence. If your voice does not rise in pitch, or does not pause slightly before and after the sentence in question, the embedding is a restrictive embedded sentence, and should *not* be separated from the outer sentence by commas. If your voice does change in pitch, or pauses slightly before and after the construction, the question may still be in doubt.[1] Then apply this second test: if the construction can be deleted from the outer sentence without drastically changing or destroying the meaning of the outer sentence, then the embedded sentence is appositive and should be marked off from the outer sentence by commas. This "deletion" test reflects the limiting power of the restrictive relative.

1   We recognized the only man on the bus, who had red hair.

Suppose you had written this sentence; your meaning was that, although the bus was packed with women, there was just one man on it, and he happened to have red hair. Here the word *only* limits the headnoun *man,* giving the sentence the meaning you desire. Note that if you drop the words *who had red hair,* the statement about how many men were on the bus does not change. *Who had red hair* is therefore an appositive, and you would separate it from the outer sentence with a comma (since the appositive comes at the end of the sentence, and is followed by a period, there is no need for a comma at the right of the appositive).

---

[1] Following A. A. Hill, *Introduction to Linguistic Structures.* New York: Harcourt Brace Jovanovich, 1958. Pp. 360–62. The lack of a pause or change of pitch with restrictives shows that the speaker thinks of the embedded sentence as an unremovable part of the noun phrase.

But if you had written

> 2 We recognized the only man on the bus who had red hair.

you would not have achieved the meaning you intended. In 2, the bus may have been full of men—but just one of them had red hair. If you drop *who had red hair* from this sentence, notice that the meaning changes, making the sentence assert that there was just one man on the bus. In this case, then, *who had red hair* is restrictive.

To summarize, restrictive relatives, whether in full form (*who was wearing a green hat*) or reduced (*wearing a green hat*), are not separated from the outer sentence. Appositive relatives, whether in full form or reduced, are separated from the outer sentence by commas:

> Appositive, outer sentence.
> Outer sentence, appositive, outer sentence.
> Outer sentence, appositive.

Since punctuation serves here as an important indication of the grammatical relationships of the parts of the sentence, to err in punctuating restrictive and appositive relatives is to commit one of the most serious punctuation errors.

Exercise

Analyze the following passages to show where RESTRICTIVE EMBEDDING and APPOSITIVE EMBEDDING have occurred.

> 1 Definite labels and features were found for the Russian substance scattered about Berlin, . . . be it merely a snatch of routine conversation, . . . or, on a summer night, a man with his head thrown back clapping his hands under a lighted window and shouting a resonant name and patronymic that made the whole street vibrate and caused a taxi to emit a nervous squeal and shy to one side after nearly running over the vociferous visitor, who had by now backed to the center of the asphalt, the better to see if the person he needed would appear

like Punch in the window. Through the Zilanovs Martin met people among whom he at first felt ignorant and alien.

VLADIMIR NABOKOV

2   Henry Jones Ford . . . was the first to call attention pointedly to the one giant force that has done most to elevate the Presidency to power and glory: the rise of American democracy. Most men who feared the proposed Presidency in 1787 were prisoners of the inherited Whig assumption that legislative power was essentially popular and executive power essentially monarchial in nature. The notion that a democratic President might be pitted against an oligarchical legislature occurred to few at the time—most notably to Gouverneur Morris, who spoke of the executive, with his tongue somewhere in his cheek, as "the guardian of the people" against the tyranny of the "great and wealthy who in the course of things will necessarily compose the Legislative body."

CLINTON ROSSITER

3   The current movement, like the women's rights movement of the 1800s, is based on an educated elite group of white, middle-class women, who have experienced a strong sense of status displacement. Much of their effort has followed the traditional pattern of concentrating on constitutional-legal reforms that most benefit middle-class women, such as the Equal Rights Amendment.

GERDA LERNER

Sub-ordination

SECTIONS 46-53

46 EMBEDDED SENTENCES IN ADVERBIALS

We saw in Section 25 that time and place adverbials can consist of prepositions followed by noun phrases. Since a sentence may be embedded wherever a noun phrase occurs, we should expect to find embedded sentences in time and place adverbials, and in fact they occur there. We will be able to derive several different surface structures in adverbials, and we will be able to use transformations that have already been introduced in the section on relative embedded sentences.

Suppose we want to derive a sentence like *John left the house at the time the sun rose*. Near the beginning of the derivation, the adverbial starts out as simply a preposition and a noun phrase. Suppose further that the noun phrase has a development such as this:

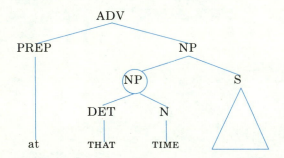

(THAT and TIME in the diagram above stand for pro-forms of definite determiners, and nouns marked with the feature •time.) Now assume that the embedded sentence is rewritten with an adverbial of its own, one with a noun phrase equivalent to the circled noun phrase in the diagram:

    1a   John left the house at THAT TIME [the sun rose at THAT TIME].

Since we have equivalent noun phrases in the outer and embedded sentences, the structure meets the condition necessary for the RE-STRICTIVE EMBEDDING transformation. First, the equivalent noun phrase in the embedded sentence is replaced by the appropriate relative pronoun:

188

1b   John left the house at THAT TIME [the sun rose at which].

Next, the relative pronoun is moved to the left of the embedded sentence, by itself or together with the preposition:

1c   John left the house at THAT TIME [at which the sun rose].

If we select *the* as the definite determiner in the adverbial, and stop the derivation at this point, we would have the rather stiff-sounding

1d   John left the house at the time at which the sun rose.

But we can, if we wish, derive an alternate form of the same sentence. In Section 39 we introduced the EQUIVALENT NOUN PHRASE DELETION transformation, which removes an equivalent noun phrase from an embedded sentence. Let us extend the scope of this transformation to include the prepositions that sometimes precede noun phrases. Now, EQUIVALENT NOUN PHRASE DELETION will remove both the noun phrase and the preposition (if the preposition also repeats the preposition before the equivalent noun phrase in the outer sentence). If we return to 1a now, we have conditions for EQUIVALENT NOUN PHRASE DELETION:

John left the house at THAT TIME [the sun rose at THAT TIME].

Deleting the repeated preposition and noun phrase gives us

1e   John left the house at the time the sun rose.

Remember that we derived the phrase *at that time* from pro-forms standing for any definite determiner and any noun with the feature •time, so this procedure would be the source for adverbials of the form ''at the *moment* the sun rose,'' ''at the *hour* the sun rose,'' and so on.

   In the same way, we can operate either the RESTRICTIVE EMBEDDING transformation or EQUIVALENT NOUN PHRASE DELETION with an embedded sentence in a place adverbial:

2a   A meteorite fell at THAT PLACE [Joan had been standing at THAT PLACE].

With EQUIVALENT NOUN PHRASE DELETION we would have

    2b   A meteorite fell at the place Joan had been standing.[1]

Or, from 2a, with RESTRICTIVE EMBEDDING:

    2c   A meteorite fell at THAT PLACE [Joan had been standing at which].

    2d   A meteorite fell at the place at which Joan had been standing.

Notice what has happened in the examples above: a pro-form in the embedded sentence adverbials carried the feature •place or •time. When the noun phrase containing the pro-form was replaced by the relative pronoun *which*, we lost the information in those features—obviously, the word *which* has no implication of time or place. But there are special relative pronouns available for noun phrases with time or place features, pronouns that preserve the feature information—*when* and *where*. We can call the process of using these special relatives the TIME-RELATIVE or PLACE-RELATIVE transformations. In operation, they are exactly the same as the regular relative transformation, with one exception: *when* and *where* replace the preposition and the equivalent noun phrase:

    3a   John left the house at THAT TIME [the sun rose at THAT TIME].

    3b   John left the house at THAT TIME [the sun rose when]. (TIME-RELATIVE transformation)

    3c   John left the house at the time when the sun rose.

With the PLACE-RELATIVE transformation, we have

    4a   A meteorite fell at THAT PLACE [Joan had been standing at THAT PLACE].

    4b   A meteorite fell at THAT PLACE [Joan had been standing where]. (PLACE-RELATIVE transformation)

    4c   A meteorite fell at the place where Joan had been standing.

---

[1] This sentence may be ungrammatical in some dialects.

46a   Application

REDUNDANCY—PRO DELETION

In Section 7, on the pro-forms of nouns, it was pointed out that the pro-forms carry relatively little information and are often deleted. At that time, no conditions were specified for the deletion of pro-forms. In the case at hand we can be more precise. One of the effects of the special relative pronouns *when* and *where* is to carry the features •time and •place to the left of the embedded sentences. In their new positions, the special relative pronouns are next to the pro-forms TIME and PLACE in the adverbial of the outer sentence. We then have a redundancy, a needless repetition of information, one that will become clearer if we explicitly mark some features from examples in Section 46:

1a   John left the house at THAT N   [when the sun rose].
                            •time   •time

2a   A meteorite fell at THAT N   [where Joan had been
                          •place   •place
standing].

In other words, sentences like 1a and 2a are unnecessarily redundant. The adverbials of the outer sentences of 1a and 2a tell us merely that the action occurred at some time or some place. But that same information is already present as a feature of the special relative pronouns. Suppose we assume then that a noun phrase composed of pro-forms (at least in the adverbial) can be deleted if the same information is present in the following noun phrase or relative pronoun. We can call this transformation PRO DELETION. By means of it we derive 1c and 2c from 1b and 2b (note that the preposition is also deleted):

1b   John left the house at THAT TIME [when the sun rose].
1c   John left the house [when the sun rose].   (PRO DELE-TION)
2b   A meteorite fell at THAT PLACE [where Joan had been standing].
2c   A meteorite fell [where Joan had been standing].   (PRO DELETION)

191

47 FEATURES IN ADVERBIALS

There is one more point to be made about time and place adverbials, one that simply notes a difference between these two kinds of modifiers that are otherwise so similar. All the examples so far have shown adverbials with the preposition *at;* the extreme generality of *at* makes it tempting to call it the pro-form of the prepositions in time and place adverbials. But what if the outer sentence adverbials have some other preposition, so that we would end up with sentences like these (after EQUIVALENT NOUN PHRASE DELETION of *at* THAT TIME and *at* THAT PLACE)?

    1a   I was busy until THE TIME [you called].
    2a   My house is near THE PLACE [you visited].

Given these sentences, how can we account for the fact that 1b, which seems to be related to a possible development of 1a, is grammatical, whereas 2b, equally likely to be related to 2a, is not?

    1b I was busy until you called.
    2b * My house is near you visited.

It would be easy enough to say that we have another instance of PRO DELETION here, and simply add the restriction that the transformation does not work for pro-forms in the place adverbials of outer sentences. But is there another way, one that will help explain why the restriction exists, or at least increase our understanding of what is involved here?

We can simplify the problem by dividing it into two parts: what is wrong with 2b, and what is right with 1b. To begin with, look at the syntactic ambiguity involved in a structure like 2b: reading or hearing the sentence, there must be a split second when we interpret the two adjacent words *near you* as a prepositional phrase. But of course the words are not a prepositional phrase at all—*near* is all that is left of the place adverbial of the outer sentence, and *you* is simply the subject of the embedded sentence. In other words, speakers of English may reject structures like 2b because such structures are intolerably misleading about the relationships of the words in the sentence.

Turning our attention to 1b, we can check to see what other prepositions can be substituted for *until. After* seems perfectly all right, as do *just as, before,* and perhaps a few more. Note that these prepositions are the ones that are most often used (in some cases, exclusively used) with noun phrases having a headnoun with the feature •time. On the other hand, a preposition like *about* can precede a noun phrase having a headnoun with either the feature •time or the feature •place:

3   Henry IV paced about the courtyard.
                                 •place

4   I saw him last about nine o'clock.
                                 •time

And prepositions like *about,* which occur with either time or place nouns, cannot substitute for *until* in 1b:

1c   * I was busy about you called.

Sentence 1c must be rejected for the same reason that 2b is unacceptable: *about you* could, in the right context, be a prepositional phrase, because *about* can be followed by either time or place nouns, and probably any concrete noun can be marked for the feature •place—for example:

5   There's a bee buzzing about you.
                                 •place

But with words like *until, before, after,* and so on, we apparently assume that they introduce a prepositional phrase only if they are followed by a noun with the feature •time. In 1b, *you* has, of course, no time feature, so we interpret *until* as the remnant of an abridged adverbial.

48   **SUBORDINATING CONJUNCTIONS AND ADVERBIALS**

We found out in Section 26 how manner adverbials—words like *impulsively*—could be derived from phrases like *in an impulsive manner.* But there are much longer manner adverbials. What are we going to do with a sentence like this?

1a   Cecelia defused the bomb as if she knew what she was doing.

Part of the structure, *she knew what she was doing,* certainly looks like something we would want to call a sentence. Also, we can account for the front of the structure, *Cecelia defused the bomb,* easily enough. All we have left to explain are the words *as if* and the relationship of the parts to one another. The transformations and phrase structure rules we have set up so far will produce sentence 1a for us if we are willing to consider *as if* as a special kind of embedder—one found only with sentences embedded in manner adverbials.

Special embedders like *as if* are traditionally called "subordinating conjunctions"—words and combinations of words like *as if, if, although, because,* and others. Suppose, to begin with, we have a sentence with a manner adverbial consisting of a preposition, a noun phrase, and an embedded sentence:

> 1b   Cecelia defused the bomb PREP THAT MANNER [she knew what she was doing].

The transformation we now use is probably a special case of the embedding transformations we have already seen. We can call it the MANNER EMBEDDING transformation; it will be obligatory any time the conditions for the RESTRICTIVE EMBEDDING transformation are not met in the embedded sentence. MANNER EMBEDDING places one of the manner embedders at the left of the embedded sentence:

> 1c   Cecelia defused the bomb PREP THAT MANNER [as if she knew what she was doing].

Other manner embedders that might have been chosen include *as though* or *like.*[1] Now, if we wish, we can delete the pro-forms in the adverbial:

> 1d   Cecelia defused the bomb [as if she knew what she was doing].   (PRO DELETION)

In the same way that we had special embedders for use with the MANNER EMBEDDING transformation, so we have a variety of other special embedders that cover other relationships of the adverbial to the outer sentence. One kind is the "condition" adverbial; example

---

[1] See *like* in the Glossary of Usage (Section 96) for an explanation of this provocative statement.

2a shows a sentence embedded in a condition adverbial:

2a   John will finish the job if he can get enough supplies.

Our derivation here is exactly like that of the manner adverbial. We begin with

2b   John will finish the job PREP THAT CONDITION [he can get enough supplies].

The CONDITION EMBEDDING transformation selects a condition embedder from a group that includes *if, unless, provided, supposing, in case,* and probably a few more:

2c   John will finish the job PREP THAT CONDITION [if he can get enough supplies].

2d   John will finish the job [if he can get enough supplies].   (PRO DELETION)

Grammarians usually distinguish a number of other adverbial relations that we can build into our system—for example, "concession." The CONCESSION EMBEDDING transformation has as embedders *though, although, even if,* and *while.* With PRO DELETION, a derivation of a concession adverbial would be

3a   Cecelia defused the bomb PREP THAT CONCESSION [it was difficult].

3b   Cecelia defused the bomb PREP THAT CONCESSION [though it was difficult].   (CONCESSION EMBEDDING)

3c   Cecelia defused the bomb [though it was difficult]. (PRO DELETION)

Similarly, the CAUSE EMBEDDING transformation selects an embedder from *because, since,* or *inasmuch as.* The same deletion is possible as with the other adverbials:

4a   Gordon reads detective stories PREP THAT CAUSE [he enjoys them].

4b   Gordon reads detective stories PREP THAT CAUSE [because he enjoys them].   (CAUSE EMBEDDING)

4c   Gordon reads detective stories [because he enjoys them].   (PRO DELETION)

With adverbials, as with many other areas, a transformational grammar seems inextricably bound up with philosophy or logic. Terms like ''time'' and ''place,'' ''cause'' and ''condition,'' reveal a search for the basic elements of thought, elements that would presumably turn up in the speech embodying that thought. Clearly, the analysis of language, so long under way, has much further to go.

Exercise

In the sentences below, identify the different kinds of adverbials:

1 As we were leaving, we heard a scratching scramble among the branches overhead.

EDWIN WAY TEALE

2 The girls, Cissy and Marcia Mae, sitting out on the side porch where they had hurried and quickly shut the curtained French doors because they weren't dressed and had no wish to talk to anybody, could hear from within the murmuring rise and fall of ladies' voices.

ELIZABETH SPENCER

3 If, for all its charm, this tale has about it a certain air of *déjà vu* banality, it is largely because the virtues it propounds have continued to form the foundations of the sensible middle-class outlook.

CHARLES T. WOOD

4 Victory in general habit leaned to the clear-sighted, though fortune and superior intelligence could make a sad muddle of nature's "inexorable" law.

T. E. LAWRENCE

5 But when I came on her sitting there, she was staring blankly ahead of her, as though she sat as a duty by the unmourned dead.

MARJORIE KINNAN RAWLINGS

6 So the last Earl of Balcairn went, as they say, to his fathers

(who had fallen in many lands and for many causes, as the eccentricities of British Foreign Policy and their own wandering natures had directed them . . .).

EVELYN WAUGH

7   A hundred years ago Courbet, artistic rebel of his day, said: "The museums should be closed for twenty years so that today's painters may begin to see the world with their own eyes."

SARAH NEWMEYER

49   WHOLE-SENTENCE MODIFIERS

It seems we never run out of problems with adverbials; we still have not considered all the kinds of words ending in -ly. What, for example, is the function of the emphasized words in the examples below?

1a   Luckily, the brakes lasted until we got to a garage.
2a   Honestly, his paintings aren't worth their prices.
3a   Generally, I eat lunch at the Automat.

Sentences like these cannot be the result of PREVERB LEFT SHIFT: if they were, they would be strange preverbs, since all the rest of the preverbs in Section 23 seemed to have something to do with time or frequency. Moreover, the relation of *luckily, honestly,* and *generally* to their respective sentences seems different from that of a verb phrase adverbial to its sentence—certainly, these words say more about the situation of the whole sentence than about the verb phrase alone. This difference suggests another kind of modification—in fact, several kinds. Note that we can paraphrase 1a by making all the words after the comma an embedded sentence in the subject position, adding the word *lucky* as an adjective, and inserting the appropriate form of *be* between the two parts:

1b   [That the brakes lasted until we got to a garage] was lucky.

In both 1a and 1b, *luckily* and *lucky* are modifying the fact reported—they modify an entire sentence. We can call words like *luckily* "sentence adverbials."

Sentence adverbials can be derived from any adjective that can occur following *be* in a sentence with an embedded sentence as its subject. The SENTENCE ADVERBIAL transformation changes the ''a'' sentences below to the ''b'' forms:

4a [That someone wants to talk when I'm studying] is inevitable.
4b Inevitably, someone wants to talk when I'm studying.
5a [That Tom didn't have a spare tire] was incredible.
5b Incredibly, Tom didn't have a spare tire.

But when we examine sentences 2a and 3a, it is clear that *honestly* and *generally* cannot be sentence adverbials. If they were, they would be derived from very strange-sounding structures:

2b *[That his paintings aren't worth their prices] is honest.
3b *[That I eat lunch at the Automat] is general.

What relation do we have between, say, *honestly* in 2a and the rest of its sentence? (See Section 50 for a discussion of 3a.) In *honestly* we have a word that describes not what is said, but the attitude of the person who says it. It is not the statement but the speaker with a claim to honesty. A transformational approach therefore derives sentences like 2a from a structure something like this:

2c I say honestly that his paintings aren't worth their prices.

Words like *honestly* in 2a are therefore simply manner adverbials of an outer sentence, most of which has been deleted. In fact, all that is left is the manner adverbial and an embedded sentence in the object position. Compare the similar examples below; it should be evident what kind of material is being deleted in each case, and why such drastic deletions are possible (each ''b'' sentence is derived from the ''a'' sentence):

6a I ask you seriously if you haven't had enough to drink.
6b Seriously, haven't you had enough to drink?
7a I say frankly that your remark was in bad taste.
7b Frankly, your remark was in bad taste.

Exercises

1. Analyze the sentences below to show the source of the emphasized words:

    1 Naturally, complex ideas sometimes are garbled in transmission.

    2 Freud certainly did not expect so much opposition in scientific circles.

    3 Realistically, Scott's expedition had little chance of success.

    4 Truly, sorrow means never having to say you're lovely.

    5 You are manifestly suffering from an allergy to horse dander.

2. Why do you suppose there are sentences like 1 and 2 below, but none like 3 and 4?

    1 Frankly, I don't care for artichokes.

    2 Honestly, I don't care for artichokes.

    3 *Falsely, I don't care for artichokes.

    4 *Deceptively, I don't care for artichokes.

3. How would you analyze the sentence below?

        Hopefully, we can settle this question in this generation.

After you have analyzed the sentence, look up *hopefully* in several dictionaries and handbooks of usage, and see if you can account for the comments you find there.

50 SENTENCE CONNECTORS

In a sentence like the following

    1 Generally I eat lunch at the Automat.

the word *generally* can be neither a sentence adverbial nor the remnant of an outer sentence, since it neither modifies the sentence as a whole nor tells us the manner of the speaker's assertion. It forms a third class of words, along with *consequently, particularly, especially, likewise, moreover, alternatively, on the other hand, never-*

theless, and many others. These words are in many respects like the conjunctions *and, or, but,* and *so.* That is, they express a connection of some kind between whole sentences. A few of the commonly recognized relationships between sentences, together with a few of the sentence connectors used with each relationship, are outlined below.

Like *and,* "additive" sentence connectors, as the name implies, join two sentences where the second simply adds more information to the first:

2   You need six hours in biology. $\begin{cases} \text{Also,} \\ \text{In addition,} \\ \text{Moreover,} \\ \text{Furthermore,} \end{cases}$ you

need three in math.

Like *or,* "alternative" sentence connectors offer or express a choice between two options:

3   Put the letter in the mail today. $\begin{cases} \text{Alternatively,} \\ \text{Otherwise,} \end{cases}$ take it over yourself.

Like *but,* "adversative" sentence connectors imply that the second sentence is in opposition to the first. With such a connector, we assert that the information of the second sentence has validity or applicability despite the information of the first:

4   Marlowe left London to escape the plague. $\begin{cases} \text{However,} \\ \text{Nevertheless,} \end{cases}$ that trip led him to his death.

Like *so,* "illative" sentence connectors present the second sentence as an effect or result of the first:

5   Thursday's agenda had some important matters. $\begin{cases} \text{Therefore,} \\ \text{Consequently,} \end{cases}$ I had asked everyone to be on time.

There are probably more types of sentence connectors that might be noted before we reached the point where the results no longer justified the effort. Two final ones worth noting are "particularizing" and "generalizing" connectors. With particularizing connectors, the second sentence offers information that exemplifies or illustrates what the first sentence states:

6   This is interesting poetry. $\begin{cases} \text{Especially,} \\ \text{For instance,} \\ \text{Particularly,} \end{cases}$

      look at these lines.

Generalizing connectors do just the reverse, placing what the first sentence says into the framework of a larger context:

7   You found her in her office? $\begin{cases} \text{As a rule,} \\ \text{Generally,} \\ \text{Usually,} \end{cases}$ she's

      not there at noon.

Exercises

1. Find some sentences using

     1   a preverb
     2   an adverbial of time, place, concession, etc.
     3   a sentence modifier
     4   a sentence connector.

Be sure to list the sources of your example sentences.

2. Diagram the following sentences:

     1   Certainly I love you.
     2   Sam reluctantly bought a fishing license.

In each case, draw a tree diagram for the deep structure first, then show the form of the sentences after each of the transformations needed to produce the surface structure.

51   **ADVERBIAL MOVEMENT AND STYLE**

Writers of English freely move some adverbials from their original positions. We have already seen how preverbs are shifted to the left or to the right (Sections 23 and 24); here we will discuss the movements of verb phrase adverbials and sentence adverbials. Time and place adverbials develop at the end of the verb phrase, according to the phrase structure rules. Generally, a time or place adverbial can be shifted to the front of the sentence:

1a   John left the house when the sun rose.
1b   When the sun rose, John left the house.
2a   Hemingway's last book was published in 1964.
2b   In 1964, Hemingway's last book was published.
3a   Marilyn saw a five-dollar bill nearby.
3b   Nearby, Marilyn saw a five-dollar bill.
4a   A meteorite fell where Joan had been standing.
4b   Where Joan had been standing, a meteorite fell.

Adverbials of manner, condition, and so on, can be shifted in the same way:

5a   Ishmael signed aboard Ahab's ship eagerly.
5b   Eagerly, Ishmael signed aboard Ahab's ship.
6a   Gordon reads detective stories because he enjoys them.
6b   Because he enjoys them, Gordon reads detective stories.

In addition, these adverbials, especially manner adverbials, are often moved to a position between the noun phrase and the verb phrase:

7a   Gauguin left for Tahiti impulsively.
7b   Gauguin impulsively left for Tahiti.

Or between any modal, *have,* or *be* on the one side, and the main verb on the other:

8a   We will get through this book somehow.
8b   We will somehow get through this book.

Sentence adverbs and sentence connectors can be shifted from their position at the beginning to the same positions within the sentence as the verb phrase adverbials: between the noun phrase and the verb phrase; or between a modal, *have,* or *be,* and the main verb:

9a Inevitably, someone will want to talk when I'm studying.

9b Someone inevitably will want to talk when I'm studying.

9c Someone will inevitably want to talk when I'm studying.

10a Thursday's agenda had some important matters. Therefore I had asked everyone to be on time.

10b I therefore had asked everyone to be on time.

10c I had therefore asked everyone to be on time.

These examples do not exhaust the possibilities for the movement of adverbials. In sentences like

11a That trip led him, nevertheless, to his death.

the sentence connector, *nevertheless,* has been moved to follow rather than precede the verb. Moving verb phrase adverbials to the left of the sentence results in no loss of clarity, but moving sentence connectors very far to the right can obscure the function of the connector—as the connector is moved farther and farther to the right, we are increasingly likely to forget the first sentence when we finally meet the connector that relates it to the second sentence. Compare the ease of comprehension of the following examples:

11b Marlowe left London to escape the plague; that trip, nevertheless, led him to his death.

11c Marlowe left London to escape the plague; that trip led him, nevertheless, to his death.

11d Marlowe left London to escape the plague; that trip, which ended at a tavern in Deptford, led him, nevertheless, to his death.

51a   Application

PUNCTUATING INTRODUCTORY ADVERBIALS

If an adverbial has been shifted to the front of the sentence, should it be followed by a comma? Should a sentence connector that is already there? Keep in mind the uses of punctuation in modern English, and the problem becomes a little simpler. First, a comma is always necessary whenever a misinterpretation of the grammar of the sentence is possible:

1   Though Marilyn left, Dick stayed till the end.

The comma after *left* makes it impossible, when we begin to read the sentence, to interpret *Dick* as the direct object of *left*.

Remember the second use of punctuation: it often mirrors the intonations the sentence would have if spoken. To tell whether you need a comma after some element that precedes the subject noun phrase, read the sentence aloud: if your instinct is to pause after that element, place a comma after the element. Try this method on the sentences below, listening to the pause that you make at the point where the written sentence has a comma:

2   Nevertheless, that trip led him to his death.
3   As if she knew what she was doing, Cecelia defused the bomb.
4   Fortunately for us, we have other means of placing a comma.

51b   Application

ADVERBIAL AMBIGUITY

Moving an adverbial to the beginning of a sentence sometimes creates ambiguities that require correction. We can illustrate the problem with time adverbials, using the emphasized words in 1a and 2a as examples:

1a   Will said something at ten o'clock.
2a   I rang the bell at ten o'clock.

Like most adverbials, these can be shifted to the front of the sentence:

1b   At ten o'clock, Will said something.
2b   At ten o'clock, I rang the bell.

Difficulties appear, though, when we have one sentence embedded in another. Note sentence 3a:

> 3a   Will said at ten o'clock I rang the bell.

Here we do not know whether *at ten o'clock* is a modifier of the outer sentence's verb phrase (*said*), or a shifted modifier of the embedded sentence's verb phrase (*rang the bell*). Note too that putting the adverbial back to the end of the sentence will not help, because both inner and outer sentences end at the same place. 3b is still ambiguous:

> 3b   Will said I rang the bell at ten o'clock.

In this particular sentence, and in others having sentences embedded by the THAT transformation, the problem is caused not by moving the adverbial, but by removing the word *that*, which shows the boundary of the embedded sentence (see Section 38b on THAT DELETION); note that the sentence can be clarified for either meaning if *that* is allowed to remain:

> 3c   Will said at ten o'clock that I rang the bell.
> 3d   Will said that at ten o'clock I rang the bell.

In 3c we have retained the meaning that Will made a particular statement and that the time when he made it was ten o'clock. In 3d we have retained the meaning that the bell was rung at ten o'clock.

The problem is somewhat more complicated if the embedded sentence has undergone the FOR . . . TO transformation (see Sections 36 and 39). In example 4a below, we have no simple marker like *that* which can be inserted to clear up the sentence:

> 4a   John promised at ten o'clock to meet Priscilla.

Here we have two possible ways to correct the sentence. First, if we intend that the meeting will take place at ten o'clock, shifting the adverbial to its original place will produce that meaning:

> 4b   John promised to meet Priscilla at ten o'clock.

If we intend to say the promise was made at ten o'clock, we can shift the adverbial to the beginning of the outer sentence:

> 4c **At ten o'clock**, John promised to meet Priscilla.

Second, we could rephrase the sentence, using the THAT transformation to embed the sentence and letting *that* mark the boundary for us:

> 4d John promised **that** at ten o'clock he would meet Priscilla.
>
> 4e John promised at ten o'clock **that** he would meet Priscilla.

Exercises

1. Section 51 shows how adverbials can be moved about rather freely. Find ten sentences with adverbials in a passage of prose by an author you enjoy, and note where the adverbials are located. Draw up a table of percentages summarizing what you found, and compare it with the tables of the other members of the class. Be sure to note the source of the passage.

2. Though sentences 1 and 2 are synonymous, do you find any difference in emphasis between the two? Even if they both contain the same information, is part of that information pushed into the foreground, so to speak, in one version?

   > 1 Gordon reads detective stories because he enjoys them.
   > 2 Because he enjoys them, Gordon reads detective stories.

   Assume that you are instructing a writer who wants to know what effect is produced by moving an adverbial to the front of the sentence. Tell him when he should do it, and when he should avoid it.

52 THE "POST HOC" ASSUMPTION

There are a number of deletions possible in sentences embedded in adverbials, but some of these deletions are invitations to what traditional handbooks call "faulty subordination" and "dangling participles." Before we look at the specific transformations involved, we need to make some very general comments about the nature of language and the nature of logic.

Everyone reading this book has surely heard of the logical fallacy called "post hoc, ergo propter hoc" ("after this, therefore because of this"), the unsound argument which asserts that because event A came before event B, therefore A caused B. Huck Finn is especially given to this argument:

> I've always reckoned that looking at the new moon over your left shoulder is one of the carelessest and foolishest things a body can do. Old Hank Bunker done it once, and bragged about it; and in less than two years he got drunk and fell off of the shot tower and spread himself out so that he was just a kind of layer, as you may say; and they slid him edgeways between two barn doors for a coffin, and buried him so, so they say, but I didn't see it. Pap told me. But anyway, it all come of looking at the moon that way, like a fool.
>
> MARK TWAIN

Now, when we see two sentences brought into the same grammatical structure—whether they are joined by a conjunction or by the embedding of one inside the other—we assume there is some purpose for having them together. That is, two absolutely unconnected thoughts will seem bizarre when grammatically joined:

1 A piano has eighty-eight keys, and legal censorship should reflect personal censorship.

To repeat, when we see two structures juxtaposed, we assume the writer had a reason for putting them together. And in the absence of any signal to the contrary, we often assume, as Huck did, that the event of the second sentence was caused by, or resulted from, the event of the first. Consider

2a The lights went out all over the Eastern seaboard, and Roger struck a match.

Despite the inadequacy of Roger's response, we feel that it was caused by the event described in the first half of the sentence. The situation becomes ludicrous, more clearly exposing the implied cause-and-effect relationship, if we reverse the sentences:

> 2b Roger struck a match, and the lights went out all over the Eastern seaboard.

Note that in neither 2a nor 2b do words like *because* or *therefore* appear; only the positions of the two sentences in each example imply the "post hoc" relationship: *because* Roger struck a match, *therefore* the lights went out. In the sections that follow, deletion transformations will be introduced that remove from the sentence words like *because, after,* and *while.* Certain problems in writing arise from the loss of these words since, without the specification of the relationships they provide, the "post hoc" assumption takes over.

The "post hoc" assumption is only one of those we sometimes make in English. But there are many more assumptions that we use systematically. Sometimes they are sources of humor, sometimes they are secret weapons used to gain an advantage. Each of the exercises that follow explores one of these "undercover" uses of language.

52a   Application

FAULTY SUBORDINATION

Consider a sentence somewhat like an earlier example:

> 1a When Roger struck a match, the lights went out all over the Eastern seaboard.

Although "faulty subordination" is the traditional term for the problem that afflicts 1a, grammatical subordination has little to do with it. The difficulty springs from the writer's inattention to the "post hoc" assumption. Note that 1a links the description of two events by means of the time adverbial *when.* No one would use a cause adverbial (*because, since,* etc.) in place of *when* by mistake:

> 1b Because Roger struck a match, the lights went out all over the Eastern seaboard.

Although we may not agree with 1b, or not understand how this cause could have such an effect, we assume that the writer means what he says.

Occasionally, though, a writer neglects the "post hoc" assumption; he unintentionally disregards our habit of thinking that a cause-and-effect relationship exists between two events connected in time, especially when the descriptions of those events are grammatically joined by time embedders, such as *when* and *after*. The solution is simple: do not make the obvious effect the grammatical cause. If the two events are unrelated, what are they doing grammatically joined? If the only connection between the two is their close occurrence in time, use a phrase such as *at the same time that* to make it explicit that causality is not involved:

1c   **At the same time that** Roger struck a match, the lights went out all over the Eastern seaboard.

Exercises

1. If we ask someone, "Have you stopped beating your wife?" we imply that he did in fact beat his wife. Every time a sentence contains the construction *stop* V-ING, where V stands for any appropriate verb, the action of the verb following *stop* is implied. Compare the sets of sentences in Group A and Group B below, and see if you can state why the first group has only normal sentences, while those in the second group seem strange.

Group A

1   Matthew says that Mary Cassatt was a French hairdresser, but she wasn't.
2   Matthew claims that Mary Cassatt was a French hairdresser, but she wasn't.
3   Matthew believes that Mary Cassatt was a French hairdresser, but she wasn't.

Group B

4 * Matthew knows that Mary Cassatt was a French hairdresser, but she wasn't.
5 * Matthew regrets that Mary Cassatt was a French hairdresser, but she wasn't.

209

6 * Matthew realizes that Mary Cassatt was a French hairdresser, but she wasn't.

2. Does *and* always mean simply "and"? Notice that, in many cases, the positions of the constructions on either side of *and* may be switched, and the meaning of the sentence does not change:

1a George collects stamps and saves string.
1b George saves string and collects stamps.
2a Ellen went to Bimini and Maria went to Steubenville.
2b Maria went to Steubenville and Ellen went to Bimini.
3a Yesterday Tony wrote letters and watched his ant farm.
3b Yesterday Tony watched his ant farm and wrote letters.

But for some sentences, if we switch the positions of the constructions, the result does not mean the same thing. Try the process with the sentences below, examine the results, and tell what *and* really means in these sentences.

4 Dan went to the station and caught a train.
5 Alice saw Tony's ant farm and laughed herself sick.
6 Susy got an A on her final paper and just barely passed the course.

53 DELETIONS IN ADVERBIALS

Suppose we have a sentence with a cause adverbial, as in the following example:

1a Anthony's line of supply was cut because Octavian had seized Corinth.

ADV-CAUSE DELETION operates on a sentence embedded in a cause adverbial by removing the embedder *because* and substituting ING-& for the tense of the embedded sentence. From 1a we would derive 1b (note that a comma marks the place of the deleted embedder):

1b Anthony's line of supply was cut, Octavian having seized Corinth.

But in the process of deletion, we have lost some of the force of the cause-and-effect relationship formerly indicated by *because*. We can restore that relationship, though, by taking advantage of the "post hoc" assumption: if we switch the adverbial to the beginning of the sentence, we will imply that the event described in the adverbial caused the event described in the outer sentence:

> 1c   Octavian having seized Corinth, Anthony's line of supply was cut.

If the outer sentence and embedded sentence have equivalent noun phrases (see Section 39), a further reduction is possible; compare the following derivation with examples 1a to 1c:

> 2a   Queeg turns the ship south, . . . because Queeg is terrified.
>
> 2b   Queeg turns the ship south, . . . Queeg being terrified.
>   (ADV-CAUSE DELETION)
>
> 2c   Queeg turns the ship south, . . . being terrified.
>   (EQUIVALENT NOUN PHRASE DELETION)

In 2c, the second of the equivalent noun phrases has been deleted. *Be* entered the embedded sentence in 2a ("Queeg *is* terrified") as a result of the PASSIVE transformation. Transformations, you will recall, change the form, but not the meaning, of the structure; elements like *being,* which change only the form, are often deletable. Here we have one such case. The deletion transformation that removes *being* probably has a more general applicability than we show here, but the conditions for its operation are not completely clear. It may be, for instance, that the many transformations that remove some form of *be* are particular instances of a general deletion transformation, one with a wide range of conditions, applicable to many structures. For now, we can say that *being* can be deleted from 2c; then, shifting what is left of the adverbial to the front of the sentence gives us

> 2d   Terrified, Queeg turns the ship south, so that it no longer heads into the wind.

> WILLIAM H. WHYTE, JR.

Most of the deletion transformations mentioned so far have taken advantage of redundancies of one sort or another; if some piece of grammatical or lexical information appears twice, a deletion transformation often works to reduce the redundancy by removing one of the sources of the information. In a sentence like

> 3a   Because she was careful, Caroline checked her results again.

there are two indicators of the causal relation between the embedded sentence and the outer sentence: the embedder *because* explicitly notes the connection, and the position of the embedded sentence, preceding the rest of the structure, also implies that Caroline's carefulness is the cause of her extra check. Since both the embedder and the ''post hoc'' assumption carry the same information, either could be dispensed with. ADV-CAUSE DELETION, as we have seen, removes the embedder and substitutes ING-& for the tense, producing

> 3b   Being careful, Caroline checked her results again.

(Of course, EQUIVALENT NOUN PHRASE DELETION has also occurred here.) In the same way, two other transformations remove embedders; one of them removes redundancy in much the same manner as ADV-CAUSE DELETION. The first of these is ADV—TIME PERFECT DELETION. To understand what is involved, first consider sentence 4a:

> 4a   Ibsen wrote *Brand* after he settled in Italy.

The adverbial shows a certain time relationship—event B, Ibsen's writing the play, followed event A, his settling in Italy. Suppose, though, that the sentence within the time adverbial had undergone the PERFECT transformation (Section 19); we would then have

> 4b   Ibsen wrote *Brand* after he had settled in Italy.

4b is now redundant, if only slightly. Remember what the perfect aspect shows in the sentence: one action is completed at a time prior to another action. But this is the same relationship between events that the embedder *after* signals. The two indicators of the time sequence, *after* and the perfect aspect, are not both needed. Hence, ADV—TIME PERFECT DELETION operates to remove the embedder and replace the tense of the embedded sentence by ING-&. Before the various elements were joined, 4b had been

Ibsen PAST-& write *Brand* [after Ibsen PAST-& have EN-& settle in Italy].

ADV—TIME PERFECT DELETION changes this to

Ibsen PAST-& write *Brand* [Ibsen ING-& have EN-& settle in Italy].

Joining the elements, after EQUIVALENT NOUN PHRASE DELETION, now produces

4c   Ibsen wrote *Brand*, having settled in Italy.

Note that a comma again marks the place of the deleted embedder. Like any other adverbial, reduced or not, the adverbial here can be shifted to other positions—for example, between the subject noun phrase and the verb phrase of the outer sentence:

4d   Ibsen, having settled in Italy, wrote *Brand*.

Often a time adverbial contains a sentence describing an event that occurs at the same time as the event described in the outer sentence:

5a   Birds . . . converge upon some small island as the entire breeding population arrives within the space of a few days.

We have no redundancy here similar to that in example 4b: in that sentence, both the embedder and the perfect aspect of the embedded sentence indicate that one event followed the other. Here, only the embedded *as* (or *while*) tells us that the event of the outer sentence happens at the same time as that of the embedded sentence. This second transformation, ADV—TIME PROGRESSIVE DELETION, provides us with a stylistic variant rather than the elimination of a redundancy. If we delete the embedder and replace the tense of the embedded sentence with the present participle element, ING-&, that element itself will imply the simultaneity of the events of the outer and the embedded sentences. From 5a, ADV—TIME PROGRESSIVE DELETION yields

5b   Birds whose winter feeding territory may have encom-
     passed the whole Atlantic or the whole Pacific con-

verge upon some small island, the entire breeding
population arriving within the space of a few days.

RACHEL CARSON

In the changes we have seen so far, some feature of the language
takes over the job of expressing the relationship between the outer
and the embedded sentences formerly shown by the deleted embedder: in ADV-CAUSE DELETION, the ''post hoc'' effect more or less
expresses what *because* did; in the ADV–TIME DELETIONS, we have
pressed the progressive and perfect aspects into service. It seems
that one more of these deletions is possible, but in this case a
rearrangement in word order replaces the deleted embedder.

This deletion is possible only with those adverbials of condition
where the embedded sentence is preceded by *if*. The transformation
is even further restricted: it operates only on an embedded sentence
where the tense is PAST-&, and is most usually found with embedded
sentences in the perfect aspect. The PERFECT transformation would
change the embedded sentence of 6a to 6b:

6a Sennett would be remembered . . . [if he PAST-& PER-
FECT do nothing else].
6b Sennett would be remembered . . . [if he PAST-& have
EN-& do nothing else].

The embedded sentence here meets all the conditions: the embedder
is *if;* the tense is PAST-&; the PERFECT transformation has occurred.
In ADV-CONDITION DELETION, the embedder *if* is removed, and in the
embedded sentence the positions of the subject noun phrase and
PAST-& *have* are switched; thus, from 6b we get 6c:

6c Sennett would be remembered . . . [had he done nothing else].

Often, as in the actual sentence used here as a model, the embedded adverbial is shifted to the left of the outer sentence:

6d Had he done nothing else, Sennett would be remembered for giving a start to three of the four comedians
who now began to apply their sharp individual talents
to this newborn language.

JAMES AGEE

53a   **Application**

DANGLING PARTICIPLES

One of the deadliest mistakes a writer can make is to be unintention-ally funny, and a dangling participle is the royal road to inadvertent humor. In our terminology, a "dangling participle" is either a re-duced adverbial that has been shifted to the front of the outer sen-tence

> 1a   Having no radiator at all, I find the cheapest car to maintain is the Volkswagen.

or the remnants of an appositive embedded sentence

> 2a   In Robinson's poem, the vines have meaning for Luke Havergal, hanging "crimson on the wall."

The emphasized structures in both 1a and 2a are embedded sen-tences from which an equivalent noun phrase has been removed. Remember that the reader has to recover the deleted noun phrase: his assumption will be (other things being equal) that the deleted noun phrase was equivalent to the *nearest* noun phrase of the outer sentence. If this had been the case, our two examples would have had, as deeper structures

> 1b   Because I have no radiator at all, I find the cheapest car to maintain is the Volkswagen.
>
> 2b   In Robinson's poem, the vines have meaning for Luke Havergal, Luke Havergal hanging "crimson on the wall."

Of course, our assumed equivalent noun phrases, emphasized in 1b and 2b, are not at all what the writer meant.

    Example 2a has become as bad as it is because the appositive embedded sentence was extraposed across another noun phrase (see Section 44c), but it is relatively simple to correct: whether the appositive is in the full form (*which are hanging "crimson on the wall"*) or reduced by WH-BE DELETION (as in the example), it should be placed immediately following the equivalent noun phrase of the outer sentence, as in 2c:

> 2c In Robinson's poem, the vines, hanging "crimson on the wall," have meaning for Luke Havergal.

In example 1a, part of the mistake was shifting the adverbial to the front of the sentence. Sentence 1a begins in a form like this:

> 1c I find the cheapest car to maintain is the Volkswagen, because the Volkswagen has no radiator at all.

From 1c, ADV-CAUSE DELETION gives

> 1d I find the cheapest car to maintain is the Volkswagen, the Volkswagen having no radiator at all.

EQUIVALENT NOUN PHRASE DELETION removes the subject noun phrase of the adverbial embedded sentence:

> 1e I find the cheapest car to maintain is the Volkswagen, having no radiator at all.

What is left of the adverbial in 1e is still closer to the equivalent noun phrase *the Volkswagen* than to any other noun phrase. It is the shift of the adverbial to the front of the sentence that moves the adverbial away from the equivalent noun phrase. Remember the assumption of the reader: he will think that the closest noun phrase of the outer sentence is equivalent to the noun phrase deleted from the embedded sentence. Of several methods of correction, the easiest may be to rearrange the outer sentence, moving the equivalent noun phrase next to the reduced adverbial; thus, one way of repairing 1a would be

> 1f Having no radiator at all, the Volkswagen is, I find, the cheapest car to maintain.

Exercise

This exercise has three steps. First, compose three sentences, each having the same outer sentence but different adverbial embedded sentences beginning with *because, after,* and *while*. For example:

1a John descended the staircase because the doorbell was ringing.
2a John descended the staircase after he read the children a story.
3a John descended the staircase while he thought about frisbees.

In the second step, transform the three sentences, using ADV-CAUSE, ADV–TIME PERFECT, and ADV–TIME PROGRESSIVE deletions on them:

1b The doorbell ringing, John descended the staircase.
2b Having read the children a story, John descended the staircase.
3b Thinking about frisbees, John descended the staircase.

In the third step, compose a supersentence, attaching the remnants of all three adverbials to a single outer sentence, thus:

4 The doorbell ringing, John, having read the children a story, descended the staircase thinking about frisbees.

Compare your final effort with those of other members of the class.

Conjunctions and Compounds

54 THE CONJUNCTION REDUCTION TRANSFORMATION

Let us suppose that the phrase structure rules allow us to generate what are called compound sentences by creating structures that consist of an indefinitely large, but finite, number of sentences connected by one of a small group of words called coordinating conjunctions. This rule, occurring before the one that writes S as NP + VP, would look like this:

$$S \rightarrow S + (C + S)^r$$

The raised *r* means that the segment inside the parentheses may be optionally repeated; C stands for *and, or, but, for, nor, so,* or *yet. And* and *or* may connect any number of sentences; the rest of the items join only two sentences.

By this rule, we would produce something like this:

1a His fellow-painters made no secret of their contempt for his work   C   he earned a fair amount of money C   they did not hesitate to make free use of his purse.

With appropriate punctuation and the insertion of a conjunction for C, we get

1b His fellow-painters made no secret of their contempt for his work, but he earned a fair amount of money, and they did not hesitate to make free use of his purse.

W. SOMERSET MAUGHAM

Here, of course, we have simply a compound sentence—three complete sentences joined by two conjunctions. But there are many other syntactic units joined by conjunctions. We can derive these from sentence conjunction beginning like this:

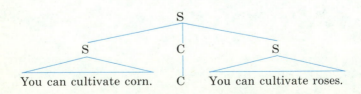

The two sentences above have identical structures because the same development of the phrase structure rules was chosen for both. They differ only in the lexical selection in the object noun phrases, *corn* and *roses*. If no further changes were made, we would end up with "You can cultivate corn *and* (*or*) you can cultivate roses." An optional transformation allows us to delete the repeated material, permitting only the dissimilar parts of the structure to remain.

This transformation is called CONJUNCTION REDUCTION. It takes compound sentences with partially similar development and deletes all the words (except the conjunction) between the elements to be joined. Examples 2 and 3 show the operation of CONJUNCTION REDUCTION:

2a You can cultivate corn C you can cultivate roses
    C you can cultivate orchards

3a who shall cultivate the mountain peaks C who shall
    cultivate the ocean C who shall cultivate the tumbling gorgeousness of the clouds.

CONJUNCTION REDUCTION now deletes all the words between the parts to be connected (emphasized in the examples above). This means that, in 2a, we delete *you can cultivate* between *corn* (the object noun phrase of the first sentence) and *roses* (the object noun phrase of the second sentence). Similarly, we can at the same time delete *you can cultivate* between *roses* and *orchards* (the object noun phrase of the third sentence). We would then have

2b You can cultivate corn C roses C orchards

Deleting the words between the emphasized noun phrases in 3a gives us

3b who shall cultivate the mountain peaks C the
    ocean C the tumbling gorgeousness of the clouds.

Rewriting C by the lexical rule as *and* gives us

2c You can cultivate corn and roses and orchards
3c who shall cultivate the mountain peaks and the ocean
    and the tumbling gorgeousness of the clouds.

If we had joined groups 2 and 3 at the beginning, and now rewrote that C as *but,* we would have

4   You can cultivate corn and roses and orchards—but who shall cultivate the mountain peaks, the ocean, and the tumbling gorgeousness of the clouds.

WALT WHITMAN

As Whitman's sentence illustrates, an *and* or an *or* introduced by the lexical rule is sometimes deleted. We will say more about this later, when we speak of the punctuation needed for conjunction.

There are some restrictions on the use of CONJUNCTION REDUCTION—for example, articles cannot be joined. We cannot put together *a dog is friendly* and *the dog is friendly* and get *A and the dog is friendly.* To handle what turn out to be complex restrictions, in Section 55 we will approach the problem from the other direction, and show some constructions where the transformation can be applied.

54a   Application

PARALLELISM

1   I am ready, and more than ready, to agree that it is for the meanings of life that one reads (and teaches) poetry.

ARCHIBALD MACLEISH

The intricate joinings of a sentence like 1 illustrate one of the most highly valued stylistic devices, ''parallelism.'' Usually defined as the conjunction of similar grammatical elements (for example, adjective *and* adjective, or noun *and* noun), parallelism is so highly admired that no commentary on style fails to illustrate the device and to correct faulty instances of it.

First, let us try to discover why parallelism is admired and how it works. Samuel Johnson compared John Dryden's knowledge with Alexander Pope's knowledge in these words:

2a   Dryden knew more of man in his general nature and Pope in his local manners. The notions of Dryden were

> formed by comprehensive speculation, and those of
> Pope by minute attention. There is more dignity in
> the knowledge of Dryden and more certainty in that
> of Pope.

In the words of critics of style, we might describe a passage like 2a in terms of its "balance," "form," "symmetry," or "proportion." If this description is correct, parallel constructions have something of the balance scale about them; one thing is matched against another. In the passage above, of course, the contrast is between Dryden's thought and Pope's. The ideas of the poets are differentiated three times. The first component of parallelism, then, is the contrasting of differences, or the comparing of similarities.

But contrast or comparison is only part of the device of parallelism. If we revise the passage, retaining Johnson's pointing out of differences but avoiding the use of similar grammatical constructions, we destroy its effect:

> 2b   Dryden knew more of man in his general nature, but
> the local manners of man were better known by Pope.
> The notions of Dryden were formed by comprehensive
> speculation, but Pope derived his ideas from attending
> to the minutest details. There is more dignity in the
> knowledge of Dryden, but Pope's knowledge has more
> certainty.

Thus, to have parallelism, we need a second element: the repetition of the same grammatical constructions.

Contrast and repetition are two of the elements of parallelism. But what is prized in effective parallel writing is *partial* repetition of grammatical constructions, not full repetition. If we place the words about Pope in constructions identical to those about Dryden, the value of the passage's style diminishes strikingly:

> 2c   Dryden knew more of man in his general nature and
> Pope knew more of man in his local manners. The
> notions of Dryden were formed by comprehensive
> speculation, and the notions of Pope were formed by
> minute attention. There is more dignity in the knowl-
> edge of Dryden than there is in the knowledge of Pope
> and there is more certainty in the knowledge of Pope
> than there is in the knowledge of Dryden.

Comparing 2a and 2c, we can observe that parallelism operates to achieve the familiar principle of economy by avoiding a vast amount of exact repetition.

It seems then that there are three requisites for effective parallelism. First, we must have contrast or comparison. Second, the contrast or comparison must be phrased in similar grammatical constructions. When we add the third element, the deletion of unnecessary repetition, we end with a well-made parallel construction.

One of the most satisfying insights into composition achieved by the transformational approach to grammar is its formalization of the tie between the simple conjunction of sentences and the stylistic device of parallelism. In Section 55, we will see how one transformation, CONJUNCTION REDUCTION, will suffice to guide us through most compounds within a sentence.

55 PARALLELISM FROM SENTENCE CONJUNCTION

Whole noun phrases in otherwise identical sentences may be joined, so long as they are in the same position—as subject, as object, or following a preposition. In the subject position, we would have an operation like this (the elements to be joined are emphasized):

1a Captain Furneaux was conducted to the chief's house
   C I was conducted to the chief's house.

1b Captain Furneaux ~~was conducted to the chief's house~~
   C I was conducted to the chief's house. (CONJUNCTION REDUCTION)

1c Captain Furneaux and I were conducted to the chief's house.

CAPTAIN JAMES COOK

Joining subject noun phrases, as in 1c, gives us what is traditionally called a "compound subject." (The details of verb agreement with a compound subject are covered in Section 35.)

If the noun phrase occurs in the object position, the procedure is exactly the same, producing a "compound object":

2a And now, concentric circles seized the lone boat itself
   C ~~concentric circles seized~~ all its crew C ~~concentric~~

circles seized each floating oar C concentric circles seized every lance pole.

2b And now, concentric circles seized the lone boat itself, and all its crew, and each floating oar, and every lance pole.

HERMAN MELVILLE

Whole prepositional phrases, or just the noun phrases within them, may be combined in this way. First, the whole prepositional phrase:

3a That government of the people shall not perish from the earth C that government by the people shall not perish from the earth C that government for the people shall not perish from the earth.

3b That government of the people, by the people, for the people, shall not perish from the earth.

ABRAHAM LINCOLN

If the prepositions introducing the prepositional phrases are the same (rather than different, as in 3a and 3b), but the noun phrases differ, the noun phrases alone may be joined:

4a Underlying college revolts of this time was a discontent with the patriarchal powers of the president C underlying college revolts of this time was a discontent with the evangelical character of the curriculum and college rules.

Here the noun phrases being joined are both preceded by *with*, so CONJUNCTION REDUCTION can remove the repeated preposition, making the noun phrases parallel:

4b Underlying college revolts of this time was a discontent with the patriarchal powers of the president C underlying college revolts of this time was a discontent with the evangelical character of the curriculum and college rules.

4c Underlying college revolts of this time was a discontent with the patriarchal powers of the president and the evangelical character of the curriculum and college rules.

LEWIS S. FEUER

The section on embedded sentences shows that sentences (or what is left of them after deletions) may occur in positions where a noun phrase occurs. We would expect then that we should be able to make embedded sentences parallel just as we can noun phrases. Example 5b shows an outer sentence with an embedded sentence in each half (at this point in the derivation, each embedded sentence has undergone the FOR . . . TO transformation and EQUIVA-LENT NOUN PHRASE DELETION. See Sections 36 and 39 for information on these two transformations if needed.):

5a One of their primary functions is [to inform the coun-try . . .] C ~~one of their primary functions is~~ [to describe important issues . . .].

5b One of their primary functions is to inform the coun-try about the conditions and problems of the nation; and to describe important issues so that we can un-derstand them.

WILLIAM J. LEDERER

In most cases, whole verb phrases in otherwise identical sentences may be joined, even if the verb phrases have been developed in different ways. In the example below, for instance, a verb phrase rewritten as a verb and a following noun phrase is joined to one developed as an intransitive verb:

6a John waved his hand C ~~John~~ disappeared.
6b John waved his hand and disappeared.

Although 6b is grammatical, and certainly a useful construction, it does not seem to be an instance of parallelism. For that, we need similarly developed verb phrases, as in the next example, where both verb phrases are developed with an object noun phrase:

7a The question whether a given opinion is a danger to society is a question of the times C ~~the question whether a given opinion is a danger to society~~ is a question of fact.

7b The question whether a given opinion is a danger to society is a question of the times and is a question of fact.

JOHN ANDREW HAMILTON

Main verbs may be formed into parallel constructions with great freedom. It makes no difference, for example, whether the auxiliary transformations have been used. In 8a and 8b, each of the sentences has undergone the PROGRESSIVE transformation:

8a the children . . . were crawling through red and yellow cylinders C the children were swinging on swings C the children were doing group calisthenics.

8b Most of the children, bare, tan, and black-haired, were crawling through red and yellow cylinders, swinging on swings, or doing group calisthenics.

IRA LEVIN

Main verbs may be joined whether or not the PASSIVE transformation has taken place:

9a Betty was born in Philadelphia C Betty was educated in Quincy C Betty was employed in Rochester.

9b Betty was born in Philadelphia, educated in Quincy, and employed in Rochester.

Verbs within the main verb may be joined with a freedom as great as that with which the whole constructions are joined. To be more precise: the verb alone is not joined to another verb, but the verb together with the tense, if any; to make this clear, the tense is marked in the next example:

10a Sandra PAST-& read Petrarch's poetry C Sandra PAST-& enjoy Petrarch's poetry.

10b Sandra read and enjoyed Petrarch's poetry.

Note that the joined verbs in the next example are in sentences that have been put into the passive voice:

11a The prerogatives of the King of Heaven were settled in the cabinet of an earthly monarch C the prerogatives of the King of Heaven were changed in the cabinet of an earthly monarch C the prerogatives of the King of Heaven were modified in the cabinet of an earthly monarch.

11b   The prerogatives of the King of Heaven were settled, or changed, or modified, in the cabinet of an earthly monarch.

EDWARD GIBBON

The next example shows the joining of adjectives:

12a   the children were bare   C   ~~the children were~~ tan   C ~~the children were~~ black-haired
12b   the children were bare, tan, and black-haired

As the sections on adverbials stress, there are many different kinds of adverbials. Whatever they may be, if the individual sentences of the compound are grammatical, the adverbials by which they differ may be joined and made parallel:

13a   something . . . makes us cling to it contentedly   C ~~something . . . makes us cling to it~~ lovingly   C ~~something . . . makes us cling to it~~ in desperation.
13b   And something about Cross Creek suits us—or something about us makes us cling to it contentedly, lovingly, and often in desperation.

MARJORIE KINNAN RAWLINGS

Of course, no one suggests that a writer goes through anything like the CONJUNCTION REDUCTION transformation when he produces a parallel structure; the only value of pulling apart joined elements and treating them as if they occurred by themselves in the sentences of the derivations is the understanding of parallel constructions the procedure gives us. If someone objects to faulty parallelism, we must know what is being objected to. If we have some means to analyze what we have written, we can resolve some very real problems that parallel constructions present.

55a   Application

FAULTY PARALLELISM

In each case of CONJUNCTION REDUCTION, the sentences were required to be identical, differing only in the wording of one particular part.

In examples 1a, 1b, and 1c, where object noun phrases are being joined, the sentences have exactly the same derivation—the only difference being that the first conjunct has *Latin* where the second conjunct has *Greek:*

> 1a   John reads Latin   C   John reads Greek.

CONJUNCTION REDUCTION deletes everything between the elements to be joined except the conjunction:

> 1b   John reads Latin   C   ~~John reads~~ Greek.
> 1c   John reads Latin and Greek.

Faulty parallelism is the name given to the problem that occurs when grammatical structures that are not identical are joined. Suppose, in examples 1a, 1b, and 1c, we had a sentence embedded in the object position of one of the conjuncts:

> 2a   John knows Latin   C   John knows [that the early bird gets the worm].

After CONJUNCTION REDUCTION, we would have faulty parallelism:

> 2b   * John knows Latin and that the early bird gets the worm.

Similarly, if embedded sentences in any position are being joined, they should undergo the same embedding transformations to produce parallelism. Compare Lederer's sentence (example 5b in Section 55) with 3 below; in the latter, one of the embedded sentences has undergone the FOR . . . TO transformation, and the other the NOMINAL transformation:

> 3 * One of their primary functions is to inform the country about the conditions and problems of the nation; and describing important issues so that we can understand them.

To correct faulty parallelism, make sure that the units joined are grammatically identical.

55b   Application

CONJUNCTION AND AMBIGUITY (1)

In some circumstances, a writer faces an extremely difficult, if not impossible, task in trying to maintain both economy and clarity in his writing. The purpose of the CONJUNCTION REDUCTION transformation is to reduce repetition, but it is possible to delete so much material that some information is lost in the process. The loss can occur in a number of ways, the most common of which are presented here.[1]

When several noun phrases have been joined, and the first of them contains an adjective, we are presented with an ambiguity:

1a   Bulletin No. 7 contains only a few items on French literature, theology, and philosophy.

Does 1a have an underlying structure like 1b or 1c?

1b   a few items on French literature C
      a few items on theology C
      a few items on philosophy

1c   a few items on French literature C
      a few items on French theology C
      a few items on French philosophy

If 1c was the meaning intended, clarity would have been better served by less deletion, despite the repetition of the word *French*. If 1b was intended, the ambiguity could have been avoided if the order of the items was changed, giving us

1d   Bulletin No. 7 contains only a few items on theology, philosophy, and French literature.

A similar problem, again having to do with what a modifier is modifying, occurs when CONJUNCTION REDUCTION is applied to pro-

[1] The examples in this section are from Norman C. Stageberg, "Some Structural Ambiguities," *A Linguistics Reader*, ed. Graham Wilson. New York: Harper & Row, 1967. Pp. 76–84.

duce a compound adverbial. 2a might be analyzed as the result of reducing either 2b or 2c:

> 2a At the dress rehearsal, she sang, danced, and tumbled very expertly.
>
> 2b she sang very expertly C
> she danced very expertly C
> she tumbled very expertly
>
> 2c she sang C
> she danced C
> she tumbled very expertly

A paraphrase like *At the dress rehearsal, she sang, danced, and tumbled, doing all of them very expertly* might serve if the meaning of 2b is intended. On the other hand, if 2c is intended, then a contrast in the sentences is not being taken advantage of—the contrast between the expert tumbling and the (presumably) less than expert singing and dancing. Here the second contrast might be expressed by joining the first two sentences by CONJUNCTION REDUCTION to give

> 2d she sang and danced C
> she tumbled very expertly

Then we further improve the parallelism, making the two structures more alike by adding an adverbial at the end of the first—for example:

> 2e she sang and danced moderately well C
> she tumbled very expertly

Now we can mark the contrast between these two groups with the conjunction *but:*

> 2f At the dress rehearsal, she sang and danced moderately well, but she tumbled very expertly.

Finally, the option that allows reduction of a repeated preposition can lead to ambiguity. We cannot tell if 3a should be analyzed as related to 3b or 3c—that is, we do not know if prepositional phrases or object noun phrases have been joined:

3a   His job is to post changes in address, telephone numbers, and performance ratings.

3b   his job is to post changes in address   C
     his job is to post changes in telephone numbers   C
     his job is to post changes in performance ratings

3c   his job is to post changes in address   C
     his job is to post telephone numbers   C
     his job is to post performance ratings

If the 3b meaning is desired, all that is necessary is to repeat the preposition, at a very slight sacrifice in economy:

3d   His job is to post changes in address, in telephone numbers, and in performance ratings.

If the 3c meaning is desired, reversing the order of the compound terms will again solve the problem:

3e   His job is to post telephone numbers, performance ratings, and changes in address.

If your paper should contain an ambiguous compound, try one of the methods used here to resolve the ambiguity. Putting the joined elements in their full form will certainly untangle the meaning, and it may then be possible to delete some repeated material if the order of the joined elements is rearranged to avoid ambiguity.

Exercises

1. Find five sentences with compound elements. Analyze them by showing how the sentences would appear if the elements were written in full as separate sentences. Remember to note the source of each example sentence.

2. Examine a first-grade reader. Do you find much compounding in it? If your answer is yes, can you discern a pattern in the kinds of compounds that are used? Contrast this with the compounding found in a passage of similar length from a reader used in the third or fourth grade.

3. Something is wrong with the parallelism in each of the following sentences. Identify the problems in the examples and revise the sentences to correct the difficulties:

1 White Americans know their ancestors' faults, and that whites cannot separate these past shortcomings from the present.

2 When the convention began, a floor fight over the seating of the California delegates and the minority platform was expected.

3 Monks were supposed to be set apart from society and very contemplative people.

4 Too many of the miners anticipated finding rich veins of gold quickly and to make large fortunes easily.

56 PHRASAL CONJUNCTION

Not all compounds come from whole sentences as conjuncts followed by CONJUNCTION REDUCTION. Consider

1a The most innocent looking Rook and Pawn endings will sometimes give rise to astounding combinations.

EDWARD LASKER

The phrase *Rook and Pawn endings* cannot possibly come from something like 1b:

1b the most innocent looking Rook endings   C
the most innocent looking Pawn endings

As chess players know, a "Rook and Pawn ending" describes a game where one player has *both* a rook and a pawn left. There must be some way, therefore, of introducing compounds into deep structure. The arguments in favor of this approach were developed by George Lakoff and Stanley Peters.[1] They note that a sentence like *Jack and Jill are alike* obviously is not derived from

2 Jack is alike   C   Jill is alike.

[1] "Phrasal Conjunction and Symmetric Predicates," *Modern Studies in English*, ed. David A. Reibel and Sanford A. Schane. Englewood Cliffs, N.J.: Prentice-Hall, 1969. Pp. 113–42.

Note that we make a comment about the subject of sentence 1a, and that comment applies to the compound subject as a unit, not to each member of the compound individually. Just as we revised the phrase structure rule (Section 54) for sentences to S → S + (C + S)^r to allow sentences to appear as deep structure conjuncts, so too we can add a rule rewriting NP as NP + (C + NP)^r. This rule will allow noun phrases to appear as deep structure conjuncts. Use of the first rule will produce a sentence conjunction. Use of our new rule will produce a phrasal conjunction, as in the next example:

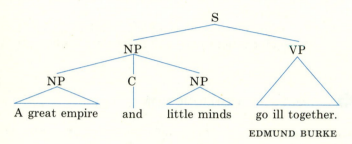

EDMUND BURKE

We need this alternative not just to produce sentences like 1, 2, and 3, but also to explain certain ambiguities that occur. When a subject noun phrase is compound, we sometimes face uncertainty. For example, if we have

4a   Lucy and Laura own horses.

should this sentence be analyzed as the result of sentence conjunction followed by CONJUNCTION REDUCTION, thus having as its source 4b?

4b   Lucy owns horses   C   Laura owns horses.

Or is 4a an example of phrasal conjunction, intended to mean that Lucy and Laura own horses as a partnership? Lakoff and Peters noticed that certain verbs and adjectives require a phrasal conjunction as their subjects: verbs such as *agree, meet,* and *differ;* and adjectives such as *alike, similar, identical, distinct,* and *equal.* Note how sentences that have these words seem incomplete with a subject that is not a phrasal conjunction:

5   * Sid differs.
6   * Maggie is identical.

On the other hand, verbs like *own* may have either sentence conjunctions or phrasal conjunctions as their subjects, giving rise to the ambiguities that occur in sentences like 4a.

56a   **Application**

INCOMPLETE COMPARISON

Some instances of what handbooks call "incomplete comparison" involve a verb or adjective requiring a phrasal conjunction as its subject. To explain what is involved here, we begin with a sentence containing such a word:

1a   *The Faerie Queene* and *The Lord of the Rings* are similar.

(In 1a, of course, we are speaking of the word *similar* as the one that requires a phrasal conjunction as the subject of the sentence.) Example 1a has a phrasal conjunction as its subject. From sentences like 1a, Lakoff and Peters derive certain other sentences by means of two transformations. The first they call PREPOSITION ADJUNCTION: it substitutes *with, to,* or *from* for the *and* in the phrasal conjunction. The choice of preposition depends on the verb or adjective in the sentence. Thus, from 1a we can derive

1b   * *The Faerie Queene* to *The Lord of the Rings* is similar.

Note that 1b is ungrammatical as it stands. The second transformation, CONJUNCT MOVEMENT, is obligatory if PREPOSITION ADJUNCTION has occurred: CONJUNCT MOVEMENT shifts the second half of the phrasal conjunction (now preceded by a preposition) to the end of the sentence:

1c   *The Faerie Queene* is similar to *The Lord of the Rings.*

As an example with a verb, we have

> 2a The president and the cabinet conferred.
> 2b * The president with the cabinet conferred. (PREPOSITION ADJUNCTION)
> 2c The president conferred with the cabinet. (CONJUNCT MOVEMENT)

If we artificially restrict our grammar to the consideration of single sentences, we would have to say that 3a is ungrammatical

> 3a * *The Faerie Queene* is similar.

or at least unacceptably incomplete, since we have no notion of what the work is similar to. But 3a could occur perfectly well in a sequence of sentences:

> 3b *The Lord of the Rings* is set in a world created solely by the imagination of the author. *The Faerie Queene* is similar.

We could say that the second sentence of 3b results from the deletion of a noun phrase from a structure like *"The Faerie Queene is similar to The Lord of the Rings,"* under conditions that reach across sentence boundaries; or that it results from drawing from the context our knowledge of what *The Faerie Queene* is similar to. The explanation does not matter as much as understanding the problem. Sentences like 3a do occur in contexts where it is *not* clear what the subject is being compared with, nor in what respect the subject is being compared. To correct this kind of incomplete comparison, decide whether PREPOSITION ADJUNCTION and CONJUNCT MOVEMENT can help to explain what is wrong. What two things are being compared? Exactly how is it that they are alike or different? The sentence can then be recast in this way: take the verb or adjective (for example, *agree, meet, differ, alike, similar, identical*) as the center of the new sentence:

> 3c . . . similar . . .

Next, place the phrasal conjunction as the subject of the sentence, adding the appropriate form of *be:*

> 3d *The Faerie Queene* and *The Lord of the Rings* are similar . . .

Finally, add some explanation of why they are similar:

3e *The Faerie Queene* and *The Lord of the Rings* are similar in that they are both set in worlds created solely by the imaginations of their authors.

56b   Application

CONJUNCTION AND AMBIGUITY (2)

In a sentence like *Lucy and Laura own horses,* we have an example of a verb, *own,* that can have either a sentence conjunction or a phrasal conjunction as its subject. Such sentences can be ambiguous. To be more precise, we should say that such sentences are always potentially ambiguous, but the intended meaning is often clear from the whole context in which the sentence appears. In example 1, there is little danger of anyone's taking *Chaucer and Shakespeare* to be a phrasal conjunction (that is, meaning that Chaucer and Shakespeare were collaborators):

1 Chaucer and Shakespeare wrote verse in iambic pentameter.

But this knowledge comes from what we know of history, not of grammar. When the knowledge we have of the compound subject is little or none, ambiguity can result. As a reader of this book, you know by now that George Lakoff and Stanley Peters worked together on an article about conjunction, but suppose I wrote:

2a Carlota Smith and Lila Gleitman wrote about conjunctions.

Is the subject a phrasal conjunction or a sentence conjunction? You cannot tell from sentence 2a alone. Each woman may have written an article on the subject, or they may have worked together to produce just one article. When an ambiguous compound like this occurs, we can resolve the difficulty by adding a few words that clarify the intended meaning; if the individuals in the compound subject have each written separate works, we could specify this by writing either 2b or 2c:

> 2b Carlota Smith and Lila Gleitman each wrote about conjunctions.
>
> 2c Both Carlota Smith and Lila Gleitman wrote about conjunctions.

On the other hand, if we are talking about the compound as a unit—if the members worked as a team—we could say

> 3 George Lakoff and Stanley Peters wrote about conjunctions together.

Words like *both* and *each* establish that a compound is the result of CONJUNCTION REDUCTION from separate sentences; words like *together* show that the compound started out as a phrasal conjunction. Add one of these words to your sentence, depending on which meaning you intend.

56c Application

PUNCTUATING COMPOUND ELEMENTS

The system given below is not the only correct way to punctuate a compound construction. In your reading you will certainly come across sentences punctuated differently, yet still punctuated correctly. Remember that advice about punctuation is more often a guide than a rule: once you know your way around, you can dispense with the guide.

One fairly firm convention is this: elements in a series are separated by commas, whether conjunctions are present or not. The important word in the convention is ''series'': it means three or more elements—three or more joined sentences, three or more joined noun phrases, three or more joined adjectives, and so on. Let's look at some sentences from Sections 54 and 55 again, this time concentrating on the punctuation:

> 1 His fellow-painters made no secret of their contempt for his work, but he earned a fair amount of money, and they did not hesitate to make free use of his purse.

The series here is

Sentence, but sentence, and sentence.

When the elements are many, the use of the conjunction together with the comma can help to reinforce the parallelism of the construction. In example 2a, the repetition of the conjunctions reminds us that each noun phrase preceded by *and* is an object of the verb *seized:*

2a   And now, concentric circles seized the lone boat itself, and all its crew, and each floating oar, and every lance pole.

2b   And now, concentric circles seized NP, and NP, and NP, and NP.

More often, a conjunction is used only before the last element in the series, but commas still separate each member:

3a   who shall cultivate the mountain peaks, the ocean, and the tumbling gorgeousness of the clouds.

3b   who shall cultivate NP, NP, and NP.

4a   The majority of men on the train worked in town all day, commuted home each evening, and seemed content with their lives.

4b   The majority of men on the train VP, VP, and VP.

5a   the children . . . were bare, tan, and black-haired

5b   the children . . . were ADJ, ADJ, and ADJ

6a   something . . . makes us cling to it contentedly, lovingly, and often in desperation.

6b   something . . . makes us cling to it ADV, ADV, and ADV.

When the elements joined in the compound construction themselves contain commas, we obviously cannot emphasize the parallelism of the structure by adding more commas. Consider a construction like this:

7a   The anarchy has sometimes been viewed merely as a reflection of Stephen's weakness of character   C sometimes as the inevitable outcome of the circumstances in which he took the throne, and of the disputed succession C sometimes as a natural reaction against the excessively autocratic rule of Henry I.

Example 7a illustrates a structure after CONJUNCTION REDUCTION (see Section 54). We could now separate the three elements by commas were it not for the fact that the second element already contains a comma. The writer does not wish to give the impression that the end of the second element, *and of the disputed succession,* is one of the parallel elements in the construction. He prevents this misreading by separating the elements by semicolons instead of commas:

7b   The anarchy has sometimes been viewed merely as a reflection of Stephen's weakness of character; sometimes as the inevitable outcome of the circumstances in which he took the throne, and of the disputed succession; sometimes as a natural reaction against the excessively autocratic rule of Henry I.

                                    CHRISTOPHER BROOKE

Our second convention is, therefore: if the elements in the series already contain commas, separate the elements by semicolons. Examples 8a and 8b show how the use of semicolons makes it clear that we are talking about three publishers, not five:

8a   She submitted the manuscript to Little, Brown C ~~she submitted the manuscript to~~ Dodd, Mead C ~~she submitted the manuscript to~~ Scribner's. (CONJUNCTION REDUCTION)

8b   She submitted the manuscript to Little, Brown; Dodd, Mead; and Scribner's.

56d   Application

COMMA SPLICES

When only two elements of less than sentence rank are joined, usually the conjunction alone is used, without any mark of punctuation:

1a   Captain Furneaux and I were conducted to the chief's house.

1b   NP and NP were conducted to the chief's house.
2a   It will be seen that the Countess Marie's resources
     were rich and abundant.

AMY KELLY

2b   the Countess Marie's resources were ADJ and ADJ.

When two sentences are joined, and neither of them is reduced, there are several possible ways to punctuate the compound. First, they may be separated by a comma and a conjunction (subject of course to the convention of Section 56c that neither of the elements has a comma within it already):

3a   I worked on that cabinet for a year, but I never got
     it right.

Second, two sentences are sometimes joined with just the conjunction:

3b   I worked on that cabinet for a year but I never got
     it right.

When omitting the comma use care that the result does not invite a false reading of the sentence:

4a   I worked on that cabinet for a year and three months
     of my time were spent fitting the doors.

In sentence 4a, a reader may be led to believe, for an instant, that the time spent on the cabinet was *a year and three months*. Note, though, that these words are parts of two grammatical units. This confusion could be eliminated by adding a comma:

4b   I worked on that cabinet for a year, and three months
     of my time were spent on the doors.

Finally, to emphasize a sharp contrast between the two sentences, join them with only a semicolon (see Section 75), omitting the conjunction:

4c   I worked on that cabinet for a year; three months of
     my time were spent on the doors.

When two sentences are joined only by a comma, as in 4d, the result is sometimes called a "comma splice":

4d I worked on that cabinet for a year, three months of my time were spent on the doors.

Many handbook writers and stylists object to the comma splice, probably because the construction frustrates our expectations. In Section 56c, we saw that a comma between joined elements usually signals a series of three or more:

5a Then, too, existence for you must be a scene of continual change and excitement, or else the world is a dungeon; you must be admired, you must be courted, you must be flattered.

CHARLOTTE BRONTË

5b the world is a dungeon; S, S, S.

The comma splice, then, leads us to expect a series but does not fulfill that expectation. To correct a comma splice, insert a conjunction before the second element, as in example 3a, or change the comma to a semicolon, as in example 5a. If there is no contrast between the two sentences, perhaps they should not be joined in the first place. A third method of correction, then, would be to punctuate the two elements as individual sentences.

Exercises

1. Find two sentences with compound elements resulting from phrasal conjunction rather than sentence conjunction. Justify your analysis of the elements as phrasal conjunctions. Remember to note the source of each example sentence.

2. Explain the ambiguity of the following sentences by listing the possible meanings they have:

    1 At the concert tonight, Renata Tormenti and Wolfgang Niednagel will sing.
    2 Nordoff and Hall wrote about the mutiny on the *Bounty*.
    3 Shakespeare and Dryden wrote about Antony and Cleopatra.

4 Shakespeare and Fletcher wrote about Palamon and Arcite.
5 The criminals of Victorian England feared Sherlock Holmes and Dr. Watson.
6 Their descendants feared Miss Marple and Father Brown.
7 Germanicus commanded the First and Twentieth Legions.
8 John Paul Jones commanded the *Ranger* and the *Alliance*.
9 Michael and Julia bought French dictionaries.

Sentence Variety

57 SENTENCE COMPLEXITY AND STYLE

Many, perhaps most, students at the college level have little trouble with the more superficial aspects of grammar: subject—verb agreement, pronoun reference, and so on. They are looking instead for ways to improve already correct writing. To put it bluntly, most of their writing is dull to read. But what makes a particular piece of writing seem dull? Probably there are many causes, but some terms appear again and again in books on writing, terms descriptive of the kind of prose the authors of those books want their students to avoid: ''flat,'' ''monotonous,'' ''thin,'' perhaps ''immature.'' One of the problems in doctoring style comes in analyzing what the claim ''immature'' implies, since if a writer knew what should be avoided, he might have a clearer idea of what to do.

Immature prose would seem to suggest first of all childish prose, meaning the kind of prose written by, or like that written by, children. Or, still more accurately, the kind of prose that in our culture is associated with children, what might be called ''primer style''—a dreary stringing together of sentence after sentence, all simple declaratives, all with little modification, all with a very restricted vocabulary. It might be something like the following:

1 Stephen walked on at his father's side.
2 Stephen was listening to stories.
3 He had heard the stories before.
4 Stephen heard again the names of the scattered and dead revellers.
5 The scattered and dead revellers had been the companions of his father's youth.

Quite different is the more complex structure that puts all these together:

6 Stephen walked on at his father's side, listening to stories he had heard before, hearing again the names of the scattered and dead revellers who had been the companions of his father's youth.

JAMES JOYCE

All that would be needed to produce a sentence like 6 would be a few simple instructions for combining sentences like 1 through

5. One way to introduce variety, then, involves the combining of simpler sentences.

A second way of introducing variety to sentence structures is to vary the normal position of elements within a sentence. The two sections that follow illustrate different methods of achieving each of these objectives.

58 COMBINING SENTENCES

In this section, we make some generalizations about the many transformations that combine sentences, together with references to the sections where those transformations are discussed in more detail.

We described earlier the three general processes that combine sentences: first, the simple joining of sentences as a result of conjunction by the phrase structure rules; second, the transformations that turn sentences into topics, allowing them to occupy noun phrase positions; and third, the transformations that turn sentences into comments, allowing them to modify noun phrases or verb phrases. Since the unrestricted combining of sentences can produce structures of (theoretically) infinite length, we find deletion transformations associated with each of these groups.

First, with sentence conjunction we have CONJUNCTION REDUCTION (see Section 54):

1a   Connie opened the door and Connie put out the cat.
1b   Connie opened the door and put out the cat.

Second, with embedding transformations, we have the following associated deletion transformations (see Sections 36, 37, 38b, and 39):

2a   I know [Ed PRESENT-& need a new car].
2b   I know that Ed needs a new car.   (THAT transformation)
2c   I know Ed needs a new car.   (THAT DELETION)

3a   No one expected [Frank PRESENT-& be on time].
3b * No one expected for Frank to be on time.   (FOR . . . TO transformation)
3c   No one expected Frank to be on time.   (FOR DELETION)

4a   Sarah resisted [Sarah PRESENT-& be transferred].

4b Sarah resisted [Sarah &-'s ING-& be transferred].
(NOMINAL transformation)

4c Sarah resisted being transferred. (EQUIVALENT NOUN
PHRASE DELETION)

Finally, with the embedding transformations that make modifiers out
of sentences, we have still other deletion transformations (see Sections 44, 44a, 45, and 45a):

5a The results [the experiment yielded the results] surprised us.

5b The results which the experiment yielded surprised
us. (RESTRICTIVE EMBEDDING)

5c The results the experiment yielded surprised us. (REL-
ATIVE PRONOUN DELETION)

6a The novel was a best-seller and the novel was praised
by critics.

6b The novel, which was praised by critics, was a best-
seller. (APPOSITIVE EMBEDDING)

6c The novel, praised by critics, was a best-seller. (WH-BE
DELETION)

Included in this last group are the many transformations that embed
sentences in adverbials, making them modifiers of verb phrases.
These will not be illustrated here, but are covered in detail in Sections
46 and 48.

One generalization to be noted about all these transformations is
this: they all preserve the original ordering of the elements of the
sentence. Although elements are removed, those that remain appear
in their original order. Now a speaker or writer may wish, often for
reasons that are easy to identify, to vary the positions of the elements. He may, for example, wish to bring a certain part of the
sentence to the beginning to give extra prominence or emphasis to
that part; he may wish to postpone a certain part to the end of the
sentence for the sake of climax or suspense. Here, too, the language
provides us with a variety of ways of rearranging the parts of a
sentence to achieve these purposes; these ways are discussed in
Section 59.

59 REARRANGING SENTENCES

This section explores what are sometimes called "stylistic transformations"—those transformations that provide us with alternate ways of saying essentially the same thing. For a variety of reasons, we may want to rearrange the parts of a sentence. We know, for instance, that we remember longest the first and last elements in a series, whether it be a series of numbers or of faces or of World Series games. The first and last positions are especially prominent, and we may wish to have a certain element in a sentence appear at the beginning or the end of that sentence to take advantage of this prominence. Some transformations will do this job for us. Some other transformations seem simply to provide us with variety—a different way of putting the sentence together.

Our first transformation, the THERE transformation, has already been mentioned in some detail on page 15. This transformation optionally changes sentences like 1a to 1b:

1a Six books are on the table.
1b There are six books on the table.

There has been inserted by the transformation, and the positions of the subject noun phrase and the verb *be* have been switched. For this transformation, the sentence also needs a word or phrase showing location, such as *on the table*. For some reason, the transformation seems to be obligatory when *be* has the meaning of "exist": 2a, for example, sounds very odd, but 2b seems acceptable:

2a Some strong points are in your argument.
2b There are some strong points in your argument.

It is this "existential" sense of *there is* which the writer uses in 3:

3 There is no country in the world where machinery is
   so lovely as in America.

                                        OSCAR WILDE

If the THERE transformation usually offers us mere variety, some other transformations make certain stylistic effects possible. Note how, in 3, Wilde holds back the name of the country until the very last word of the sentence. It would be useful to have some device to postpone a noun phrase, even if that noun phrase is the subject of the sentence, until suspense builds through the whole sentence.

The next two transformations shift a subject noun phrase to the right. The first of these we might call TOPIC POSTPONEMENT, since it frequently serves to introduce a new noun phrase into a discourse. This transformation operates on sentences having a verb showing location or movement, such as 4a:

> 4a   A tall dark stranger strode down the middle of the street.

TOPIC POSTPONEMENT shifts the adverbial of location or direction to the front of the sentence, and shifts the subject noun phrase to the end:

> 4b   Down the middle of the street strode a tall dark stranger.

Suppose we want to describe a surprising change of scene, then, and to build to a climax to postpone the description of that scene until the end of the sentence. Instead of saying

> 5a   An empty field of snow stretched before the observer, and in the twinkling of an eye the tents disappeared completely.

we can use TOPIC POSTPONEMENT to say

> 5b   In the twinkling of an eye the tents disappeared completely, and before the observer stretched an empty field of snow.
>
> **THOMAS R. HENRY**

We might formulate a rule of thumb, then: any element out of its usual position will call attention to itself.

We saw that TOPIC POSTPONEMENT, besides shifting the subject noun phrase to the end of the sentence, moves any adverbial of location or direction to the front. As the sections on adverbials showed, almost any adverbial can be shifted to the front of the sentence.

The first half of the conjunction in 5b has had a time adverbial, *in the twinkling of an eye,* shifted in this way. We can call the transformation that does this ADVERBIAL PREPOSING. All that ADVERBIAL PREPOSING will call attention to is the adverbial itself. If we use ADVERBIAL PREPOSING on 5a, we get

> 5c   In the twinkling of an eye the tents disappeared completely, and before the observer an empty field of snow stretched.

Note how much less emphasis the subject *an empty field of snow* receives in 5c than in the second half of 5b.

The second transformation to shift a subject noun phrase to the end of the sentence is EXTRAPOSITION, outlined in Section 38. In this case, though, the sentence must have an embedded sentence in the subject noun phrase position. By EXTRAPOSITION, then, we derive 6b from 6a:

> 6a   [That there are two types of flowers among the higher plants] is well known.
>
> 6b   It is well known that there are two types of flowers among the higher plants.
>
> KARL VON FRISCH

If TOPIC POSTPONEMENT and EXTRAPOSITION maintain suspense by shifting subject noun phrases to the end of the sentence, there may be times when we want to accomplish just the reverse: to get some other noun phrase right at the beginning of the sentence. The first element in a series is also prominent, and we may wish to establish our topic immediately. Again, at least two transformations serve this purpose.

The first of these two transformations is called TOUGH MOVEMENT, and both its formulation and even its existence have been questioned. But there are some strong arguments in its favor. To begin with, suppose we reflect on the benefits derived from embedded sentences in the first place; they provide us with a way of forming complicated topics, and indeed we often have to talk about complicated things. We may not always want to talk about *someone* or *a good man,* as in 7a:

> 7a   Someone finds a good man.

Rather than merely talking about this or that noun phrase, we may want to say something about the action, event, or state described by the whole sentence. If we have a sentence embedded in a noun phrase position, a position where topics occur, then we can make a comment about the whole sentence as topic:

> 7b [SOME ONE PRESENT-& find a good man] is hard.

With FOR . . . TO transformation, we get

> 7c [For SOME ONE to find a good man] is hard.

The words SOME and ONE in 7b and 7c stand for pro-forms and, as Section 46a explained, noun phrases made up entirely of pro-forms can be deleted. Thus we would have

> 7d [To find a good man] is hard. (PRO DELETION)

With EXTRAPOSITION, we can shift an embedded sentence in the subject position to the right of the sentence, leaving *it* in the original subject position:

> 7e It is hard to find a good man.

What started out as the verb phrase of the outer sentence, *is hard*, is now in the middle of what was an embedded sentence! But there is more to come. 7e is a member of a highly restricted class of sentences; these are sentences including, as 7e does, a predicate adjective describing capability, such as *tough, easy, difficult, hard, possible,* and so on. Some other examples include

> 8a It is easy for you to say that.
> 9a It is difficult for Susan to peel pomegranates.

This class also includes sentences with a noun phrase following *be* that describes a psychological state, such as *a delight, a treat, fun, a torment:*

> 10a It is a torment for me to study grammar.
> 11a It is a pleasure (for SOME ONE) to visit Philadelphia.

Sentences 7e and 8a through 11a have a number of things in

common: they all had a sentence embedded in the subject position; each of those sentences was embedded by the FOR . . . TO transformation; each embedded sentence was moved to the right by EXTRAPOSITION; finally, each embedded sentence had a transitive verb followed by an object noun phrase: *a good man, that, pomegranates, grammar,* and *Philadelphia.* Now, here is what TOUGH MOVEMENT does: when all these conditions are fulfilled, and all these transformations have occurred, TOUGH MOVEMENT shifts that object noun phrase of the embedded sentence to the front of the outer sentence, replacing *it.* With this transformation, we would have

7f   A good man is hard to find.
8b   That is easy for you to say.
9b   Pomegranates are difficult for Susan to peel.
10b   Grammar is a torment for me to study.
11b   Philadelphia is a pleasure to visit.

The second transformation to shift noun phrases to the front of the sentence is the PASSIVE transformation, outlined on pages 16 and 17. As mentioned there, the PASSIVE transformation switches the position of subject and object noun phrases and adds several elements to the sentence:

12a   John PAST-& fly a plane to Reno.
12b   A plane PAST-& be EN-& fly to Reno by John.

When the elements in 12b are joined, we get

12c   A plane was flown to Reno by John.

A lot has been said about appropriate and inappropriate uses of the passive. Section 59a makes some comments about the stylistic implications of the PASSIVE transformation.

59a   **Application**

USING PASSIVES

Many handbooks and rhetorics contain stern injunctions against the use of the passive voice; their objections are based on an impression that the passive is static and lifeless. The active voice, these handbooks claim, is forthright and dynamic. Statements about style as simple as this are seldom wholly correct. Like almost every kind of construction, the passive is sometimes appropriate, even almost necessary, while at other times the passive is hardly defensible.

To begin with acceptable uses: the passive is justified when the writer wishes to stress the results of an action, rather than who performed the action:

> 1   The temperature of the peculiarly sandlike snow was taken daily to a depth of one inch, and was found consistently to lie about 5° lower than that of the air immediately above the surface.
>
>   THOMAS R. HENRY

Here it is absolutely immaterial who did the measuring; the author wants to tell us the results, and hence moves the noun phrase *the temperature of the peculiarly sandlike snow* to the subject position by the PASSIVE transformation. Again, the PASSIVE transformation often allows us to eliminate a noun phrase that is perfectly clear to the reader:

> 2   Vivienne Michel, the breathless French-Canadian girl who narrates *The Spy Who Loved Me,* may be intended as a representation of the typical James Bond fan.
>
>   GEORGE GRELLA

It is certain who did the intending in example 2: it can only have been Ian Fleming, author of the James Bond novels. The PASSIVE transformation and the removal of a clearly understood agentive phrase allow us to dispense with a redundant noun phrase.

Sometimes grammatical considerations make the use of the PASSIVE transformation judicious. Note how the author of 3a uses the passive voice:

> 3a   If the Elizabethans believed in an ideal order animating earthly order, they were terrified lest it should be upset, and appalled by the visible tokens of disorder that suggested its upsetting.
>
>   E. M. W. TILLYARD

CONJUNCTION REDUCTION was possible in 3a because both conjuncts on either side of *and* are passive. The first conjunct (*they were terrified*) does not have an expressed agentive phrase; to return it to the active voice we would have to supply some weak-sounding noun phrase like *the thought* as subject. Although the second conjunct does have the agent expressed, CONJUNCTION REDUCTION would no longer be possible if it were active:

> 3b they were terrified lest it should be upset, and the visible tokens of disorder that suggested its upsetting appalled them.

In example 3a, the subordinated construction beginning with *if* has as its subject noun phrase *the Elizabethans;* the PASSIVE transformation clarifies pronoun references in the rest of the sentence by putting the pronouns referring to *the Elizabethans* in the subject positions of their conjuncts (the subject pronoun and *be* in the second conjunct—*they were appalled*—have been removed by CONJUNCTION REDUCTION). We often see the PASSIVE transformation used this way—to focus attention on a particular noun phrase by making it the subject of its sentence—especially when that sentence is one of a series, all the sentences of which have related noun phrases as their subjects:

> 4 The most successful of R. P. Blackmur's early poems were modeled on those of Yeats. Their style was at once too open and too subjective for the material and temperament of the poet. . . . Many of Mr. Blackmur's later poems were written as the man in the story played the violin, by main force; they seemed interesting as an awkward, tortured, and honest diary, but surprisingly unsuccessful as works of art.
>
> RANDALL JARRELL

Why doesn't Jarrell open with *Blackmur modeled the most successful of his early poems on those of Yeats?* Notice that he contrasts Blackmur's early poems with his later ones, and the mention of each group is followed by a comment on the style of each group. Jarrell, using the passive voice, has focused our attention on the poetry, which he wants to talk about, rather than on the poet, who is of marginal importance to this discussion. Through the passive voice, some facet of the poetry is made the subject of each of the four sentences in the example: *the most successful of R. P. Blackmur's early poems, their style, many of Mr. Blackmur's later poems,* and *they.*

In cases like those above, the PASSIVE transformation produces a better sentence than would otherwise have been possible. When the transformation cannot be justified by some purposeful use, the sentence should be left in the active voice.

One particularly inappropriate use of the PASSIVE transformation allows for a kind of intellectual dishonesty (or laziness). Suppose you had written a sentence like this:

> 5a Middle-class Americans are charged with complacency and indifference.

If we reverse the transformation, putting the sentence back into the active voice, what happens? We get

> 5b SOME ONE charges middle-class Americans with complacency and indifference.

Who is doing the charging? Here it is neither unimportant nor at all clear who is leveling the charge. Perhaps the sentence, to be completely honest, should read:

> 5c I have heard some people charge middle-class Americans with complacency and indifference, but I can't remember who they were, and I haven't bothered to look it up.

The PASSIVE transformation should not be a cloak for rumors. If you wish to use the passive in a certain context, make sure the agentive phrase is immediately clear from the context (as *by Ian Fleming* is in example 2), or leave the phrase in the sentence (*by the visible tokens* in 3a).

Exercises

1. Virginia Woolf's style is notable for its many inversions—shifts of parts of the sentence from their normal position to some other place within the sentence. In the sentences below, from her novel *To the*

Lighthouse, mark the parts that are shifted, and rewrite the sentences in their normal order:

1 It was not easy or snug this world she had known for close on seventy years. Bowed down she was with weariness.

2 Visions of joy there must have been at the washtub, say with her children.

3 For now had come that moment, that hesitation when dawn trembles and night pauses, when if a feather alight in the scale it will be weighed down.

4 It annoyed her, this phrase-making, and she said to him, in a matter-of-fact way, that it was a perfectly lovely evening.

5 It was as if the water floated off and set sailing thoughts which had grown stagnant on dry land, and gave to their bodies even some sort of physical relief.

6 What had made it like that? Thinking, night after night, she supposed—about the reality of kitchen tables, she added, remembering the symbol which in her vagueness as to what Mr. Ramsay did think about Andrew had given her.

7 It seemed to rebuke her with its cold stare for all this hurry and agitation; this folly and waste of emotion; it drastically recalled her and spread through her mind first a peace, as her disorderly sensations . . . trooped off the field; and then, weariness.

2. After revising the sentences in exercise 1 to a normal order, write sentences of your own modeled on those revisions, and then see if you can rearrange the parts to the order of the Woolf originals.

3. Henry James' style is notable for its many interruptions. In these interruptions, the sentence is split and some grammatically unrelated material separates the parts of the sentence. In the sentences below, from his novel *The Ambassadors,* remove the parts that interrupt the sentence, noting where the interruptions occur:

1 Chad brought her straight up to him, and Chad was, oh yes, at this moment—for the glory of Woollett or whatever —better still even than Gloriani.

2 Then he had remarked—making the most of the advantage of his years—that it frightened him quite enough to find

himself dedicated to the entertainment of a little foreign girl.

3   The deep human expertness in Gloriani's charming smile—oh, the terrible life behind it!—was flashed upon him as a test of his stuff.

4   Of course experience was in a manner defiance; but it wasn't, at any rate—rather indeed quite the contrary!—grossness; which was so much gained.

5   There could be not a better example—and she appeared to note it with high amusement—than the way, making things out already so much for himself, he was at last throwing precautions to the winds.

6   But there was something he wanted to know, a need created in him by her recent intermission, by his having given, from the first, so much, as now more than ever appeared to him, and got so little.

7   "I've left you wholly alone; haven't, I think I may say, since the first hour or two—when I merely preached patience—so much as breathed on you."

4. Write some Jamesian sentences of your own, modeled on those in exercise 3. Be ready to explain how your sentences are like the examples.

5. The style of William Faulkner is marked by a number of features. In the sentences below, from his novel *Light in August,* note where RESTRICTIVE EMBEDDING and WH-BE DELETION have occurred. Note also the repetitions of certain elements in slightly changed form.

1   In the middle of the sermon she sprang from the bench and began to scream, to shriek something toward the pulpit where her husband had ceased talking, leaning forward with his hands raised and stopped.

2   So when during the following two days she could seem to look nowhere and be nowhere without finding the child watching her with the profound and intent interrogation of an animal, she foisted upon him more of the attributes of an adult.

3   It was new, painted red, with gilt trim and a handpower siren and a bell gold in color and in tone serene, arrogant, and proud.

4   Then he could smell smoke, and food, the hot fierce food, and he began to say over and over to himself *I have not eaten since I have not eaten since* trying to remember how many days it had been since Friday in Jefferson, in the restaurant where he had eaten his supper.

5   Approaching, Byron thinks how the mute chair evocative of disuse and supineness and shabby remoteness from the world, is somehow the symbol and the being too of the man himself.

6   He feels no particular pain now, but better than that, he feels no haste, no urgency, to do anything or go anywhere.

6. Write some sentences in the Faulkner manner, marked by those features you found in exercise 5. Be ready to explain how your sentences are modeled on the examples.

7. Ernest Hemingway's style is so strongly marked that it has often been parodied. In the selections below, from his novel *The Sun Also Rises,* note what he does in joining sentences, what kinds of sentences are joined, and what elements are deleted by CONJUNCTION REDUCTION.

1   At five o'clock I was in the Hotel Crillon waiting for Brett. She was not there, so I sat down and wrote some letters. They were not very good letters but I hoped their being on Crillon stationery would help them. Brett did not turn up, so about quarter to six I went down to the bar and had a Jack Rose with George the barman. Brett had not been in the bar either, and so I looked for her upstairs on my way out, and took a taxi to the Cafe Select.

2   We climbed up and up and crossed another high Col and turned along it, and the road ran down to the right, and we saw a whole new range of mountains off to the south, all brown and baked-looking and furrowed in strange shapes.

3   At the end of the street I saw the cathedral and walked up toward it. The first time I ever saw it I thought the facade was ugly but I liked it now. I went inside. It was dim and dark and the pillars went high up, and there were people praying, and it smelt of incense, and there were some beautiful big windows.

4   During the morning I usually sat in the cafe and read the

Madrid papers and then walked in the town or out into the country. Sometimes Bill went along. Sometimes he wrote in his room. Robert Cohn spent the mornings studying Spanish or trying to get a shave at the barber-shop.

8. Using the information you gained from exercise 7, write some sentences imitating Hemingway. Tell what constructions you tried to duplicate.

60 SENTENCE FRAGMENTS

Many competent writers occasionally add variety through the use of parts of sentences, or sentence fragments. But first the word ''sentence'' has to be defined, since it means too many things to be helpful without further discrimination; there are too many kinds of ''sentences.'' An orthographic, or written, sentence is a word or group of words beginning with a capital letter, and ending with a period, question mark, or exclamation point. Compare this with our handbook's definition of a grammatical sentence—a structure producible by correct operation of the phrase structure rules, together with the application of all relevant obligatory transformations.

In the great majority of cases—probably over 90 percent in almost any extended piece of writing—an orthographic sentence is the same as a grammatical sentence. But some written sentences are only parts of grammatical sentences, perhaps only a verb phrase, perhaps only a noun phrase, perhaps only a reduced embedded sentence. These sentence ''fragments,'' as they are sometimes called, reflect the fact that in spoken language our utterances are not always full, grammatical (in the sense defined above) sentences. Every day we hear such things as the following:

"Do anything yesterday?"
"Took my English test."
"Pass?"
"Tried to."
"No luck?"
"Don't think so."
"Tough."
"Yep."

Obviously, writing convincing dialogue sometimes requires this kind of construction. But there are other kinds of acceptable written sentence fragments; sometimes they occur in descriptive passages:

> 1 Solemn beauty, full-starred night. Celestial blues reds whites and yellows. Self-luminous dwarfs and giants. In the show overhead the Big Dipper appears upside down.
>
> WALTER TELLER

Note, though, that the effect is not long sustained. After the series of noun phrases, the author moves to a complete grammatical sentence.

A third use of the sentence fragment adds an extremely studied, oratorical quality to the writing:

> 2 But what do we want, finally? To kill the institution? No, not at all. To resurrect it. To heal those parts that are sick. To further strengthen those already healthy. These are our aims.

Note that example 2 simply punctuates parallel embedded sentences (with the subject noun phrase deleted) as independent orthographic sentences.

If you aim at effects like those above, do not be afraid to write a sentence fragment. The only sentence fragments to be avoided are those that result from losing track of the structure of the sentence. Sometimes writers have the embarrassing experience of writing a long, involved introductory adverbial and quite literally forgetting, during the writing of it, that they have not finished the sentence they intended to form. So something like this might result:

> 3 * Although wealth in the United States, despite the aims of the graduated income tax, despite mass ownership of corporate stocks and bonds, and despite inheritance taxes, remains in relatively few hands.

The danger here is that the reader is as likely as the writer to lose himself in the sentence. If you have a sentence marked as a fragment, check to see if it is not an embedded sentence punctuated as an independent orthographic one or, as in 3 above, a sentence that started out in one way but finished in another.

60a   Application

ADVERBIALS AND SENTENCE FRAGMENTS

It sometimes happens that an adverbial with an embedded sentence forms a separate utterance in speech, especially as the answer to a question:

> 1a   Why does Gordon read detective stories? Because he enjoys them.

Perhaps because of the frequency of a separate adverbial in speech, students occasionally punctuate the adverbial as a separate written sentence:

> 1b   Gordon reads detective stories. Because he enjoys them.

Because he enjoys them in example 1b is one of the constructions sometimes called ''sentence fragments,'' and probably the kind of sentence fragment most strongly objected to by stylists. Their objections stem no doubt from the failure of this kind of fragment to follow any of the three uses of punctuation in modern English (for more information on these uses, see the unit on punctuation, beginning with Section 74).

First, the fragment in 1b fails as a guide for oral reading. Someone who spontaneously uttered 1b or read it aloud without punctuation to guide him would probably have a level voice pitch between the words *stories* and *because*. The transition between the two words would be short and smooth, with the voice neither rising nor falling in pitch. But the period signals the end of a construction in written English, and is the usual counterpart, in spoken English, of a falling voice pitch and diminishing volume. Thus, the punctuation in 1b does not lead one to read the sentence aloud in a natural way.

Second, the punctuation fails to indicate the syntax of the two parts. The period after *stories* falsely implies that the two parts have equal grammatical standing, two independent structures developed from two separate sentences. But *because he enjoys them* is only a cause adverbial with an embedded sentence, developed ultimately from the same sentence that includes *Gordon reads detective stories*.

Third, there is no arbitrary accepted convention (like hyphenation or syllable division) governing cases like 1b. The punctuation of example 1b as two written sentences fails on all three counts.

It is simple to correct, though, by removing the period and starting *because* with a lower-case letter. The structure would then be punctuated in a way that suggests the close grammatical relationship between the outer sentence and the adverbial embedded sentence:

1c   Gordon reads detective stories because he enjoys them.

At the same time, the punctuation will not mislead anyone who reads the sentence aloud. As a general rule, place no punctuation between an adverbial developed in its normal position (following the verb phrase) and the rest of the sentence.

A
Practical
Rhetoric

About Communication

SECTIONS **61-63**

61 A THEORY OF COMMUNICATION

When we examine any complex activity, we usually begin by trying to analyze it, to break it down into its components. Then, by mastering one part at a time, we gradually achieve mastery of the whole. From golf to brain surgery, the process of acquiring a skill begins with analysis. When we are successful, the skill can be demonstrated in synthesis—putting the parts together again, perhaps in a better form than the one we started with.

Many books on writing start, though, with a synthetic procedure; they start with sentence-writing, go on to paragraph-building by showing the relations between sentences in a paragraph, and finally work from the paragraph to the whole paper. It may be that there is a flaw in going about the study of composition in this way: it may not be basic enough in its analysis. To talk about topic sentences, concrete detail, exemplification, and the like, is to concentrate entirely on what is in the paper. But there are people—the writer and his audience—involved in a composition. To exclude them turns students of composition into theme-writing machines.

Almost all composition texts, of course, have something to say about the people involved: the student is told to pick a topic that interests him, to consider his readers, perhaps to distinguish the different kinds of themes—narrative, descriptive, expository, and so on. But if he wants to know—to be consciously aware of—what is involved in the job of writing, he needs to start with a theory broad enough to encompass all the considerations of authorship, audience, and material.

In essence, the purpose of a composition is to communicate. Anything we will ever write is some kind of communication. The term "communication" covers the menu at a restaurant, the words scratched on a wall, a newspaper headline, and a lyric poem. If we can define the factors involved in any kind of communication, we can examine writing in the light of those factors, and we will be able to relate the manifold activities common to a personal letter, a job application, a committee report, and a two-volume history of philosophy.

A helpful analysis of the communication act originates with Roman Jakobson.[1] We will follow his outline and adopt his terminology for

[1] Roman Jakobson, "Closing Statement: Linguistics and Poetry," *Style in Language,* ed. Thomas A. Sebeok. New York: The Technology Press of Massachusetts Institute of Technology, 1960.

the various parts and uses of information transmitted from one person to another.

Most messages begin with someone who has something to say—"most," not "all," because too many college themes begin with a reluctant student who is writing only to complete an assignment. But for the sake of the analysis, let us assume that this student is the exception, and that most items of communication start as an idea in the mind of someone who wants to convey that idea: call this person the "addresser."

Before that idea can be transmitted (excluding the possibility of extrasensory perception), it has to be turned into something concrete, something perceptible to the senses. Since no one can look into our minds, we express the idea to others by the process of "symbolization": finding a set of symbols appropriate for conveying the idea. This set of symbols, whatever it is, Jakobson calls the "code." Example: Suppose I behaved badly to a friend at a party; the next day I feel the need to apologize. As I go to meet him to do just that, I turn over in my mind different ways of putting into words what I have to say—I think of one way to begin, then another. Technically, what I am doing is called "encoding": putting the idea into symbols that I know and that I presume the other person knows. The particular code here will be English, but it need not be. If the other person and I shared a knowledge of French or Spanish, I might select one of those codes. Nor are the natural languages the only codes in common use: a code is *any* system of symbols used for conveying information. Seen in this perspective, mathematics is a code; so is symbolic logic; even the colors and lines on a topographic map are parts of a code.

So I, the addresser, am going to apologize, and I'm thinking, in English (the code), of the words I'm going to use. There is still no message: the whole thing is still inside my head. I need some way to get the message from me to its intended receiver—the addressee. I have to choose a means, a medium, to carry the message. Some of the media have been around a long time. If I simply speak my apology and the addressee listens to me, we are making use of our oral and aural faculties, plus the sound-conducting properties of the air. This system for transmission is an example of a channel: a medium for conducting messages. Only a short time ago (in relation to the lifetime of our species) writing was invented, and another channel became available. With this invention, a single code—Russian, Arabic, Esperanto, or whatever—can be transmitted by either of two channels, speech or writing. Most inventions in communication since that time have done nothing more than expand the range of our voices, as radio and television do, or make written language more available, as the printing press and xerography do. There are, though, other channels: the Braille system uses the sense of touch, and sign languages depend on sight without the intermediary of a written language.

One last factor affects communication—the context. The context is the background for the communications act: it is anything else that might have a bearing on the message—what the speaker and the hearer know about each other, for example, or their knowledge of the world outside them. If the person to whom I apologize decides, from my past conduct, that I am a lying snake and does not believe me, the context has had an effect on my communication. Ordinarily, though, we try to foresee, as best we can, how the context will influence the message.

Now we can try to relate each of the communication factors to our particular situation: our addresser is, of course, the writer of the composition. Similarly, the addressee is the audience that the writer has in mind, even if that audience never sees the paper he writes. Our particular channel is a piece of paper and a writing instrument, together with a set of conventions that govern our use of them—the fact that we write from left to right and arrange our lines from top to bottom is among the most obvious of these. Some of these conventions are followed almost universally by writers; others a teacher may require of his students; still others the writer may adopt or not, as he prefers. The context is the background of the writing activity: most often we will use it as an information source; a finished paper becomes a part of it. The problem of controlling and utilizing our context to help us in our job of writing is the problem of research. When we write a composition, the language we use is the code. But English has many varieties: the whole grammar section of this book, for instance, represents in effect an abstraction, a way of using English, rather than the way any individual actually uses it. All these factors—addresser, addressee, channel, context, and code—have implications for the message, the composition itself. Specifically, we can classify the composition by its relation to one or another of the factors that have been outlined.

Exercises

1. Identify the addresser, addressee, channel, context, and code for each of the following messages:

   1 the message to Garcia
   2 "One, if by land, and two, if by sea"
   3 a horn blowing in Roncesvalles
   4 "Mr. Watson, come here; I want you."
   5 "The Italian navigator has arrived in the New World."
   6 "Call me Ishmael."
   7 "I am thy father's ghost."
   8 Bong, bong, bong, bong, bong
   9 "Good night, good luck, and good news tomorrow."

2. What channel finally succeeded in the attempt to establish communication with Helen Keller? Who was the addresser, and what was the message?

3. Below is a reproduction of a plaque attached to the Pioneer 10 spacecraft, whose mission is a flight past Jupiter, and beyond into

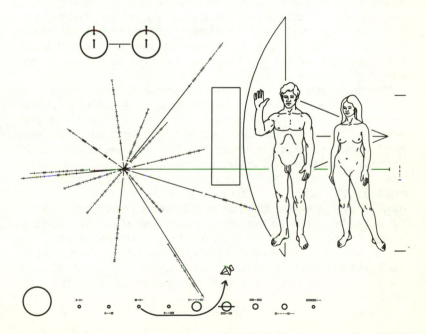

interstellar space. Without worrying about the code, which is rather complicated, and who the addressee might be, tell what you think the message is.

62 THE PURPOSES OF COMMUNICATION

Looking first at the different purposes or functions of messages, we can probably determine the primary job each message is supposed to do, and we can relate that job to one of the factors of the communications act. Suppose we first consider those messages that direct our attention primarily toward the writer himself—not his opinions (those are grounded, we hope, in fact or reason, and can presumably be checked), but the writer's feelings, his experiences—the things we can never know unless he tells us. The best example of a message focused almost exclusively on the writer is the lyric poem. We often find prose selections, too, that concentrate on "how I felt." It is easy to scorn a topic like "How I Spent My Summer Vacation," but from St. Augustine's *Confessions* to Claude Brown's *Manchild in the Promised Land,* people have been telling us how they spent summer and winter, youth and age, and readers show no signs of wearying of autobiography. Remember this: If someone is an expert on no other subject, he is still the world's authority on himself. All such messages—those that focus our attention on the writer—are primarily "emotive" in function.

Next come those messages that direct our attention toward the reader. Jakobson mentions two of the possible relationships that may be covered here: if the writer has some kind of authority or preeminence over the reader, the message teaches. Jakobson's term for this relationship is "hortatory": in this class we would include sermons, textbooks, and practical information of the how-to-do-it type. On the other hand, where the reader holds authority, the message is "supplicatory": an apology, a request for a job or interview. Finally, when our attention is still directed toward the reader, but when the writer and reader are on an equal plane, the message is "persuasive": it attempts to convince, or influence, or affect the reader in thought or behavior. Rather than command, messages of this kind try to produce agreement from within the reader. All such messages—those directed toward the reader—are "conative" in function.

When the message points to the channel, it is called a "phatic" message—that is, it performs a sort of housekeeping function. Our "Hello" when we answer the phone shows only that the channel is open and operative. Similarly, when someone listening to us speak replies, "Oh," "umhmm," "yes," and so on, he is telling us that he is attentive (the channel is open) and that we are supplying him with information at a satisfactory rate. Although spoken English has many phatic signals, there appear to be very few in written English. From this difference between the written and spoken channels arise very special requirements for the writer, as we shall see later.

If the message directs us to the code itself, its function is called "metalingual." Here again, the clearest examples of this function come from spoken English, such as "Do you follow me?" or, on the part of the listener, "What do you mean?" A construction that glosses or explains some part of language has a metalingual function; each entry in a dictionary, for example, is a metalingual message. In composition class, the questions, corrections, or suggestions that the instructor writes on student papers are the most frequent metalingual messages students will see.

Most student compositions will probably point to the context, having what Jakobson calls a "referential" function. Books on rhetoric distinguish many varieties of referential messages: descriptive and narrative are just two of them. A work of fiction implies its own context, usually a context like that of nonfiction, to a greater or lesser degree: the world as we know it, with the physical laws and human behavior we are familiar with. But in fantasy or science fiction, writers often create a radically different context, unique to the particular work.

No matter what the purpose of your writing is, each of the factors outlined above will have a bearing on it. You can avoid a number of writing problems if you know what decisions need to be made before you begin your task. The factors involved in all communication can be your guide here. They can help you ask the right questions; when you have supplied the answers to these questions, you will not just be ready to begin—you will have begun. In the section that follows, a checklist based on these factors provides questions to which you should have an answer before you start your composition. Run through them before you begin. If you are in doubt about the answer to any of these questions, refer to Sections 64 to 69, which discuss these matters, and make a decision before you continue.

Exercises

1. Identify as best you can the function of the following messages:

  1 "Help!"   6 "Beg pardon?"
  2 "Many happy returns." 7 "Now hear this . . ."
  3 "CQ, CQ, CQ"   8 "Damn it!"
  4 "Z-z-z-z-z-z-z"   9 "I dub thee Sir Hector."
  5 WET PAINT   10 "Up, up, and away!"

2. How does the function of this text differ from the function of, say, a chemistry text? How does the function of a love letter differ from the function of a draft notice?

63 A CHECKLIST OF QUESTIONS FOR THE WRITER

Who is the writer?
 Are you interested in this topic?
  If yes, which aspect of your personality are you drawing on?
   Some special knowledge?
   Some special reaction?
   Some special observation?
  If no, can you use a persona? (See Section 65.)

Who is the reader?
 Does he know anything about this topic?
  If yes, how can you best use his specialized knowledge?
  If no, will you be using any words or terms in a specialized way that he may be accustomed to using in a different, more general, sense?
  If no, what general information does he have that you can make comparisons with?
 What does the reader need or want to know about your topic?
  How will the topic affect him?
   Will your treatment support or deny what he already believes?
   Will he be sympathetic or hostile to what you say?
 Are you honestly writing for the reader you have in mind, or are you writing what you think your instructor expects you to say?

Addresser: The Writer

64 CHOOSING A TOPIC

If you want to produce an essay that will interest no one, choose a topic that does not interest you. The reverse, of course, is not true—just because you have an intense interest in a subject, do not assume that everyone shares your concern. But you can hardly hope to produce an essay that is not a chore to read unless you care about its subject.

Suppose you are in an ideal situation: you can write on anything you please. Subjects for a composition are all around you. On the reasonable assumption that what vitally affects you is also of interest to you, then each day's newspaper has a dozen topics of interest. Nor do you need to avoid a topic simply because it is controversial. Jonathan Swift's "A Modest Proposal" came from the fires of controversy; if John Stuart Mill were writing today, he would be called an agitator; John Henry Newman stood at the center of the religious arguments of his day, as did Thomas Huxley in scientific quarrels. There is plenty of room and plenty of need for restraint and caution in writing, but not in the matter of choosing a topic. Finally, writing on a subject you feel strongly about has a reward to offer: although every piece of writing requires a certain amount of inescapable drudgery, the passion of your conviction will help you at least to endure, if not enjoy, the dull parts of the task.

65 THE ASSIGNED TOPIC

Suppose that your class is assigned to write on a topic you care nothing about. If this is the case, use the occasion to learn something about yourself. This can be done in at least two ways: the first of these is to focus on your personal knowledge of the topic, your own reactions and observations.

Take a topic of stunning dullness: "Freshmen Registration." Do not fall into the trap of thinking that your point of view of the registration procedure was the same as everyone else's. No one saw it exactly the same way. The first step is to comb your memory for the reactions and observations you had. Start with what went on inside you: what were your first feelings? Were they apprehension and uncertainty, or confidence and exhilaration? Now move from the emotions you felt to the effect those emotions had on your behavior. (Remember, you're not writing this down—you're just thinking it over for the moment.) Suppose you were confused; that confusion may have betrayed itself in a physical reaction. Were your steps hesitant? Did you find yourself moving aimlessly? Or did you try to give the impression of ease by being a little more boisterous, by laughing a little louder, than the occasion really warranted?

If you have found something of interest about your thoughts and movements, extend that awareness to the other people you saw. How did they look? Could you see your own feelings in anyone else's face? Your movements in anyone else's actions? Think about the others again. How were they dressed? What were they doing? Most of them, no doubt, were acting in their own interest, taking care of their own forms, and so on, but were any of them acting together? You are beginning to classify them already, according to their looks, their dress, their actions. All this thought on the subject constitutes a sort of experimentation with different classifications.

Now, since you probably thought first of those closest to you, the ones near you in line, think of those who were farther away in space and whose duties were different from yours. What about the people who were running the registration? How did they look? Did they appear efficient or confused? Interested or bored? Fresh or tired?

Move next to the physical surroundings. What about the size or the color of the buildings, the color and amount of the light, both inside and out? Were the stations of registration grouped closely together, or were they far apart, perhaps in different parts of the campus? If you had to walk any considerable distances, did you find yourself getting tired or footsore? Now we are back to the feelings inside you.

These few paragraphs have tried to present a method for recovering and eventually reproducing the immediacy of any experience. Your thoughts were directed in a particular way, beginning with thoughts about yourself, and moving outward in ever widening circles: your body, the people close to you, those farther away, the groups you formed, the buildings you were in, the scene around the buildings. The only virtue of the procedure is its completeness— leave out nothing that may prove to be of interest. The hope behind the method is that you will assemble a mass of details, and that from these details you may find certain patterns or repetitions around which a theme may be organized. When their proper arrangement is found, these details (they are not yet a composition) will be a unique blend: you will have filtered the raw material of the experience through your own consciousness, ending with a result like no one else's.

There is another way of handling a topic: a writer sometimes adopts what is called a "persona" (from the Latin word for an actor's mask)—he pretends to be someone else. If you were bored by registration, try adopting a persona: who would you be if you *were* interested in registration? Now you have a chance to exercise your imagination. What would the procedure be like to one of the administrators or instructors behind the tables? Suppose you were one of them, and instead of your first, it was your twentieth registration. How would you feel then? Or try another viewpoint. What does the registration season mean to someone who sells business forms, or dormitory fixtures, or textbooks? If you find a perspective that intrigues you, ask yourself the questions from the first part of this section, this time supplying details about your new identity not from memory but from your imagination. You may not, of course, decide to write the composition pretending to be someone else, but your thoughts will help you to enlarge your own viewpoint.

66 THE SIZE OF THE TOPIC

Most classes in composition have a ritual that occurs the first time themes are mentioned: a student will ask, "How long is the paper supposed to be?" There are just two answers, and even they differ only superficially: the instructor will specify a length—no less than a paragraph, five hundred words, or whatever it may be—or he will say something like "Long enough to cover the material." In reality, both answers are the same; obviously you are not going to take up a subject and then stop at the five-hundredth word. No, whether you write one paragraph or one volume, the reader expects something whole, not merely a fragment.

If you have trouble gauging the amount of material you should try to cover in a theme of a certain length, look first at your textbooks—not just this book, but the textbook you enjoy the most, the one for your favorite subject. Now, suppose your assigned theme is to be approximately five hundred words; your task then is to find out how much material an experienced writer will try to cover in five hundred words. Open the text, then, and beginning at the start of a section or chapter division, count the words in the text, stopping at the end of the paragraph in which the five-hundredth word appears. Examine the section you have just counted off, noting how much material the author gives, and in what detail.

To illustrate the procedure in more depth, look at the following paragraph from a psychology text, containing about one hundred and fifty words:

> The study of associative learning can be carried on in the *conditioned-response* experiment. This experiment was originated by the Russian physiologist and Nobel Prize winner Ivan Pavlov. While studying the relatively automatic reflexes associated with digestion, Pavlov noticed that the flow of saliva in the mouth of the dog was influenced not only by food placed in the dog's mouth but also by the sight of food. He interpreted the flow of saliva to food placed in the mouth as an unlearned response, or, as he called it, an *unconditioned response*. But surely, he thought, the response to the *sight* of food has to be learned. Hence this is a learned or *conditioned response*. Pavlov experimented to find out how conditioned responses are formed. He taught the dog to salivate to various signals, such as the onset of a light or the sound of a metronome, thereby proving to his satisfaction that a new stimulus-response association could be formed in the laboratory.[1]

Notice that the authors of the paragraph assume that the reader already knows what "associative learning" means: the phrase occurs in the first sentence and is not subsequently defined. What information do they convey in the paragraph? Note that they introduce and exemplify two terms, "conditioned response" and "unconditioned response." They give almost no information about Pavlov himself, nor do they attempt to go into the technical details of his work. Although they describe the general nature of the experiment, they do not explain how Pavlov taught his dog to salivate, simply that he did. Nor are the details of his proof introduced. If you were beginning a five-hundred-word theme with this paragraph, you could probably follow only one of these possible developments: you might say more about the man himself; you might describe the physical set-up of the equipment: the harness for the dog, the feeding mechanism, and so on; you might say more about Pavlov's method of inducing a conditioned response: how long it took, what methods

[1] Ernest R. Hilgard, Richard C. Atkinson and Rita L. Atkinson, *Introduction to Psychology*, 5th ed. New York: Harcourt Brace Jovanovich, 1971. P. 189.

279

he used, or his first attempts at the procedure. Any of these would be appropriate, and follow sensibly from the original paragraph, but you could not cover them all, since that would run the composition far past the limit.

If you start from the other end, with a general topic in mind, then you would progressively narrow down your scope until you have something that seems to fit. Suppose you have been asked to write a theme about some kind of work experience. You want to write about working on a newspaper. Think about the range of activities the topic covers: the more time spent considering your topic, the better prepared you will be when the time comes to start writing. Obviously, ''Newspaper Work'' is too large a topic—what kind of work do you mean? If you do not want to write about newsboys or distribution systems, you can narrow down the topic to how newspapers are made. Reporters ''make'' the paper, in one sense; compositors and pressmen ''make'' the paper, in a different sense. Any of these employees' duties, if you know enough about them, will easily fill five hundred words. One way, though, of adding interest to your topic is to seek out the unusual.

What unusual jobs does a newspaper offer? One way of finding the unusual is to start with, and eliminate, the usual: we have been talking about the production of newspapers, so the unusual here would be someone who worked for a newspaper, but had nothing to do with producing it—for example, the person who takes complaints from the customers about editorial policy. We will have more to say about the question of unusual topics when we consider the composition from the reader's standpoint.

In summary: When you begin with a subject and want to narrow it down, see what divisions you can make within the subject matter itself. If you know something about one of the parts, can you make further divisions? In general, the smaller the topic, the better.

Addressee: The Reader

SECTIONS **67-69**

67 THE KINDS OF READERS

In 1963–64, a group of scholars decided to compile a sample of modern American writing. They wanted to cover the great number of different kinds of writing currently being done, with each selection large enough to insure that it accurately reflected its own type of writing. They wanted the collection to be an adequate representation of the English language as written in the United States. The Standard Corpus of Present-Day Edited American English, as the collection is called, is composed of five hundred samples, each about two thousand words in length, coded on magnetic tape. Among many other things, the Brown Corpus (as it is usually referred to) reveals the astonishing variety of writing presently being done. Of particular interest to us is the fact that each kind of writing implies a different kind of reader.

The producers of the corpus selected material from fifteen general categories:[1]

Press: Reportage
Press: Editorial
Press: Reviews
Religion
Skills and Hobbies
Popular Lore
Belles Lettres, Biography, etc.
Miscellaneous
Learned and Scientific Writings
Fiction: General
Fiction: Mystery and Detective
Fiction: Science
Fiction: Adventure and Western
Fiction: Romance and Love Story
Humor

Each of these is divided into subcategories. But before we examine the list more closely, consider who might read material from one of the categories. Consider too that the subject matter of articles in different categories might be similar, yet the readers of one category may not be the readers of the others.

---

[1] Figures, list, and samples are from one of the first studies of the tape, from Henry Kučera and W. Nelson Francis, *Computational Analysis of Present-Day American English.* Providence: Brown University Press, 1967.

One of the samples from the Learned and Scientific Writings category, entitled "Micrometeorites," is from the *Satellite Environment Handbook,* and is presumably intended for astronautical engineers or designers of satellites. How would this article differ from a story about micrometeorites in *If: Worlds of Science Fiction?* Or from an article about them in *Mechanix Illustrated?*

Another of the samples comes from the 1961 *Technical Manual of the American Association of Textile Chemists and Colorists.* Colors and dyes are sure to be discussed there, but they might also be discussed in an article on home decorating in *House Beautiful.*

The point of all this is that your topic will not direct you to your reader: you need to pick your audience. Suppose you are the manager of an industrial plant, and one of the workers has been injured. You have to write several accounts of the accident, and each one will differ according to its intended reader. No dishonesty is involved here: it is just that different readers will want to know different things about the accident. The grievance committee from the union will want to know what benefits the injured man is entitled to; it will want to know what the company intends to do about the hazard, if one exists, to prevent similar accidents. The company safety director will get another report. He too will want to know about the correction of any hazard, but he will also be interested in disseminating your information to the other plant managers, perhaps as part of an educational program or campaign, since his responsibility extends to the whole company, not just your plant. A third report may have to be sent to your immediate superior—say a regional manager—who will want to know the effects of the accident on production (did a shutdown occur?), on the costs of repairs or modifications (will large-scale changes be necessary?), on employee relations (has morale suffered?). The form and content of each report, then, depends partly on who is going to read it, and what that reader needs or wants to know.

68 IDENTIFYING YOUR READER

Who is your reader? What does he already know? What does he want to know? What does he need to know?

The writers of the sample paragraph in Section 66 knew who their readers would be—college freshmen or sophomores taking their first psychology course. They also knew, in general, what information or misinformation their readers would bring to the course. They knew that their technical terms had to be defined. So too do you have to visualize your readers, decide what they already know about the subject of your composition, and assess the value to them of what you have to say.

What audience are you aiming for? Suppose your composition is about a short story or novel you have just read, or a movie you have just seen. We can begin here by thinking of the people who do this sort of thing professionally: people who write about the arts. What kinds of readers do they have? These reviewers have presumably read the books and seen the movies before their readers have, and their task is well defined. Their audience wants to know if the book is worth reading or the movie worth seeing. The reviewer has to give some idea of the story, the characters, the setting, and so on.

But critics also write about books everyone has read, plays and movies hundreds of thousands have already seen: the author of the latest book on Shakespeare's plays realizes that his readers know who Hamlet is, know what the setting of the play is, even have familiarity with a great many of the speeches. One of the frequent mistakes made by beginning writers involves the distinction between these two kinds of writing: the student's essay treats, say, *Antigone* as if it had been written last week. Unless you are specially assigned the task of reviewing a new book or movie or play, assume that your audience is familiar with your subject matter; do not tell them what the story is—they already know that.

When we consider the needs of the reader, many clear examples present themselves: a doctor writing a book on dieting or exercise feels that his audience vitally needs the information he presents; political columns and works, news commentaries, outlines of and solutions to current problems—all take the approach that their subjects are a matter of necessity, not choice, to the reader. Again, we are not speaking of some vague notion of "the general reader." Take, for example, a subject like pollution. We will suppose that you have narrowed it down to a manageable limit: you have decided to write about a fish kill caused by the dumping of industrial wastes from a certain company's factory into a local stream. Who are your readers? What would you say if your composition were to be read by the executives of the company that did the dumping? What arguments could you present to convince the company to stop the dumping? Pick a different audience, and you end up with a different essay: if your readers were local fishermen, you would have an easy audience to visualize, one ready to agree with you. Are they sport fishermen or commercial fishermen? In addressing each, you would use slightly different arguments because the two audiences differ slightly in their need for your information: in the one case, people are deprived of enjoyment; in the other, they may lose their jobs. Your audience may even be hostile to your composition: what if you were writing for employees of the offending company? How would you go about convincing them to actively oppose their company's practices? The details of marshaling your evidence and presenting your arguments belong to the section on context, but we can say this much now: the clearer your idea of your reader, the easier the organizing of your paper will be.

Exercise

Judging from the price, the advertisements, and the articles of one of the pairs of magazines listed below, what are the differences between their readers:

> *Ms.* and *Woman's Day*
> *Playboy* and *Esquire*
> *National Geographic* and *Holiday*
> *Glamour* and *Vogue*
> *Sports Illustrated* and *Sport*
> *Humpty Dumpty* and *Weekly Reader*
> *Teen* and *Boy's Life*
> *Consumer Report* and *Money*
> *The National Review* and *National Observer*
> *Mechanix Illustrated* and *Scientific American*
> *Silver Screen* and *TV Guide*
> *Ladies Home Journal* and *Cosmopolitan*

69 WHAT YOUR READER ALREADY KNOWS

Consider the situation of the fish kill in Section 68. What information would you need to supply to each of the audiences listed there? The executives of the company know their own business operations; they are unlikely, though, to know much about the extent and nature of sport fishing in the area unless fishing is their hobby; they are even less likely to know much about commercial fishing downstream.

If you write for sportsmen, you would face a different problem: the technical names of the chemical wastes will mean little; they must be defined as they are used. If you were writing for the workers at the factory, on the other hand, you would take into account that the workers use those chemicals—they know their own materials and methods. This special knowledge may even suggest a line of argument: chemicals potent enough to kill fish are probably toxic to humans, too. The workers are already familiar with safety regulations governing the handling of any dangerous substances they use. It is a short step from safety regulations that protect human life to those that protect other forms of life.

Starting with something your reader understands and developing your composition in those terms put his knowledge to work for you. Where you depart from the reader's field of knowledge, make sure new terms are defined, and connect your new material to his understanding whenever possible.

If your readers share no common specialization, you can still draw on the general knowledge they possess just by being members of our society. The writer of the next example wanted to explain the advantage of multiple-stage rockets; he introduces a comparison that is almost certain to be helpful:

> Space flight requires both muscle and speed. Whether the payload is a grapefruit-sized satellite or a manned capsule, it must be pushed to a speed of 25,300 feet per second to reach a 160-mile high orbit around the earth. To go to the moon, it must hit 36,000 f.p.s.
>
> The muscle is supplied by a launch vehicle whose initial push, defined in pounds of thrust, must be sufficiently greater than the total weight of the vehicle, fuel and payload to overcome the pull of gravity.
>
> The heavier the combination, the more thrust is needed to get it started against the pull of gravity and to keep it moving fast enough to reach its destination.
>
> Just adding more propellant to a single stage vehicle would ultimately make the propellant containers so heavy that the vehicle could not reach the necessary velocity.
>
> So for speed, a second stage is used.
>
> This tandem combination can be compared to a sports car being pushed by a truck. The truck goes as far and as fast as it can. When both vehicles reach the top speed

of the truck, the fully fueled sports car starts, adding its own acceleration to carry its driver farther and faster.

Centaur's "truck" so far has been an Atlas, the same General Dynamics' launch vehicle that boosted the first American astronauts into orbit.

Fully fueled on the ground, Atlas, Centaur and a two-ton payload weigh a total 303,000 pounds. Atlas' 380,000 pounds of thrust, provided by a kerosene-derived fuel, push the combined vehicles to 91 miles and a speed of 12,700 f.p.s. before it drops off and Centaur's hydrogen fueled engines take over.

The high energy of the smaller Centaur now need push only the 36,500 pounds of itself and the payload against less gravitational effect and without the resistance of the atmosphere. After 440 seconds of firing, Centaur is traveling at 36,000 f.p.s., fast enough to send its payload along its orbit to the moon.[1]

The writer of the example probably had little difficulty in deciding what his readers already know: in trucks and sports cars he found a simple comparison, and its use saved him hundreds of words of explanation.

Exercises

1. Examine the political cartoon from a recent issue of your daily newspaper. List all the information a reader would require to understand it. Bring the cartoon to class and see if your list meets with general agreement.

2. Bring to class a magazine that appeals to a specialized interest, such as electronics, high fidelity, or motorcycling. Distribute different articles from the magazine to members of the class, making sure that each student has an article on a subject with which he is completely unfamiliar. Ask each student to underline the words in one paragraph for which he would need further explanation.

[1] From "High Energy for Space: A Report from General Dynamics," an advertisement in *Saturday Review* (11 June 1966). P. 32. Reprinted by permission of General Dynamics.

Channel:
The
Mechanics

SECTIONS **70-73**

If we lived in the world that some science fiction writers dream of, we would communicate by reading each other's minds. Besides eliminating misunderstandings, transferring our thoughts directly would have another advantage: we would not have to worry about the channel. A channel imposes certain limitations on the messages it carries. For example, look at the color comic strip section in the Sunday paper: a close inspection reveals that blue and red and yellow are printed in solid blocks of ink, but shades of brown, pink, orange, and so on, are mixtures of tiny colored dots. The channel, in this case the high-speed press, limits the effect the comic strip artist can achieve. His shading cannot be as subtle or as varied as that of an artist who uses water colors or oil paints as a medium.

But a particular channel has its own conventions that use its limitations to aid communication. Consider one of the most basic problems involved in writing. In the history of the species and the history of each individual, speech comes before writing. Writing is for each of us the conversion of speech to a more permanent form. When we write, we have to adapt speech, which comes to us in successive waves of sound, to the two-dimensional surface of the writing material, a surface that we perceive all at once. The most basic convention of written English is that we begin at the left end of the top line, move to the end of the line, return to the left end of the next line down, and so on to the bottom of the page. We have agreed, then, to begin our perception of the surface at an arbitrary point. To use the upper left-hand corner as a starting place seems like the most natural thing in the world to us, but it is entirely conventional: if our conventions were different, we could, like the Chinese, arrange our letters in columns rather than rows, or print words right to left, as in Hebrew. Even reading always in the same direction is a habit that not all cultures have developed, as Thomas Pyles points out:[1]

> Sometimes the early Greeks would change direction in alternate lines, starting, for instance, at the right, then changing direction at the end of the line and going from left to right, and continuing this change of direction throughout. Solon's laws were so written. The Greeks had a word for the fashion— *boustrophedon,* ''as the ox turns in plowing,'' a wondrous word indeed, which may even be used in English if one is

[1] *The Origins and Development of the English Language,* 2nd ed. New York: Harcourt Brace Jovanovich, 1971. P. 52.

skillful enough to steer conversation in such a way as to make occasion for its use.

But any convention relieves the reader of the necessity of having to decide anew where to begin on each page. The conventions we cover in this chapter are not nearly as basic as the left-to-right, top-to-bottom order of reading, of course, and the instructor may therefore ask you to modify some of them. But whatever the practice of your particular school, conventions like these are not stumbling blocks strewn by student-hating pedants, but guidelines woven from the experience of many writers and editors. The purpose of such guidelines is not to hinder your expression, but to free you from worry about the limitations of the channel.

70 THE FORMAT OF THE PAPER

The advice given below in glossary form is mostly applicable to a documented, typewritten paper written as a semester project. A short handwritten paper of only a few pages obviously will not include many of the features explained here. But information about the general appearance of the paper—margins, cover sheet, and so on—will be pertinent no matter what the format or length.

Appendixes.   See **Back matter.**

Back matter.   A number of items that may appear in a long paper are collectively called "back matter," since they are items that follow the end of the text. The University of Chicago *Manual of Style* suggests that they be arranged in the following order if more than one are added to a paper or manuscript:

> Appendixes
> Notes
> Glossary
> Bibliography
> Index

An "appendix" is the place for data that you suspect the reader may want to refer to, but that is too bulky for inclusion in the body of your paper. For instance, a sociological study based on a survey may have a specimen of the survey form as an appendix. The raw data (if needed at all) of a psychological experiment reported in the paper belongs in an appendix. It is likely that you will seldom, if ever, need an appendix in a freshman paper. Nor is it a good policy to add appendixes in an effort to give some heft to your research paper.

''Notes'' you will have. Unless asked by your instructor to type them at the foot of the page on which their numbers occur, type your notes, double-spaced, on sheets following the last page of the text (or appendix, if there is one). The notes thus form a separate section of their own; on the first line of the first page of this section, type the word ''Notes.'' The notes should be numbered consecutively throughout the text of your paper. Scholarly books usually number notes consecutively through each chapter, but even your research paper will not be long enough to warrant following that practice. Most, if not all, of your notes will simply document your source material (see Sections 71 to 73 for the composition of source notes, and the sample papers in Section 105).

A ''glossary,'' if included, follows the notes. It is conceivable (but again, not likely) that a freshman term paper would need a glossary. If you have many technical words to define, or words used in a special sense, such as in an essay on slang, a glossary is the place to gather them for quick reference.

The ''bibliography'' is the next section in the back matter. Find out from your instructor whether the bibliography is to be a list of all the works you checked, or only those from which you cited material. The form of bibliographical entries is covered in Sections 71 and 72. The bibliography, like the rest of the paper, should be double-spaced. Type the first line of an entry flush with the left-hand margin. Subsequent lines of the same entry are indented at least three spaces. Unless your bibliography runs to several pages, do not divide it into sections such as ''Books'' and ''Articles''; list all entries in a single, alphabetically arranged sequence.

The last section of all in a scholarly work is the ''index.'' Unless you write a book, you will never need one.

Bibliography. See **Back matter.**

Chapters. In a paper of about ten pages or more, you may find it convenient to divide the material into several sections. Your reader may find it easier to comprehend as well. Begin each section on a new sheet; the sections may simply be headed with consecutive roman numerals, centered on the page. Occasionally, a few words explaining the material of the section are added, like this:

I. The First Settlers

Ordinarily, though, a fifteen-page paper made up of five three-page chapters, each with its own chapter title, seems a little pretentious.

Charts. See **Front matter.**

Contents, table of. See **Front matter.**

Cover sheet. See **Front matter.**

Dividing a word at the end of a line. See Section 81a.

Drawings. See **Front matter.**

Endorsement. Another name for the information that identifies the paper for the purposes of the course. See **Front matter.**

Footnotes. See **Back matter.**

Front matter. Those items in a long paper that precede the first page of text. Arrange the ones you use in the following order:

> Cover sheet
> Table of contents
> List of illustrations
> List of tables

For the ''cover sheet,'' regardless of the length or format of your paper, place a blank sheet before the first page of text. Your school may specify the placement and arrangement of the information this sheet will carry, but it should include at least the title of the paper, your name, your class and section number, and the date. It will also help to include the instructor's name; if you do, make sure you have it correctly spelled.

A ''table of contents'' will not be necessary unless the paper has a number of divisions in the text. Do not use one just to pad out your paper, but if you feel a contents page is justified, list on it the separate chapters or parts of the text, together with the beginning page numbers of each one, plus the beginning page numbers for any back matter: notes, bibliography, and so on. All material before the first page of the text is marked with lower-case roman numerals; arabic numbers begin with the first page of the text. Thus, a table of contents is numbered ''i.''

The ''list of illustrations'' notes the page numbers of maps, charts, graphs, drawings, and so on, that appear in the paper. Unless the figure is only the depth of a few typed lines, put it on a separate sheet, numbered consecutively with the rest of the paper and bearing a title that identifies the figure and explains its relationship to the text. This same title will then be given with the page number in the list of illustrations. The heading of the sheet will depend on the kind of figures used in the paper: it may be headed simply ''Charts,'' or ''Graphs,'' rather than ''Illustrations.'' The list, if included, is numbered ''ii'' if a table of contents is also used. Otherwise, of course, it is simply ''i.''

The ''list of tables,'' headed ''Tables,'' gives the page numbers of data arranged in tabular form, just as the list of illustrations does for figures or data in graphic form. List here the tables with the titles that appear beneath them. Again, unless the tables are very small, place each one on a separate sheet. If a contents page and a list of illustrations have been used, the list of tables will be numbered ''iii.''

Glossary. See **Back matter.**

Graphs. See **Front matter.**

Handwritten papers. See **Paper.**

Illustrations. See **Front matter.**

Indentation. For typed material, indent the first line of a paragraph at least five spaces. Quotations set off from the text in block style should also be indented at least five spaces. If your paper is handwritten, be sure your indentation is apparent, since the reader will have no other indication of where you intend to begin a new paragraph.

Index. See **Back matter.**

Maps. See **Front matter.**

Margins. Your paper needs ample margins—at least an inch on all four sides. On an elite typewriter, a margin of an inch would be twelve spaces from the left and right edges of the paper; on a pica typewriter, ten spaces. The typing should begin no higher than the seventh line from the top edge of the paper, and end on the seventh line from the bottom, to maintain top and bottom margins of at least an inch.

Notes. See **Back matter.**

Numbering of notes. See **Back matter.**

Numbering of pages. Number your pages consecutively, beginning with ''1'' on the first page of the text. The front matter is paged separately, with lower-case roman numerals. The page number is usually located at least three or four lines from the top of the sheet, next to the right-hand margin. Your instructor will also appreciate it if you write your name just before the page number on each page of the manuscript. Then, if the sheets are accidentally mixed with those of another student, the two papers can be sorted out easily.

Pagination. See **Numbering of pages.**

Paper. Unless your course uses a special regulation paper, use an $8\frac{1}{2}'' \times 11''$ sheet of unlined white paper. Type on one side of the sheet only. "Erasable" papers should be avoided, since a casual touch can smudge the typing or remove it entirely. A handwritten theme should use the same size paper, with about twenty-five or thirty ruled lines to the sheet. Write on every other line, on one side of the paper, and observe the same margins as for typed themes.

Poetry, quotations of. Three or more lines of poetry should be centered on the page. Observe the same indentations that the passage has in the original, since it often indicates the rhyme scheme or stanza pattern—for example:

> Despisèd love struck not with woe
> That head of curly knots,
> Nor stomach troubles laid him low,
> Young Stephen Dowling Bots.

Two lines of poetry may be run into the text, separated from it by quotation marks, of course, with a slash showing the line division: "Despisèd love struck not with woe / That head of curly knots." Note that capitalization in the quoted matter follows the original.

Preliminaries. See **Front matter.**

Spacing. All material, including notes and bibliography, should be double-spaced. The spacing allows a word that has been omitted to be typed above the line at the spot where it should occur, with the place of omission marked with a caret pointing to the added word in the line above.

Syllabification. See Section 81a.

Symbols not on typewriter keyboards. Insert by hand and in ink any special symbols or characters not found on the typewriter.

Tables. See **Front matter.**

Title. Besides giving the title on the cover sheet, repeat it on the first line of the first page of the text. Do not underline it or enclose it in quotation marks. Begin the text about four lines below the title. Follow the same procedure for chapter titles, if any.

Title page. See **Front matter.**

Typewriter. It is a courtesy to your reader to make sure that the keys of your typewriter are clean and produce a clear impression. The ribbon should be replaced if the typing is noticeably lighter than that produced by a new ribbon. It should go without saying that the care you put into the physical appearance of your theme is well worth while. Finally, if you have any choice in the matter at all, avoid typewriters with bizarre typefaces, such as those designed to look like handwriting. Productions on these typewriters lack both the individuality of handwriting and the clarity of type.

71 CITATION FORMS

A well-made note enables the reader to find the source you cite. Since the reader always needs certain items of information to locate a work, all citation forms, whatever system is used, contain these items. Because of tradition and editorial preferences, the arrangement and placement of details of the information differ from journal to journal and publisher to publisher. More impressive than the differences, though, are the similarities between the systems. We can condense the many methods of documentation into two general formats, each used by a large number of disciplines. Use the form recommended by your instructor or, if you are given a choice, follow the form appropriate to your field of study.

As you read material for all your courses, begin to familiarize yourself with the periodicals and publications in your field. There you will find examples of the customary styles of documentation used in the discipline, as well as the special problems encountered by writers in that area.

Finally, remember that a reference note serves its purpose if it has the information your reader needs. More information than is necessary, such as repeating in a note material already given in the text, simply wastes space. Less information than is needed, no matter how elegantly phrased, frustrates the whole purpose of the note.

The description of the two systems below should be sufficient for almost all your needs. Should you require additional help for particular problems, you can certainly find an answer in *A Manual of Style,* published by the University of Chicago Press, twelfth edition, revised, 1969. The Chicago *Manual* covers much more material than has been possible to explain here, including the specialized reference systems used to document judicial decisions, public laws, government reports, proceedings, and many other matters.

72 A FORM FOR THE HUMANITIES

With some variations, the form for the humanities is based on *The MLA Style Sheet,* second edition, 1970, published by the Modern Language Association of America. *The MLA Style Sheet* serves as a guide in matters of style for most journals of literary interest, both scholarly and popular, and for books published by many university presses, often on subjects of general as well as specialized interest. It presents a useful format for writers on subjects in the humanities. Departures from the MLA recommendations are noted as they occur.

72a FIRST REFERENCE

One characteristic of the MLA system is the listing of the essential bibliographic information in the first note from each source. Subsequent notes from the same source can be shortened as shown in Section 72b. First references are arranged as follows:

Books. Take your information from the title page of the book itself. Arrange it in this order.[1]
(1) Name of the author or authors in normal order, followed by a comma:

[1] Kenneth Muir, *Introduction to Elizabethan Literature.* New York: Random House, 1967. P. 38.
[2] W. Gordon Whaley, Osmond P. Breland, Charles Heimsch, Austin Phelps, and Glenn S. Rabideau, *Principles of Biology.* New York: Harper & Row, 1954. P. 106.

---

[1] *The MLA Style Sheet* punctuates a note as a single sentence, while a bibliography entry is punctuated as several sentences. The system here does away with this distinction, making the punctuation of references uniform, whether in a note or in the bibliography.

Since note 2 documents a work with more than three authors, it could have been abbreviated as follows:

> [2] W. Gordon Whaley et al., *Principles of Biology.* New York: Harper & Row, 1954. P. 106.

(2) Title of the book, underlined, followed by a period. If the book has a subtitle, separate it from the main title by a colon. Lengthy subtitles, like the one in note 3, may be omitted from the reference note if the paper includes a bibliography where the subtitles are given in full:

> [3] Charles Vereker, *Eighteenth Century Optimism: A Study of the Interrelations of Moral and Social Theory in English and French Thought Between 1689 and 1789.* Liverpool: Liverpool University Press, 1967. P. 88.

If the book is edited by someone other than the author, or if it is a translation, place a comma after the title, then the abbreviation ''ed.'' or ''tr.,'' followed by the name of the author or translator and, finally, the period:

> [4] John Milton, *Paradise Regained, the Minor Poems, and Samson Agonistes,* ed. Merritt Y. Hughes. New York: Odyssey Press, 1937. P. 185.
> [5] Alexander Herzen, *Memoirs,* tr. J. D. Duff. New Haven: Yale University Press, 1923. P. 144.

If your citation concerns the particular edition or translation you are using rather than any other, the name of the editor or translator may be placed first, making the note look like this:

> [4] Merritt Y. Hughes, ed., *John Milton: Paradise Regained, the Minor Poems, and Samson Agonistes.* New York: Odyssey Press, 1937. P. 185.
> [5] J. D. Duff, tr., *Alexander Herzen: Memoirs.* New Haven: Yale University Press, 1923. P. 144.

When you are not using the first edition of the work, put a comma after the title, then the information about the edition you are using: the abbreviations ''rev. ed.'' (for revised edition), ''2nd ed.,'' and so on, follow the name of the editor or translator, if any. Of course, you should be using the latest edition of a work, if at all possible.

⁶ Oscar Ogg, *The 26 Letters,* rev. ed. New York: Thomas Y. Crowell, 1971. P. 120.

⁷ John Gerard, *The Autobiography of a Hunted Priest,* tr. Philip Caraman, S.J., Image Books ed. Garden City, N.Y.: Doubleday, 1955. P. 219.

(3) The information above—title, author, editor or translator, and edition—identifies the book. The information in the examples below gives the data of its publication. List first the city where the book was published, including the abbreviation of the state or country if the city is not well known or is ambiguous (Cambridge, England or Cambridge, Massachusetts), followed by a colon; then the name of the publisher (shortened forms in general use may be used), followed by a comma; then the year of publication, followed by a period. (*The MLA Style Sheet* encloses the publication data in parentheses, followed by a comma after the closing parenthesis.)

⁸ Kenneth H. Cooper, *Aerobics.* New York: Bantam Books, 1968. P. 112.

⁹ Samuel Gorovitz et al., *Philosophical Analysis,* 2nd ed. New York: Random House, 1965. P. 71.

(4) If the work you are citing has more than one volume, give the volume number (abbreviated "Vol."), followed by a comma, then the page number or numbers (preceded by the abbreviation "p." or "pp."), followed by a period:

¹⁰ Thomas Wright and James Orchard Halliwell, eds., *Reliquiae Antiquae.* London, 1843. Vol. 2, p. 45.

¹¹ C. S. Lewis, *The Pilgrim's Regress,* 7th ed. London: Geoffrey Bles, 1950. Pp. 138–39.

An article in a collection by a different editor: List first the author of the article you are citing, followed by a comma; then the title of the article, in quotation marks, with a comma inside the final quotation mark; then the information about the title of the whole book and its editor, in the normal way for the first reference to a book. Take the title of the article from the first page of the article itself, not from the table of contents, where the title may have been abbreviated.

[12] James Sledd, "Syntactic Strictures," *Readings in Applied English Linguistics,* ed. Harold Byron Allen, 2nd ed. New York: Appleton-Century-Crofts, 1964. P. 416.

An article from a journal or periodical.   List first the author and the title of the article, just as in note 12. Then list the title of the journal, preceded by a comma, underlined, and followed by a comma. Next comes the volume number (without the abbreviation "Vol."), followed by the date in parentheses. No comma precedes the parentheses.

The next item, the date, requires some explanation: usually it will be sufficient to indicate only the year, as in note 13:

[13] James W. Carey and John J. Quirk, "The Mythos of the Electronic Revolution," *American Scholar,* 39 (1970). P. 406.

Libraries usually bind together the issues of a periodical by volume. When one volume of the periodical appears each year, there is no problem. But the volume numbers of some publications run across two calendar years—*College English,* for example, appears monthly from October through May of the following year. Also, most journals are paginated consecutively throughout one volume, but some are paginated separately beginning anew with each issue. It is always helpful, therefore, and sometimes necessary, to include the issue number and the month or season of the issue together with the date. Compare the form of the note below with the one just given:

[13] James W. Carey and John J. Quirk, "The Mythos of the Electronic Revolution," *American Scholar,* 39, No. 3 (Summer 1970). P. 406.

Following the date in parentheses comes a period, then the page number, also followed by a period:

[14] Gerald L. Bruns, "Silent Orpheus: Annihilating Words and Literary Language," *College English,* 31, No. 8 (May 1970). P. 825.

Articles from newspapers and magazines. For daily or weekly publications, or monthly magazines of general interest, the date sufficiently identifies the issue cited:

15 "Atlantic Divers View Volcanic Activity," *The New York Times* (15 August 1973). [or (August 15, 1973).] P. 4.

16 "Nigeria," *Time* (27 July 1970). [or (July 27, 1970).] P. 26.

As notes 15 and 16 show, citations for unsigned articles begin with the title of the article. But be sure to notice if the author's name appears at the end of the article, as is often the case, even in newsmagazines, when personal opinion is being expressed.

Information from encyclopedias or dictionaries. A reference to a work that is alphabetically arranged can be simplified, since information in such works is easily found: volume and page numbers need not be included, but the heading under which the entry is listed should be indicated (note that it follows the publisher and date):

17 Harold Wentworth and Stuart Berg Flexner, eds., *Dictionary of American Slang,* supplemented ed. New York: Thomas Y. Crowell, 1967. "Earduster."

Citations from the Bible and the classics. Citations from the Bible simply list the book (not underlined), followed without a comma by the number for chapter and verse. The chapter and verse are separated by a period with no space on either side:

18 Proverbs 9.1.

In quoting from the classics (or from any work of which many translations have been made), you give little information to your reader if you supply him with a page number. He may have the work you refer to, but not the edition or translation you are using. Notes 19 and 20 illustrate the preferred procedure in this case:

19 William Shakespeare, *The Complete Works,* ed. G. B. Harrison. New York: Harcourt Brace Jovanovich, 1968. "All's Well That Ends Well," III.iv.55.

In note 19, the capital roman numeral indicates the act, the lower-case roman numeral the scene, and the arabic numeral the line referred to. With this information, your reader can check the passage he desires in whatever edition he may have.

Note 20 cites a work that has been frequently translated. As is the case with many of the prose classics, the work is divided into books, the books into chapters, and the chapters into sections. Here the numbers identify the book, the chapter, and the section, in that order:

[20] St. Augustine, *Confessions,* tr. Vernon J. Bourke. Washington, D. C.: Catholic University of America Press, 1953. XI.xviii.23.

72b SECOND REFERENCE

Second and subsequent notes from a source are usually shortened. The simplest way, particularly appropriate to short papers, is to give the last name of the author, the volume number (if your citation is from a multivolume book), and the page number. Second references to the book cited in notes 10 and 11 above would look like 1 and 2 below:

[1] Wright and Halliwell, vol. 2, p. 88.
[2] Lewis, p. 29.

Second references to the articles cited in notes 12, 13, and 15 would look like this:

[3] Sledd, p. 414.
[4] Carey and Quirk, p. 410.
[5] "Atlantic Divers," p. 4.

If you have cited from two or more works by the same author, this system will not be adequate. For example, suppose two of your references are

[6] Kenneth W. Cameron, "Thoreau and Orestes Brownson," *Emerson Society Quarterly,* 51 (1968). P. 55.
[7] Kenneth W. Cameron, "Thoreau's Harvard Friends and Temperance," *Emerson Society Quarterly,* 51 (1968). P. 140.

These two articles can be referred to in subsequent citations by the last name of the author together with an abbreviated version of the titles. For example:

[8] Cameron, "Thoreau and Brownson," p. 60.
[9] Cameron, "Thoreau's Harvard Friends," p. 141.

72c BIBLIOGRAPHY

If you are instructed to include a bibliography with your paper when you use the MLA system, the entries in the bibliography will be the same as the notes, with three exceptions. First, the bibliography is arranged alphabetically by the authors' last names. Second, the references to individual pages are omitted. Third, in the case of articles, the inclusive page numbers for the article as a whole are given. Below is a sample bibliography compiled from the notes used in the illustrations:

"Atlantic Divers View Volcanic Activity," *The New York Times* (15 August 1973). P. 4.

Augustine, *Confessions,* tr. Vernon J. Bourke. Washington, D.C.: Catholic University of America Press, 1953. (Note that this entry is not alphabetized under *Saint.*)

Bruns, Gerald L., "Silent Orpheus: Annihilating Words and Literary Language," *College English,* 31, No. 8 (May 1970). Pp. 821–27.

Cameron, Kenneth W., "Thoreau and Orestes Brownson," *Emerson Society Quarterly,* 51 (1968). Pp. 53–65.

————, "Thoreau's Harvard Friends and Temperance," *Emerson Society Quarterly,* 51 (1968). Pp. 137–41. (Note the use of the long dash in preference to the repetition of an author's name.)

Carey, James W., and John J. Quirk, "The Mythos of the Electronic Revolution," *American Scholar,* 39 (1970). Pp. 395–424. (Note that the name of only the first co-author is reversed.)

Cooper, Kenneth H., *Aerobics.* New York: Bantam Books, 1968.

Gerard, John, *The Autobiography of a Hunted Priest,* tr. Philip Caraman, S.J., Image Books ed. Garden City, N.Y.: Doubleday, 1955.

Gorovitz, Samuel, Ron G. Williams, Donald Provence, and Merrill Provence, *Philosophical Analysis,* 2nd ed. New York: Random House, 1965.

Herzen, Alexander, *Memoirs,* tr. J. D. Duff. New Haven: Yale University Press, 1923.

Lewis, C. S., *The Pilgrim's Regress,* 7th ed. London: Geoffrey Bles, 1950.

Milton, John, *Paradise Regained, the Minor Poems, and Samson Agonistes,* ed. Merritt Y. Hughes. New York: Odyssey Press, 1937.

"Nigeria," *Time* (27 July 1970). P. 26.

Shakespeare, William, *The Complete Works,* ed. G. B. Harrison. New York: Harcourt Brace Jovanovich, 1968.

Sledd, James, "Syntactic Strictures," *Readings in Applied English Linguistics,* ed. Harold Byron Allen, 2nd ed. New York: Appleton-Century-Crofts, 1964. Pp. 414–22.

Vereker, Charles, *Eighteenth Century Optimism: A Study of the Interrelations of Moral and Social Theory in English and French Thought Between 1689 and 1789.* Liverpool: Liverpool University Press, 1967.

Wentworth, Harold, and Stuart Berg Flexner, eds., *Dictionary of American Slang,* supplemented ed. New York: Thomas Y. Crowell, 1967.

Whaley, W. Gordon, Osmond P. Breland, Charles Heimsch, Austin Phelps, and Glenn S. Rabideau, *Principles of Biology.* New York: Harper & Row, 1954.

Wright, Thomas, and James Orchard Halliwell, eds., *Reliquiae Antiquae.* London, 1843.

73 A FORM FOR THE NATURAL AND SOCIAL SCIENCES

This next method of documenting material is sometimes called the "name and year" system. It is commonly used by publications in the physical and social sciences; for example, this is the system recommended by the American Institute of Biological Sciences in its *Style Manual for Biological Journals,* second edition, and the American Psychological Association in its *Publication Manual.* Where the references are many and a bibliography will be included, it is much more economical of space than the system for the humanities.

73a BIBLIOGRAPHY

Since this system depends on the organization of its bibliography, we will begin with the form of entries there. The bibliography is again alphabetically arranged according to the authors' last names. The author's name, in inverted order, is followed by a period. Next comes the year of publication, followed by a period. The rest of the information is arranged as in the system for the humanities.

Books.

> Richardson, Moses. 1966. *Fundamentals of Mathematics,* 3rd ed. New York: Macmillan.

Articles.

> Bennett, William H. 1970. "The Stress Patterns of Gothic," *PMLA,* 85:463–72. (Note that the volume number is separated from the inclusive page numbers by a colon.)

Articles and books by the same author are arranged in chronological order by publication date:

> Chomsky, Noam. 1957. *Syntactic Structures.* The Hague: Mouton.
>
> ———. 1961. "Some Methodological Remarks on Generative Grammar," *Word,* 17:219–39.
>
> ———. 1962. "Explanatory Models in Linguistics," *Logic, Methodology, and Philosophy of Science,* ed. E. Nagel, P. Suppes, and A. Tarski. Stanford: Stanford University Press.

Articles and books by the same author published in the same year are differentiated by arranging them in alphabetical order by title, and adding letters after the year of publication, as in the examples below:

> Arnold, B. H.: 1962a. *Intuitive Concepts in Elementary Topology.* Englewood Cliffs, N.J.: Prentice-Hall.
>
> ———. 1962b. *Logic and Boolean Algebra.* Englewood Cliffs, N.J.: Prentice-Hall.

73b REFERENCES

In the "name and year" system, do not separate notes from the text. Instead, give in parentheses the last name of the author and the year of publication of the work you are citing. Place this reference at the point in the text where you have cited the material. Examples 1 and 2 show acceptable ways of citing a source and identifying a direct quotation using this system:

1 Early generative grammars were concerned with a simple, declarative structure called a kernel sentence (Chomsky 1957). Even negative questions began their derivations from kernel sentences.
2 As Chomsky said, "It is, of course, impossible to prove that semantic notions are of no use in grammar. . . ." (1957: p. 100).

The reader who wishes to locate the sources of your references then finds in the bibliography the work by Chomsky published in 1957.

Channel: Punctuation

74 PUNCTUATION: A SHORT HISTORY

Under the heading of "Punctuation" belong the various marks—comma, period, question mark, and so on—and typographic devices like italics and brackets. These are areas where the channel of written English requires different conventions from those used in spoken English. Speech has no doubling of forms to correspond to the written *Mister* and *Mr.*, for example, nor do we pronounce proper nouns any differently from common nouns. Conversely, normal English writing allows us to capture some features of the spoken language only imperfectly: unlike some written languages, English contains no device for showing where the stress of a word falls when the word is spoken; we have no means, in written English, of indicating changes in the pitch of the voice. To capture information like pitch and stress, or at least part of it, we have recourse to the devices described in this section.

By far the oldest surviving writings in the Germanic languages (of which English is one) are those of Gothic. At the time these writings were made, the fourth century, the Goths lived in southeastern Europe. In the centuries that followed, the Goths moved westward, becoming better known to the Romans and to history in the process. Most of the Gothic manuscripts contain translations of the New Testament; if by some chance the conventions of writing found in these earliest specimens of the Germanic languages had survived to our time, we would have printing that looked like this:

> inthedaysofkingherodofjudeatherelivedapriestcalled
> zechariahwhobelongedtotheabijahsectionofthepriesthood
> andhehadawifeelizabethbynamewhowasadescendantofaaron.
> bothwereworthyinthesightofgodandscrupulouslyobserved
> allthecommandmentsandobservancesofthelord. butthey
> werechildlesselizabethwasbarrenandtheywerebothgetting
> oninyears.

In a time when people who could read were rare, and manuscripts to read from were even rarer, the contact that the many had with books most probably came secondhand: someone read to them. Picture a monastery at mealtime: the monks sit eating silently, while a lector, standing at one end of the hall, reads to them from Scripture. The first marks of punctuation (which had already appeared in pre-Christian times) served the very practical purpose of letting the lector pause for breath occasionally.[1] Rather than being faced with unbroken lines like those of the Gothic example, the lector saw a manuscript with word divided from word by spaces, and various marks that made concessions to the limits of human lung power. The first marks of punctuation, then, were guides for oral reading. If they happened to come at grammatical divisions of the sentence, their occurrence at those spots was due to coincidence, not intention.

Down to the sixteenth and seventeenth centuries, writers on punctuation thought of the marks partly as devices for indicating breath pauses of different lengths, as Richard Mulcaster did in 1582:

> *Comma,* is a small crooked point, which in writing followeth som small branch of the sentence, & in reading warneth vs to rest there, and to help our breth a little. . . . *Period* is a small round point, which in writing followeth a perfit sentence, and in reading warneth vs to rest there and to help our breth at full.[2]

Yet, like Mulcaster, the grammarians often said that the marks also had something to do with the structure of the sentence, since it had been suggested that punctuation be used to help indicate the syntax as early as the seventh century. So for a thousand years, most grammarians tried to make punctuation serve these two very different functions—to mark pauses for oral readings and to indicate elements of grammar. Thus John Brightland, in 1711, claimed: "The Use of these Points, Pauses, or Stops, is not only to give a proper Time for Breathing; but to avoid Obscurity, and Confusion of the Sence in the joining Words together in a Sentence."[3]

Typesetters, who had an immediate need for clear and unambiguous instructions for punctuation, suffered most from the attempt to make the system of "pointing," as it was called, do two jobs at once. It was no encouragement to them to have grammarians despair of the task, as John Buchanan did in 1762: "Pointing a Discourse is a Province beyond the Capacities of mere Youth."

---

[1] See Walter J. Ong, "Historical Backgrounds of Elizabethan and Jacobean Punctuation Theory," *PMLA,* 59 (1944). Pp. 349–60.

[2] Cited in Ong, p. 355.

[3] This and the two subsequent quotations are cited in Park Honan, "Eighteenth and Nineteenth Century English Punctuation Theory," *English Studies,* 41 (1960). Pp. 93–96.

Although the situation was obviously unsatisfactory, and recognized as such, the source of the problem was not identified and clearly stated until later in the eighteenth century. David Steel, in his *Elements of Punctuation* (1786), noted what theorists had been trying to do with the system and what they ought to do:

> Grammar, which ought to be the basis of punctuation, has seldom been considered as adequate to the purpose: too much accommodation to the reader, and too little attention to grammatical construction have usually been the sources whence the doctrine of points has been deduced.

Despite Steel and some others who followed him, it was not until a hundred years later—not until the middle of the nineteenth century—that there was a general agreement that the first purpose of punctuation is to provide grammatical information, and even now that agreement is far from complete. In relatively few cases is it possible to say, "This punctuation is wrong." Take the following sentence, for example; it stands here presumably as the author wrote it:

1a   But she was still looking up at him then; and his words tailed off into silence.

JOHN FOWLES

The sentence could just as grammatically have been punctuated like this:

1b   But she was still looking up at him then, and his words tailed off into silence.

Or even left unpunctuated, like this:

1c   But she was still looking up at him then and his words tailed off into silence.

Modern punctuation, although streamlined by comparison with that of years past, still has its sharp edges and hidden crevices. Primarily, it shows grammatical structure, but it still retains traces of the old oral reading system. To these two purposes have been added, again rather recently, certain marks that neither indicate a syntactic construction nor allow a pause for breathing, but are wholly arbitrary: we hyphenate some words, for instance, because everybody does it. Unfortunately, the same mark is often made to serve more than one of these purposes: in one instance, it sets off a grammatical unit; in another, it indicates a pause for breath; in still a third, its use is a matter of convention. To aid the student who is trying to correct a paper, the pages that follow are organized according to the mark of punctuation—first come all the uses of commas, then those of semicolons, and so on—but in each section the purpose of a particular usage will be given, together with some indication of its importance.

Since many of the syntactically determined uses of punctuation are detailed in the grammar section, that material will not be repeated here in full. Instead, these usages will be illustrated, and a short statement of the principle involved will be given. If you need more information or a fuller discussion, follow the reference to the applicable section of the grammar.

Exercises

1. At the library, examine a facsimile copy of some Elizabethan work. (A convenient one would be the Norton facsimile edition of *The First Folio of Shakespeare,* ed. Charlton Hinman [New York, 1968].) Copy a short passage exactly, being especially careful with the punctuation. Then compare the passage with the same lines in a modern popular edition. Note any variations in punctuation. See if you can judge why the modern editor punctuated it differently.

2. Be your own editor of Shakespeare's works! Revise one of the following passages by modernizing the spelling and punctuation. All are from *The First Folio:*

   1 Hee hath Ribbons of all the colours i'th Rainebow; Points, more then all the Lawyers in Bohemia, can learnedly handle, though they come to him by th'grosse: Inckles, Caddysses, Cambrickes, Lawnes: why he sings em ouer, as they were Gods, or Goddesses: you would thinke a Smocke were a shee-Angell, he so chauntes to the sleeue-hand, and the worke about the square on't.

   2 Doe not thinke so, you shall not finde it so:
   And Heauen forgiue them, that so much haue sway'd
   Your Maiesties good thoughts away from me:
   I will redeeme all this on Percies head,

> And in the closing of some glorious day,
> Be bold to tell you that I am your Sonne,
> When I will weare a Garment all of Blood,
> And staine my fauours in a bloody Maske:
> Which washt away, shall scowre my shame with it.

3 If he did not care whether he had their loue, or no, hee waued indifferently, 'twixt doing them neyther good, nor harme: but hee seekes their hate with greater deuotion, then they can render it him; and leaues nothing vndone, that may fully discouer him their opposite. Now to seeme to affect the mallice and displeasure of the People, is as bad, as that which he dislikes, to flatter them for their loue.

75 COMMA

75a TO SET OFF AN APPOSITIVE ELEMENT

In the grammar of written English, the most important use of the comma is to separate an embedded appositive from the outer sentence, whether the appositive is in full form (traditionally called a nonrestrictive relative clause), as in 1, or in reduced form, as in 2:

1 The French, who care pertinently for this subject, have produced, as might be expected, a spokesman with a flair for definition.

VERNON YOUNG

2 The machine tool industry, mainly a congeries of small shops employing highly skilled labor, has notoriously resisted innovation.

BEN B. SELIGMAN

Example 2 has an appositive reduced from its full form, *which is mainly a congeries of small shops employing highly skilled labor,* by WH-BE DELETION (see Section 45a).

Often, as in example 1, only the commas tell us that we have an appositive relative rather than a restrictive relative (see Section 45b), and herein lies the importance of this rule of comma placement.

75b TO SET OFF INTRODUCTORY ELEMENTS

A second use of the comma is to mark elements of syntax that have been shifted by stylistic transformations. Whenever we move an element from one position to another, it is advisable to separate it from the rest of the sentence by commas.

In sentence 1a below, the adverbial is in the position in which it is generated by the phrase structure rules—following the main verb. Shifting the adverbial to the left of the sentence (1b) moves it from this position and explains the presence of the comma after *stands*. If we had shifted the adverbial to follow the subject noun phrase, as in 1c, commas would be needed both before and after the adverbial:

1a The bridge is concededly one of the most beautiful structures in America as it stands.

1b As it stands, the bridge is concededly one of the most beautiful structures in America.

JOHN A. KOUWENHOVEN

1c The bridge , as it stands, is concededly one of the most beautiful structures in America.

What are sometimes called parenthetical elements are set off from the rest of the sentence in the same manner. In the case of parenthetical elements, we have a drastic rearrangement of the original word order, since the construction begins as an outer sentence with a sentence embedded by the THAT transformation in the object position. Subsequently, THAT DELETION removes the embedder. At this stage, we would have a sentence like 2a:

2a We may say [art does away with unnecessary complications].

An optional stylistic transformation may now shift the outer sentence to at least two different positions *within* the embedded sentence.

In either of these cases, since the outer sentence has been moved from its normal position, it is separated from the rest of the construction by commas. It may be placed between the subject noun phrase and the verb phrase of the embedded sentence:

> 2b   Art, we may say, does away with unnecessary complications.
>
> ABRAHAM KAPLAN

Or, it may be moved to come between the main verb and the object noun phrase of the embedded sentence. Compare 3a and 3b:

> 3a   I think [in its essence it is not a particularity of our time and place].
> 3b   But in its essence it is not, I think, a particularity of our time and place.
>
> ABRAHAM KAPLAN

Similarly, constructions from sentences embedded in adverbials are set off from the rest of the sentence when they are shifted to the left of the sentence:

> 4   Octavian having seized Corinth, Anthony's line of supply was cut.

Constructions resulting from the operation of deletion transformations on adverbial embedded sentences are set off, even when they appear in their normal position. As Section 53 explained in detail, the emphasized construction in example 5 below results from ADV—TIME PROGRESSIVE DELETION.

> 5   One can never forget Keaton wearing it, standing erect at the prow as his little boat is being launched.
>
> JAMES AGEE

Here the comma seems to mark the place of the deleted embedder *while* or *as*. The remains of a heavily deleted adverbial sentence, when shifted to the left of the sentence, are of course set off by a comma in the same way that any shifted construction is set off:

6 Terrified, Queeg turns the ship south, so that it no
   longer heads into the wind.

WILLIAM H. WHYTE, JR.

Finally, sentence connectors (*also, alternatively, however,* and so
on—see Section 50) and whole-sentence modifiers (*certainly, truly,
fortunately,* and so on—see Section 49) are separated from the rest
of the sentence, whatever their position. In example 7, we have a
sentence connector, *in other words,* and a sentence modifier, *obviously:*

7 In other words, it was not Sophocles who was inspired
   by Freud but, obviously, the other way round.

EUGENE IONESCO

75c   TO SEPARATE ELEMENTS IN A SERIES

When three or more grammatical units of the same kind appear in
the same sentence, they are separated by commas, a device which
serves to emphasize the parallelism of the construction. The units
in the series may be simple ones—nouns or verbs—or more complex
ones like noun phrases, verb phrases, or even whole sentences. The
commas are frequently used even when coordinating conjunctions
appear between the elements, as in sentences 2, 3, and 4, when
commas would not be grammatically required:

1 One saw great crowds of prosperous, well-dressed,
   extremely sophisticated people. (pattern: ADJ, ADJ,
   ADJ *people.*)

ALFRED KAZIN

2 They must be able to go from shelf to shelf, tracking
   down an idea, a name, or a picture. (pattern: *tracking
   down* NP, NP, *or* NP.)

JACQUES BARZUN

3 I lingered round them, under that benign sky: watched
   the moths fluttering among the heath and hare-bells,

listened to the soft wind breathing through the grass, and wondered how anyone could ever imagine unquiet slumbers for the sleepers in that quiet earth. (pattern: *I lingered round them, under that benign sky:* VP, VP, *and* VP.)

EMILY BRONTË

4   Two stags fighting for a harem of hinds, or a man murdering another man, or a dozen dogs fighting over a bone, are not engaged in war. (pattern: NP, *or* NP, *or* NP, *are not engaged in war.*)

JULIAN HUXLEY

5   A carefully written program on parallelism should be able to teach a student what parallel structure is, how to recognize it, how to check it for accuracy, how to correct instances of faulty parallelism. (pattern: *to teach a student* S, S, S, S.)

ALBERT R. KITZHABER

More information about punctuating compound elements and more examples can be found in Section 56c.

The most difficult problem in punctuating elements in a series is deciding how to punctuate a noun phrase with several adjectives before its headnoun. Strictly speaking, the term ''series'' does not apply here: in some instances, a comma separates only two adjectives. The purpose of the convention seems to be to indicate that each of the adjectives modifies the headnoun directly:

6   The common defense against such a criticism is that the critic is timid, an old fogey, that we live in new times, which call for daring, uninhibited experimentation and the generating of new forms.

WALTER GOODMAN

In the noun phrase emphasized in sentence 6, both the adjectives modify the headnoun. We could just as grammatically switch their positions thus: ''which call for *uninhibited, daring* experimentation.'' But commas do not come between two adjectives that precede a headnoun when the first adjective modifies not the headnoun but a noun phrase composed of the second adjective and the headnoun:

7   No family enemy could have been harder on John Quincy Adams than his son Charles, who . . . urged him not to state publicly his mistaken Antimasonic views.

PETER SHAW

In the noun phrase in 7, the punctuation (or, rather, the lack of it) suggests that Adams' son thought that only the Antimasonic views of his father were mistaken, not that all his father's views were both Antimasonic and mistaken. Note that here we cannot interchange the positions of the two adjectives without changing the meaning of the phrase: "his *Antimasonic mistaken* views." Compare the difference between the structures of the two phrases in sentences 6 and 7:

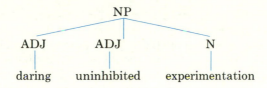

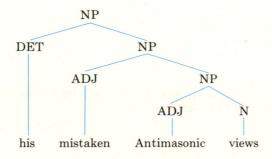

For a means of testing particular noun phrases to determine which structure applies and whether a comma is needed, see Section 9a.

Comma placement in sentences like 6 has only minimal importance in most cases. Writers now use fewer commas than formerly, particularly within noun phrases. Thus, even noun phrases like that in 6 often appear without a comma between the adjectives, even though both adjectives directly modify the headnoun:

8 He wanted to make sure that the truth—the essential elemental truth without which men cannot be restored—should never be lost or distorted.

GERALD VANN

9 Mr. Thompson was a tough weather-beaten man with stiff black hair and a week's growth of black whiskers.

KATHERINE ANNE PORTER

75d   TO SEPARATE COMPOUND SENTENCES

According to the traditional handbook rule, when two sentences are joined by a coordinating conjunction, they are to be separated by a comma. But in few handbooks is the statement unqualified; most say that only "long" sentences should be so punctuated. Thus, we could account for the comma's absence in 1 and its presence in 2 by pointing to the greater length of the joined sentences in 2 (in the examples below, the brackets are included to show each of the sentences joined in the construction):

1 [The sky was a dying violet] and [the houses stood out darkly against it].

FLANNERY O'CONNOR

2 [The current snatched him as though he had been a wisp of grass], and [I saw the body roll over twice before I lost sight of it forever].

JOSEPH CONRAD

But this seemingly simple definition fails. There is no way to determine when a sentence is "long" enough to justify the comma before the conjunction. In example 3, the first of the joined sentences takes more time to say than the first sentence in 2, yet here O'Connor omits a comma where, presumably, Conrad would have placed one:

3 [He preferred its threadbare elegance to anything he could name] and [it was because of it that all the

neighborhoods they had lived in had been a torment
to him].

FLANNERY O'CONNOR

Even the same writer may sometimes use the comma in this position
and sometimes omit it. Note that the following two examples have
exactly the same number of words and the same number of syllables
in their first sentences:

4   [In the fall the war was always there], but [we did
    not go to it any more].
5   [It was cold in the fall in Milan] and [the dark came
    very early].

ERNEST HEMINGWAY

Obviously, we cannot be guided by the "long sentence" rule: to
say that writers used such a guide would mean that often a writer
agreed neither with others nor with himself on what constitutes a
long sentence.

With this instance of comma placement we apparently have a
survival of the "breath pause" system of punctuation: a comma is
placed where the reader would pause if the sentence were read
aloud. But there has been an increased subtlety in employing punctuation to mark pauses—the writer in many cases seems to use (or
not to use) commas and semicolons to vary the pace at which a
sentence moves, often matching in some way the pace of the actions
described in that sentence. In the following example, Elleston Trevor
pictures many things happening simultaneously, pictures movement
and confusion. Because the short sentences are not set apart one
from another by commas, the descriptions of the different actions
are brought as close together as possible; each description crowds
on the heels of the one before, and the reader is moved without
interruption from one of the joined elements to the next:

6   [Then everyone was craning suddenly] and [the mur-
    mur swelled] and [people grabbed at their children
    while the porters struggled to clear the edge of the
    platform].

But it is the lack of punctuation, not the shortness of the sentences,
that sweeps us along. Compare example 7, by the same author,

where the semicolons slow the pace down almost to that of separate sentences ended by periods, although the sentences themselves are very short:

> 7   [It had not succeeded]; [it had not failed]; [there had
> been no ground gained nor any lost]; [there were as
> many dead in the German lines as lay out here under
> the last soft easing of the rain].

When John Fowles wrote *The French Lieutenant's Woman,* he intended the novel to be leisurely, in the Victorian manner. One of the devices he used to give it an unhurried tempo was the joining of many sentences by *both* semicolon and conjunction:

> 8   [His income from his father's estate had always been
> sufficient for his needs]; but [he had not increased
> the capital].

A general description of punctuation for joined sentences would therefore go something like this: a neutral pace, neither fast nor slow—what we might call "normal"—is effected by placing a comma before the conjunction:

> 9a   The pig was eat, and Tom was beat, and Tom went
> crying down the street.

The sense of a faster tempo is reinforced by omitting the commas:

> 9b   The pig was eat and Tom was beat and Tom went
> crying down the street.

Semicolons rather than commas lend a slower than normal pace:

> 9c   The pig was eat; and Tom was beat; and Tom went
> crying down the street.

Slowest of all, of course, would be punctuating each construction as a separate sentence:

> 9d   The pig was eat. And Tom was beat. And Tom went
> crying down the street.

75e WITH DIRECT QUOTATIONS

By convention, direct quotations are separated from the outer sentence by commas:

> 1   Josie said, "There aren't any to find, fellow."
>
>   PETER TAYLOR
>
> 2   "I'm no engineer," Mr. Visconti said. "I cannot judge
>   it practically, but I challenge anyone today to make
>   so beautiful a drawing of a dredge."
>
>   GRAHAM GREENE

Note that when a comma follows quoted matter, as in 2, the comma is placed inside the closing quotation mark.

The University of Chicago *Manual of Style* lists one exception to this practice: when the verb of the outer sentence is *be,* no commas are used, whether the quoted matter precedes or follows the verb:

> 3a   "Business before pleasure" is Walter's motto.
> 3b   Walter's motto is "Business before pleasure."

75f UNNECESSARY COMMAS

Appositives and elements shifted from their normal positions are preceded and followed by commas:

> 1   Captain Zack, whose mechanical skill barely sufficed
>   to open a jar of olives, thereupon burst into tears and
>   hid in his cabin.
>
>   S. J. PERELMAN

But such constructions can also be set off by dashes or enclosed in parentheses:

> 2   Good English—unless *good* is defined circularly as
>   *that which the schools consider good*—is not neces-
>   sarily taught in schools.
>
>   BRADFORD ARTHUR

3 It is not mere chance that Hitler (like his predecessor Wilhelm II) was an enthusiastic disciple of kitsch.

HERMANN BROCH

Only one of these three devices is needed in any one situation. It would be unnecessary duplication, for instance, either to precede or to follow the parentheses in 3 with a comma.

Unless you can justify the placement of a comma by reference to one of the preceding rules, leave it out.

76 SEMICOLON

76a TO SEPARATE ELEMENTS CONTAINING COMMAS

One of the uses of commas is to indicate elements in a series—for example, NP, NP, *and* NP. But if one of these elements already contains a comma, then the separation of the elements by the same punctuation mark may be misleading. We find, then, that when the elements in a series contain commas, the elements are often separated by semicolons:

1a Typical industries relying heavily on chemical engineering include those producing chemicals, polymers, metals, drugs, glass, food, gasoline, rocket fuels, paper, soap, and cement; those producing energy from nuclear fuel; and those processing materials by methods involving chemical reactions.

Note that if we did not have the long string of products in the first element, commas would have been sufficient to separate the members of the series:

1b Typical industries relying heavily on chemical engineering include those producing various consumer goods, those producing energy from nuclear fuel, and those processing materials by methods involving chemical reactions.

76b TO SEPARATE COMPOUND SENTENCES

For a slower than normal pace to a sentence, use a semicolon preceding the conjunction between joined sentences (see Section 75d):

1   What Camp taste responds to is "instant character" (this is, of course, very 18th century); and, conversely, what it is not stirred by is the sense of the development of character.

SUSAN SONTAG

A more common use of the semicolon is to join sentences when the conjunction is omitted:

2a   It belonged to all; they had only to use it well, humbly and with pride.

WILLIAM FAULKNER

3a   Julian was fifteen minutes beforehand at the rendezvous; this annoyed him.

HOWARD NEMEROV

Examples 2a and 3a could equally well have been punctuated with periods at the point of the semicolons, or with commas and coordinating conjunctions:

2b   It belonged to all, and they had only to use it well, humbly and with pride.

3b   Julian was fifteen minutes beforehand at the rendezvous, and this annoyed him.

To use simply a comma in the position of the semicolon in 2a or 2b would be an example of what is sometimes called a comma fault or comma splice. For an explanation of the objections to comma splices, see Section 56d.

77 COLON

77a TO INTRODUCE A LIST, ILLUSTRATION, OR EXAMPLE

The colon indicates a relationship of sense rather than of grammar between the constructions that precede and follow it. In fact, the construction following the colon is sometimes no more than a string of noun phrases. In this usage, the colon serves merely to separate the name of a list from the members of that list:

1   Prerequisites: Math 120, Math 121, and at least junior standing.

The list may not be explicitly named; often, the part before the colon describes the contents of the list. Compare example 2 with a formal list headed with something like "Personal Pronouns with Analogical Genitives."

2   The personal pronouns in *-r* developed new analogical genitive forms in *-es* rather late in Middle English: *hires, oures, youres, heres* (Northern *theires*).

THOMAS PYLES

In addition to introducing a list, the colon may precede a single example or illustration of what the first part of the construction has stated. In example 3, the writer gives some specific situations to support his contention that nothing is truly abstract:

3   Perhaps nothing we do with point or line is ever, in the common meaning of the word, "abstract": the simplest formula or the most abstruse, carried through, turns out to imitate some piece of nature.

HOWARD NEMEROV

Words like *thought, idea, sentence,* and so on, refer to language units or units of something expressible by language. Often, the colon separates two constructions where the first contains one of these words, and the second construction is the unit of language the word refers to:

324

4   I had answered the first question that a poet must
    ask himself: Is this poem necessary?

LOUIS SIMPSON

5   In Part Three we have the result: the simple, practical
    life of the pioneers.

In example 4, Simpson uses the word *question;* following the colon
we have the question itself. Similarly, in example 5 we have the
word *result;* the phrase following the colon tells us what the result
is.

Occasionally we find just the reverse of this usage. The construction before the colon is described or named in the second part:

6   He explained that the extreme of psychological ad-
    justment is suicide: and he saw nothing strange in
    this notion.

WYLIE SYPHER

The *notion* is what precedes the colon; here we have an ordering
of THING: NAME, rather than NAME: THING, as in 4 and 5.

77b   TO INTRODUCE A QUOTATION

In Section 75e, we described the use of the comma to separate
a quotation from the outer sentence:

1   Josie said, "There aren't any to find, fellow."

But sometimes with quotations that form complete sentences, and
especially with extended quotations, a colon separates the introductory construction from the quotation:

2   On March 11, 1952, Albert Einstein wrote to Carl
    Seelig: "Between the conception of the idea of this
    special relativity theory and the completion of the
    corresponding publication, there elapsed five or six
    weeks."

GERALD HOLTON

78b PUNCTUATION

78 PERIOD

78a TO END A DECLARATIVE SENTENCE

The commonest use of the period is to end a grammatically connected group of words that is neither a question nor intended by the writer to have extraordinary emphasis:

> 1 While all the rest were pretty obviously intellectual, he came from a society which hunted birds, animals, and, in his case, girls.
>
> QUENTIN BELL

Periods are also used with sentence fragments, discussed in Section 60.

78b TO END AN INDIRECT QUESTION

A period ends an indirect question—an embedded sentence that begins with an interrogative pronoun but that is phrased in normal word order. Note that in example 1a, the emphasized embedded sentence begins with *how,* but the word order of the sentence differs from that of 1b, where the question is quoted directly:

> 1a He asked me how we would manage with a smaller allotment.
> 1b He asked me, "How would we manage with a smaller allotment?"

Similarly, the indirect question differs from a direct, quoted question in that the DO-INSERTION transformation does not apply to indirect questions. Compare 2a and 2b:

> 2a He asked if Shirley had received her appointment.
> 2b He asked, "Did Shirley receive her appointment?"

78c WITH ELLIPSES

An arbitrary use of periods is to mark the place where something has been omitted from quoted material. To illustrate the use of ellipses, suppose that you want to quote material from part of this sentence:

> 1a "If we limit ourselves to the hallucinogens, however, we usually find that up to half of the students listed as 'users' turn out to have 'used' drugs no more than three times, and have no plans to continue."
>
> KENNETH KENISTON

If you want to quote some, but not all, of this sentence, there are only three possible ways you can abridge it: you can leave some off the beginning, leave some out of the middle, or leave some off the end. If the omission comes at the beginning of the quotation, the place of the omitted material is marked with three spaced periods:

> 1b ". . . We usually find that up to half of the students listed as 'users' turn out to have 'used' drugs no more than three times, and have no plans to continue."

There is one space between the final period of the ellipses and the first letter of the word following it.

Three spaced periods are also used if material is omitted from the middle of the sentence:

> 1c "If we limit ourselves to the hallucinogens, . . . up to half of the students listed as 'users' turn out to have 'used' drugs no more than three times, and have no plans to continue."

Note here that the comma following the introductory adverbial is retained, and a single space is left between it and the first period of the ellipses.

If material is omitted from the end of the quotation, a period is placed immediately after the last word quoted, to end the sentence;

then follow the three periods of the ellipses—four in all:

> **1d** "If we limit ourselves to the hallucinogens, however, we usually find that up to half of the students listed as 'users' turn out to have 'used' drugs no more than three times**. . . .**"

79 QUESTION MARK

The most common use of the question mark, as end punctuation for a question, needs no illustration here. Some of the more infrequent uses, however, give occasional trouble. First, an interrogative sentence sometimes occurs within a declarative sentence as a parenthetical element, an element unconnected to the syntax of the larger sentence. In such a case, it is not correct to speak of "embedded" and "outer" sentences, since the declarative and interrogative do not develop from a common S symbol. The one sentence simply interrupts the other (as shown by the dashes). Here the interrogative is followed by a question mark:

> **1** Thomas Malory—could there have been more than one Thomas Malory?—seems hardly the man to have written *Morte Darthur.*

If a question is quoted directly, the sentence ends with the question mark, within the closing quotation mark:

> **2** The first line of the poem is "I'm nobody! Who are you?"

A question mark follows a doubtful or conjectural date:

> **3a** Miltiades (540?–489? B.C.): Athenian general.

This usage is more often seen in tables or lists than in prose passages. A reader prefers to read words, not symbols, and the appropriate phrasing can indicate the uncertainty of the date:

> **3b** Miltiades, who was born about 540 B.C. and died about 489 B.C., was an Athenian general.

In addition, there are two situations where question marks are omitted. A period, not a question mark, follows an indirect question:

    4   They wanted to know where you were last night.

Usually a period follows a sentence when the sentence is a covert order, expressed as a question only for the sake of courtesy:

    5   Will you please send me another mongoose.

80   EXCLAMATION POINT

The exclamation point follows a sentence intended to have unusually heavy emphasis or indicate unusual excitement. Like underlining a word, the device is not heavily used by capable writers. They do not need to. They rely on their words to lend the sentence the emphasis, the excitement, the surprise, the force, that an exclamation point provides so mechanically. In the whole novel *The Old Man and the Sea,* Hemingway found it necessary to use only one exclamation point.[1] Contrast his practice with the style of comic strips where every sentence ends with an exclamation point, and it is not hard to decide which usage is more effective.

81   HYPHEN

81a   WITH DIVIDED WORDS

When a word must be divided at the end of a line, carrying the end of the word to the beginning of the next line, the place of division is marked by a hyphen. Typesetters use a complex set of rules to decide where to divide words, chiefly so that the reader will not be misled about what word is being divided. The rules are not a matter of concern for your purposes in writing a paper; a few guidelines will suffice:

(1) Do not divide a single-syllable word.

[1] C. P. Heaton, ''Style in *The Old Man and the Sea,*'' *Style,* 4 (Winter 1970). Pp. 22–23.

(2) Do not carry a single syllable to the next line if the syllable represents only a grammatical ending, as in fish-*ing* or lift-*ed*.

(3) Otherwise, divide words at syllable boundaries, as indicated in your dictionary.

81b WITHIN COMPOUND WORDS

There is no certain way of telling whether compound forms should be written as two words (*tar paper*), written with a hyphen (*tar-paper*), or written as a single word (*tarpaper*). The University of Chicago *Manual of Style* says, ''There are, quite literally, scores if not hundreds of . . . rules for the spelling of compound words. Many of them are nearly useless because of the great numbers of exceptions.''[1] Obviously, it makes little sense to pontificate in the face of such confusion. Dropping a hyphen or placing one where it is not usually found is not a matter of great consequence. In the interest of consistency, consult your dictionary whenever the question of the spelling of one of these forms arises. If the compound form needed is not listed there, follow the usage of the most similar compound given.

When the compound form consists of two adjectives, the hyphen can be used to reduce ambiguity. A phrase such as *a slow moving van* could be derived from two sources, either 1 or 2:

1   a van moves slowly
2   a moving van that is slow

If the meaning of example 1 is intended, a hyphen between the two adjectives gives the ·desired result: *a slow-moving van*. On the other hand, for the meaning of example 2, a hyphen between the second adjective and the headnoun will serve: *a slow moving-van*.

82 DASH

Dashes are often used in place of the commas to set off an appositive embedded sentence, full or reduced, especially if that appositive

[1] P. 132.

provides an example or a definition of the noun phrase in the outer sentence:

1 Animals which use their forelimbs extensively—especially tree climbing mammals—have a well developed larynx.

PETER B. DENES AND ELLIOT N. PINSON

2 Along each of these avenues, and along each major side street—116th, 125th, 135th, and so on—bars, stores, pawnshops, restaurants, even little luncheonettes had been smashed open and entered and looted.

JAMES BALDWIN

Note that commas to set off the appositive might prove a source of confusion in 2, because commas are already used to separate several items in a series. The dashes offer an alternative punctuation for appositives when commas must be used for some other purpose.

Dashes are commonly used when the outer sentence and the embedded appositive have equivalent noun phrases, and the embedded appositive repeats the noun phrase in a sentence that further restricts it, defines it in a new sense, or justifies its presence in the sentence:

3 The great artist—or at all events the great literary artist—cannot be a man shallow either in his thoughts or his feelings.

C. S. LEWIS

4 We can look beyond the trivia of daily life—beyond entanglements with wives and children and employers, beyond neighbors, bond issues, tax bills, and the rest.

BENJAMIN DEMOTT

5 I talked with several old-timers—one of them over eighty and a native son—in Sacramento, Placerville, Auburn, and Fresno.

ERIC HOFFER

Dashes frequently set off an appositive that defines any word, not just a noun phrase, at greater length:

6 In spite of this, however, most of us cannot help believing that the philosophers were right—right when

331

they proclaimed, amid all their differences, that most
of the things we bother about are not worth bothering
about.

ROBERT LYND

83 PARENTHESES

The general principle of parentheses is this: we usually think of a
piece of writing as moving in a certain direction; parentheses enclose
material that deviates from the general course of the writing. Parentheses may enclose whole sentences that provide information which,
while having little or nothing to do with the point at hand, is helpful
for comparison:

1 The population of Indian California was small: over
the whole of the state there were probably no more
than a hundred and fifty thousand people, perhaps as
many as two hundred and fifty thousand. (In 1860,
ten years after the beginning of the gold rush, the
white population of the state was already three hundred and ninety thousand.)[1]

THEODORA KROEBER

On the same principle, an embedded appositive containing digressive
material may be enclosed in parentheses rather than set off by
dashes or commas:

2 Salvador Dali (whom, in general, I do not greatly
admire) once made the remark that Picasso's great-
ness consisted in the fact that he had destroyed one
by one all the historical styles of painting.

JOSEPH WOOD KRUTCH

Notice that no commas set off the appositive in example 2: the
parentheses eliminate the need for them. As a general rule, no mark
of punctuation precedes the opening parenthesis.

Parentheses often enclose a phrase, a word, or even figures used
to refresh the reader's memory, direct him to another part of the

---

[1] Note that since the whole sentence is enclosed in parentheses, the period of that
sentence is placed within the closing parenthesis. Compare examples 3, 4, and 5.

same work, point out a conclusion not immediately apparent, or qualify a statement. All these usages are illustrated below:

3   Thus the first sentence is built around a handsome triplet of alliterative abstractions ("the implicit, the imponderable, and the unknown").

WALKER GIBSON

4   For more information on the topic, see the section on single-cell organisms (pp. 328–38).

5   No clearer proof of his hold upon the popular imagination may be seen than what emerged one catastrophic week in March 1955, when New York's WOR-TV programmed *Kong* for seven evenings in a row (a total of sixteen showings).

X. J. KENNEDY

6   When two carriers of the same gene marry and bear children, one quarter of their children (on the average) will be normal, one quarter will be afflicted, and one half will be carriers like themselves.

PETER J. MEDAWAR

84   BRACKETS

Normally, you would use brackets only to enclose material that you insert into quoted matter. There are several reasons why you may need to modify a quotation. The portion you wish to cite may include a pronoun with an antecedent in an earlier, unquoted sentence. In this case, an explanation of the pronoun reference can be supplied in brackets immediately following the pronoun:

1   "She [Mrs. Post] is a considerable imaginative writer, and her book has some of the excitement of a novel."

EDMUND WILSON

A smoother sentence results if you simply substitute the bracketed antecedent for the pronoun:

2   "[Mrs. Post] is a considerable imaginative writer, and her book has some of the excitement of a novel."

If you feel it necessary to provide more information than the quotation does, brackets again enclose your comments:

> 3 "She is a considerable imaginative writer, and her book [*Etiquette,* first published in 1922] has some of the excitement of a novel."

Finally, if you wish to avoid having the reader think that you overlooked an error in the quotation, place the word *sic* (Latin for "thus"—that is, "as it stands in the original") in brackets after the erroneous material:

> 4 "In 1066, after a squabble over rights to the throne, William of Orange [*sic*], a Norman whose claims had been denied, crossed the Channel and conquered 'Englaland.'"

Use brackets to avoid placing parentheses within parentheses. For example, some material in references is customarily placed within parentheses:

> 5 Thomas Pynchon, "A Journey into the Mind of Watts," *The New York Times Magazine* (12 June 1966). Pp. 34–84.

Suppose that you wanted to enclose this citation within the text, in parentheses. The date, already in parentheses, would be enclosed in brackets instead:

> 6 Pynchon discusses the incident that touched off the riots ("A Journey into the Mind of Watts," *The New York Times Magazine* [12 June 1966]. P. 34).

Since brackets do not appear on a standard typewriter keyboard, they may be inserted by hand, or formed with the typewriter slash mark and underline keys above and below the line: [ ] Do not try to get by with parentheses when brackets are called for.

85 QUOTATION MARKS

85a WITH QUOTED MATTER

Quoted matter of any length, from a single word on up, is enclosed in double quotation marks:

> 1 "In human beings as in horses," Lord Birkenhead was moved to comment on the Cecil record, "there is something to be said for the hereditary principle."
>
> BARBARA TUCHMAN

A quotation within a quotation is enclosed in single marks:

> 2 Leacock illustrates his point with an anecdote that ends: "One day on going in to luncheon it was discovered that there were thirty guests present, whereas the table only held covers for twenty-one. 'Oh well,' said the Duke, not a whit abashed, 'some of us will have to eat standing up.'"

If a third level of quotation is used, it is enclosed once again in double quotation marks.

85b BLOCK QUOTATIONS

Quotations of prose that extend longer than seven or eight lines are often set as a block quotation: each line of the block quotation is indented from the left margin a space at least equal to the space for paragraph indentation. Quotation marks are omitted when the excerpted material is set as a block:

> 1 Greenough and Kittredge then propose a test, proving whether language is inherently poetical:
>
> > Literature has been attentively studied, as *literature*, for hundreds and even thousands of years. Hence there has grown up among scholars a set of

technical terms—the names of the so-called "figures of speech"—which designate what are commonly regarded as the ornaments or devices that characterize the poetical style.

Two lines of poetry, and sometimes parts of three lines, are usually not set off, but run into the text, enclosed in double quotation marks, with a slash marking the end of the lines:

2   Just as baseball box-scores have a place for errors, poetry needs a place for memorable stumbles, like the lines from Wordsworth's "Peter Bell": "Once more the Ass, with motion dull, / Upon the pivot of his skull / Turned round his long left ear."

Three or more lines of poetry are usually set as a block quotation:

3   Thomas Holley Chivers, an imitator of Poe (or vice-versa), let his passion for exotic-sounding words carry him beyond reasonable limits:

> In the music of the morns,
> Blown through Conchimarian horns,
> Down the dark vistas of the reboantic Norns,
> To the Genius of Eternity,
> Crying: "Come to me! Come to me!"

When quoting poetry in block form, adhere as closely as possible to the poem's stanza form or pattern of indentation:

4   Eliza Cook's poetry provides an example of the sort of verse likely to be rewarded with a government pension in the nineteenth century:

> There's a mission, no doubt, for the mole in the dust,
>   As there is for the charger, with nostrils of pride;
> The sloth and the newt have their places of trust,
>   And the agents are needed, for God has supplied.

85c   WITH DIALOGUE

Enclose dialogue in double quotation marks. The words of each speaker are considered a paragraph in themselves, no matter how short the statement, and indentation signals that a new speaker is talking, as in this Hemingway passage:

"That girl with the phony title who was so rude and that silly drunk with her. They said they were friends of yours."

"They are. And she *is* very rude sometimes."

"You see. There's no use to make mysteries simply because one has drunk a few glasses of wine. Why did you want to make the mysteries? It isn't the sort of thing I thought you would do."

"I don't know." I wanted to drop it. Then I thought of something. "Were they rude about your tie?" I asked.

"Why should they have been rude about my tie? I was wearing a plain black knitted tie with a white polo shirt."

85d   WITH WORDS USED IN A SPECIAL SENSE

Words used in a special sense, a sense different from their ordinary use, are often enclosed in quotation marks:

In fact, looking at the broadened part of the Milky Way in the region of Sagittarius you would think first that the mythical celestial road branches here into two "one-way traffic lanes."

GEORGE GAMOV

Since Gamov had previously compared the appearance of the Milky Way to a road, the traffic lane analogy was not unexpected, but obviously he is not talking about literal one-way streets. If he continued to use the comparison, no quotation marks would be necessary the second time he wrote of one-way traffic lanes, since the special sense in which the phrase is used has already been established.

85e WITH NAMES OF PARTS OF WORKS

When a book has chapters or sections with titles, these titles are enclosed in double quotation marks. On the same principle, articles, essays, or reviews in periodicals are enclosed in double quotation marks:

1 He got the idea from "The Modern Theory of Politics," Part Two of *The Structure of Political Thought*.
2 I read it in the "Scorecard" section of *Sports Illustrated* for 2 November 1970.
3 The latest *Papers in Linguistics* has an article on the subject "Constraints on Constituent Ordering."

85f WITH OTHER PUNCTUATION

Arbitrarily, periods and commas are always placed inside a closing quotation mark:

1 Such is perhaps the most frequently underlying reason why expressions are approved of or objected to as "euphonious" or "cacophonous," "harmonious" or "inharmonious."

W. K. WIMSATT

Colons and semicolons, on the other hand, always follow a closing quotation mark:

2 The grammarian then resorts to "prefabrication": a sentence put together not to communicate but to illustrate grammar.
3 There was such a complex event as "Charles I's death on the scaffold"; hence the judgment "Charles I died on the scaffold" is true.

BERTRAND RUSSELL

The placement of exclamation points and question marks depends on the syntax: if the construction within the quotation marks is an exclamation or a question, then the end punctuation goes inside the closing quotation mark. If the whole sentence, not just the part within quotation marks, is an exclamation or a question, the end punctuation is placed outside the closing quotation mark:

4 Fans close to the field began to yell "Foul!"
5 Pilate answered, "What is Truth?"
6 Did she ask anything about "The Miller's Tale"?

86 APOSTROPHE

86a WITH OMITTED LETTERS

The original use of the apostrophe in English was to show where letters or numbers were omitted in contractions; we still retain this use in *isn't, aren't, can't, there's* (there is), *sou'wester* (southwester), the class of *'73,* and so on:

I'll take these two big lads, as does nought but fight, home to my missis for tonight, and I'll get a jug o' tea.

ELIZABETH GASKELL

86b WITH GENITIVES

An apostrophe is also found in modern English with noun phrases in their genitive forms: *General Electric's* new air conditioner, *Sheila's* uncle, *today's* special. (See Section 11 for an explanation of the genitive.) It is likely that this use of the apostrophe also springs from a desire to mark omitted letters: when the practice of using apostrophes with genitives began in the sixteenth century, phrases like *John his brother* also occurred. Early grammarians may have erroneously thought that a phrase like *John's brother* was a shortening of *John his brother,* and therefore used the apostrophe to mark the "missing" letters. That this explanation would not account for *Mary's brother* apparently did not occur to them.

Spelling words in the genitive form is simple: with noun phrases that do not end in *s,* simply add *'s* to the phrase: *Bath + 's →*

Bath's;   *women* + *'s* → *women's;*   *Sheila* + *'s* → *Sheila's;*
husband + *'s* → *husband's*. In current usage, noun phrases that
end in *s* show some variation in the way they form the genitive.
However, from material in the Brown Corpus (Section 67), a simple
rule, followed by the great majority of American writers and editors,
may be stated: if the word to which *'s* is to be joined already ends
in *s* (no matter whether the word is singular or plural), add only the
apostrophe: *Moses* + *'s* → *Moses';*   *Jones* + *'s* → *Jones';*
Paris + *'s* → *Paris'; princess* + *'s* → *princess'; princesses* + *'s* →
princesses'.

86c   WITH PLURALS OF SYMBOLS

There is one final arbitrary use of the apostrophe: it is used in forming
the plural of symbols—that is, letters, numbers, and words as words:

1   The children learned about 3's and M's on *Sesame
    Street* today.
2   Krupp's most pleasant surprise was the astonishing
    versatility of the six batteries of 88's he had contrib-
    uted to Franco.

WILLIAM MANCHESTER

3   Legal writing is studded with *shall's*.

The use of the apostrophe with symbols may be diminishing; we often
find plurals of these symbols written with just an *s:*

4   The documents don't specify whether American B-52s
    and F-111s, or the mosquito-like Cambodian T-28s
    supplied by the United States, are supposed to attack
    the hospitals.

JACK ANDERSON

87   ITALICS

Italics (or underlining, the equivalent in typewriting), have four uses,
the most common of which is to distinguish titles of published works.

"Published works" has a very broad meaning here: it includes books, plays, movies, television shows, reports, speeches, and so on:

> 1 In the school of Philosophical Bawdry, so prominent in our fiction during the past decade, *Giles Goat-Boy* is probably the best American example so far.
>
> HAYDEN CARRUTH

> 2 NBC will bring back its noteworthy *Experiment in Television* series for a short run on Sunday afternoons starting January 24.
>
> NEIL HICKEY

Names of ships, airplanes, trains, and so on, are similarly italicized:

> 3 And it had been just our evil luck that the *S. S. Campari* had called in at Savannah on the afternoon of the day the crime had been committed.
>
> ALISTAIR MACLEAN

A second use of italics is the marking of foreign words and phrases. As a foreign word becomes "naturalized"—more and more familiar to readers of English—it is less and less likely to be italicized. Up-to-date dictionaries can give you some aid in determining whether a particular word is commonly italicized.

> 4 Historians say that the post-impressionists expressed the *Zeitgeist* of the late nineteenth century, but at that time they were scarcely known.
>
> LESTER D. LONGMAN

Third, a word being referred to as a word—in a definition, say—is commonly italicized:

> 5 *Simile* is involved in the great class of English adjectives that end in *-ly*, which is an abraded form of *like*.
>
> GREENOUGH AND KITTREDGE

> 6 *Occasion* is found on most lists of difficult words to spell.

A fourth function of italics involves adding emphasis to a word or phrase. Italics or underlining provides a mechanical means of giving a word an appearance different from that of the words around it; the difference in appearance catches the reader's attention, just as heavy stress on the word would arrest the hearer's attention if the sentence were spoken:

> 7 Is government by the people *practicable* in the world as it is today and as it is likely to become?
>
> MORTIMER ADLER

> 8 It is the only case we know of in which the Nazis met with *open* native resistance, and the result seems to have been that those exposed to it changed their minds.
>
> HANNAH ARENDT

A writer can make good use of italics for emphasis—but there is a limit: its value lies in its relative rarity. Employ the device too much and you ruin its effectiveness. Consider what a page of prose would look like if every noun were set in italics: the typeface of each noun would resemble that of every other noun, and no one of them would strike the reader's eyes with more force than any other. To be effective, the use of italics for emphasis should be sparing.

88 ABBREVIATIONS

88a TITLES

When followed by a proper name, certain titles are almost always abbreviated: *Mr., Messrs., Mrs., Mmes., Dr.,* and *St.* (*Saint*). Other titles are usually spelled out:

> 1 In the study Father Rothschild and Mr. Outrage were plotting with enthusiasm.
>
> EVELYN WAUGH

2 Professor Richards can reasonably take for granted
that he agrees too.

WILLIAM EMPSON

The new title *Ms.,* used by some to replace *Mrs.* or *Miss,* has no full form, and is not therefore an actual abbreviation. It will probably find most use in name plates, addresses, the salutations of letters, and the like. The lack of an unabbreviated form should not itself prove a handicap, since there is seldom occasion to spell out other comparable titles.

After proper names, use *Sr., Jr.,* and the abbreviated forms of academic titles: *M.A., Ph.D.,* and so on:

3 Anne Askew, M.D., specializes in pediatrics.

88b DATES AND TIMES

With dates and numbers, use the abbreviated forms A.D., B.C., A.M., P.M. (sometimes a.m., p.m.):

> At the beginning of this story, round about 4000 B.C.,
> there was no civilized community living anywhere on
> earth.

LEONARD COTTRELL

88c ORGANIZATIONS AND UNITS OF MEASURE

The names of familiar organizations, some units of measure, governmental agencies, and so on, are usually abbreviated (without periods): *AFL–CIO, BTU, mph, HEW, UNESCO.*

1 Hoover disapproved of intercepting letters for reasons
that make the ACLU blush.

MARY MCGRORY

With new or infrequently used abbreviations of this kind, present practice is to spell out the term fully the first time it is used, enclosing the abbreviation in parentheses immediately following the name:

> 2 In Boston, where the temperature reached 97 degrees, the New England Power Exchange (NEPEX) reduced power by 5 percent for four hours in the afternoon.
>
> UNITED PRESS INTERNATIONAL

Subsequent uses of the same name are simply abbreviated, as in example 3, which followed example 2:

> 3 A spokesman said the reduction was ordered because NEPEX had provided the New York City power pool with needed voltage.

88d   TERMS SELDOM ABBREVIATED

When used as parts of a sentence, the following terms are almost never abbreviated: proper names and parts of proper names, such as the words *Street* and *Company;* units of time, such as days of the week and months; familiar units of measure, such as *feet, inches,* and *pounds;* and, except in footnotes and bibliographies, the words *Chapter, page, verse,* and *Volume:*

> On Tuesday, March 13, Charles copied Chapter Three of *Moby Dick* onto a scroll eight feet long, and mailed it to the New Depths Publishing Company on Staunton Avenue in Fulton, Missouri.

89   CAPITALIZATION

89a   PROPER NAMES

Words used as proper names or parts of proper names are capitalized. "Proper name" here includes the names of persons, states, and countries, of course, but it also covers the name of any specifically identifiable entity: a topographical feature, such as the *Mississippi;* a historical period—the *Renaissance;* ships, planes, monuments, and the like:

1 Libra Exploratory Mission Base, come in please, this is Passerine launch.

URSULA K. LE GUIN

2 Symmetry is an accident of disorder, yet accident is the order of non-symmetry—what Hans Arp calls the "Laws of Chance," or the scientist approximates with his "Second Law of Thermodynamics."

RICHARD LIPPOLD

When preceding a name, titles are thought of as part of that name, and are therefore capitalized. Following a name, titles are not capitalized, since they become merely descriptive terms:

3 The following year he entered the service of Cardinal Luigi d'Este in Ferrara. . . . One of his critics [was] Silvio Antoniano, professor of eloquence in Rome and a future cardinal.

JOHN CHARLES NELSON

Titles of literary, musical, or graphic works, student papers, movies, television shows, and the like, identify their particular works; capitalize the first word in the title and all succeeding words except articles, short prepositions, and conjunctions:

4 The German scholar Joachim Jeremias in his pamphlet "The Lord's Prayer" and his book, *The Central Message of the New Testament,* makes much of the word *abba*.

ANDREW M. GREELEY

5 Take for another example that picture of Seurat's which I saw two years ago in Chicago—"La Grande Jatte."

E. M. FORSTER

345

89b WORDS DERIVED FROM PROPER NAMES

Words derived from proper names are often capitalized: *McLuhanism, Sapphic, Appalachian;* yet the practice of modern writers may vary from word to word. In the sentence that follows, it is hard to say, for example, why *Hebraism* is capitalized while *puritanism* is not:

> 1   His peculiar and characteristic blend of classicism, romanticism, puritanism, modernism, individualism, Hebraism, Hellenism, Republicanism, egoism, indignation, sensuous aestheticism, and passion for a liberty of speech and thought . . . made him an arrogant, self-dedicated solitary, a superb and monstrous alien.
>
>   **ROSE MACAULAY**

There are some guidelines that can be followed in this maze, however: words derived from the proper names of places seem always to be capitalized:

> 2   Both the Russian and the American in those positions are subject to the common delusion that those two entities comprise the entire world or at least the entire world that matters.
>
>   **FRANK GETLEIN**

About the only exception to this practice occurs with the names of regions—the *Midwest,* the *Northeast*—where derived forms may or may not be capitalized:

> 3   As integrated school systems were introduced in most southern districts, many black teachers were fired or transferred to lower-level jobs.
>
>   **VERNON E. JORDAN, JR.**

There seems to be a practice of capitalizing words derived from proper names when they are used as adjectives (*Leibnizian, Byronic*) but not when used as other parts of speech (*raglan, macintosh, macadamize*). This practice carries over into scientific writing, where names used as adjectives are capitalized (*Mach* speed. *Curie* point), while names used as nouns for units of measurement are not (*curie, hertz, joule, roentgen).* When a particular word is in question, the safest guide in this matter is your dictionary.

89c   FIRST WORD IN A SENTENCE

The first word of a sentence (including quoted sentences) is capitalized:

1   But all I could say was "It's not true. It's just not true."

SUSAN HOWATCH

2   His questions had invariably been answered with the infuriating *What will be will be.*

PHILIP JOSE FARMER

When only parts of sentences are quoted, their first words are not capitalized:

3   Freud can thus define psychoanalysis as "nothing more than the discovery of the unconscious in mental life."

NORMAN O. BROWN

90   NUMBERS

Numbers should be given as figures unless they can be spelled out in one or two words:

1   Find ten errors in this paragraph.
2   Find 135 errors in this paragraph.

In a sentence that cites several numbers, if one has to be in figures, put them all in figures for consistency:

3   There were 3 errors in the first paragraph, 13 in the second, and 488 in the last.

Some single-word numbers are always given in figures: the time, when A.M. or P.M. is used; addresses; percentages; and dates: *12:30 A.M.; 14* Union Street; 7 percent; June *17, 1973* (or) *17* June *1973.*

Exercises

1. Pretend that you are an editor at Harcourt Brace Jovanovich responsible for getting manuscripts ready for publication. Suppose further that you receive a manuscript containing the material below. Try, using the comments on punctuation and typographical devices in Sections 75 to 90, to prepare these passages for the typesetter. Your instructor will supply you with references to the sections of this text where you can compare your finished effort with what the actual editor did.

   1 modern punctuation although streamlined by comparison with that of years past still has its sharp edges and hidden crevices primarily it shows grammatical structure but it still retains traces of the old oral reading system to these two purposes have been added again rather recently certain marks that neither indicate a syntactic construction nor allow a pause for breathing but are wholly arbitrary we hyphenate some words for instance because everybody does it unfortunately the same mark is often made to serve more than one of these purposes in one instance it sets off a grammatical unit in another it indicates a pause for breath in still a third its use is a matter of convention to aid the student who is trying to correct a paper the pages that follow are organized according to the mark of punctuation first come all the uses of commas then those of semicolons and so on but in each section the purpose of a particular usage will be given together with some indication of its importance

   2 the sentence as it is written or spoken is organized by the surface structure it seems that we understand surface structures because we know two things we know all the meaningful elements as they are organized by the deep structure even though all the elements may not appear on the surface and we know the changes necessary to convert the deep structure to the surface structure the exact nature

of deep structure is a matter of controversy among language investigators at the deepest level it may turn out that the organization of language is unlike anything in this book if that is the case the grammar that this book assumes is simply that of an intermediate level but since important insights are yielded our analysis will have value no matter how deep our deep structure is

3   it has often been noted that many perhaps most americans feel guilty about their language an english teacher who is supposed to be the umpire of usage continually hears people say i know i don't talk as well as i should but such people accept as facts of nature the inferiority of their pronunciation and grammar they live in a mudville of the mind where pronunciation is slovenly where the best writers make common errors and where the english language is ever threatened by linguistic chaos

2. Occasionally a reader runs across a book using a slightly different system of punctuation. European typesetters, for example, employ their own set of conventions. Some of these are illustrated in the passage below, from James Joyce's short story "The Dead." Point out the major differences between the system of punctuation in the selection and the system you are familiar with:

> She raised her head from her arms and dried her eyes with the back of her hand like a child. A kinder note than he had intended went into his voice.
> —Why, Gretta? he asked.
> —I am thinking about a person long ago who used to sing that song.
> —And who was the person long ago? asked Gabriel smiling.
> —It was a person I used to know in Galway when I was living with my grandmother, she said.
> The smile passed away from Gabriel's face. A dull anger began to gather again at the back of his mind and the dull fires of his lust began to glow angrily in his veins.
> —Someone you were in love with? he asked ironically.

3. Section 74 discussed the three kinds of punctuation in modern English; we have marks that indicate a breath pause, marks that show some unit of grammar in the sentence, and marks that are completely arbitrary conventions. Identify the marks of punctua-

tion in the next passage and classify them as to which of the three kinds they are:

Afterward, over a cup of tea in the red *sala,* Mrs. Moreno told her that the ladies had accepted her as an unlooked-for gift, more delightful for being so improbably what they wanted and so neatly timed. Like successful collaborators, they smiled at each other, enumerating fringe benefits as they occurred to either one of them.

"So I can have most of the day when the light is good enough for painting—"

"If you look on the evenings as amusement rather than work—"

"Of course, a ready-made social life—"

"—with very nice people. At least the Filipinos will be of good family. Who knows? You might meet someone—"

"You're incorrigible! Whom could I meet? A lonely soldier? A good bridge partner?"

"Not necessarily a *bridge* partner," Mrs. Moreno said naughtily.

SANTHA RAMA RAU

Code:
The
Language

SECTIONS **91-96**

In the section on grammar we pretended that there existed a perfect English, an ideal kind of language where speakers could always unequivocally label a construction as right or wrong. We pretended further that when a construction was judged ungrammatical, it had that status under all conditions, for all speakers, and in all situations. Finally, we pretended that anyone with equal information and sufficient reflection would agree with our judgments. Of course, none of these suppositions is true.

English is not a kind of sausage, exactly the same no matter where we cut it. Most of us distinguish at least two varieties—good and bad. But the varieties of English are many, and distinguishable in several ways. The first set of distinctions we want to examine is that covered by the term "dialect."

91 DIALECT

If we take people at their word, no one in the United States speaks a dialect. We associate the term with people who are "quaint," who live in out-of-the-way places, poling flat-bottomed skiffs through swamps or whittling whimmy-diddles to sell to tourists. As Raven I. McDavid, Jr., notes, scholars investigating regional dialects are always being told, "We don't speak no dialect around hyur; if you want *rale* dialect you gotta go down into Hellhole Swamp!"[1] The fact is that every one of us speaks slightly differently from every other speaker of English throughout the world.

The way a particular individual talks is called his "idiolect." But on closer investigation we find that many features of his speech are also found in the speech of his neighbors, but not in the speech of, say, the people in the next state. When we examine the speech of a particular region, we find that its people have in common certain pronunciations, certain meanings, and certain syntactic constructions. Since the speakers share these features, and since we can define the group geographically, we say that they speak a particular "regional dialect."

On further investigation we find that some features of an individual's speech are found in the speech of his neighbors of the same economic class, but not in the speech of those who are much richer

---

[1] "Sense and Nonsense About American Dialects," *PMLA*, 81, No. 2 (May 1966). P. 10.

or much poorer. In this way—analyzing speech not by region, but largely by the particular rung of society in which it occurs—we can distinguish "social dialects."

In brief, every American speaks a dialect—or, more accurately, several dialects, depending on which system of classification one uses. There is no such thing as "Standard American English." The misguided person who succeeds in eradicating from his speech all traces of regional pronunciation would be rewarded by sounding like a foreigner.

But can we consider one of the dialects of American English as a standard because it is in some way better? Before we answer that question, we have to consider another: what do we mean when we say that one dialect is "better" than another?

It might be argued that the preferred dialect, the one we want to call standard, is better because it *sounds* better—because its sounds are more pleasing, more beautiful, than those of the other dialects. But this can hardly be maintained:

> Beauty in linguistic forms is due to the associations they arouse. Such a form as "goil" is ugly only if the hearer happens to dislike Brooklyn. To realize the truth of this statement, one has only to consider variants where we have no such associations. If a child in the New Mexican pueblo of Santa Clara puts the sentence "I am going to town" in the form *bupiyeummang,* the "ugly" pronunciation is immediately corrected to *bupijeummang.* The Tewa parents are not being merely arbitrary; they are objecting to an unacceptable dialect. I doubt if any English speaker can seriously maintain that he finds one Tewa form more beautiful than the other.[2]

This is not to say, obviously, that people do not prefer the sound of one dialect over that of another. Quite clearly they do. But these preferences are matters of taste; the "beauty" or "ugliness" is in the ear of the listener, not in the mouth of the speaker. It is folly of the silliest sort to attempt to change someone's pronunciation to a "more euphonious" sound.

A second argument in favor of recognizing a particular dialect as standard is based more on syntax than on sound. It goes like this:

[2] Archibald A. Hill, "Correctness and Style in English Composition," *A Linguistics Reader,* ed. Graham Wilson. New York: Harper & Row, 1967. P. 50.

dialect *X* is better than dialect *Y* because certain grammatical distinctions are made in *X* that are not made in *Y*. While this argument shows a little more sophistication than the one based on ''beautiful sounds,'' it is equally invalid. If one man says, ''I have three *brother*,'' while another says, ''I have three *brothers*,'' both have the concept of plurality in their dialects. The first speaker, however, has a rule in his dialect that prevents the plural forms of nouns from occurring after numbers. If we can argue that the second dialect is better because *brothers* shows plurality, we can just as easily argue that the second dialect is worse because the plural *brothers* is redundant after the number three. Neither argument would be correct.

As far as is known, anything that can be said in one dialect or language can be said in another dialect or language. There are no untranslatable concepts. All that we can say is that some languages and dialects express certain distinctions as part of their system, while other languages or dialects express those distinctions only as they are needed. As an example, consider the English sentence *I read the book*. The sentence would have precisely the same form regardless of whether the speaker was a man or a woman. But that sentence in Russian would have the form *Ya chital knigu* if the speaker is a man, and *Ya chitala knigu* if the speaker is a woman. In other words, an indication of whether the speaker is a man or a woman is part of the Russian past tense verb system. That information is expressed every time a speaker of Russian uses the first person singular pronoun as the subject of a past tense verb. Obviously, the same meaning could be conveyed in English: *I, a man, read the book; I, a woman, read the book*. But is Russian more precise because it makes this distinction all the time? No. Is English more concise because it makes this distinction only when necessary? No. The systems of grammar of the two languages are simply different, and what holds for separate languages holds for dialects of the same language: their grammars are simply different, and by no known yardstick can we measure whether one grammar is better than another.

A final argument for a standard is based on literary classics. If we do not insist on a standard dialect, so the argument goes, we will cut ourselves off from great works of literature. This line of thinking has two flaws: first, it overestimates the differences between American dialects. The differences that do exist are neither so many nor so profound that they impair mutual intelligibility. Second, the proponents of the argument have not really thought deeply about the literary works they think they are defending, especially the American works. If we wanted to select the greatest American novel, many votes would be cast for *The Adventures of Huckleberry Finn,* which is written in dialect from beginning to end. Apparently the dialect of the Okies in *The Grapes of Wrath* did not deter the Nobel judges from awarding the prize for literature to its author, John Steinbeck. Even the works of Henry James can be considered to exhibit a highly artificial dialect, found only in writing.

From an objective point of view, then, all dialects are equal. But one of the truest statements that can be made about American manners is that many people believe that a speaker's dialect tells you something about his intelligence, his character, or his ability. And one of the saddest statements that can be made about American education is that this widely held belief is untrue.

One final point: If all that we have said here about dialects is true, what about the grammar in the first part of this book? Sentences are called grammatical or ungrammatical on nearly every page. Doesn't that imply a standard against which the constructions of other dialects are judged? Again, the answer is no. When a transformational grammarian makes a decision about the grammaticality of a sentence, he is in most cases talking about the status of that sentence *in his own idiolect.* Whether his comment is applicable to a wider class of speakers is a judgment that each reader must make.

The systematic study of English dialects is barely a century old. The study of social dialects in the United States is much younger still. Great gaps in our knowledge wait to be filled. Students who speak a stigmatized dialect can best help themselves and the cause of learning by serious investigation of the grammar of their own speech.

91a   REGIONAL DIALECTS

Ideally, the study of American dialects should begin with the study of British regional dialects, as settlers from different parts of England brought their various dialects with them to the New World. Yet correlations of this kind are difficult to make, largely because of gaps in our knowledge of English folk speech at the time of the settlements.[1]

[1] See, for example, Hans Kurath, "British Sources of Selected Features of American Pronunciation: Problems and Methods," *Readings in American Dialectology,* ed. H. B. Allen and G. N. Underwood. New York: Appleton-Century-Crofts, 1971. Pp. 265–72.

Whatever their counties of origin, though, the settlers carried their dialectal differences with them as the colonies extended their territories westward. The history of their movements is often illustrated by the study of present-day dialects.

Beginning in the 1930s and continuing to the present, a vast amount of painstaking fieldwork has succeeded in showing the dialect regions of much of the eastern half of the United States. The map on page 357 shows the three large dialect regions of American English, and the subdivisions within them. The Northern dialect area includes all of New England, the northern part of New Jersey, and the northernmost counties of Pennsylvania. The Midland dialect area embraces the rest of New Jersey and Pennsylvania, and the northern parts of Delaware, Maryland, and Virginia. It then spreads southwest through the valleys of the Appalachians. The Southern dialect area covers the rest of Virginia and North and South Carolina, as far west as the mountains. Listed below are just a few of the many characteristics in pronunciation, vocabulary, and syntax used to distinguish the various areas.

THE NORTHERN DIALECT (REGIONS 1–6)[2]

PRONUNCIATION

> *with:* the final sound is voiced—that is, it is the same as the first sound in *though,* rather than the first sound in *thought*
> *grease, greasy:* with the final sound of *cease.* rather than *seize*
> *roots:* has the vowel sound of *boots.*

VOCABULARY

> *pail:* (Midland and Southern *bucket*)
> *swill:* ''garbage'' (Midland and Southern *slop*)
> *brook:* ''small stream'' (rare in Inland North)

SYNTAX

> *dove:* as past tense of *dive*
> *see:* as past tense (not heard from well-educated informants)
> *sick to the stomach*

THE MIDLAND DIALECT (REGIONS 7–13)

PRONUNCIATION

> *r:* pronounced after vowels

[2] The material that follows is from W. Nelson Francis and Raven I. McDavid, Jr., *The Structure of American English.* New York: Ronald Press, 1958. Pp. 512–22.

THE REGIONAL DIALECTS OF THE UNITED STATES

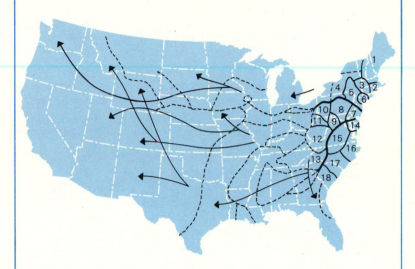

Atlantic Seaboard areas identified below; black dashed lines mark tentative boundaries; arrows indicate direction of migrations.

THE NORTH

1. Northeastern New England

2. Southeastern New England

3. Southwestern New England

4. Inland North (Western Vermont, Upstate New York, and derivatives)

5. The Hudson Valley

6. Metropolitan New York

THE MIDLAND

7. Delaware Valley (Philadelphia)

8. Susquehanna Valley

9. Upper Potomac and Shenandoah

10. Upper Ohio Valley (Pittsburgh)

11. Northern West Virginia

12. Southern West Virginia and Eastern Kentucky

13. Western Carolina and Eastern Tennessee

THE SOUTH

14. Delmarva (Eastern Shore)

15. Virginia Piedmont

16. Northeastern North Carolina (Albemarle Sound and Neuse Valley)

17. Cape Fear and Peedee Valleys

18. South Carolina Low Country (Charleston)

with: the final sound is voiceless—that is, it is the same as the first sound in *thought*

VOCABULARY

blinds: ''window shades''
skillet: ''frying pan''
green-beans: ''string beans''

SYNTAX

you-uns: second person plural (heard from older, poorly educated speakers, and from some younger, better-educated speakers)
want off: for *want to get off* as in *I want off at Tenth Street*
quarter till (in telling time)

THE SOUTHERN DIALECT (REGIONS 14–18)

PRONUNCIATION

r: words in Midland region pronounced with *r* are here pronounced without *r* except before vowels
Mrs: pronounced *miz*

VOCABULARY

chittlins: ''edible intestines''
harp, mouth harp: ''harmonica'' (except in Charleston)
snap beans: ''string beans''

SYNTAX (heard mostly from older, poorly educated informants)

heern tell (also Northeastern New England)
on account of: as in ''I like him *on account of* he's so funny''
all two, all both: for *both*

91b SOCIAL DIALECTS

Despite its limitations, our knowledge about regional dialects is vast in comparison with what is known about social dialects. From the beginning of the dialect surveys of the eastern states in the 1930s, the attempt was made to sample the usage of three distinct social groups. Informants were listed as one of the following:

Type I: Little formal education, little reading, and restricted social contacts

Type II: Better formal education (usually high school) and/or wider reading and social contacts

Type III: Superior education (usually college), cultured background, wide reading, and/or extensive social contacts.[1]

Although some conclusions about social dialects can be drawn from this material, we are limited by the reliance of the survey on just one measure of social class—education. Yet social groups are definable by other standards—for example, wealth versus poverty, or travel versus isolation.

Students of dialect have begun to investigate one special area—the English spoken by many American blacks. Unlike the children of European immigrants, who were physically indistinguishable from the children of the oldest families, American blacks—marked by their color, suppressed by slavery, denied education, and segregated by law and custom—were forced into isolation from the larger society around them. This isolation, even in the hearts of cities, contained all the factors needed to preserve a distinctive dialect. The investigation of American black dialects is currently one of the most exciting and controversial fields of language study.

It is necessary at this point to stress that American black dialects are not racial dialects. Nothing in the physiology of blacks (or any other race, for that matter) makes them speak in a distinctive way. Probably hundreds of thousands of blacks speak the same regional dialect as others in their area. Yet greater numbers speak dialects born in and preserved by their enforced isolation.

Increased knowledge will probably allow the dialectologist to define several varieties of Black English. It would be astonishing if millions of people, spread through a country the size of the United States, did not show regional variation in their speech. Yet given the present infancy of dialect studies, we can only state that there appears to be more than one dialect of Black English.

Recent studies trace the origin of American black dialects to pidgin or trade languages common among the slavers of the West African coast in the seventeenth century. There is evidence that at least some of the slaves spoke a pidgin English before their importation to America. In the century that followed, increasing numbers of native-born blacks grew up speaking a creole English that contained elements from both English and the languages of their West African

---

[1] E. Bagby Atwood, "The Methods of American Dialectology," *Readings In American Dialectology*, ed. H. B. Allen and G. N. Underwood. New York: Appleton-Century-Crofts, 1971. Pp. 12–13.

homelands. Speaking about current dialects, William A. Stewart says, "At least some of the particular syntactic features of American Negro dialects are neither skewings nor extensions of white dialect patterns, but are in fact structural vestiges of an earlier plantation creole, and ultimately of the original slave-trade pidgin English which gave rise to it."[2]

Exercise

In the correspondence below, from The Los Angeles Times Syndicate (29 April 1973), what responsibility is the writer from Jamaica taking on herself? What does she mean by the word *wrong* in her last sentence? Does Amy Vanderbilt appear to agree with her?

> Dear Miss Vanderbilt: I have a girlfriend who speaks of "making" her daughter's wedding. It sounds funny to me, but a number of her friends use the same expression. How can I explain to her that it is wrong?
>
> JAMAICA, N.Y.
>
> I have written about this before. The expression puzzled me, and I thought that it was a translation from the German, that perhaps it came from people with a German background. I found that this was not the case. The expression "to make a wedding" or "to make a party" seems to be a direct translation from Yiddish. Perhaps the best thing is to show this column to your friend.

Some other questions that might be explored are these: What is the relationship between German and Yiddish? Is Miss Vanderbilt factually correct about the origins of the phrase? Why, do you think, did the writer of the letter show an uncanny appropriateness in sending it to Amy Vanderbilt?

92 LEVELS OF USAGE

When we turn from regional and social dialects to the different ways of speaking and writing each individual has, we are turning to "levels

[2] "Continuity and Change in American Negro Dialects," *Contemporary English: Change and Variation,* ed. David L. Shores. Philadelphia: J. B. Lippincott, 1972. P. 104. See also Stewart's "Sociolinguistic Factors in the History of American Negro Dialects," in the same volume, pp. 86–95. The two taken together are a brief but well-done introduction to the study of American black dialects.

of usage'' or ''styles,'' but whatever term we use, we recognize that the language of *True Teen Romances* is not the same as that of *The Ecclesiastical Review.*

Why levels of usage exist at all is a difficult question to answer. A very old theory maintains that different subject matters have appropriately different styles; thus, a ''high style'' suits subjects of epic sweep and grandeur, while a ''low style'' suits matters of a domestic or comic nature. Another theory says that the level of usage is determined by the age or status of its intended audience. A third holds that the occasion influences the work's level of usage. Certainly all of these are partially true, at least, and there may be many other reasons for the differences we feel. But to recognize and use different styles, we need first a system of classifying them, simply to know what we are talking about.

It should be mentioned that it is not (and never was) sufficient to simply check a dictionary for enlightenment on levels of usage, for often the label indicating level will differ from dictionary to dictionary. Suppose you wanted to know whether *mad* in the sense of ''enthusiastic about'' should be used in an essay you are writing. If you consult *Webster's New Collegiate Dictionary,* eighth edition, or *The Random House Dictionary,* you will find no restrictive label. On the other hand, if you check *Funk & Wagnalls Standard College Dictionary,* or *The American Heritage Dictionary,* you will find it marked ''informal.''

Obviously we cannot hope to list the status of every word or construction; what we need is a set of guidelines, one that will help us identify the level of usage of specific passages, and aid us in selecting a level or style for our own use.

Since so many elements contribute to the effect of a piece of writing, we will not find a single yardstick by which we can measure style. As a start, Sections 92a to 92c examine three elements— organization, syntax, and choice of words, or diction. Each of these comprises an entire range or scale of possibilities along which an essay may be classified. In terms of organization, for example, consider a very humble piece of writing—a grocery list. If the list has been pinned up somewhere, with items jotted down as they occur, it will have no apparent order, and it will thus be near one end of the scale of organization—the naturally ordered end. On the other hand, if someone were to sit down and make up the list—grouping all the meats together, all the vegetables together—the list would be ordered, and it would be closer to the artificially ordered end of the scale than the first list. Similarly, some of an essay's syntactic constructions may seem spontaneous (that is, like the syntax of speech), while others may seem studied. We will call the essay's syntax spontaneous or studied according to the preponderance of one or the other quality. So too the diction of the essay may be more or less limited or more or less general in terms of the size of the audience that would understand it. By combining the classifications of the essay on these three scales, we arrive at an estimate of its overall effect.

92a ORGANIZATION

To begin at one end of the scale of organization, consider a naturally ordered example of writing—one day's entry in a diary. Of course, the sentences of the entry would have order within themselves, and several consecutive sentences might deal with the same event, but it would not be surprising if the events of the day were set down as they occurred. Similarly, a casual letter to a friend might discuss the events that have occurred since the writer last saw his correspondent, but he would probably deal with his material as it occurred to him—almost certainly he would not outline and classify it.

Material near one end of the scale, like diaries or friendly letters, is seldom revised, and has little or no planned arrangement of topics —postscripts take care of the subjects forgotten until the last minute. The English monks who, centuries ago, wrote chronicles of the events of each year were producing a naturally ordered record. But a historian who reads those chronicles, and selects, arranges, and interprets the same events, is introducing an artificial order to the material.

Material at the artificially ordered end of the scale is revised by the writer before it is released; its topics are arranged and classified, with introduction, transitions, and conclusions. Most of your compositions will be artificially ordered. This broad subject of arrangement and classification is handled in more detail in Sections 99 to 103.

92b SYNTAX

Some syntactic constructions we associate more with speech than with writing, and these constructions consequently lend an effect of spontaneity and immediacy to the written passages in which they occur. Other constructions are rarely if ever heard in speech. Writing that contains a number of them produces an effect of care and consciousness—a studied effect. Compare, for example, the way just one syntactic device, sentence conjunction, might be handled in the two styles. Language that attempts to suggest speech may have, as one of its characteristics, the simple stringing together of sentences using *and:*

> 1 I gave the whole thing a good goin'-over 'fore we bought her. Didn' listen to the fella talkin' what a hell of a bargain she was. Stuck my finger in the differential and they wasn't no sawdust. Opened the gear box an' they wasn't no sawdust. Test' her clutch an' rolled her wheels for line. Went under her an' her frame ain't splayed none.
>
> **JOHN STEINBECK**

The studied style, making use of sentence conjunction, often deletes all repeated elements by CONJUNCTION REDUCTION (see Section 55), thereby producing parallel constructions, like the three noun phrases in the next example:

> 2 I was so stunned I could barely react; stunned not by the blow nor the intent, but by the absurdity that I, a grown man, had just been hit in the head with a frozen veal chop.
>
> **NEIL SIMON**

As a rule, the spontaneous style lacks subordination; when subordination does appear (as a result of embedded sentences in adverbials), it is likely to be limited to adverbials of time, place, or cause. The spontaneous style characteristically lacks connectors of purely grammatical function; heavy use is made of RELATIVE PRONOUN DELETION (Section 44a) and WH-BE DELETION (Section 45a):

> 3 There's little choice between the philosophy [which] you learned from Broadway loafers, and the one [which] Edmund got from his books.
>
> **EUGENE O'NEILL**

4   At a place [which was] known only to them they
     buried Crazy Horse somewhere near Chankpe Opi
     Wakpala, the creek [which was] called Wounded Knee.

DEE BROWN

The studied style tends to retain elements like those bracketed in
sentences 3 and 4. Note that we have a full, not a reduced, relative
embedded sentence in the example that follows:

5   The thesis of Professor Edel is that James had deeply
     buried doubts about his own masculinity which were
     triggered to the imaginative level of art by the trau-
     matic failure of *Guy Domville* in the theater.

MILDRED E. HARTSOCK

Contractions are almost the hallmark of the spontaneous style;
notice the change from example 6a to 6b, when we expand the
original contractions:

6a   No. I couldn't get it going. It's harder to do than my
     first book. I'm having a hard time handling it.

ERNEST HEMINGWAY

6b   No. I could not get it going. It is harder to do than
     my first book. I am having a hard time handling it.

Note too the reverse effect when we take a sentence in the studied
style and introduce contractions:

7a   It is only in the intermediate sections that we feel he
     has blurred his effects.

EDMUND WILSON

7b   It's only in the intermediate sections that we feel he's
     blurred his effects.

Finally, the spontaneous style might be described as closely adher-
ing to the order of elements as produced by the phrase structure
rules: a subject noun phrase followed by the main verb, with adverbials, if any, last of all. Transformational variations from this order
produce a more studied effect, as in the next example, where two
time adverbials, one containing an embedded sentence, have been

364

shifted to the left of the outer sentence:

8 In my second year at Queen's, when I gave up Celtic Studies in favor of Psychology, I became secretary of the Gaelic Society.

BERNADETTE DEVLIN

Naturally, the syntax of any piece of prose is a mixture of what we have called spontaneous and studied. Hardly any single construction is always found in one or the other style. The possible exception to this generalization is the absolute construction, which is limited almost exclusively to the studied style. The following sentences illustrate absolute constructions, which are explained in more detail in Section 53.

9 Having entered the House of Commons in the customary manner for peers' sons, . . . he had little personal experience of vote-getting.

BARBARA TUCHMAN

10 Having said this, I will now say that I think a big, unabridged dictionary is a fine thing to have in any home or classroom.

JOHN HOLT

92c CHOICE OF WORDS

The individual words that are chosen for a passage have an effect on the style of that passage. If you announce that you have built a *natatorium* in your back yard, you will obviously get a different reaction than if you announce you have built a *swimming pool.* Both words in one sense "mean" the same thing, yet in another sense they have entirely different meanings. Before we can talk about the limitations of diction, we have to explore how words, parts of language, are related to things outside language.

Our first notion might be that words refer directly to things—that they substitute for pointing; by saying, "Chair," I direct your attention to that object in much the same manner as pointing does. But this cannot be the answer. We have words for abstractions— *courage*—that no one can point to; we have words for things that no longer exist—*the Colossus of Rhodes, the Wabash Cannonball;* we even have words for things that (as far as we know) cannot exist—*time machine.* A word then must be related to a concept, something that exists in the mind. It is this concept that is related to the physically existing object, if there is one. But how are these relationships established in the first place?

Some information on how we go about connecting a word with a concept, and the concept with the thing, can be gained by observing the errors very small children make in learning a language. Suppose a baby sees the family pet and hears her father call it *Rover.* On another occasion, the dog is present again, but this time mother calls it *doggy.* As far as the child knows, these two terms are interchangeably applicable to the concept, whatever form it may have, associated with the terms. When the baby sees the neighbor's dog and hears it called both *Rex* and *doggy,* she must begin to formulate the idea of class membership: that some terms—*Rex, Rover*—are applicable to concepts of individuals, while others—*doggy*—are applicable to concepts of sets or classes of individuals. The child may still have a very fuzzy notion of the limits of the class, though. If she sees a cat and calls it *doggy,* her definition of the class might consist of something like "small, furry, four-legged animal." And when she is corrected, the limits of her definition are revised. In fact, she continually revises them until her notion of the class *doggy* roughly corresponds to the notion of that class held by her elders.

Probably the great majority of the words we know are learned in this casual, haphazard way—by inference from the contexts, verbal and nonverbal, in which we encounter them. Suppose you were a clerk in a large store that sells music and musical instruments. A customer entered and said, "Do you have any tosh?" From the verbal context of the word, you knew already that *tosh* is a noun; you also knew that it is either a mass noun like *sheet music,* as in "Do you have any sheet music?" or perhaps a mass noun derived from a proper noun, as in "Do you have any Mozart?" From the nonverbal context, you assumed that the word has something to do with music. But you still did not have a concept to link it to. Under the circumstances, you did the safest thing—you turned to the manager and said, "Do we have any tosh?"

The manager said to the customer, "No, we haven't carried it in years. I don't know if it's used any more." The manager's reference to *tosh* by the pronoun *it* eliminated the proper noun possibility. Your information became a little more precise, but more contexts would be needed before you finally came to understand the concept related to the word.

Since we have been talking about meaning, we have raised the question of the capacity of language to communicate. If you write only for your own amusement, it does not matter a bit whether your definitions of the words you use coincide with other people's definitions of them. But usually we write with some intention of being read and understood. Now that others have been brought into the picture, we have a method of classifying style according to diction —we can specify whether your meaning for a particular word is generally shared, or limited in some way.

Exercises

1. The following quotation is from *Time* (25 June 1973):

> Who is a Jew? Talmudic scholars, rabbinical courts and even the Israeli Cabinet have long argued the question. The English language has answers of its own—some of them offensive to Jew and non-Jew alike. For 35 years, the Board of Deputies of British Jews, Britain's equivalent to the American B'nai B'rith, has tried to persuade lexicographers to change certain definitions in dictionaries. . . . Next month Marcus Shloimovitz, a 67-year-old textile salesman from Manchester, will take the argument one step further—to the High Court of Justice.
>
> Shloimovitz has no complaint about [*The Oxford English Dictionary*'s] first definition of a Jew: "A person of Hebrew race; an Israelite." He does, however, object to the second: "As a name of opprobrium or reprobation; spec. applied to a grasping or extortionate money-lender or usurer, or a trader who drives hard bargains or deals craftily." Acting as his own lawyer, Shloimovitz will ask the court to force the *O.E.D.* to delete definition No. 2 from all future printings.

Discuss the passage above in light of how definitions are formed and learned. You might want to check your dictionary's definition of words like *nigger, kike, spic,* and *wop.* You should consider questions like these: What is the purpose of a dictionary? Do people who use these words learn them from a dictionary? Does the presence of such words in a dictionary sanction their use or increase their respectability?

2. A complete definition of a word in a reputable dictionary will include the following parts (compare the sample entries in Section 98b): the main form of the word in its typical spelling; the pronunciation; the part of speech; any restrictive labels that identify it as the jargon of a particular field, as occurring on a particular level of usage, or as heard in a geographical region; the etymology; the meaning or meanings; and sentences illustrating its use. Find three specimens of current slang not listed in your dictionary and write entries for them (as completely as you can) according to the form listed above.

3. As a class project, read "The Principles of Newspeak," an appendix to George Orwell's novel *1984*. (The appendix will be much clearer if you have also read the novel.) Discuss the procedure outlined there for fixing the definitions of words. Does it seem possible to you? Ultimately you will be led to consider the connection between words and concepts. You should be able to support your opinion with sound arguments.

93 DICTION

93a SLANG

Words can do more than convey meaning. Consider a device like a password. Here the meaning of the word is unimportant. The only purpose served by the word is identification: the word identifies the speaker as a member of a particular group—namely, us rather than them. But you cannot talk in passwords. For private or secret messages, humans invent codes: the sender and receiver have prearranged, private meanings for the terms in the code, and the resulting system serves the double purpose of communicating information and identifying the sender as a member of the group.

Consider the large group of words that we might call "adolescent" slang. It has an audience limited by age, and serves to identify the speaker himself as a member of the group. (The speaker may not be an adolescent chronologically, but he shows where his sympathies lie.) The glamour of being a teenager, in the United States at least, attracts the eleven- or twelve-year-old, leading him to adopt the speech habits of those a few years older. But time does not stand still. As the child's sixteen-year-old models increase in age and join the adult community, their juniors desire identity with them less and less. The ''new'' teenagers invent or adopt slang of their own. This new slang will itself automatically become obsolete as its inventors reach maturity.

Since the primary function of slang is to identify the speaker, it acts like an informal code in seeking to exclude those not in the group. As slang is codelike, there is almost always a corresponding term with the same or similar meaning in the general vocabulary for each slang term. In fact, in those rare cases where the general vocabulary offers no good match, the slang word may eventually be adopted for general use, losing its status as slang.

Of course, it would be a Herculean job to invent slang terms to match every word in the general vocabulary, nor do the makers of slang attempt the task. A small number of words will serve the purpose of identifying the speaker. This handful, though, must be pressed into service in a great number of contexts, giving slang its characteristic looseness of meaning and adaptability to different parts of speech. Suppose for illustration we invent a slang term of our own—say, *word*. *Word,* we will suppose, means ''a pleasurable experience from literature,'' so that one might say, ''I got a real word out of that book.'' We would not be surprised to find, almost immediately, that it comes to mean any pleasurable experience: ''I got a real word out of that game.'' Or that it is soon used as an adjective: ''That's a wordy movie.'' Or even as a verb: ''Word with your friends at the New Mountain Coffee House.''

Not all slang is adolescent in origin, of course. Any community with a sense of common identity—college students, nationality groups, craftsmen, carnival workers, even pickpockets—is likely to have slang terms of its own. These are not technical terms: when a doctor refers to an artery as a *spurter,* he does not do so for accuracy; he is using language to experience the same sense of community and privacy as the teenager of the middle 1960s who called his new record *groovy.*

The problems that arise from the use of slang in composition come not from any unacceptable qualities in the words themselves, but from the fact that slang separates the writer from the audience for which the writing is intended. Especially in the case of adolescent slang, the use of such words is ill-advised unless the writer seeks to limit his audience to those a few years older or younger than himself. It is not that others will fail to understand—most probably they will know what is meant; they will just feel that they have not been invited to the party.

The looseness of slang presents another problem: usually the writer wants to be as precise as he can. When someone says he is *hung-up,* we do not know if he has a phobia, a frustration, an aversion, or, as they say on television, a technical difficulty.

Of course, there are circumstances where slang is appropriate in a composition: to characterize a speaker, for instance, or as a sudden shift in style for comic effect. But without a purpose, slang may make the reader feel anything from offense to embarrassment.

There is no clearly marked dividing line between slang and the general vocabulary, but these tests can be used: Is there some corresponding term that is unquestionably in general use? Would the term's use by a faculty member or public official sound strained, foolish, or condescending? Does the mere use of the term help you to identify the speaker as a member of a particular group? The word is probably slang if the answer to all these is yes.

93b JARGON

Like slang, jargon also has a limited audience, but for a different reason. The concepts symbolized by slang terms present no problem —it is the words we may not know. But jargon can be meaningless because the concept is unfamiliar. Whereas slang words have matching general words, there are no corresponding general terms for most items of jargon. A physicist may not know what *optimal k-category analysis* means for the same reason that a grammarian does not know what *mesotron* means. Each of them, as far as the special competence of the other is concerned, belongs to the general public, and is quite understandably not as familiar with the terminology of the other's profession as the specialist would be. Neither the physicist nor the grammarian is trying to keep secrets from anyone; it is just that most people have no desire to talk about these things. If the public should become interested in these matters, the words would soon pass from jargon to the general vocabulary, as *neurotic* and *transistor* already have. Be careful, though, that your reader knows whether you are using a word like *neurotic* in the general sense or in the technical sense.

A paper full of jargon can be as bad as a paper full of slang—in fact, it can be worse: while slang may bore or antagonize your reader, jargon may mystify him. How much would the following sentences mean to any reader who knew nothing about electronics?

There are twelve electromagnets also on the CRT neck mounted in a convergence yoke. They cure outer edge bleeding.

ART MARGOLIS

If your subject requires you to use technical terms, common sense demands that you define them.

93c PLAIN AND ORNATE DICTION

When we examine the large class of words that we might consider in general circulation, we still find sizable groups of words that produce different reactions in the reader. Compare the words on the left below with those on the right, for example:

sleepy	somnolent
poor	impoverished
drunk	intoxicated
hairy	hirsute

We might call the words on the left ''plain'' and those on the right ''ornate.'' The plain words are usually shorter, usually the ones we learn first, and usually native in origin rather than borrowed from a foreign language. A certain kind of mind prefers the ornate words whenever possible, perhaps for the veneer of learning they spread thinly over the context. Remember two things in connection with ornate words. First, be sure of their meaning before you use them. Unintended humor is a deadly thing, and a pompous word misused does you more harm than most errors of grammar. As one freshman wrote:

1 Man's only use as an instrument of nature is to profligate the race.

Second, and more important, never use an ornate word in the belief that it is somehow more sophisticated, more official, more scientific, than the plain word. There is an old joke about a plumber who wrote to the Department of Commerce to find out if he could clean out pipes with sulfuric acid. A bureaucrat answered, ''The use of sulfuric acid is strongly contraindicated.'' The plumber thanked him for his reply and said he would try it the first chance he got. After several exchanges of this nature, the bureaucrat finally wrote, "Don't use sulfuric acid—it will eat hell out of the pipes!" It sounds like no more than a funny story about stuffy government officials, but the label of a widely used medicine bears these words:

> 2 Continuous dosage over an extended period is generally contraindicated since codeine phosphate may cause addiction.

The overuse of ornate language is no laughing matter here; this folly could have serious consequences.

93d LEVELS OF STYLE

The table below lists some of the characteristics of language level or style measured by the three scales we have discussed:

ORGANIZATION

Naturally Ordered	Artificially Ordered
Never revised	Always revised
Simple statement of thesis	Formal introduction
Little arrangement of topics	Classification
Abrupt shift of topics	Transition
Postscript	Conclusion

SYNTAX

Spontaneous	Studied
Sentence conjunction in full	CONJUNCTION REDUCTION and parallelism
Little subordination other than time or place	Subordination not limited to time and place
Relative sentences in reduced form	Relative sentences in full form
Contractions	No contractions
Little use of stylistic transformations	Frequent use of stylistic transformations

DICTION

Limited: Loose	General		Limited: Precise
Slang	Plain	Ornate	Jargon

Exercises

1. Without consulting a dictionary, make up your own definition of "colloquial"; then check your definition against the dictionary, and report on any misconceptions you may have had.

2. Look up each of the words listed below in at least four different dictionaries. Make a table of your results, showing whether the dictionaries list the words as standard, slang, or colloquial. Discuss your results.

boondoggle	snide	rummy
corny	jerk	spang
frisk	enthuse	nobby
pinhead	galore	scram
carpetbagger	scads	goof
pleb	scrumptious	soused
slush fund		

3. Look at the words in exercise 2. How many of them do you know? How many of them do you use? How many of them have you ever heard? How many of them have you met in writing? On the basis of your answers, what difficulties does a dictionary face in listing slang?

4. Classify the styles of the following paragraphs, using the three scales discussed in this section:

1   One would almost think that the great benefit modern man seeks in collective living is the avoidance of guilt by the simple expedient of having the state, the party, or the class command us to do the evil that lies hidden in our heart. Thus we are no longer responsible for it, we imagine. Better still, we can satisfy all our worst instincts in the service of collective barbarism, and in the end we will be praised for it. We will be heroes, chiefs of police, and maybe even dictators.

THOMAS MERTON

2   I have it on the authority of the head barber at the most elegant children's barber shop in New York that you don't have to shampoo children's hair at all, provided you get a wet hot washcloth, wring it out well, and rub it over the kid's hair every night. This assumes that you prefer going through minor hell every night, as opposed to major hell once a week.

If you do go through major hell once a week, or once a month, several things might help:

shampoo goggles, if you can find them,

cold cream smeared on the eyebrows, which deflects water away from the delicate little eyes,

a rubber hose attachment for the faucet, which doubles as a handy thing to beat the child with if he won't let you shampoo him.

Compared to shampoos, baths are child's play, which brings up the problem of what to do with all those toys, particularly if you share the same bath and your husband does not dig bathing with a rubber duck.

CAROL G. EISEN

3   I have accepted it as a principle that the great commonplaces, like *ut pictura poesis* or the "garment of style," which sum into comparison or metaphor a whole theory of ornament, embody the serious aims of intelligent men and that the poems can show us what they meant. So, too, if we find that "Imitation" was seriously and carefully defined to include formal excellence in design, coherent ordering, statement of truth, then that definition was in all probability useful and regulative, and we shall do well to consider every image as possibly explicable in terms of it.

ROSEMOND TUVE

4   With Madeleine, Herzog had made his second attempt to live in the country. For a big-city Jew he was peculiarly devoted to country life. He had forced Daisy to endure a freezing winter in eastern Connecticut while he was writing *Romanticism and Christianity,* in a cottage where the pipes had to be thawed with candles and freezing blasts penetrated the clapboard walls while Herzog brooded over his Rousseau or practiced on the oboe. The instrument had been left to him at the death of Aleck Hirshbein, his roommate at

Chicago, and Herzog with his odd sense of piety (much heavy love in Herzog; grief did not pass quickly, with him) taught himself to play the instrument and, come to think of it, the sad music must have oppressed Daisy even more than the months of cold fog.

SAUL BELLOW

5   That is what makes it so weird when all these black pan-thuhs come around to pick up "surfing styles," like the clothing manufacturers. They don't know what any of it means. It's like archeologists discovering hieroglyphics or something, and they say, god, that's neat—Egypt!—but they don't know what the hell it is. They don't know anything about . . . *The Life.* It's great to think of a lot of old emphysematous pan-thuhs in the Garment District in New York City struggling in off the street against a gummy 15-mile-an-hour wind full of soot and coffee-brown snow and gasping in the elevator to clear their old nicotine-phlegm tubes on the way upstairs to make out the invoices on a lot of surfer stuff for 1966, the big nylon windbreakers with the wide, white horizontal competition stripes, nylon swimming trunks with competition stripes, bell-bottom slacks for girls, the big hairy sleeveless jackets, vests, the blue "tennies," meaning tennis shoes, and the . . . *look,* the Major Hair, all this long lank blonde hair, the plain face kind of tanned and bleached out at the same time, but with big eyes.

TOM WOLFE

6   One high preemptive opening bid is given different treat-ment—the opening bid of 4 spades. Here there is a ready-made takeout bid available. This is the overcall of 4 no-trump, which uses up no bidding room. Therefore, if you bid 4 notrump, partner will respond at the five-level in his best suit. If you double 4 spades, this is strictly for penalties. Partner needs extremely freakish distribution to override your decision and take out into a suit.

EDGAR KAPLAN

7   Lise is thin. Her height is about five-foot-six. Her hair is pale brown, probably tinted, a very light streaked lock sweeping from the middle of her hair-line to the top of her

crown; her hair is cut short at the sides and back, and is styled high. She might be as young as twenty-nine or as old as thirty-six, but hardly younger, hardly older.

MURIEL SPARK

94 PROBLEMS WITH DICTION

94a INCONSISTENT DICTION

Your diction, like the other elements of style, should be consistent throughout the composition. Sudden shifts from plain to ornate, ornate to slang, plain to jargon, and so on, are always distracting and occasionally comic. Archibald A. Hill records the following example from a student paper:

> Mrs. Jackson devoted many years of endeavor to establishing and supporting a home where unfortunate women who had made mistakes (which they often sincerely regretted) could go to have their bastards.[1]

A variation in style need not be as noticeable as this one to be disturbing. If a word is marked for inconsistency, consult your dictionary or thesaurus for a more appropriate synonym. A feeling for the style levels of words comes through practice, and one of the advantages of having your instructor read your paper is the guidance offered in this respect by someone with more experience.

94b MISTAKEN MEANINGS

Looking up a new word in a dictionary is an admirable practice that few of us manage to make habitual. We infer the meaning of a word from its context, revising and modifying our understanding of it as we continue to find it in new contexts. But when we see an unfamiliar word, the two or three sentences in which it occurs may give us

[1] "Correctness and Style in English Composition," *A Linguistics Reader,* ed. Graham Wilson. New York: Harper & Row, 1967. P. 53.

an inaccurate idea of its meaning. Or we may misinterpret the contexts, and go our way thinking that we understand the word perfectly. Sometimes a careful observer can even tell how a particular mistake was born.

One student of writing must somewhere or other have read a sentence like this:

1   Public opinion is beginning to polarize on this issue.

Webster's New Collegiate Dictionary, eighth edition, defines *polarization* as "a: division into two opposites.   b: concentration about opposing extremes of groups or interests formerly ranged on a continuum." The student realized that *polarize* implies something of a coming together, but he did not connect the word with the concept of magnetic poles, hence a coming together into two opposing groups. Rather, he interpreted the sentence to mean a forming of a single group, something like putting many parts together to form a whole. Some time later he was writing about a basketball player who had improved greatly during the course of the season, and wrote:

2   His talents are beginning to polarize.

A new word should therefore be employed with some circumspection. Of course you can and should take advantage of the reference books that deal with the meanings of words. But the better, if longer, way is to read and talk. "The way to build your vocabulary is to build your experience, moving much among men and women and taking interest in their interests, with a courteous grave inquiry like that of a child."[1]

94c   UNFAMILIAR REGIONALISMS

Occasionally one meets a term well known in a particular geographical region and almost unknown elsewhere. Students of dialect use words like *cooter* ("turtle") or *spider* ("frying pan") to help them determine the boundaries of different dialect regions. Occasionally

[1] Donald J. Lloyd and Harry Warfel, *American English in Its Cultural Setting*. New York: Knopf, 1957. P. 438.

a well-known word may be regionally used in a different sense or different construction. In the region that includes North Carolina, you can find *right* used as an intensifier (*he faced a right hard problem*) on all levels of style, even in newspaper editorials.

The use of regionalisms is not automatically wrong. On the contrary, our language would be poorer if they were homogenized out of existence. They are a problem only when they present a barrier to understanding. The experienced writer does not stop his story to define one of these terms; he tries to work enough information into the context to make the meaning of the term apparent. One British novelist began a story with a description of a character wearing a *trilby*. A few more sentences made it evident that a trilby is some kind of hat made from a soft material, which is all the reader needed to know. Regionalisms need not be avoided, then, especially when you are writing about the area where those words are used. Simply make sure, as you would with jargon, that the word will not leave the reader guessing.

94d MONOTONOUS DICTION

Often a sequence of sentences leaves something to be desired when no individual sentence can be called wrong. The diction of the passage is marred by an excessive repetition of the same words. The cause of the problem is often an inordinate use of those word groups sometimes called "idioms." The language readily accepts idioms, combinations of old words with a new meaning imposed. Consider all the verbs that can be formed by linking *put* with different particles, adverbs, or prepositions: you can *put someone up* or *put someone on, put something up* or *put up with something, put something over* or *put someone out*. You can *get back, get even,* or *get away.* You can *look down on someone, look out for someone, look someone up,* or *look something up.* Each of the word groups has a different meaning, of course, and there can be no objection to the use of one or another of them. But the repeated use, close together, of idioms made up of the same words makes for a passage that is monotonous at best:

> 1 The Reeve is put out with the Miller's tale, and tries
> to get back at him by telling a story that puts down
> millers. In *The Reeve's Tale,* two students get even

with a miller who has tried to get the best of them. They pretend to put up with it, but get an idea for revenge. When he puts them up for the night, they put the scheme over on the miller and his wife and get away in the morning.

Finding a few synonyms for some of the idioms (not necessarily all of them) will not turn the paragraph into model prose, but it will at least make it endurable. Compare:

2 The Reeve is angered by the Miller's tale, and tries to repay him by telling a story that mocks millers. In *The Reeve's Tale,* two students get even with a miller who has tried to defraud them. They pretend to endure it, but plan their revenge. When he puts them up for the night, they dupe the miller and his wife and escape in the morning.

The remedy for monotonous diction is the same as that for any problem in diction: thinking about exactly what you want to say and using the tools that give you information about words.

94e WORDINESS

Often, people use more words than they need as a sort of mental time-marking, stringing out words that do not mean anything until they find something to say. This is common in speech, and not particularly objectionable. In writing, however, your readers do not need those words. They want you to say what you have to say and be done with it. If your style tends to sprawl, try these three syntactic methods of tightening it up. First, watch out for words deriving from noun pro-forms, those extremely general words like *reason, thing, place, time,* and so on. They add little if anything to the sentence, and you are almost always better off without them. Compare the long and the short versions of the examples below; in each case, the shorter the better:

1a The reason that we are meeting is that we need to consider

1b We are meeting because we need to consider

1c   We are meeting to consider
2a   The growing enthusiasm on the part of many teachers
      of English
2b   The growing enthusiasm of many teachers of English
3a   This is the place where Washington met
3b   This is where Washington met
3c   Here Washington met

Second, see if you can use a verb form rather than a related nominal. Give special attention to prepositional phrases following the verbs *be* or *have:*

4a   The next point is of obvious concern to anyone
4b   The next point obviously concerns anyone
5a   The language has a ready acceptance of new idioms
5b   The language readily accepts new idioms

Finally, take advantage of the various methods of deletion, especially WH-BE DELETION in relative sentences:

6a   Idioms, which are combinations of old words with
6b   Idioms, combinations of old words with
7a   The characteristics which are determined by the material
7b   The characteristics determined by the material

Make the cutting of unneeded words part of your habit in revision.

Exercises

1. An old word game takes advantage of the fact that some words referring to the same concept can be arranged in triads, where one of the words refers to the concept in an unfavorable light, one refers to it fairly neutrally, and one regards it favorably. Thus we have sets like the following:

Favorable	*Neutral*	*Unfavorable*
venerable	old	over-the-hill
challenging	difficult	backbreaking
youthful	underage	callow

Favorable	Neutral	Unfavorable
officer of the law	policeman	pig
healer	doctor	quack
captain of industry	businessman	fat cat

In May 1969, The New York Times Wire Service carried an article, one sentence of which read:

> One nationally known educational expert, who wished to be anonymous, put it this way: "Faculties, despite their yelling in public for more authority, are dishonest. They egg the kids on to fight the president."

Without changing the factual content of what either the writer of the article or the "nationally known educational expert" said, see if you can reword the sentence by switching terms with favorable connotations for those with unfavorable, and vice versa.

2. Try the procedure of exercise 1 on three excerpts from a current newspaper.

3. In each of the following passages, the writer has mistaken the meaning of one of the words. Discover what that word is, give its actual meaning, and substitute a word or phrase that will correct the sentence:

1   Like a great play, the Debutante Ball makes its return engagement each year, parading its cast. . . . The last cloying moments of waiting wear many faces. There is the wistful face of D____ . . . and there is the exultant face of M____, caught forever on film.

2   While freckled Jim O'Brien is a sharpshooter and deft ball handler, McMillen unquestionably is the Terps' most offensive player.

3   Other less flashy declarations of love are also available in heart-shaped jewelry. One of the most unusual is a unisex ring featuring two enjoining hands which open to reveal a sterling silver heart beneath.

4   Both teams flash strong front lines and sound backcourts. Both have a wealth of depth. And both revel in a fast tempo, perpetuated by pressure defense.

95 USAGE AND THE MAN FROM MARS

It has often been noted that many, perhaps most, Americans feel guilty about their language. An English teacher (who is supposed to be the umpire of usage) continually hears people say, ''I know I don't talk as well as I should but. . . .'' Such people accept as facts of nature the inferiority of their pronunciation and grammar. They live in a Mudville of the mind where pronunciation is ''slovenly,'' where the best writers make ''common errors,'' and where the English language is ever threatened by ''linguistic chaos.'' There is a curious reverse side to their attitude, though, for these people are also sure that somewhere in this favored land the sun is shining bright; they believe we could all reach the promised land of good usage if—if dictionary-makers were vigilant, if influential writers held the line, and especially if their children's teachers were as strict as *their* teachers had been. While many have given up hope for themselves—they are content to remain linguistic Caseys, strikeouts in the game of grammar—they want their children to succeed where they failed, apparently by suffering as they suffered.

How much of this attitude is true is the question that now concerns us. First we need to specify what we are talking about. This is no easy task, since usage drifts across our categories like smog across county lines. Some questions—''Should I say none *is* or none *are?*'' —seem to be matters of grammar. Others—''Does *cute* really mean 'bow-legged'?''—obviously involve the meaning of words. Still others—'' What will people think of me if I use *finalize* as a verb?''— seem to be social questions. Yet determining the answers to all of these requires the same procedures we use in determining the answers to any question about language.

Suppose we conjure up one of the grammarian's favorite devices, the man from Mars come to Earth to learn English. He first must decide on method. If he wanted to learn carpentry, he would undoubtedly seek out the most skillful carpenter he could find. If he followed the same method with language, he would look for those who use language with success to serve as models.

This implies that the only guide we have in matters of usage is the practice of competent, respected writers and speakers. If we want to know what a word means, we need to see what contemporary users of the word mean by it. We might consider whether there are any alternative methods of deciding what to do. Could we, perhaps, take some general principle such as precision and apply it as a test in all doubtful matters? It does not seem that we can.

Consider an example: Suppose I notice that some people say "It's a quarter *of* three," and some say "It's a quarter *to* three." Now suppose that I adopt the practice of saying *of* to indicate time before noon, and *to* to indicate time after noon. Thus, in my usage, "a quarter *of* three" unambiguously indicates 2:45 A.M., and "a quarter *to* three" always refers only to 2:45 P.M. Would my usage be more precise than that of others? Certainly. But would it be worth it? Hardly. As long as no one else knows my system, it is a wholly wasted effort. I can advise others to adopt the usage, but the work needed to compel everybody to observe it would be all out of proportion to the benefits achieved. Three centuries of striving has been insufficient to change certain usages in English.

We need to discover what current practice is. Inevitably, we will find some instances of a split in usage, like *quarter of* versus *quarter to*. Of course, no one really cares how you say that it is fifteen minutes before the hour; here your choice is perfectly free. But for reasons that are often mysterious, some usage items become fossilized—people continue to make pronouncements about them without the slightest evidence or reflection about the facts. The glossary in Section 96 attempts to provide some evidence to help you make your decisions about a selection of items of usage.

Exercises

1. Here are some miscellaneous comments that were all called forth by a single event. What can you say, based solely on the comments listed here, about the nature of the event?

   1 "We are robbing ourselves of all righteous indignation against evil."

   SYDNEY J. HARRIS

   2 "Opening the floodgates . . . like the printing of paper money backed by no sound value. . . . deplorable. . . . the refuge of the indolent or the result of confused thinking."

   AMERICAN BAR ASSOCIATION JOURNAL

   3 ". . . Bolshevik. . . ."

   THE NEW YORK TIMES

   4 "A very great calamity. . . . the questionable, the perverse, the unworthy, and the downright outrageous. . . . a scandal and a disaster. . . . subversion and decay."

   WILSON FOLLETT

5 "The bolshevik spirit. . . . corrupted at center."

THE RIGHT REVEREND RICHARD S. EMRICH

6 "Anarchy. . . . [It] can only be viewed with alarm."

HOKE NORRIS

Your instructor will tell you what the event was after you have discussed the question.

2. Lois says, "No wonder I can't communicate with them!" Does she really mean what she says? Before you answer, consider two things: Ditto's first speech is "Mom, can Billy and me have a cookie?" Is it successful as communication—that is, does his mother understand what he wants? After three panels of corrections, he says, "May I have a cookie?" Does this speech succeed in communicating, as far as Billy is concerned? What is Lois really objecting to when she overhears Chip on the phone?

3. Each of the sentences below contains a word or construction that has irked some self-appointed guardian of English. How many can you identify?

1 The yells of the mob could be heard clearly within the palace.

2 Next to the main building was a dilapidated shed, its shingles fallen, and its planks hanging loose.

3 There is not much variation in departmental requirements for graduation on this campus.

4 When the severity of his injuries was fully known, Williamson realized he would need several months to recuperate.

5 The hands who had been to town were so rowdy, and the ones who had stayed in camp so riled, I could only hope that nothing happened to stampede the herd.

6 Galileo considered the Earth's rotation around the sun a proven theory.

7 John descended the staircase slowly, his hand gripping the banister.

8 From the standpoint of those responsible for security, anything less than several reliable telegraphers at each stop along the railroad would jeopardize the safety of everyone aboard the presidential train.

4. Discuss the different ways in which we use the word *incorrect*. In what sense is it used in this comic strip? What is Kelly implying about the importance of "correct" usage?

KELLY   **by Jack Moore**

96   **A GLOSSARY OF USAGE**

Sources of information for the usage comments are abbreviated as follows:

AH: *The American Heritage Dictionary of the English Language.* 1969.

B: Margaret M. Bryant, *Current American Usage.* 1962.

K: Henry Kučera and W. Nelson Francis, *Computational Analysis of Present-Day American English.* 1967.

M: Walter E. Meyers, ''A Study of Usage Items,'' *College Composition and Communication.* 1972. Pp. 155–69.

RH: *The Random House Dictionary of the English Language,* college ed. 1968.

SCD: *Funk & Wagnalls Standard College Dictionary.* 1966.

WNWD: *Webster's New World Dictionary of the American Language,* 2nd college ed. 1970.

W3:   *Webster's Third New International Dictionary.* 1961.

W8:   *Webster's New Collegiate Dictionary,* 8th ed. 1973.

For purposes of comparison, the following sources are sometimes referred to:

L: Sterling A. Leonard, *Current English Usage.* 1932.

M&W: Albert H. Marckwardt and Fred Walcott, *Facts About Current English Usage.* 1938.

agendum, agenda, agendas   As borrowed from Latin, the singular was *agendum* (a form that does not occur in the Brown Corpus), with *agenda* as plural. The latter word is now completely ''naturalized'' for many speakers and writers: all sources agree that *agenda* is standard English when used as a singular form meaning ''a list of things to be done or considered.'' It may be used as a singular without restriction. By analogy with the great majority of English nouns, the plural form *agendas* has been created (*B, RH, SCD, WNWD*).

antenna, antennae, antennas   For the sense of the word having to do with radio transmission or reception, all sources list the plural form as *antennas.* Most show *antennae* as the plural form for the meaning of moveable sensory appendages, although two (*W8* and *WNWD*) list either form for this meaning. The borrowed word therefore has two plurals, the native *antennas* and the borrowed *antennae.* Most cases of competing usage end with one of the forms becoming obsolete, but here both plurals continue to exist, apparently because each form has become limited to a separate meaning of the word. Compare *agendum, medium.*

anticipate   Some commentaries contend that the word *anticipate* should not be used to mean ''look forward to'' or ''expect,'' but be limited to those contexts where a countering reaction is expressed, as in

> He had anticipated being revealed as the cat burglar
> by burying his black mask and tools.

Americans do not limit their use of the word in this way. All dictionaries record the meaning of ''look forward to'' or ''expect'' as standard, and that meaning seems to be by far the most frequent use of the word. In *M, anticipate* and related forms have the so-called precise sense only about one-fifth of the time.

back of, in back of   Since there is a difference in opinion about these two items, they will be handled separately. The first, *back of,* was listed as ''established'' in English usage as early as 1932 (*L*), yet the *AH* usage survey found it unacceptable in writing to almost half the judges. This survey illustrates the variation between opinion and practice—people do not always write the way they think they write, even people as aware of language as the editors of dictionaries. According to *AH* and *RH, back of* would not usually be acceptable in writing, yet both sources give ''back of'' as the definition of the word *behind,* and it is difficult to conceive of a more formal use of language than the definitions of a dictionary. *WNWD* also defines *behind* as ''back of'' without restriction.

In back of was ranked ''disputable'' in 1932, and is listed as ''informal'' in *RH* and ''unacceptable for writing'' to an even half of the *AH* judges. In *RH,* the first definition of *behind* is ''in back of,'' and the form is listed without restriction in *W3.*

If we limit ourselves to observing what writers do, rather than what they say they do, we would have to decide that *back of* has been acceptable for a generation, and *in back of* is now in use by reputable writers. This agrees with the findings in *B;* it is noted there that the construction is obviously modeled on *in front of,* a completely acceptable expression. The following sentence, mentioned in *M,* shows with great clarity how speakers and writers of English are led to use *in back of* by the natural desire for parallelism:

> Silence stood *in front of* her waiting, and *in back of*
> her blocking her retreat.

better than   *Better* is sometimes used in the metaphoric sense of ''more,'' as in

> The distance was better than a mile.

Some commentaries strongly object to this use of the word, probably because the construction occurs very infrequently in writing (*M*). However, *RH, SCD, WNWD, W3,* and *W8* list this meaning without restriction, and there would seem to be little reason to bar it from the kind of writing done in college composition courses.

between, among   In grade school we were all given a simple description of the usage of these two words: ''Use *between* with two things, *among* with more than two things.'' The description was sufficient for our simple understanding at the time, but as adults we should not feel bound by its inaccuracies. In fact, *between* is often used with more than two things, and has been so used since Old English; *between* in a construction like

A treaty was concluded *between* the four powers.

is correctly used, according to *AH, RH, SCD, WNWD, W3,* and *W8.* ''It is still the only word available, according to [*The Oxford English Dictionary*], to express the relation of a thing to many surrounding things severally and individually, *among* expressing a relation to them collectively and vaguely'' (*B,* p. 38).

can't seem to   The expression *can't seem to,* as in

He *can't seem to* find his glasses.

occurs only in dialogue or in quotations of speech in the Brown Corpus (*M*). That finding is consistent with *B,* where the same uses are noted. The construction marks the context in which it appears as spontaneous and naturally ordered, and would therefore introduce an undesirable variation in style in a composition that is studied and artificially ordered.

comparison of absolutes   Sometimes it is maintained that adjectives like *perfect, round,* and *unique* should not be used in a comparative or superlative sense. That is, a thing is either perfect or it is not (so the argument goes), and therefore it is illogical to speak of something as ''more perfect.'' Despite the assertion in *B* that these words are ''freely compared,'' it is probably inaccurate to make a blanket statement about all these absolute adjectives, since the comparison of some of them is much more acceptable than that of others, and much more frequently found in writing. *Perfect* is probably most often compared, since to ban it would deny the stylistic authority of the Preamble to the Constitution:

. . . in order to form a *more perfect* union. . . .

M found the comparative use of these words to be very infrequent. Two of the uses cited illustrate opposite extremes on the studied–spontaneous scale: one was the quotation from the Preamble; the other was

> Holy mackerel, that's the *most unique* dog I ever saw.

Several sources suggest that forms like *more nearly unique* are more appropriate when a studied, organized prose style is being attempted.

compensate　The verb *compensate* has passed from psychological jargon into general diction, meaning something like "make up for some real or imagined inadequacy by some form of action," as in the following sentence:

> Jim *compensated* for his short stature by his boisterous conduct.

All sources list this particular meaning without restriction.

contact　The use of *contact* as a verb meaning "to get in touch with" is listed without restrictions by *RH* and *W8*. All sources note that the verb is widely used in this sense, but *SCD* and *AH* would bar it from use in formal contexts. *M* finds *contact* used as a verb five times in the corpus, and in each case it has the meaning "to get in touch with." Two of those instances are from newspaper reporting, two from government publications, and one from a scholarly source.

continual, continuous　All dictionaries except *W8* distinguish between *continual* and *continuous* on grounds exemplified by the comment from *AH: "Continual* can apply to uninterrupted action but is now chiefly restricted to what is intermittent or repeated at intervals: *the continual banging of the shutters. Continuous* implies either action without interruption in time or unbroken extent in space: *a continuous vigil, a continuous slope of terrain.*"

M's findings flatly contradict this distinction. In thirty occurrences, far from being "chiefly restricted to what is intermittent," *continual* and *continually* are used to mean "uninterrupted" just as often as they are used to mean "intermittent." *Continuous* and *continuously* are used to mean "intermittent" in one-quarter to one-third of the contexts out of sixty-seven occurrences. (The exact percentages are unimportant, since there would be disagreement about the meaning of the word in a few contexts.)

It would seem that *continual* is used acceptably in either sense. *Continuous*, if these figures are representative, is used without differentiation in at least one-fourth of its contexts. The distinction between the two words can therefore be described as "sometimes made."

criterion, criteria   All dictionaries list two plural forms, the foreign *criteria* and the native *criterions*, a form that does not occur in the Brown Corpus. Unlike *agenda*, however, *criteria* is not used as a singular. In every case where a pronoun or verb showed agreement and made it possible to distinguish number, *criteria* was used as a plural.

datum, data   As originally introduced to English from Latin, *datum* was a singular count noun, with *data* as its plural form. *B*, gathering evidence from written English from about 1935 to 1960, cites one study that shows *data* used as a mass noun (*this data was*) 16 percent of the time, and as a plural count noun (*these data were*) 84 percent of the time. From material written in 1960, *M* shows usage to be about evenly divided between mass and plural count. In general writing, at least, the mass-noun use of *data* appears to be rapidly increasing.

In scientific writing, on the other hand, *data* is predominantly used as a plural count noun. There is reason to suspect, though, that even in scientific writing the plural usage is sometimes an afterthought rather than the writer's natural practice: two writers who consistently used *data* with a plural verb form also wrote the phrases "the large *amount* of data" and "the *mass* of data" rather than "the large *number* of data," which would have been consistent with their use of the word as a count noun.

different from, different than   All sources (except *W8*) that comment on whether *different* should be followed by *from* or *than* indicate a preference for *from*, in all but one situation: *AH* and *SCD* note that *than* can sometimes be used to eliminate one or more unnecessary words before an embedded sentence. Thus, sentence 2 would be preferred to 1 by the editors of these dictionaries:

1   There was no evidence that anything was different *from what* it had been.
2   There was no evidence that anything was different *than* it had been.

Different from appears to be the habitual usage of Americans, at least in writing. *M* shows that sentence 2 is the only use in the

Brown Corpus of *different than,* as opposed to thirty uses of *different from.* Two of the latter are followed by an embedded sentence:

3 different *from what the state exacts*
4 different *from what we encounter on earth*

doubt if, doubt whether, doubt that No dictionary except *AH* repeats the statement sometimes found in handbooks that these three constructions are not interchangeable. Some commentaries maintain that *doubt that* implies a denial, others that *doubt whether* should be reserved for positive statements intended to convey real doubt or uncertainty. In statements where it was possible to determine real doubt or uncertainty, *M* found *that* occurring roughly as often as *whether,* and *if* occurring half as often as each of these.

In negative contexts, such as *I do not doubt, There is no doubt, There is little doubt,* or *no room for doubt,* American writers overwhelmingly use *that.* In positive statements, a writer need not hesitate to use whichever word comes naturally.

due to *Due to* is used without objection following any form of the verb *be;* in such a case, *due* functions as an adjective:

1 Dwight's problems are *due to* his absent-mindedness.

The use of *due* as an adjective is centuries old. Its use to replace *because of* in an adverbial phrase, however, is recent, and new usages will generally meet with objection if they are recognized as new. Thus, *AH* considers a sentence like 2 unacceptable in writing:

2 Dwight stumbled *due to* his absent-mindedness.

All sources commenting on *due to* agree that it is widely used informally.

fault Occasionally an instructor or text may insist that *fault* should not be used as a transitive verb meaning "to find fault with." *RH, SCD, WNWD, W3,* and *W8* all list this use of the verb without restriction, however. The word is used as a verb once in the Brown Corpus, and it is used with this meaning:

Chicago . . . could not be *faulted* on the choice of artists.

gotten   As a past participle, *gotten* is apparently limited to American use, and has been for over a generation (*L, M&W*). Although most dictionaries simply list the form as an alternate past participle form with *got, B* notes that *gotten* is never used when the meaning of the verb is ''to possess, have.'' *M* confirms that observation. To begin with, the form is comparatively infrequent in writing: *got* occurs 482 times in the Brown Corpus, *gotten* only sixteen times. How many of the occurrences of *got* are simple past tense uses is not known, but if only one-quarter of the 482 were past participles, *gotten* would still be far outnumbered.

Of the sixteen occurrences, however, the word is each time part of an idiomatic use; none of them have the sense of ''to possess, have.'' Some examples of the idioms include:

> had gotten into his car
> had gotten him on the phone
> had gotten a look at him
> had gotten away with it
> had gotten the jump on him.

hisself, theirselves   Although *hisself* and *theirselves* are heard in some speech, the forms do not normally occur in edited written English. In the table below, the numbers following each word indicate the number of times that word occurs in the million-word text of the Brown Corpus (*K*):

Word	*Occurrences*
himself	603
hisself	1
themselves	270
theirselves	0

The one occurrence of *hisself* reported appeared in dialogue.

For an explanation of why *hisself* and *theirselves* appear at all, see Section 31a.

hopefully   One sentence from *M* illustrates the use of *hopefully* in question here:

> 1   *Hopefully*, the perennial battle of rule 22 then would be fought to a settlement once and for all.

The use of *hopefully* as a sentence adverbial is parallel in syntax to the unobjected-to use of *frankly* in a sentence like 2:

2   *Frankly,* the battle then would be fought to a settlement.

For no apparent reason, however, the use of *hopefully* as a sentence adverbial has become a target for guardians of the purity of the language. The construction is listed without restriction in *RH, SCD,* and *W8,* and *hopefully* occurs twice as a sentence adverbial out of eight appearances in the Brown Corpus. *WNWD* comments of *hopefully* that it is ''regarded by some as a loose usage, but widely current.''

in back of   See *back of.*

in regard to, in regards to   *B* labels *in regard to* as standard, *in regards to* as nonstandard. *M* supports this distinction. *In regard to* occurs frequently in the corpus, *in regards to* not at all.

like   Perhaps better than any other word, *like* demonstrates the unpredictable and arbitrary nature of some usage judgments. If *like* is used as a conjunction, as in sentence 1a, it will be widely regarded as inappropriate for formal written usage (*AH*), though the usage has occurred in the works of reputable writers since the sixteenth century (*The Oxford English Dictionary*):

1a   He runs his company *like* a general runs his army.

But if CONJUNCTION REDUCTION (see Section 55) operates to remove the repeated verb, the sentence becomes acceptable for formal writing:

1b   He runs his company *like* a general his army.

Similarly, there is little objection to the prepositional use of *like:*

1c   He runs his company *like* a general.

B finds constructions like 1a rare in formal written English, but frequent in written dialogue.

The frequency of the usage in speech (it is standard spoken English in all dialect regions but New England [*B*]) doubtless explains the fact that objections to sentences like 1a in writing appear to be diminishing. Almost fifteen years ago, the slogan ''Winston tastes good, like a cigarette should'' brought a tidal wave of criticism of (and free publicity for) the R. J. Reynolds Company. But the 1973 advertisement of Benson and Hedges—

''The Parliament recessed filter. It works like a cigarette holder works''—has gained no such notoriety. *Like* as a conjunction is listed as colloquial by *WNWD,* and cited without restriction by *W8,* which quotes examples from the modern writers John Keats and Norman Mailer. Similarly, President Nixon's promising to ''tell it like it is'' in a major address has tended to upgrade the usage.

Some teachers of composition may, however, prefer *as* (or *as if,* where applicable) in such constructions.

medium, media   All dictionaries list two plural forms, the foreign *media* and the native *mediums.* The native plural is the only form used for the meaning ''spiritualists.'' The plurals of this word have begun a development parallel to that of *datum, data. W8* records *media* as singular in the sense of ''means of mass communications,'' a usage called ''now sometimes heard'' by *WNWD,* which lists *medias* as its plural. We will probably see the increasing use of the word as a mass noun rather than a plural count noun through the next several decades. The singular use of *media* (used as a mass noun) is unacceptable to *AH,* however.

more perfect, most perfect, *etc*.   See *comparison of absolutes.*

none   In surprisingly unanimous agreement, all sources state that *none* as a subject can take either a singular or a plural verb, depending on the sense in which the word is used. *M* lists twenty-seven occurrences of *none* with singular and eight with plural. The same freedom applies to pronouns referring to *none:* of five pronoun references, two are plural and three singular.

phenomenon, phenomena   All sources list *phenomenon* as a singular count noun with two plurals: *phenomenons* for the meaning of ''marvelous things or persons,'' and *phenomena* for other senses. *M* notes *phenomena* as the only plural form occurring in the corpus. *B* reports one clear and one doubtful use of *phenomena* as a singular, and *SCD* notes that the form is sometimes ''erroneously used as a singular.''

The process by which borrowed words become changed as they are naturalized is clearly illustrated by comparing this word with *data. Phenomenon* and *phenomena* are probably heard about equally often: the first occurs in the corpus thirty-five times, and the second twenty-six times. Here the unfamiliar plural has a good chance of being clearly recognized as an exception and therefore of being preserved. With *data,* on the other hand, that form is a hundred times likelier to be heard than *datum.* But *data* just does not sound like an English plural, although the context makes it clear that the speaker is not referring to a single count item.

The road is open for the interpretation of the word as a mass noun.

rate   In question here are two meanings for the verb *rate:* the transitive sense meaning "to deserve," as in

> 1   Wisconsin Dells . . . *rates* a stopover when traveling from Chicago.

and the intransitive sense meaning "to have value or status," as in

> 2   The second level, senior engineer, *rates* slightly below first level supervision.

The intransitive sense is probably now established for use in any kind of writing: despite a label of "informal" by *SCD,* and objections to its use in writing by *AH, M* reports that the sense occurs as frequently in writing as any other meaning of the word, and *WNWD, RH,* and *W8* give this meaning without restriction.

The transitive sense probably occurs less often in edited writing. *M* reports only one occurrence (example 1 above); the restrictions for intransitive in *SCD* and *AH* apply here as well, and *WNWD* labels it "colloquial." But *RH* and *W8* give this meaning without restriction also.

shall, will   The "rules" governing the use of *shall* and *will* show the persistence of linguistic myth. The usage statements found in several dictionaries are not to be trusted. Reliable statements are given in *AH, SCD,* and *WNWD.* American usage of *shall* and *will* may be stated as follows: (1) *Will* is far more frequently used with all personal pronouns and in all contexts, with the exception of (2). (2) In laws, official directives, and public proclamations, *shall* predominates so heavily that the word may almost be classified as legal jargon. (3) In nonlegal writing, *shall* is much more frequently used with first person pronouns than with others. (4) *Shall* in conversation strikes some Americans as affected or otherwise unusual, as revealed by this passage from a fiction sample in the Brown Corpus:

> "Nevertheless, there is no bath."
> "But a young American has a bath next to his room and I shall ask him if you might use it this once. And then we shall see."
> The Gräfin was partial to the word "shall."

In summary, use whichever word comes naturally to you. As *B* comments, "There is no *shall-will* 'error' . . . to make the speaker or writer conspicuous" (p. 182).

slow, slowly   Every so often, a newspaper will carry a letter to the editor complaining about the highway signs that read DRIVE SLOW. In Middle English, there were two ways of forming adverbs by adding a suffix; one of those suffixes was entirely lost as the language changed, leading to adverb forms like *slow,* identical to the adjective form. But no one is born knowing the history of the language; the great majority of adverbs in modern English end in -*ly*. People come to think of the -*ly* form as the rule, and adverbs that do not end in this way have to be learned as exceptions. Adverbs like *fast* are learned individually; but since *slow,* unlike *fast,* also has an -*ly* form, there is a tendency to think of *slow* exclusively as the adjective form, and to consider its use as an adverb erroneous. Thus, although *slow* as an adverb has had continual use since Middle English, it occurs much more infrequently than *slowly*. *M* finds only one such use in the Brown Corpus:

> He smiled very sweet and *slow* at Mr. Skyros.

Slow frequently occurs in speech as an adverb, often, as *AH* comments, in "commands, exhortations, and where forcefulness is otherwise sought." The one exception to the prevalence of *slowly* in writing is in phrases where a participle results from the transformation of an embedded sentence:

> a ball bounced slow ⟹ a slow-bouncing ball

In phrases of this kind in the Brown Corpus ("a relatively *slow* growing market," "the *slow* moving British column"), *slow* was found about twice as often as *slowly* ("a *slowly* increasing load").

someplace, somewhere   *W8* lists *someplace* without restriction, but the word is to a large extent confined to speech. *RH* comments that "precise speakers prefer *somewhere,*" but precision has obviously nothing to do with it. The two words simply identify the style of the passage in which they occur as either casual and spontaneous (with *someplace*), or thoughtful and studied (with *somewhere*). *B* labels *someplace* as colloquial, *AH* and *SCD* label it as informal. The word is found in the Brown Corpus only six times, two of those in dialogue; *somewhere,* by comparison, occurs sixty times. *Somewheres,* found in dialogue to suggest that the speaker has little formal education, occurs once (*M*).

sustain *Sustain* is sometimes objected to in the sense of ''experience'' or ''suffer,'' as in

> It is the clumsy child who *sustains* the worst injuries.

The objection seems to be groundless: *RH, SCD, WNWD,* and *W8* list this meaning without restriction, and the word occurs with this meaning in about one-quarter of the *M* occurrences.

theirselves See *hisself.*

who, whom When in doubt about the correct form, many writers fall into two groups—some use *who,* and others use *whom:*

> 1 [She was] the kind of girl *who* people would describe as having a terrific personality when they tried to fix you up with her.
>
> WILLIAM GOLDMAN
>
> 2 Now that the CAB is squeezing more passengers into fewer planes at higher fares, it is wiping out all discounts for passengers *whom* it figures will have no alternative.
>
> LOUIS M. KOHLMEIER

Neither of these usages could be predicted by the rules of pronoun formation: in sentence 1, *who* is the object of the verb *describe,* as in

> 3 People would describe *her* as having a terrific personality.

In sentence 2, *whom* is the subject of an embedded sentence, as in

> 4 It figures *they* will have no alternative.

When the surface structure of the sentence is transformed from its deep structure order, many native speakers of English rely on word order alone to convey their meaning. This is especially true in questions; sentence 5 was approved for speech by 59 percent of the *AH* Usage Panel:

> 5 *Who* did you meet?

Both *W8* and *WNWD* note that the use of *who* as the object of a verb or preposition is widespread on all educational levels in speech. In addition, this usage has a long history in the work of many reputable writers. The only accurate generalization that can be made is that usage is divided, no doubt an indication that a change is occurring in the language: *whom* is becoming obsolete in writing. As for its use in speech, as far back as 1927, *The Oxford English Dictionary* commented that *whom* was "no longer current in natural, colloquial speech."

Context:
The
Background
and
Research

SECTIONS **97-105**

When you write a paper, the whole world is the context of your message. But unless you choose to be limited to the tiny segment of the universe that constitutes your own experience, you will need help to find what you need from that context, to select the information appropriate to the question at hand, to preserve that information without distortion by errors, and to arrange it in the best order.

The next three sections in this part aim to do just that—first, by helping you to judge whether evidence is sound and what conclusions can be drawn from it; second, by directing you to the reference works that can either give you information on your topic or tell you where to find the information; and third, by giving you some hints about efficient methods of note-taking. The remaining sections deal with different methods of writing the composition—getting it down on paper, arranging it in a sensible fashion, and revising it so that it shows to best advantage.

97 THE LOGICAL USE OF EVIDENCE

When searching for evidence for your topic, you will have to evaluate carefully what you find for its truth and applicability. The same caution will be needed in your own use of evidence. A mispunctuated sentence is "wrong" in a very specialized and ultimately trivial way, but an invalid argument can be wrong in a moral sense; it may not be just a lie, but a particularly subversive kind of lie, since it masquerades as an objective statement of the evidence.

97a INAPPROPRIATE EVIDENCE

The evidence that you find and adapt for your own use should always be pertinent, accurate, and complete. It will most certainly be of different kinds: it may include the citation of authorities, generalizations from typical examples, and statistics. No one kind of evidence is superior to the others, and all of it is subject to the same kinds of misuse. There is no substitute for a thorough understanding of the rules of logic, nor can that understanding be provided in a few pages in a handbook. But some of the more common and more pernicious errors of argument and evidence can be touched on, and some guidelines offered for an honest use of your evidence.

Lack of evidence   A frequent error, one by no means limited to student papers, stems from presenting an opinion with no evidence at all. For example, the Canadian Movement for Personal Fitness says (on the back of milk bottles), ''The average Canadian male at 28 is only about as fit as the average Swede at 60.'' Not a shred of evidence is presented for the claim; in fact, it is hard to imagine the kind of evidence that could possibly support it. The use of the word *average* and the precision of the figures *28* and *60* lend a kind of clinical tone to the statement, but we should note that averages are abstractions and, by definition, cannot be either fit or unfit, healthy or falling down from sickness.

Irrelevancy   Sometimes, instead of no evidence at all, a writer or speaker provides information that has nothing whatever to do with the question at hand. Advertising writers are particularly prone to this fallacy:

> It's high time for Hires! The honest root beer.

The reader may speculate on how a root beer could be dishonest. Or he may ponder what the writer of the next example sees as the connection between peaches and people:

> Discover the softness of the peach experience. New! Pond's Creamy Peach Facial Moisturizer. Feel it. Touch it. Discover it. This new super-wet, milky white moisturizer from Pond's. With just a hint of peach fragrance. Your skin feels so soft. So lusciously alive!

In the photograph accompanying the advertisement, a model is being kissed on the temple while holding a peach to her chin.

Begging the question   A similar fallacy involves begging the question—that is, assuming that the question under discussion is already proven or disproven. During the My Lai investigations, questions were begged in abundance as disputants argued that (1) American boys could not have done it because American boys would not do things like that, or (2) the soldiers massacred the civilians because soldiers are mercenary butchers who massacre civilians.

Non sequitur   Saying that the evidence must be pertinent means that it must be connected to the question at hand. If someone points out that the crime rate and the number of known drug addicts have increased over a particular period, he is making a covert claim that one event has caused the other. While this may be true, the conclusion—that drug addiction causes crime—does not follow (in Latin, *non sequitur*) from the statistical evidence: the mutual rise of the two sets of figures does not show their connection. For the statistic to be pertinent, it would have to be proved that addicts were responsible for the crimes.

Appeal to authority   The use of authority sometimes runs afoul of the requirement that evidence be pertinent. To count as an authority, the speaker must be discussing a subject within his competence; if we wanted to learn about playing tennis or throwing a football, we might consult Billie Jean King or Joe Namath, but their recommendations for Colgate toothpaste and Noxzema shaving cream would not carry much weight. Such endorsements are not citations from authorities—simply testimonials. And on a subject where experts differ, the use of authority is fallacious if only the opinion of a competent authority is given, rather than the reason for his opinion.

Doubtful evidence   The information you present must be accurate. Statistics furnish good examples of inaccuracy, because, while figures seem authoritative and unbiased, we often misunderstand either their use or their method of collection. It is sometimes pointed out that the number of sex crimes in some particular country declined when the sale of pornography became legal in that country. We should question the accuracy of this claim, since arrests for the sale of pornography would certainly have been counted as sex crimes. When pornography-selling became legal, arrests for it were no longer made, and a whole category was removed from the heading of "sex crimes." We would therefore expect the total number of sex crimes to decline simply as a result of the legislative action and, to be valid, the statistics would need to show that *other* sex crimes, such as rape or indecent exposure, had declined in number.

The following example shows a fallacy that frequently arises from a misunderstanding of probability in statistics:

> The fear of inadvertent inflation [of airbags in automobiles] is a real fear and must be met with candor. Until this [one reported malfunction, causing partial inflation] happened, the risk of inadvertent inflation had been estimated at one in 3.3 billion vehicle miles, or once in the lifetimes of 6,000 typical drivers. It should not have happened in the first nine months of testing 1,831 cars.
>
> JAMES J. KILPATRICK

To see why this is fallacious, consider the case of two coins thrown into the air: in an infinite number of trials, they should land as two heads 25 percent of the time, two tails 25 percent of the time, and one head and one tail 50 percent of the time. Now pretend that in four trials we get a perfect distribution of the probable results: they land two heads once, two tails once, and one head and one tail twice. There is nothing about the law of probability that enables us to predict the order of the results—two heads might appear on the first trial, or on the last, or in the middle. If the estimate in the Kilpatrick quotation is accurate, that one expected failure is as likely to appear in the first mile as in the last mile or in any single mile between. What needs to be watched is the rate of failure, and the quotation states that the failure rate expected with the device had not been exceeded.

Evidence out of context   Evidence may be inaccurate simply because it is removed from the larger context in which it occurs, with important qualifications or limitations deleted. In "Abortion on Demand" (*Time*, 29 January 1973), we find the following sentences:

> Psychologist David points out that while psychosis after childbirth develops in 4,000 U.S. mothers each year, there are few cases of post-abortion psychosis. Nor is there much evidence even of less serious emotional trouble.

The quotation as given makes it seem better, from a mental health standpoint, to have an abortion than to have a baby. But the quotation has been taken from context. Three paragraphs earlier, in the same essay, we read:

> "While the literature is immense," says Psychologist Henry David of the Transnational Family Research Institute in Washington, D.C., there is "undue reliance on impressionistic case reports." The one certainty, he says, is that "there is no psychologically painless way to cope with an unwanted pregnancy."

In other words, *Time* cites a statistic from a speaker who is questioning the validity and trustworthiness of statistics.

Incomplete evidence   Finally, the evidence should be complete. One can make a case for anything if he presents only one side of the argument or only part of the evidence. An advertisement for a margarine reads:

> New Promise Margarine can help lower cholesterol. Promise tastes like butter. Yet when hundreds of people used Promise Margarine *instead* of butter in clinical tests, the average cholesterol level for the group went down. In just three weeks.

Accompanying the words is a graph showing two human outlines, partially shaded to show cholesterol levels. The figure on the left, labeled "With butter," appears to be almost half shaded; the figure on the right, labeled "With Promise," appears to be about one-quarter shaded. But the scale does not start at zero—in the graph, the scale at the side runs from about 190 to 250. (The units of the graph are nowhere specified; cholesterol is usually measured from a blood sample in milligrams per 100 cc.) What the graph actually shows then is not a drop of nearly 25 percent, but a drop from about 218 to 208, or about 4 percent, a much less dramatic decline.

Straw man technique A subtle variation of the flaw of incomplete evidence is the use of a "straw man." The straw man technique consists in taking the weakest arguments of your adversary and, after demolishing them, pretending that the whole question has been resolved. Thus, someone opposed to changes in the university system might focus on campus riots and characterize those in favor of change as bomb-throwing anarchists; the writer would conveniently forget about peaceful demonstrations and respectable opponents. An honest evaluation of a question requires that you consider those arguments that your opponent judges to be most important.

97b DRAWING CONCLUSIONS

Drawing conclusions, whether to a particular argument or to a paper as a whole, should be handled with the same care as in choosing evidence. Here are four of the most common ways of arriving at fallacious conclusions:

Post hoc fallacy Many faulty conclusions spring from the difficulty of drawing necessary connections between possible causes and effects. The post hoc fallacy (discussed in detail in Section 52) claims that the earlier of two events caused the later, simply on the basis of their relationship in time.

False analogy   A second kind of faulty conclusion derives from the use of analogies. An analogy is the comparison of two essentially unlike things that are similar in some ways. The user of an analogy hopes that one part of the comparison will illumine the other; it is invalid, however, to draw a conclusion from one part of an analogy and then to apply that conclusion to the other part. For example, consider the following:

> Last Friday the Washington Post was inveighing away against Nixon and his court, but ran also an editorial in defense of the acquittal of the so-called "Camden 28." The situation there, briefly stated, was that a jury, prodded by the judge, refused to convict a couple of dozen citizens who had come together to burn draft cards.
>
> What happened was that someone had got hold of the plot to burglarize the Selective Service office, and reported to the FBI. The FBI urged the informer to infiltrate the group and egg it along. He did so—so successfully as to overcome the protesters' misgivings about the practicality of the project. In due course they broke in, destroyed the records, were apprehended—and then tried. It is the point of the Washington Post that having been encouraged to commit the crime by the government itself, i.e., the FBI, the defendants should indeed have been let off. . . .
>
> One wonders then: Why does not the Washington Post importune Judge Sirica to acquit the Watergate felons? These were men who were asked by government officials far more exalted than FBI agents to commit their burglary. And they were asked to do it in the name of national security. What is missing in the analogy?
>
> WILLIAM F. BUCKLEY, JR.

What is missing in the analogy is, first of all, an exact correspondence between the parts: in the Camden case, the conspirators—the FBI and its informer—urged people to commit a crime so that they could be caught and jailed, an extremely unusual intention, to say the least. But in the Watergate case, the conspirators had the ordinary criminal intention of not getting caught. The analogy is inexact in a second way: if we say that the Watergate felons were urged by government officials to commit a crime, then these felons are analogous not to the Camden 28, but to the FBI informer, because, as far as the Camden 28 knew, no government officials had asked them to break into the Selective Service office. Buckley's analogy could be applied more logically to urge a stiff sentence for the FBI informer, like those handed down to the Watergate burglars.

False dichotomy   In the fallacy of false dichotomy or false dilemma, one pretends that there are only two (or at most just a few) possible conclusions to an argument, and that if we reject the one alternative, we must necessarily accept the other. Bumper stickers lend themselves to this flaw; ''America—love it or leave it'' is a familiar instance. Here is a second example:

> John Wesley Dean III chose to make himself the chief spider in the web of the Watergate cover-up. . . . And why? He's no ideologue like Gordon Liddy, the lawyer-adventurer he recruited as campaign committee counsel. No fanatic like the perjuror Bart Porter, who wore a Nixon button from the age of eight. Dean is a cool young man, with no visible loyalty either to men or ideas.
>
> Ambition seems the only explanation. Dean might have seen in the mess, created and administered by desperadoes and blunderers, the main chance—to make himself the indispensable man, to render service that would give him the pick of the spoils when the horror was finally buried, although he always thought it might not work.
>
> MARY MCGRORY

The argument assumes that a man would do something illegal for only two motives, loyalty or ambition, a patently false assumption. Among famous felons who acted from neither motive we could include Robin Hood, the Forty Thieves, and Iago.

Everybody does it   A final error in drawing conclusions is familiarly called ''everybody does it.'' It consists of justifying a particular act because someone else has done it before. Thus, committing premarital intercourse or cheating the Internal Revenue Service is all right because our friends do it, and killing civilians in a war zone or tapping telephone lines is all right because our enemies do it. Surveys of public opinion lend themselves to this misuse, but should be approached with care—everybody may be right, but then again, everybody may be wrong. If we judge an action to be wrong in itself, the repeated performance of that action will not make it right. The following example describes, with some force, a speaker whose mind is possessed by this fallacy. In 1973, the National Collegiate Athletic Association severely punished the University of Southwestern Louisiana for 125 recruiting violations. Beryl Shipley, the former USL basketball coach, stated:

> We wanted major college basketball, and in our haste to move quickly we made mistakes. But I should point out that anyone who is familiar with the structures of major college athletics knows that every major college basketball power in the nation has at one time or another committed violations in their programs.

97c PROPAGANDA

Propaganda uses the same misleading or invalid arguments mentioned in Sections 97a and 97b, and often adds characteristic flaws of its own. An argument degenerates into propaganda in a variety of ways, some of which are listed here:

Exaggeration Exaggeration occurs all the time in commercials and advertisements, of course. We might expect it any time someone is trying to sell us something, from a presidential candidate to a baseball game. When a capacity crowd turned out to see the pitching debut of David Clyde on June 28, 1973, the Associated Press reported the next day:

> American League President Joe Cronin put it another way: "Maybe this is God's way of bringing major league baseball to Dallas–Fort Worth."

Appeal to emotion Perhaps the shortest way for an argument to turn into propaganda is through an appeal to emotion. Emotion in an argument is not wrong in itself—passion can infuse a valid opinion as well as a false one—but when emotion replaces evidence, the argument has left the realm of rational discussion. An appeal to emotion may take many forms: it may tug at the loyalty of the audience, urging us ''to rally behind. . . .'' Or it may appeal to the audience's greed:

> A woman has her own special reasons for owning a Cadillac. Not the least of which is the peace of mind that comes

with knowing she is driving the car of cars. Isn't that reason enough to visit your Cadillac dealer?

Or the emotion appealed to may be more basic, as in the advertisement for Gordon's gin that shows a man in a tuxedo drinking what may be a martini while being nuzzled by a blonde in a low-cut dress. What all this has to do with gin will not withstand rational examination, but the implication is clear emotionally—good things happen to people who drink Gordon's. The argument has the same basis and power as carrying a rabbit's foot or consulting an astrology chart.

Ad hominem appeal   The emotion appealed to may be hate—for example, the character of the opponent, rather than his argument, is attacked. An attack on the person rather than the ideas of an opponent is called the ''ad hominem'' fallacy (from the Latin for ''to the man''). A prime example of the ad hominem fallacy occurred when Senator Jennings Randolph, in a debate on the Equal Rights Amendment, characterized women's liberationists as a ''small band of bra-less bubbleheads.'' As Howard Kahane notes, ''This line may have been good for a laugh in the almost all-male Senate, but it was irrelevant to arguments the women's lib representatives had presented. Randolph attacked *them* (through ridicule) rather than their arguments.''[1]

Loaded language   Propaganda uses, more or less subtly, loaded language—that is, arguments employing words that in themselves prejudice the statement the sentence is making. For example, in the *Time* article mentioned in Section 97a, we find this sentence:

> The view of the fetus as a person has spawned a nationwide, Catholic-dominated, Right to Life movement whose partisans insist that abortion deprives the fetus of due process under the Constitution.

Words like *dominated, partisans,* and probably *insist* have negative connotations for most readers—they are associated with unpleasant news about unpleasant people—and they drag these associations with them into whatever context they appear in. The use of *spawned,* especially, forfeits the claim of the sentence to objectivity. Here is

---

[1] *Logic and Contemporary Rhetoric: The Use of Reason in Everyday Life.* Belmont, Cal.: Wadsworth, 1971. P. 27. Kahane's book is an excellent introduction to its subject.

a second example:

> Although several dozen [Democratic Study Group] members could best be described as moderates, the group's leaders are staunch liberals, and the DSG's base is in the Northeast-Midwest-Pacific axis which has keynoted the left tilt of the national Democratic Party.
>
> KEVIN PHILLIPS

Consider the associations of the word *axis* in the Phillips quotation. Yet all the sentence actually states is that members of the Democratic Study Group are representatives from the Northeast, the Midwest, and the Pacific states.

Propaganda rarely bears up under close examination, even on a grammatical level. The advertisement for the detergent that washes dishes ''better'' uses the comparative form of the adverb when there is no comparison. The advertisement that calls a brand of liquor ''the thinking man's drink'' uses the definite article *the* to imply that there are no other drinks in that class. And the host of products heralded by words like *now* and *new* and *modern* play on our childlike faith that each dawn begins a better day.

Exercises

1. What logical fallacies do you find in the following examples?

    1   Professor Brown gave me an F on my last paper. I guess he just doesn't like me.
    2   Four out of five New York doctors think Abysmalac is better for your cold.
    3   Cascadia State has a three-week spring practice for their swimming team. We need spring practice too, if we are to continue to compete.
    4   Jolie Belle, star of stage and screen, votes a straight Democratic ticket.
    5   How can you think that Gauguin was a great artist? Don't you know that he abandoned his wife and children?
    6   As Lincoln said, "You can fool . . . all of the people . . . all of the time."

7 Do you think we should squander billions of welfare dollars on a bunch of loafers?
8 Highly placed White House officials expect taxes to be cut next year.
9 If marijuana isn't bad for you, why is it illegal?
10 Sudso contains no hexachlorophene.
11 If a player didn't follow the training rules, the coach would throw him off the team, so anybody who doesn't like what the President's doing should be deported.
12 Sales of liquor should be banned because it's wrong to sell intoxicating beverages.

2. Select some particular news event and compare the handling of it by a national network newscast, your local newspapers, and a weekly newsmagazine. Include the treatment by any syndicated columnists or editorials you may find. From your comparison of these sources, report to the class on any differences in coverage, attitude, or evaluation you discover.

3. Discuss the associations you have for the following words; specify which ones you would consider "loaded." Supplement the list with items of your own choosing.

authoritarian	law and order	politico
Black Power	liberation	progressive
clique	longhair	pundit
Establishment	militant	radical
hardhat	militarist	redneck
jackleg	paternalistic	utopian
junta	permissive	welfare

98 **REFERENCE WORKS**

No matter how much information on a subject is available, you have to be able to find it. Machines may someday help, but we are far from the day when a friendly robot brings us just the books and articles we need. There are two steps to finding the information you need: first, determine what books and articles have been written on your subject; second, locate them. Many undergraduates wrongly reverse the order of these steps. They locate a number of books in the card catalogue that seem by their titles to be helpful; they obtain those books and start looking for useful information in them. This procedure is faulty for a number of reasons. First, it limits you to only those books listed in the card catalogue. Second, it limits you to works published in book form; you won't find material published in newspapers, magazines, or scholarly and popular journals, by looking in the card catalogue. Third, it wastes time: you have to browse through volume after volume, not in the knowledge that what you want is there, but in the hope that it might be. And finally, you are left to evaluate the material on your own: the catalogue will not tell you whether the book is reliable or sketchy, written by a scholar or by a crackpot.

Your trip to the library ought to begin in the reference room or section. The shelves there hold dictionaries of all kinds, general and special encyclopedias, handbooks, atlases, gazetteers, yearbooks, indexes, and bibliographies. Whichever one you start with, read the introduction first. These books use a variety of different systems to classify their contents; they have their individual methods of using symbols and abbreviations; they vary in range and depth of coverage. Before you can use any of them intelligently, you have to know their particular strengths and limitations. Once again: Read the introduction.

Keep in mind the publication dates of the works you examine: some journals appear every week, some every month, and some only once a year. If your topic deals with a contemporary question, an outdated index will be of no value. Naturally, you want the most recent volume, edition, or supplement of any particular reference source. Since many reference works are frequently revised, always cite the most recent copyright date in the edition you are using.

98a ENCYCLOPEDIAS

For a general outline of the problem you are exploring, you may choose to begin by reading the pertinent material in a general encyclopedia. The great virtue of an encyclopedia is the ease of use that its alphabetical arrangement provides. You can gain background knowledge quickly, but do not let your search stop with an encyclopedia article: more recent and more specialized sources are available, and will probably be needed before you are finished.

Revisions of encyclopedias

A complete revision of a thirty-volume encyclopedia is enormously expensive—and consequently, infrequent. Instead, some encyclopedias have yearbooks or supplements listing the events since publication of the main set or last supplement. As the name implies, these usually appear annually. Check the most recent yearbook or supplement after reading the article in the main set.

Using encyclopedias

It will save you time if you note how the various encyclopedias arrange their material, since they differ in their handling of information. For instance, the *Encyclopedia Americana* separates general subjects into small, specialized articles, each of which is listed alphabetically. The *Encyclopaedia Britannica,* on the other hand, uses longer, more comprehensive articles. Thus, having read a *Britannica* article, you would be fairly sure that you had covered the most important aspects of a subject. To gain the same coverage, you might have to read several entries in the *Americana.*

Indexes for encyclopedias may follow the rest of the volumes in a volume of their own, or they may appear at the back of each volume. Indexing practices differ, so read the introduction to the index first, to save time and to make certain that you note all references to your topic.

An encyclopedia can help you get started finding more specialized sources. But the bibliographies in encyclopedias should be only a first step; at the very least, you will have to check for information appearing since the publication of the encyclopedia.

Some General Encyclopedias

Collier's Encyclopedia, 24 vols. 1965. Annual supplement published. Bibliography and index in Volume 24.

Columbia Encyclopedia, 3rd ed. 1963.

Encyclopaedia Britannica, 14th ed., 24 vols. 1929. Despite the date, this encyclopedia is continually revised, so that some articles are much more current than others. Since important scholars have contributed to the *Britannica,* the eleventh and thirteenth editions are sometimes still useful. Annual supplement published. Index and atlas in Volume 24.

Encyclopedia Americana, 30 vols. 1963. Bibliographies follow the more important articles. Annual supplement published. Index in Volume 30.

Specialized Encyclopedias

The following encyclopedias are limited to the subject matter described by, or related to that described by, their titles. They are extremely useful for their fields and associated subjects.

The Catholic Encyclopedia, 16 vols. 1907–14. Two supplements, 1922 and 1951. Covers subjects related to Catholic history, doctrine, and interest. Valuable for subjects in medieval history, literature, philosophy, and art. Before consulting it for topics where current information is important, check against *New Catholic Encyclopedia,* below.

Cyclopedia of American Agriculture, 4 vols. 1907–09.

Cyclopedia of American Government, 3 vols. 1914.

Cyclopedia of Education, 5 vols. 1911–13.

Dictionary of American History, 6 vols. 1942. First supplement, Volume 6, 1961.

Encyclopedia of Educational Research, 3rd ed. 1960.

Encyclopaedia of Religion and Ethics, 13 vols. 1908–27. Contains articles on all religions, ethical systems and movements, religious beliefs and customs, philosophies, moral practices, and related subjects in fields of anthropology, mythology, and folklore. Bibliographies included.

Encyclopedia of the Social Sciences, 15 vols. 1930–35.

Grove's Dictionary of Music and Musicians, 9 vols. 1954. Supplement, 1961. Articles on musical terms, history, theory and practice, instruments, musicians, and individual compositions, from about 1450. Special emphasis on English music and musicians. Bibliography included.

International Encyclopedia of Music and Musicians, 9th ed. 1964.

Jewish Encyclopedia, 12 vols. 1901–06.

McGraw-Hill Encyclopedia of Science and Technology, 15 vols., rev. ed. 1960. Authoritative articles on the natural sciences and their major applications in engineering, agriculture, forestry, industrial biology, and other technologies. Annual supplement published.

New Catholic Encyclopedia, 15 vols. 1967. Bibliographies follow articles; index in Volume 15. Especially useful for post–Vatican II subjects.

New Schaff-Herzog Encyclopedia of Religious Knowledge, 13 vols. 1908–12.

Thorpe's Dictionary of Applied Chemistry, 12 vols. 1937–56.

Universal Jewish Encyclopedia, 11 vols. 1939–43.

98b DICTIONARIES

Most of the time we consult a dictionary for one of three things: word meaning, pronunciation, or spelling. Dictionaries contain much more information, though, in a readily accessible form.

The same two general precautions that apply to encyclopedias should be taken with dictionaries: be sure you read the introduction (dictionaries make heavy use of rather specialized symbols), and be sure the dictionary is up to date. Dictionaries are regularly revised to include new words and new meanings for old words. *Webster's Third New International Dictionary,* for instance, includes some 100,000 words not recorded in *Webster's Second.* The great majority of these words are technical terms from the sciences and professions.

Changes in dictionaries occur as a result of editorial decisions as well. *Webster's Third* eliminated entries of biographical, fictitious, and mythological characters. It also deleted geographical references, common abbreviations, and foreign words, except for those words that have become naturalized.

Collegiate or Desk Dictionaries

The desk dictionary, the kind you will use most frequently, lists a great deal of information about words: consider, as a typical example, this definition from *Webster's New Collegiate Dictionary,* eighth edition:

> **oce·an·ic** \ˌō-shē-'an-ik\ *adj* **1 :** of, relating to, produced by, or frequenting the ocean and esp. the open sea as distinguished from littoral or neritic waters **2 :** VAST. GREAT

The dots or raised periods within the word being defined show the places where the word may be divided at the end of a line. Note that these breaks do not necessarily coincide with syllable division.

Inside the slanted lines is a guide to the pronunciation of the word.

Since the symbols used to represent particular sounds differ from dictionary to dictionary, it is important to read the key to the symbols that appears at the bottom of each page, with a more comprehensive explanation in the prefatory material. Remember that the job of a dictionary with respect to pronunciation is to record what is generally heard, not to prescribe or dictate the editor's favorite sounds. Naturally, the way words are spoken will vary from one geographical location to another, and sometimes a single entry will list two or more pronunciations for the same word. Your safest guide in such cases is to follow the practice of respected speakers from your own region.

The entry gives the part of speech of the word as the third piece of information, followed by the definitions. In the case of *oceanic,* two different senses of the word are distinguished by the arabic numerals. The small capitals for the words following **2** indicate not only that those words are synonyms for *oceanic,* but that the reader should compare the entries for *vast* and *great.*

By chance, this entry did not show four other pieces of information customarily obtained from a dictionary: etymologies, time labels, usage labels, and illustrative quotations. Compare the first and last parts of the definition for *of* in the same dictionary:

> **of** . . . *prep* [ME, off, of, fr. OE, adv. & prep.; akin to OHG *aba,* off, away, L *ab* from, away, Gk *apo*] . . . **12** *archaic* : on ⟨a plague ∼ all cowards —Shak.⟩

The etymology—the history of the form of the word—is the string of symbols and abbreviations within the square brackets. Translated, the etymology tells us that the word comes from a Middle English (ME) word meaning ''off'' or ''of,'' and, in turn, from an Old English (OE) word used both adverbially and prepositionally. We are also told that *of* has related forms: in Old High German (OHG), *aba,* meaning ''off'' or ''away''; in Latin (L), *ab,* meaning ''from'' or ''away''; and in Greek (Gk), *apo.* The twelfth definition of this many-sided word is ''on,'' with the time label ''archaic,'' meaning that (as determined by this dictionary) the word *of* has been used with this sense only sporadically since 1755. If no instances of this usage had been recorded since 1755, the word would have been marked *obs* for ''obsolete.'' A quotation (in this case, from Shakespeare) showing the use of the word in context is provided within the pointed brackets. Remember that symbols differ from dictionary to dictionary. Another dictionary may use a completely different set to show pronunciation, to trace etymologies, to mark illustrative quotations.

Always check the introduction first to be sure you understand what set your dictionary uses.

The last bit of information the dictionary provides is the usage label. A usage label always marks some restriction in the use of the word. If the restriction is geographical, the word would be called ''dialect''; if the word is seldom heard in the speech of the powerful and prestigious, it would be marked ''substandard'' or ''nonstandard''; or if the word is limited to certain contexts or certain uses, it would be labeled ''slang'' or ''technical,'' as the case might be. Editors exercise their judgment in marking words with these labels; the only way to begin to understand the standards they use for your particular dictionary is to read the discussion of those labels found at the front of the book.

Unabridged Dictionaries

The desk dictionary usually consists of a selection of the word entries in an unabridged dictionary. The unabridged dictionary offers, of course, more words, plus more definitions of the words listed in its abridgement; in addition, the unabridged offers many more illustrations of the word in context. Compare the following entry for *oceanic* from *Webster's Third New International Dictionary* with that of the *New Collegiate:*

> **oce·an·ic** \-ˌanik, -nēk\ *adj* [F *océanique*, fr. MF *oceanique*, fr. *ocean, ocean* ocean + *-ique* -ic] **1 a :** of, relating to, occurring in, living in, or frequenting the ocean ⟨∼ currents⟩ ⟨∼ depths⟩ ⟨∼ rock⟩ ⟨∼ birds⟩ **b :** affected by or produced by the ocean ⟨a wet, windy, ∼ climate —C.D.Forde⟩ **c :** resembling the ocean esp. in immensity of size or extent ⟨October gives the grain belt an ∼ vastness of gold —W.W.Haines⟩ ⟨the ∼ violence of his rage against the miseries of man's life —Walter McElroy⟩ **2** *usu cap* **:** OCEANIAN **3 :** of, relating to, constituting, or living in the open sea as distinguished from littoral or neritic regions ⟨∼ waters⟩ ⟨∼ life⟩ — compare ABYSSAL, PHOTIC **4** *usu cap* **:** relating to, belonging to, or characterizing the Austronesian family of languages or the Melanesian and Polynesian divisions of that family

One dictionary took from 1858 to 1928 to complete. This, which Albert C. Baugh called ''the greatest dictionary of any language in the world,'' was *The Oxford English Dictionary,* or the *OED,* as it is more often called. The aim of its compilers was ''to record every word which could be found in English from about the year 1000 and to exhibit the history of each—its forms, its various spellings, and all its uses and meanings, past and present.''[1] Compare the

[1] *A History of the English Language,* 2nd ed. New York: Appleton-Century-Crofts, 1957. P. 396.

OED citation for *oceanic* with the Webster definitions:

Oceanic (ōuʃiˌæˑnik), *a.* [ad. med. or mod.L. *ōceanic-us*, f. *ōceanus* OCEAN : cf. F. *océanique* (1548 in Hatz.-Darm., also in Cotgr. 1611) and -IC.]

1. Of or pertaining to, situated or living in or by, the ocean ; flowing into the ocean.

1656 [see OCEANINE]. **1755** in JOHNSON. **1772–84** COOK *Voy.* (1790) VI. 2116 Gulls, petrels, and other oceanic birds. **1830** LYELL *Princ. Geol.* I. 244 The population of all oceanic deltas are particularly exposed to suffer by such catastrophes. **1834** MRS. SOMERVILLE *Connex. Phys. Sc.* XV. (1849) 135 The Gulf-stream and other oceanic rivers. **1851–6** WOODWARD *Mollusca* 12 The oceanic-snail, and multitudes of other floating molluscs, pass their lives on the open sea. **1859** DARWIN *Orig. Spec.* iv. (1873) 82 An oceanic island at first sight seems to have been highly favourable for the production of new species. **1869** RAWLINSON *Anc. Hist.* 12 The rivers of the circumjacent plains are..oceanic, i. e. they mingle themselves with the waters of the great deep. **1880** W. B. CARPENTER in *19th Cent.* No. 38. 596 The proper oceanic area is a portion of the crust of the earth..depressed with tolerable uniformity some thousands of feet below the land area.

2. Of the nature of an ocean, ocean-like ; of immense extent or magnitude ; vast.

a **1834** COLERIDGE *Notes Eng. Divines* (1853) I. 209 His reading had been oceanic. **1834** — *Table-t.* 15 Mar., The body and substance of his [Shakspere's] works came out of the unfathomable depths of his own oceanic mind.

3. Of or pertaining to Oceania ; = OCEANIAN *A.*

1842 PRICHARD *Nat. Hist. Man* 332 The Oceanic race, is, on the other hand, the most beautiful..of all the nations who inhabit the isles of the Great Southern Ocean. **1857** *Chambers' Inform.* II. 296/1 The native inhabitants of all these islands..forming the Oceanic section of the Mongolidæ in Dr. Latham's classification.

The *OED* was revised and reissued in 1933 in thirteen volumes.

General Dictionaries

The following list groups reputable and reliable dictionaries by size. The first three are unabridged; *The American Heritage* is intermediate in size between the unabridged and the desk dictionaries that follow it.

New Standard Dictionary of the English Language, unabridged ed. New York: Funk & Wagnalls, 1963.

The Random House Dictionary of the English Language, unabridged ed. New York: Random House, 1966.

Webster's Third New International Dictionary, unabridged ed. Springfield, Mass.: G. & C. Merriam, 1961.

The American Heritage Dictionary of the English Language. Boston: American Heritage and Houghton Mifflin, 1969. The dictionary lists 155,000 entries, about the same as the desk, or college, editions that follow.

The American College Dictionary. New York: Random House, 1966.

Funk & Wagnalls Standard College Dictionary, text ed. New York: Harcourt Brace Jovanovich, 1966.

The Random House Dictionary of the English Language, college ed. New York: Random House, 1968.

Webster's New Collegiate Dictionary, 8th ed. Springfield, Mass.: G. & C. Merriam, 1973.

Webster's New World Dictionary of the American Language, 2nd college ed. Cleveland and New York: World, 1972.

Specialized Dictionaries

From time to time you may need more specific or more comprehensive information about some language question than the general dictionaries provide. For questions concerning usage, synonyms, or dialect, check the appropriate titles below:

Berrey, Lester V., and Melvin Van den Bark, eds., *American Thesaurus of Slang,* 2nd ed. 1953.

Bryant, Margaret M., *Current American Usage.* 1962.

Craigie, William, and J. R. Hulbert, eds., *A Dictionary of American English on Historical Principles,* 4 vols. 1938–44.

Mathews, Mitford M., ed., *A Dictionary of Americanisms, on Historical Principles,* 2 vols. 1951.

Partridge, Eric, *A Dictionary of Slang and Unconventional English,* 5th ed. 1961.

Roget's Thesaurus of English Words and Phrases, new ed., rev. by Robert A. Dutch. 1965.

Webster's New Dictionary of Synonyms. 1968.

Wentworth, Harold, and Stuart Berg Flexner, *Dictionary of American Slang,* supplemented ed. 1967.

98c BIOGRAPHICAL REFERENCE WORKS

Biographical information can be found in the following works, which are divided into three groups: those listed under "Universal" are not limited to persons of a particular nationality, as are the works listed under "American" and "British."

Universal Biography

Current Biography. 1940—. Living persons. Issued monthly with annual cumulations.

A *Dictionary of Universal Biography of All Ages and People,* 2nd ed. 1951.

The International Who's Who. 1935—. Living persons.

Twentieth Century Authors: A Biographical Dictionary of Modern Literature. 1942. Supplement, 1955. Living authors.

Chambers' Biographical Dictionary, rev. ed. 1961. Dead persons.

Webster's Biographical Dictionary, rev. ed. 1964. Both living and dead persons.

World Biography, 5th ed. 2 vols. 1954. Living persons.

American Biography

Dictionary of American Biography, 20 vols. 1928–37. Two supplements, 1944 and 1958. The authoritative biographical work about dead Americans. With the supplements, it includes persons whose deaths occurred before December 31, 1940.

National Cyclopaedia of American Biography. 1891—. Both living and dead Americans.

Who's Who in America. 1899—. Brief entries on living Americans, with addresses. Published every other year. For dead Americans, see *Who Was Who in America,* 3 vols. 1951–60.

Who's Who of American Women. 1958—. Living women.

British Biography

Dictionary of National Biography, 63 vols. 1885–1900. If the library you use has the reprint, rather than the original, edition, the set will consist of 21 volumes. First supplement, 3 volumes, 1901. Errata volume, 1904. Second supplement, 3 volumes, 1912. Additional volumes appeared about every ten years from 1927 to 1959, covering persons who died between 1900 and 1950.

Who's Who. 1849—. Contains information on living British subjects (and a few persons of other nationalities), with addresses. Published annually. For dead Englishmen, see *Who Was Who.* 1920—.

98d INDEXES TO PERIODICALS

Indexes to periodicals are among the most valuable of the researcher's tools, helping him to find what he wants from the mass of material continually appearing in magazines, journals, and newspapers. Of course, exactly which periodicals are examined differs from one index to another. Read the prefatory material of an index carefully to make sure that it surveys the important periodicals in the field you are working in. The dates indicated below are the years of coverage, not of publication.

General Periodicals

International Index to Periodicals, 1907–65. Succeeded by *Social Sciences and Humanities Index,* 1965—. Author and subject indexes.

The New York Times Index, 1913—. A useful guide for dating events, which can then be researched in other newspapers. Index gives date, page, and column, with cross references to related topics.

Nineteenth-Century Readers' Guide to Periodical Literature, 2 vols., 1890–99. Author and subject indexes.

Poole's Index to Periodical Literature, 1802–1881, 5 vols. Supplements cover period from 1882 to 1907. The first index to American and English periodicals, covering 479 magazines. The system of locating material used in the set was cumbersome and time-consuming, but has now been made obsolete by the publication of Marion V. Bell and Jean C. Bacon, *Poole's Index Date and Volume Key.* 1957. Use Bell and Bacon to locate material in the index.

Readers' Guide to Periodical Literature, 1900—. An author and subject index to more than one hundred well-known general American periodicals.

Specialized Periodicals

The following works are listed alphabetically by the word in the title that describes the subject matter. For example, *International Abstracts of Biological Sciences* is listed as if the first word were *Biological.*

International Aerospace Abstracts, 1961—.

Agricultural Index, 1916–64. Succeeded by *Biological and Agricultural Index,* 1964—. Subject index.

Bibliography of Agriculture, 1941—.

Art Index, 1929—. Author and subject indexes.

Bibliographic Index, 1937—. Alphabetical subject list of both separately published bibliographies and bibliographies included in books and periodicals, many in foreign languages.

Biological Abstracts, 1927—. Succeeds *Botanical Abstracts,* 1918–26, and *Abstracts of Bacteriology,* 1917–26.

International Abstracts of Biological Sciences, 1954—.

Book Review Digest, 1905—. Index to reviews of fiction and nonfiction in over fifty American and English periodicals, classified by the author of the reviewed work. Subject and title indexes.

Book Review Index, 1965—.

Technical Book Review Index, 1917–29 and 1935—.

Index to Book Reviews in the Humanities, 1960—.

Business Periodicals Index, 1958—. Prior to 1958, part of *Industrial Arts Index.*

Catholic Periodical Index, 1930—. Subject index.

Chemical Abstracts, 1907—.

Economic Abstracts, 1951—.

Index to Economic Journals, 1886–1963. Six volumes published to date.

Education Abstracts, 1949—.

Education Index, 1929—. Subject index to articles in about 150 magazines in the fields of education and psychology. Also includes references to selected books, bulletins, and reports on education.

Engineering Index, 1884—.

Electrical Engineering. See *Science Abstracts.*

Geological Abstracts, 1953–58. Succeeded by *GeoScience Abstracts,* 1959—.

Bibliography and Index of Geology, Exclusive of North America, 1934—.

Bibliography of North American Geology, 1919—.

Historical Abstracts, 1955—.

International Bibliography of Historical Sciences, 1926—.

Writings on American History, 1902—. Annual bibliography of articles and separately published books on American history.

Writings on British History, 1934—.

Annual Bibliography of Language and Literature, PMLA, 1919—. Up to 1955, the PMLA bibliography was restricted to books and articles by Americans. The coverage is now international, including writings about and in an astonishing number of languages and national literatures.

Index to Legal Periodicals, 1908—. Author and subject indexes.

Excerpta Medica, 1947—. An index to medicine and associated subjects.

Index Medicus, 1879–1926. Succeeded by *Quarterly Cumulative Index Medicus,* 1927—. Author and subject indexes.

Meteorological and Geoastrophysical Abstracts, 1950—.

Music Index, 1949—. Author and subject indexes.

Bibliography of Philosophy, 1934—.

Physics. See *Science Abstracts.*

Psychological Abstracts. 1927—. Partially overlaps the coverage of *Psychological Index,* published from 1894 to 1935, when the two journals merged.

Bulletin of the Public Affairs Information Service, 1915—.

Index to Religious Periodical Literature, 1949—.

Science Abstracts, 1898—. Includes *Physics Abstracts* and *Electrical Engineering Abstracts.*

Applied Science and Technology Index, 1958—. Prior to 1958, part of *Industrial Arts Index.* Subject index.

International Bibliography of the Social Sciences. A United Nations publication. Includes economics, 1952—; political science, 1952—; social and cultural anthropology, 1955—; and sociology, 1951—.

Sociological Abstracts, 1952—.

Technical Translations, 1959—. A United States government publication.

United Nations Documents Index, 1950—.

United States government publications. Research reports are listed in the *Index to Federal Research and Development Reports,* 1965—. Between 1949 and 1964, the subjects now collected in this index were listed in *Nuclear Science Abstracts, Scientific and Technical Aerospace Reports, Technical Abstract Bulletin,* or *United States Government Research and Development Reports.* See also *Monthly Catalog of United States Government Publications,* 1895—, and *Monthly Checklist of State Publications,* 1910—. Locating government publications can be a difficult job. For help with the job, consult Laurence F. Schmeckebier and R. B. Eastin, *Government Publications and Their Use,* rev. ed. 1969.

Zoological Record. 1864—.

98e ALMANACS, YEARBOOKS, AND ATLASES

Often in research, you need a specific fact, a location, a statistic, a date. Two general reference aids supply information of this type—yearbooks, chiefly for material that can be chronologically arranged; and atlases or gazetteers, for material that can be geographically fixed. Almanacs usually combine information of both varieties.

Yearbooks record contemporary events, changes or trends in many different fields, and a wide variety of statistics. Below are selected lists of the more important almanacs, yearbooks, and atlases.

Almanacs and Yearbooks

The Americana Annual: An Encyclopedia of Current Events, 1923—. The annual supplement to the *Encyclopedia Americana.*

The American Yearbook: A Record of Events and Progress, 1910–19 and 1925—.

The Annual Register: A Review of Public Events at Home and Abroad, 1758—. Published in London, with concentration on English events.

Britannica Book of the Year, 1938—. Summaries of political, social, economic, and scientific developments, including statistical information. The annual supplement to the *Encyclopaedia Britannica.*

Collier's Year Book, 1939—.

Facts on File: A Weekly Synopsis of World Events, 1940—.

Information Please Almanac, 1947—.

The New International Year Book: A Compendium of the World's Progress, 1907—.

The Statesman's Year-Book: Statistical and Historical Annual of the States of the World, 1864—. Published in London, this yearbook gives concise data about countries, their governments, economic conditions, education, religion, defense, agriculture, commerce, industry, and so on. Bibliography for each country.

Statistical Abstract of the United States, 1878—. The largest readily accessible collection of statistical information.

The World Almanac and Book of Facts, 1868—. A standard reference almanac of miscellaneous information. Useful and compact enough to deserve a place on the student's desk beside his dictionary and thesaurus.

Yearbook of the United Nations, 1947—.

Atlases

Atlases are devoted to geographical information. In addition to maps, atlases usually contain general and statistical information on climate, vegetation, agriculture, industry, ocean depths, ocean and air currents, seismic areas, highways, railways, population densities, and so on. Historical atlases contain maps showing various political boundaries and their changes through time.

In order to make the best possible use of an atlas, note the table of contents, index, and copyright date. Atlases are copyrighted as other books are; since geographical boundaries, population figures, and the like change rather steadily, it is important that any atlas you use should be up to date and accurate.

Some atlases provide indexes in the margins of the maps, but the majority have a comprehensive index to all the maps at the back of the volume. Wherever the index is, the names of cities, rivers, mountains, lakes, and so on, are arranged alphabetically. Directions for finding the place sought follow the name. Often the index includes a pronunciation guide to the names. Dates following titles below indicate year of publication.

Advanced Atlas of Modern Geography, 3rd ed. 1956.

Atlas of American History. 1943.

Atlas of World History. 1957.

Collier's World Atlas and Gazetteer. 1953.

Columbia-Lippincott Gazetteer of the World. 1962. Lists over 130,000 names of places and geographic features, including the ancient world; pronunciation and variant spellings are given. Covers population, altitude, history, trade, industry, natural resources, and cultural institutions.

Encyclopaedia Britannica World Atlas. 1963.

Goode's World Atlas, 12th ed. 1964.

Historical Atlas, 8th ed. 1956. One of the best of the historical atlases, covering from 200 B.C. to A.D. 1955. Especially good for war campaigns, treaty adjustments, and development of commerce.

Macmillan World Gazetteer and Geographical Dictionary, rev. ed., ed. T. C. Collocott and J. O. Thorne. 1961.

National Geographic Atlas of the World, ed. M. B. Grosvenor. 1963.

The Times Atlas of the World, ed. John W. Bartholomew, 5 vols. 1955–59. The leading English-language atlas, with major emphasis on physical features. Special attention is given to islands and island groups.

98f   GUIDES TO LITERATURE AND MYTHOLOGY

Guides to mythology are useful chiefly in explaining allusions. The literary histories and guides have wider applications: they give brief accounts of the lives of authors, provide background material to aid interpretation, identify particular works, and explain terms used in criticism. Listed below are the most frequently consulted guides to literature and mythology.

Bartlett's Familiar Quotations, 13th ed. 1955. A standard collection, arranged chronologically by author, from about 2000 B.C.

Cambridge Bibliography of English Literature, 4 vols. 1940. Supplement, Volume 5, 1957. Usually the first step in investigating a topic in English literature, the *CBEL* lists works by authors, a selection of the editions of those works, and an extensive selection of criticism of the works.

Cambridge History of American Literature, 4 vols. 1917–21.

Cambridge History of English Literature, 15 vols. 1907–27. The most important general history of English literature from its beginnings to the end of the nineteenth century. Each chapter is written by a specialist in the field. Includes bibliographies.

Encyclopedia of Poetry and Poetics. 1965.

Essay and General Literature Index. 1934. Covers 1900–33. Supplement, 1941—.

Granger's Index to Poetry and Recitations, 5th ed. 1962. Poetry found in anthologies is indexed by title and first line, by author, and by subject.

Literary History of the United States, 3rd ed., 2 vols. 1963. The first volume is a survey of American literary history; the second is a bibliography that is especially valuable for its sections on individual authors, with critical and evaluative comments on editions, biographies, etc.

The New Century Handbook of English Literature. 1956.

Oxford Classical Dictionary. 1949.

Oxford Companion to American Literature, 4th ed. 1965.

Oxford Companion to Classical Literature, 2nd ed. 1937.

Oxford Companion to English Literature, 3rd ed. 1946.

The Reader's Encyclopedia, 2nd ed. 1965. Brief articles on writers, philosophers, plots and characters, literary and mythological allusions, art, music, and other topics.

The Year's Work in English Studies. 1921—. Annual summary of criticism, published by the English Association.

Exercises

1. Visit your library and write a brief report on two or more reference books. Using either an encyclopedia, a yearbook, or an atlas, answer the following questions:

    1 What is the reference work's title?
    2 What is its copyright date?
    3 What is the frequency of its publication?
    4 What does the work attempt to cover?
    5 What is its method of arrangement?
    6 What is the location of its index?
    7 Where is the key to its abbreviations located?

2. Investigate a handbook in a field that interests you, then give an oral report on two or three of its entries. Be prepared to describe the handbook's system of organization well enough to explain its use to a fellow student.

3. Locate reference books that will provide the information asked for below, and also give the page numbers where the information may be found:

    1 the latest magazine and newspaper articles on airline safety
    2 an account of agriculture in a foreign country
    3 the five largest cities in the United States
    4 a photograph of John Barth
    5 the biography of Margaret Mead
    6 the developments of the past year in the space program
    7 an illustrated article on witchcraft

4. Collaborate with a fellow student on the following two exercises, each of you doing one of them. Then check each other's work and compare notes on your findings:

    1 Which of the following reference works is published most frequently?
    Who's Who
    Current Biography
    Biographical Index
    2 Compare entries for any historical figure in each of the following works. Which has the longest entry? Which has the shortest?

Webster's Biographical Dictionary
Dictionary of American Biography
one of the multivolume encyclopedias

99 TAKING NOTES

All the material in this section is designed to help in the preparation
of a long paper with many references. Shorter papers with only a
few notes may be handled in a less elaborate fashion, as long as
care is taken to avoid the problems that will be mentioned.

Reference Cards

Your first step is to make sure you get your references right. Before
taking notes from any source, fill out a reference card on the work.
If you take the time to list the information about the work in the
correct form for documentation, it will be simpler for you to prepare
the bibliography later, since the reference cards can be arranged
in alphabetical order, and the bibliography typed directly from them.

The reference cards (3″ × 5″ index cards or slips are large
enough) should list all the bibliographical information taken from the
title page of the work itself, together with the library call number
of the work in case you need to refer to the book again.

Williams, Charles, *War in Heaven.*
New York: Pellegrini + Cudahy, 1949.

PZ3

W67144

If, after examining the book, you find no pertinent information in it, and you will not be using or citing it, make a note on your reference card that it contains nothing that you need. Later on, this card and its notation may save you a trip to the library if you have forgotten whether you checked the work.

Note Cards

As you find information you wish to use, list that information on note cards. These cards or slips should be larger than the reference cards, large enough to accommodate a good-sized note; 5″ × 8″ is a convenient and readily available size. The top of the note card needs only a brief heading, directing you to the appropriate reference card, and an indication of the page or pages where the information comes from. For the example given above, your note card might look like this:

> Williams, p. 102
>
> "He took off his cassock and put on--in a fantastic culmination-- the dinner jacket he had been wearing." (Needs liturgical clothing for magic rites.)

Of course, if your bibliography includes works by another author named Williams, you would need to head this card "Williams, C., p. 102," or if you cited several works by Charles Williams, information identifying this particular work would appear in the heading as "Williams, *War in Heaven*, p. 102."

When you copy material verbatim from the work, always enclose it in quotation marks and copy it carefully and accurately. Check it against the original when you have finished copying it, and give it a final check before the book leaves your hands. Whenever you include your own words or comments on the note cards, it is a good idea to use some method such as enclosing them in parentheses (as has been done in the example). This will help you to distinguish an exact quotation from your paraphrase or commentary, and may save you from inadvertently plagiarizing from your source.

Limit yourself to one piece of information or evidence for each card. Although two pieces of information may seem closely related when you copy them, you cannot be sure that they will not be separated by several pages in your paper. You will end up by cutting note cards in half if two pieces of information needed at different places in your paper are on the same card.

Finally, when you are in doubt whether to take a note or not, take it. If it turns out that you don't need it, you will have wasted a few minutes. If you need it and have not taken the note, you may waste a great deal more time making a special trip to the library.

100 WRITING THE PAPER

Assuming that you have selected your topic, that your notes are taken and your material gathered, the largest part of the job is still before you—the actual writing of the paper. What is perhaps the commonest method requires you to begin by constructing an outline, a logical arrangement of the topics and subtopics to be discussed in their proper order. But many students find this method difficult, if not impossible, to use, and it does seem that there are at least two flaws in the procedure.

First, outlining an essay in a book is a simple enough job: all the ideas, all the connections, are there in front of you. But it takes a different kind of imagination to outline something that has not been written yet, even if the planning for the essay-to-be has been as thorough as you can make it. It is entirely possible that you do not know exactly what you are going to say until you have said it. In writing, part of the process of thinking the subject through involves putting it into words—actually writing something about it. In the writer's head is a notion, clear or foggy, of what he wants to say—a notion that can take full shape only when it is externalized, when it is out of the writer's head and onto the paper.

Second, although an outline does, in a sense, support the paper to be written, it can also limit the possibilities of that paper. Suppose you have a perfect outline—as sharp in its details, as accurate in the joining of one part to another, as a blueprint. You begin to write, and halfway through the paper a new idea occurs to you. It should be no surprise that the creative act of writing can itself engender new ideas. Any writer would hope to be absolutely inundated with insights, whenever they come. But what are you to do? Stop at that point and begin again from scratch, constructing a new outline to accommodate the new idea? Or do you just throw up your hands, say that you cannot fit it in, and keep moving on? An outline can chain a writer to one particular development of a topic and rob the essay of any chance of spontaneity. We will consider outlines at the proper place, but for the moment, let's consider a different way: let's see if we can devise a method that will allow new material to be incorporated if some new ideas turn up.

101 THE PRELIMINARY DRAFT

If you find it comfortable and convenient to make an outline first, and write the paper to fit it, do so by all means. But if you have had difficulties writing that way, the method proposed here may help.

You probably already have a pretty accurate idea of how much time it takes you to write a paper of a given length. Whatever amount of time you have for a particular writing task, there are good and bad ways of spending it: an hour an evening for three evenings, say, will produce a better paper, other things being equal, than a three-hour stretch the night before the paper is due.

The great majority of old sayings about how to get a job done could probably be reduced to a single precept: "Begin." This is sound advice for writing as well as for anything else. Writers say they are afraid of beginning: they stare paralyzed at a blank sheet of paper. The only way to overcome this fear is also the simplest way: begin to write anything at all about the topic you are dealing with. It may be the first thing that comes to your mind, or what seems to you the most important point of your topic, or perhaps even the conclusion you hope eventually to reach. Exactly what you write matters less than the physical action of writing and the mental action of putting your thoughts into words.

Once you have started (leave plenty of room between the lines on this draft) keep it up: write next whatever occurs to you next. At this stage, plan on writing more than you need. Suppose your task is to write a five-hundred-word theme. Figuring it out, you think that your theme will have to cover almost two typewritten pages, double-spaced. If you write only about five hundred words on the preliminary draft, chances are your final version will be thin, drawn-out stuff. Do this instead: let these sentences you write first, the material you are just trying to get down on paper, equal about half again as much as your final total. Aim then, at writing about 700 to 750 words. Now fill out that total; write anything, so long as it has to do with your topic. For a research paper, insert your notes whenever one seems to apply.

Do not worry about the sentences being connected. Do not worry at this point about transitions between sentences or paragraphs, or the grouping of sentences into paragraphs. Do not worry about development or examples or anything but filling that space. As an idea occurs to you, write it down. If a line of thought presents itself, follow that line of thought to its conclusion. In short, let your mind work freely on the topic, not letting any notions of order restrict you, but letting the essay develop itself, as it were. The intention here is to get the information out of your head and onto the paper in front of you. When you have filled your allotted amount, stop. Reward yourself by doing something else. If you can, put the preliminary draft aside till the next day, and begin the second step then.

102   THE OUTLINE

When you next take up your preliminary draft, look it over. With some material in front of you, you can begin arranging that material, putting each section into its proper place. Some of the sentences, certainly, will be more closely related than others. Group the related sentences. You can do this physically if you like, by cutting the pages apart. Focus your attention on one of these groups of sentences, and try to summarize in one statement the idea of that group. What you are doing here is producing an outline, or as much of an outline as you can make from the material you have. Remember, at this stage, you are not rewriting the sentences themselves, but trying to extract the central ideas from groups of sentences, and arranging those ideas on your outline.

102a THE INTRODUCTION

When sorting the groups to determine where they should go, ask yourself questions like these:

Do any of the sentences or groups place a limitation on the topic, as examples 1 to 3 do?

> 1   Let me first say, however, that I have no intention whatever of trying to show that one national system is, on balance, better than the other; only that they are much more different than is usually realized.
>
> GEOFFREY CROWTHER
>
> 2   What I have to say here touches mainly lyric poetry.
>
> OWEN BARFIELD
>
> 3   We may begin by ruling out of consideration one way of treating fictions as sources of knowledge.
>
> C. S. LEWIS

Do any of the sentences formally or informally define or explain terms in the topic, as examples 4 to 6 do?

> 4   The richness of Shakespeare's language, as Empson uses that term, is presumably its tendency to yield complicated "net impressions."
>
> CHARLES L. STEVENSON
>
> 5   One of the attempts at a standard of poetic value most often reiterated in past ages has been the doctrinal— the explicitly didactic.
>
> W. K. WIMSATT
>
> 6   The bullfight is not a sport in the Anglo-Saxon sense of the word, that is, it is not an equal contest or an attempt at an equal contest between a bull and a man.
>
> ERNEST HEMINGWAY

Do any of the sentences state how many parts there are to the topic or question, how your material is going to be arranged, how much ground you plan to cover, as examples 7 and 8 do?

7 These can be subdivided into (1) questions about their capabilities; (2) questions about their moral and other propensities; and (3) questions about what it is like to *be* a member of such and such a race in such and such a situation.

RICHARD M. HARE

8 Two great maxims emerge from his treatment.

WILLIAM JAMES

All such material—whatever limits or restricts the topic, whatever defines or explains it, and whatever shows how it will be arranged—is properly introductory, and can be used to form the first part of the outline and, eventually, the first part of the paper.

102b THE BODY OF THE PAPER

The scope of this book allows us to mention only a few of the methods by which the body of the essay can be developed. Among the common ways are the following:

(1) Chronological organization: Here the material, say a narrative or a process, is arranged in order of time, beginning with what happens first, then explaining what happens next, and so on.

(2) Spatial organization: Often in describing the appearance of a scene or a character, the writer begins at some particular point and moves his focus from that point in some orderly direction, perhaps top to bottom, or outward from a central point, or just the reverse—''closing in'' on the subject.

(3) Comparison or contrast: The writer notes the similarities or differences between two attitudes, characters, solutions to problems, and so on.

(4) Cause and effect: First the factors contributing to an event, action, or problem are presented, and then the results of those factors.

These are only a few methods, and all of them have variations. The existence of order in the arrangement of your material is more important than the type of order you choose. Always consider first what it is you are trying to explain, then consider alternative ways of ordering your material to fit the explanation.

Suppose, for example, you want to write about human behavior, say the actions of characters in a drama. Perhaps you have an assigned topic, such as analyzing the character of Creon in Sophocles' play *Antigone*. There are only two possible sources of evidence—the words and actions of the play. You examine what Creon says, what others say about him, what he does, and how he reacts to what others do; you then make some generalization about the character of Creon on the basis of that examination—what is important to him, what influences him, how he thinks, or how he does not think. There are at least two ways of presenting your material to the reader. The first way would be to state your generalization, followed in the outline by summaries of the groups of sentences that support the generalization. The second way would be just the reverse: to lead up to the generalization by giving the evidence first— that is, by beginning with the concrete parts of the argument, followed by the abstraction, your comment on the evidence. This second method may be a little better for the beginning writer; at least the material appears to be going somewhere, to be leading to a conclusion.

By pulling your sentences together like this, you are in effect creating an outline. At this point, pause a little and look over the outline as it is taking shape. Compare the points you discuss with the points listed in the introduction. If you say there that you will cover questions 1, 2, and 3, do not surprise the reader by introducing a fourth question unannounced. Consider at this time whether you have left out any obvious parts. Perhaps more to the point: Are there any parts in the outline that you do not need? For example, in the Creon paper, a digression on the purpose of the Greek chorus would hardly advance your argument. Eliminate any sections that do not move the essay forward to its conclusion. By the same token, consider whether the topic itself may need to be changed in light of your current thinking. You may discover that the topic you have written about is not quite the topic you started with. Make any modifications necessary in the topic itself.

102c THE CONCLUSION

Do any of the groups of sentences make predictions about what is likely to happen in the future? Do any of the sentences summarize what has happened? Do any of the sentences draw general inferences, or make statements whose applicability goes beyond the limits of the body of the paper? Do any of the sentences propose solutions to problems, suggestions for action, or the like? All such sentences are properly concluding material, and can serve as the basis of your outline of the ending of the paper.

After all this, you will probably have some sentences left over, sentences that do not seem to fit in anywhere—throw them away.

102d SAMPLE OUTLINES

Your instructor may ask you to hand in a formal outline with your paper. The following two samples show acceptable outline forms: the first, for obvious reasons, is sometimes called a "phrase" outline; the second puts all information in full sentences, and is therefore called a "sentence" outline. Find out if your instructor prefers one method over the other.

Phrase Outline

Existentialism in Jean-Paul Sartre's *No Exit*

I. Thesis paragraph: Object of the paper
    A. A definition of existentialism
    B. Adherence to existentialism in Sartre's *No Exit*
II. A definition of existentialism
    A. Five fundamental themes
        1. A quest for being
        2. A commitment to finitude
        3. Transcendence
        4. Coexistence
        5. Destiny
    B. The principle of freedom
    C. The importance of existence over essence
    D. Man's capacity for change
III. Sartre's *No Exit*
    A. Adherence to existential attitudes
        1. Being's confrontation with death
        2. Man's rejection of other men
        3. Acceptance of the responsibility of freedom
        4. The characters' capacity for change

B. Conclusion: Presence of chief existential themes in Sartre's *No Exit*

Sentence Outline

The Shape of the Globe Theater

I. Thesis: The shape of Shakespeare's Globe Theater has long been controversial, and is relevant to the interpretation of his plays.

II. Evidence of the shape of the Globe may be divided into three groups.

    A. Was the Globe round?

        1. Contemporary references suggest a round building.

            a. Some Shakespearean references suggest a round building.

            b. Other contemporary references suggest a round building.

                (1) Such evidence occurs in non-Shakespearean plays performed at the Globe.

                (2) The name "Globe" suggests a round building.

            c. Pictorial evidence for a round building exists in the drawings of Norden, Hondius, and Hollar, and the background sketches of Jones.

        2. Evidence against a round building includes the difficulties of a round shape for wooden construction and the possibility of a misinterpretation of the drawings.

    B. Was the Globe polygonal?

        1. Pictorial evidence for a polygonal building exists in Norden's drawing, Visscher's drawing, Ryther's Bankside drawing, and Delaram's *View of London*.

        2. E. K. Chambers' research suggests a polygonal building.

    C. Was the Globe specifically hexagonal?

        1. Mrs. Thrale's account of the property identifies the building as hexagonal.

2. The plan of design of a hexagonal building
has specific advantages.
III. Conclusion: The Globe was probably polygonal.

103 THE FIRST DRAFT

Now you are ready to write the first draft of your paper. Of all the steps, this is probably the simplest, since all you need to do at this point is rearrange the sentences you have decided to keep, writing them in the order of your outline. Naturally, some revision will be needed to make the parts fit together. Some paragraphs will need expansion or development, and you will need to make the paragraphs fit smoothly together.

103a PARAGRAPH DEVELOPMENT

Introduction

The purpose of language can hardly be anything but getting ideas from one mind to another. But written language is at a disadvantage, compared with spoken, in serving this purpose. When a reader does not understand something he sees on the page, he cannot immediately ask the writer what he meant. Using a term from the communications industry, we might say that the writer gets no feedback: he is unable to find out immediately how well he is making himself understood. Of course, a writer has some compensating advantages—he can plan in advance, so that the progression of his thoughts is more orderly, and the connections between those thoughts is more explicit, than those of all but the most skillful speakers. The paragraph, well put together, is an important element in the development of your paper.

The paragraph is not a natural unit of language in the way that the sentence is. Yet the skillfully written paragraph gathers related material into a unit that can be perceived by the eye, setting particular sections apart from others. The indentation of the paragraph acts as a signal that the author's thought is taking a slightly different turn from what has gone before.

Paragraphs aid in another way, one more directly connected with the overall structure of the paper. If we think about the way sentences work, we begin to see the usefulness of a device like the paragraph. In Section 1, we spoke about topics and comments: what we want to talk about, and the things we want to say about them. In that section, we saw that often a noun phrase serves as a topic and the rest of the sentence serves as the comment on that topic. Section 42 showed that a sentence can itself be turned into a topic. Suppose, then, that this complex sentence is what we want to speak of; the rest of the paragraph can serve as a comment on that "topic sentence."

As an example, consider a noun phrase like *The Shadow*. As the subject of a sentence, it is a topic, and the rest of the sentence comments on it:

> 1   The Shadow used the identity of Lamont Cranston, a wealthy lawyer.

Now we can take the whole of sentence 1 and add an adverbial to it, making the comment more complex:

> 2   The Shadow used the identity of Lamont Cranston, a wealthy lawyer, as his cover in a relentless war on crime.

Now we can take the whole of sentence 2, put it into a larger context, and make sentence 2 the topic by applying another comment:

> 3   The Shadow used the identity of Lamont Cranston, a wealthy lawyer, as his cover in a relentless war on crime—a fact known only to his faithful Xinca Indian servants and his readers.

Now suppose this sentence to be the first one in a paragraph (as indeed it is); the rest of the sentences of that paragraph can then form a complex comment by telling us more about the subject expressed in sentence 3:

> 4   The Shadow used the identity of Lamont Cranston, a wealthy lawyer, as his cover in a relentless war on crime—a fact known only to his faithful Xinca Indian

servants and his readers. He also disguised himself as the police-station janitor, and as Henry Arnaud, another mysterious figure. The Shadow, who wore a bat-like black cloak and a black hat, cracked crimes the police could not. He possessed the power of surrounding himself with darkness, and his "bloodchilling laugh," accompanied by two red-lit eyes glowing out of the dark, unhinged crooks and destroyed their will to resist. (In case they recovered too soon, The Shadow carried four pistols.)

RUSSEL B. NYE

The paragraph can serve as a larger component in the development of your paper; each paragraph should act like a complex comment, explaining the topic, defining it, giving examples of it, and so on. The rest of this section deals with several ways in which paragraphs can be extended and developed.

Through Definition and Example

One of the commonest flaws in student writing is the underdeveloped paragraph. Such paragraphs often have a clearly stated topic, but fail to say much about it. Here we want to look at different ways of forming comments extending through a whole paragraph. One thing to remember is that when we talk about putting language together, we are also talking about putting thoughts together, since language gives concrete form to ideas. Therefore, when in Sections 46, 48, and 50 we discussed some relations between sentences and parts of sentences, we might just as well have been talking about the relations between actions or events or concepts. It is natural for us to join larger ideas embodied in sentences in the same way that we join smaller ideas within sentences.

To begin with, let us note what happens in very simple sentences built around the verb *be,* such as the following:

5   Allan is a student.

We can describe what example 5 does in several ways: we can say that it partially defines Allan, or describes him, or identifies him as a member of a particular class. In the same manner, one of the common paragraph types defines or identifies something:

> 6   A phoneme is a class of sounds which: (1) are phoneti-
> cally similar and (2) show certain characteristic pat-
> terns of distribution in the language or dialect under
> consideration. Note that this definition is restricted
> in its application to a single language or dialect. There
> is no such thing as a general /p/ phoneme. There is,
> however, an English /p/ phoneme. Likewise there is
> a Hindi /p/ phoneme. They are in no sense identical.
> Each is a feature of its own language and not relevant
> to any other language.
>
> H. A. GLEASON, JR.

Note that the formal definition in example 6 is entirely contained in the first sentence. Often the definition can itself be handled in a sentence or two, leaving some room in the paragraph for the writer to expand, refine, or further clarify what he means. In this case, Gleason continues in the second and third sentences to stress a particularly important part of the definition. He then gives examples in the next two sentences, and finishes with two statements that link the examples to the part of the definition he originally emphasized.

Note also the movement from general to particular and back again in the paragraph. We often find examples occurring in paragraphs that begin with a definition, since the concrete instance that the example provides gives us an immediate application of the definition. Often, too, the paragraph does not end with the example, but returns to the definition, re-emphasizing it. We can observe this movement in example 7:

> 7   In the same spirit of literal undertaking, saints spend
> their lives and their burning abilities on every sort of
> necessity they find at hand. They care for lepers,
> foundlings, prisoners of war, idiots, orphans. They
> defend Jews as did Hugh of Lincoln, who, single-
> handed, cowed armed and angry mobs in England of
> the twelfth century or sheltered fugitives in his epis-
> copal palace. They found hospitals. They teach the
> ignorant. Like Raymond Nonnatus they give them-
> selves up as hostages for the ransom of slaves and
> captives. Imagine the most enormous of the corporal
> acts of mercy, and some saint or whole contingent of
> saints has committed it.
>
> PHYLLIS McGINLEY

The first sentence is extremely general: *saints spend their lives; every sort of necessity*. The next sentence states some of those necessities, although it is still general in its statement of who does these things: the subject is simply *They*. The third sentence links a particular act with a particular person. After two short, general sentences, we have the second example within the paragraph, which ends with a final generalization that restates what the opening sentence said.

Identifying something, by definition or example or both, is a common paragraph strategy, especially at the start of the essay or the beginning of some section of it. Like a debater, the writer uses such places to make sure that his audience does not misunderstand the terms and topics he is using.

Through Repeated Examples

A writer may use an example to give concrete substance to a definition, as we saw in examples 6 and 7. A second use of examples is to support an argument or statement. Usually more elaborate, such examples appear as evidence to prove what the writer says. Note the examples that occupy everything after the first two sentences in the next paragraph:

> 8 Among Negroes the tradition was to give presents to children going only from one grade to another. How much more important this was when the person was graduating at the top of the class. Uncle Willie and Momma had sent away for a Mickey Mouse watch like Bailey's. Louise gave me four embroidered handkerchiefs. (I gave her crocheted doilies.) Mrs. Sneed, the minister's wife, made me an undershirt to wear for graduation, and nearly every customer gave me a nickel or maybe even a dime with the instruction "Keep on moving to higher ground," or some such encouragement.
>
> MAYA ANGELOU

Furnishing a number of examples in sequence is the counterpart on the paragraph level of the simple device of joining one noun phrase to another by *and*. In both cases, the writer's technique is additive, simply joining one thing to another.

441

Through Comparison and Contrast

The additive use of examples is a simple and straightforward way of developing a paragraph. A more complex use involves taking two illustrations or examples and comparing them point for point. The writer may wish to draw our attention forcefully to similarities between the two, or to emphasize differences. Example 9 shows such a contrast; note that the first sentence is again general, telling in what respect the two men are to be compared. The detailing sentences that follow support the first sentence by a series of three contrasts:

> 9 In character, the two Emperors were totally unlike. Nicholas was gentle, shy and painfully aware of his own limitations; the Kaiser was a braggart, a bully, and a strutting exhibitionist. Nicholas hated the idea of becoming a sovereign; William all but wrenched the crown from the head of his dying father, Frederick III. As Tsar, Nicholas tried to live quietly with his wife, avoiding fuss. William delighted in parading about in high black boots, white cloak, a silver breastplate and an evil-looking spiked helmet.
>
> ROBERT K. MASSIE

A well-chosen example gives the reader a second chance at understanding what you mean. Definitions and examples work from opposite ends, so to speak. When we know what a definition covers, and supply an instance to fit it, we are moving from general knowledge to a particular application of that knowledge. On the other hand, when we have a group of particulars and decide what they all have in common, we are generalizing about the data that we have. Readers can probably be divided into those who particularize better and those who generalize better, but a careful writer can make provision for both kinds by including both thoughtful definitions and well-chosen examples.

Through Specification of Time and Place

Consider what adverbials of time and place do for the sentences in which they appear. For a sentence like

> 10a The four of them founded a commune.

we have no specific information about the time and place of the event described. But if we add two adverbials, we can locate the event in terms of the world we know:

10b   In 1961, the four of them founded a commune in Utah.

When we organize the materials of a paragraph by placing them in a time or space relationship, we are using one of the most common means of paragraph development.

What are sometimes called ''process'' paragraphs are simple instances of time development. In such paragraphs, often found in instruction sheets, how-to-do-it books, and the like, we are told what to do first, what to do second, what to do third, and so on. Step A precedes step B, which precedes step C, until the end of the process is reached:

11   When the jar is filled, cover the cabbage with a clean white cloth, large cabbage leaves, or a saucer. Then place a flat flint rock or other weight on top of this to hold the cabbage under the brine. Let this stand ten days, or as long as is necessary to get it as sour as you want.

When this is completed, take the kraut out and pack it in canning jars. Then put the jars in a pot of water and bring it to a boil to both seal the jars and cook the cabbage.

The Foxfire Book

Note the simple relation between events in the above paragraphs, signaled by words like *when* and *then*.

Paragraphs dealing with the actions of real people (in short, history) are often developed chronologically. Note how the author of example 12 avoided a long list of dates, however, by inserting relevant geographical material:

12   In 1829 Serbia had also become a semi-independent principality after a generation of struggles for freedom, and by mid-century she was raising the issue of southern Slav unification. Her rights were reaffirmed by the powers in 1856. To her southwest lay the tough mountain people of Montenegro, relentless fighters

against the Turks; to the west the provinces of Bosnia and Herzegovina were inhabited by Slavs under Turkish rule; on the north were Slavs under Austrian and Hungarian rule; on the east and south lived Slav minorities in territories held by Turkey. The internal politics of Serbia, as of Greece, were an explosive mixture of ferocious domestic feuds and excitable nationalist claims. Prince Alexander of the "Black George" dynasty ruled from 1842 until 1858, when he was deposed by popular uprising. He was replaced by Milosh, of the rival Obrenovich dynasty, who had ruled from 1817–1839. He reigned only until 1860, when his son Michael succeeded to his turbulent inheritance. With the aid of the western powers he contrived, in 1867, to have the last of the Turkish garrisons withdrawn from Serbia. He was assassinated the following year.

DAVID THOMSON

Note that both kinds of material appear, not in a haphazard fashion, but in a carefully arranged order. The organization of the events located in time is, of course, obvious: it is arranged chronologically for the most part and, in those cases where events overlap, we are provided with dates to keep us straight. But notice the organization of the geographical material that tells us about Serbia's neighbors: beginning with Montenegro in the southwest, the description proceeds clockwise around the compass, ending in the south. Both organizations are clear and orderly. The most important consideration is to avoid confusion on the reader's part about just where the material is going.

Summary

This section has illustrated just a few of the methods of organizing and extending your material. All the relations between parts of sentences discussed in Sections 48 and 50 can be found in extended form between the sentences of a paragraph.

As you examine the work of skillful writers, note how often their paragraphs combine several methods of development. Try to decide, as you look at the work, just why the writer began and ended the paragraph at the places he did. Try to imagine what organization underlies the paragraphs as you analyze them. Especially when you are researching a long paper, note how writers discussing the same subject as yours organize their material.

103b TRANSITIONS

The simplest way of effecting transitions and unifying the paper at the same time is by the use of numbers; even the best writers sometimes have recourse to the method used in example 1, by Edward Hallett Carr. Carr uses ordinal numbers to set forth his points:

> 1   This searching critique, though it may call for some serious reservations, brings to light certain neglected truths.
>
> In the first place. . . .

At the end of this paragraph, Carr begins his next paragraph with the words *The second point is. . . .,* and the next paragraph with *The third point is. . . .* Certainly, the connection is clear.

Transitional statements in a theme organized chronologically can be simply stated, too:

> 2   Such, then, would be my diagnosis of the present condition of art. I must now, by special request, say what I think will happen to art in the future.
>
> KENNETH CLARK

It is not necessary, however, for a section to begin with some explicit statement of its relation to the preceding one. In fact, paragraphs beginning with such a phrase as *Our next consideration is. . . .* are the exception rather than the rule. Good writers usually have some subtler means of referring to what has gone before. In the next example, Robert Frost uses enumeration, but a covert kind of enumeration. In speaking of different kinds of belief, he defines the first in the same paragraph in which he raises the subject. But instead of the words *In the second place,* he begins the next paragraph with

> 3   There is another belief like that, the belief in someone else.

445

The phrase *another belief* connects this paragraph with the one just before. After discussing *belief in someone else,* he opens the third paragraph by writing

> 4   Then there is literary belief.

Finally, in the paragraph following the one on literary belief, he repeats and summarizes all three, relating them to the conclusion of his essay:

> 5   Now I think—I happen to think—that those three beliefs that I speak of, the self-belief, the love-belief, and the art-belief, are all closely related to the God-belief.

Frost's device for transition is the simple repetition of the word *belief,* together with words like *another* and *then.* Note how Edith Hamilton's repetition of the word *truth* effects a transition between two paragraphs and allows a contrast to be exploited at the same time:

> 6   . . . What [Thucydides] knew was truth indeed, with no shadow of turning and inexpressibly sad. But Xenophon's truths were true, too. . . .

Transitional statements, well handled, can serve a double purpose: they not only link one paragraph to the next and map changes of direction in the essay, but they can indicate what position a particular paragraph has in relation to the essay as a whole. Often, the repetition of a word or phrase connects two paragraphs. This same device, simple repetition, can clearly mark the turns of thought in the essay. William B. Willcox, in writing of the process of historical research, gives the reasons that led to his investigations of Sir Henry Clinton, British commander-in-chief during the Revolutionary War. After discussing the accessibility of materials about Clinton, he begins a new paragraph with

> 7   Another consideration strengthened the case for focusing on Clinton.

Willcox uses partial repetition to link this paragraph with the next, which discusses the general as one of the causes of the British defeat. It begins

> 8   **Clinton thus became the focus of my inquiry.**

The difficulties Willcox encountered are introduced in the next paragraph, again by using repetition to connect the part with the whole:

> 9   **Although my field of inquiry was established and its limits apparently set, I soon discovered that research can develop as unpredictably as if it had a life of its own.**

The early English printers used a device called a catchword to guide them in assembling the finished book. At the foot of each page, following the last line, was printed the first word appearing on the next page: this was the catchword. The repeated word told the printer what came next; it connected the old page with the new. In his transitions, Willcox uses a signal much like a catchword. To the old subject, Clinton, he adds mention of the new subject, his inquiry. To initiate the movement of the essay toward another facet of the topic, the problems he had not foreseen, Willcox reminds us of the subject just covered, the inquiry.

Willcox guides the reader from one paragraph to the next by changes as simple and as clearly marked as a road map. Note how new developments are signaled by linking them to a phrase from the first sentence of the preceding paragraph: *focusing on Clinton, the focus of my inquiry,* and *Although my field of inquiry.*

In summary, when making transitional statements, remember these practices:

(1) Use enumeration explicitly, connecting your paragraphs with phrases like *in the first place.*

(2) Use enumeration implicitly, linking your paragraphs with phrases like *another point* or *the next consideration.*

(3) Use repetition, either by repeating a word or a phrase from the end of one paragraph in the beginning of the next, or by repeating a word or phrase from the topic sentence to return to the main idea of your paragraph.

When you have finished rewriting for continuity, set the essay aside again.

104 THE SECOND DRAFT

104a REVISION

A writer's work can suffer from his being too close to it. After a job of writing, your essay exists both in your mind and on the paper. If you read it through immediately, checking either for sense or for mechanics, you may miss a needed correction because you unconsciously supply from your memory what is lacking on the paper. A writer needs to gain some distance from his work to turn himself into an editor, so you must remove yourself from your essay in some way. A few means of achieving this distance will be suggested in Section 104b, but the best way is to put some time between the writing and the editing, and, if possible, between one stage of the writing itself and the next.

When you take up the essay again to make the second and final draft, read through your pages, considering whether you want to add or remove any points. This is the last time you will check the structure of the essay.

After making any last-minute changes, rewrite the essay. You should still have much more material than you need, despite the loss of the sentences discarded when you set up the outline. Now cut the essay down to the five-hundred-word limit (see Section 94e for advice on eliminating phrases that mean nothing). Consider whether some sentences cannot be condensed by the conjunction transformations, or by rewriting them as outer sentences with adverbials.

As an example, consider the following paragraph: Does it sound like the way you write?

> The painting of the ancient Aztecs was divided into two primary types: the first was not really an art form, but was primarily a writing system, used for records, history, and the like. These codices, as they are properly called, range from primers concerning child care to the intricacies of ritual. These codices were intended primarily for reading, and for that reason, and for the reason that they were both religious and secular, I have considered them a different class from the symbols painted on priests' robes, decorative

motifs on buildings, and the like, which were symbolic rather than representational, and always religious in character.

The paragraph has several problems: the repetition of *prim-* in *primary, primarily,* and *primer* creates monotony. But the writer can solve that problem with a thesaurus. More serious are two problems you may share: padding, with words like *types, reason,* and *class* that add nothing but length to the paragraph; and the altogether redundant repetition of phrases (*these codices, and the like*).

We can start revising with the first sentence, as far as the colon. Although the writer tells us there are two types of Aztec art, the types remain unnamed until the last sentence. We can incorporate that information into the first sentence:

> The painting of the ancient Aztecs was divided into two primary types: either representational or symbolic.

The reader surely will not lose count with two names as short as these, so we can drop the word *two.* Nor do the words *primary types* add anything. And why do we need *divided into?* If we want to say that no Aztec art was both symbolic *and* representational, as *divided into* implies, the words *either . . . or* will show that. The sentence would now read

> The painting of the ancient Aztecs was either representational or symbolic.

The subject noun phrase thumps along, too. The *of* phrase is needless, since there is no danger of ambiguity in *ancient Aztec painting.* We can further condense, then, to

> Ancient Aztec painting was either representational or symbolic.

The facts we need to preserve from the rest of the original sentence are what the first kind of painting was and what it was not. The second sentence provides us with a term for representational paintings. Suppose we combine these, making the phrase *These codices, as they are properly called* an appositive embedded sentence. Changing the number to agree, we arrive at

> Representational paintings, which are properly called codices

WH-BE DELETION now gives us

> Representational paintings, properly called codices, were not really an art form, but were primarily a writing system.

Now think about the words *really* and *primarily:* the writer is using them nearly synonymously, and if we substitute the second for the first, we have a structure on which CONJUNCTION REDUCTION can operate:

> Representational paintings, properly called codices, were not primarily an art form, but were primarily a writing system.

Deleting everything but the conjunction between *an art form* and *a writing system* gives us

> Representational paintings, properly called codices, were not primarily an art form but a writing system.

Now consider the uses of the codices: to begin with, *primer* is used incorrectly here—a primer is a book for, not about, children. The word *records* is vague enough to mean anything (*records* of what?), so we really have only three uses listed: *history, child care,* and *the intricacies of ritual.* Obviously, these details are meant to exemplify a variety of purposes to which the paintings were put. And the details are subjects, not uses. Sorting out our changes, then, would give us something like this:

> The writing system expressed subjects. The subjects ranged from history to child care to the intricacies of ritual.

Changing the verb *ranged* in the second sentence to *ranging,* and deleting the equivalent noun phrase will cut a few more words:

> The writing system expressed subjects ranging from history to child care to the intricacies of ritual.

This too can become a relative sentence, a nonrestrictive one, if inserted immediately following *a writing system:*

> Representational paintings, properly called codices, were not primarily an art form but a writing system, which expressed subjects ranging from history to child care to the intricacies of ritual.

Just as we changed *ranged* to *ranging,* we can change *expressed* to *expressing,* provided we delete *which:*

> Representational paintings, properly called codices, were not primarily an art form but a writing system, expressing subjects ranging from history to child care to the intricacies of ritual.

As it is obvious all the way through the paragraph that the author considers representational and symbolic paintings to make up two different classes, we can remove the sentence beginning *I have considered them.* But if we are to lose no information in our revision, we need to retain the causes that led the writer to make the division:

> These codices were intended primarily for reading, and for that reason, and for the reason that they were both religious and secular

Do we really need the second reason? We have given the subject matter, at least examples of it: child care hardly seems religious, but ritual obviously is. Suppose we simply drop the second reason—it only states what our examples already demonstrate. The first reason can stand as it is. The short sentence provides a nice variation from the rather lengthy one preceding it:

> Representational paintings, properly called codices, were not primarily an art form but a writing system, expressing subjects ranging from history to child care to the intricacies of ritual. These codices were intended to be read.

The symbolic paintings contrasted with representational ones for two reasons: rather than being information-carriers, they were decorative, and they were exclusively religious in character. We would like to include the original examples, too. We can simply say they were decorative, and put the examples in an adverbial embedded sentence:

> Symbolic paintings were decorative, whether on priests' robes or on buildings.

Suppose now we have a stylistic change, moving the adverbial between the subject noun phrase and the verb phrase of the outer sentence:

> Symbolic paintings, whether on priests' robes or on buildings, were decorative. Symbolic paintings were exclusively religious in character.

Joining the sentences, and using CONJUNCTION REDUCTION on them, will give us

> Symbolic paintings, whether on priests' robes or on buildings, were decorative and exclusively religious in character.

By beginning our sentence with an adversative sentence connector—something like *but* or *on the other hand*—we can make sure that the reader does not miss the contrast between representational paintings and symbolic paintings. The whole paragraph, revised, now reads

> Ancient Aztec painting was either representational or symbolic. Representational paintings, properly called codices, were not primarily an art form but a writing system, expressing subjects ranging from history to child care to the intricacies of ritual. These codices were intended to be read. But symbolic paintings, whether on priests' robes or on buildings, were decorative and exclusively religious in character.

While retaining all the information of the original, we have cut its size from 103 words to 60. And this revision is only one of the many possible. In fact, it is not hard to see how it could be improved further. With representational paintings, we find out first their subject matter and then their purpose. We could arrange the material about symbolic paintings in that same order, revising the last sentence to read

> But symbolic paintings, whether on priests' robes or on buildings, were exclusively religious in character and intended to be decorative.

When you have finished your own revisions, your paper should be at or near the word limit set by the instructor. This is a good time to make sure you have not omitted any of the mechanical details required for the assignment: margins, footnote form and numbering, cover sheet, and so on.

This is not, however, the best time to proofread. If you can afford the time, put the paper aside for one more day. Even an hour or two, if time is precious, will help you approach the material with a fresh eye.

104b PROOFREADING

When you begin to proofread, read first to check the syntax of your sentences, making sure no inadvertent omissions or repetitions have occurred. Corral a friend to listen while you read it aloud—the act of reading will itself focus your attention on the material. When you reach a quotation, compare it carefully with your note. Check to see that beginning and ending quotation marks have not been omitted, and that you have cited the source in each case.

If you spell poorly, a second proofreading to curb this one problem alone may be the answer. Here the danger is just the reverse of that for which the first reading was designed. When checking for spelling, you want nothing to distract you from the form of the individual words. It becomes important not to get caught up in the meaning of the lines, letting the sense of the words draw your attention away from their images. To escape this snare, start at the end of the last sentence in the paper, and move to the start, examining each word in turn.

Your paper is finished now. It may not be perfect, but it should at least represent your best efforts. And ''efforts'' is the right word. Most often, writing comes hard—at least, writing that says something close to what you mean comes hard. But much of that hard work requires time, not genius; attention, not inspiration. Before you decide that the task exceeds your powers, look at the pages on pages of print all around you, and remember that the author of each of them once faced a sheet of paper as blank as the ones you began with. You can share two things, if nothing else, with even the best of those writers: a respect for your work and for your readers.

105   SAMPLE PAPERS

This final section includes samples of two short papers done in the two formats described in Sections 70 to 73. For purposes of illustration, the notes in the first paper have been cited at the foot of each page on which they occur. Your instructor may want you to group all your notes at the end of the paper. If this is the case, the section (headed "Notes") follows the last page of the text and precedes the bibliography.

Experience and Change in James Dickey's <u>Deliverance</u>

Marianne Fonville

English 112H, Section 15

Professor Charles Handler

November 13, 1973

Experience and Change in James Dickey's Deliverance

In the span of a man's life there may occur an event that will redefine his present existence and determine his future course. This experience, whether pursued or stumbled into, can provide him with insight that alters and clarifies his life. James Dickey's novel Deliverance tells of such an experience. It is the story of a single horrifying excursion down the Cahulawassee River by four ordinary, city-dwelling men. Although dismissed by at least one critic as simply a blood-and-thunder adventure story,[1] the novel is more than that. It is even more than the "modern Gothic horror story"[2] another reviewer saw, if we consider the effect of the trip on the novel's narrator, Ed Gentry.

Prior to the trip, Ed is a "get-through-the-day man."[3] Though he does appreciate the pleasure of creating, of shaping things to his will, he has never set for himself any great goal. As he puts it, "I am mainly interested in sliding. . . . Sliding is living by anti-friction. It is finding a modest thing you can do, and then greasing that thing. On both sides. It is grooving with comfort" (p. 48).

Still, Ed seems dissatisfied with this nonchalant way of life. He is aware that merely getting by is making him a prisoner. Whatever he sets out to do will have little consequence in the world. He has "a sense of being someone else, some poor fool who lives as unobserved and impotent as a ghost, going through the only motions it has" (p. 19). Possibly this is why he admires

---

[1]Benjamin DeMott, "Book Reviews," Saturday Review (28 March 1970). P. 25.

[2]Warren Eyster, "Two Regional Novels," Sewanee Review, 89 (Summer 1971). P. 39.

[3]James Dickey, Deliverance. New York: Dell, 1970. P. 39. In this paper, page numbers of all quotations from Deliverance refer to this edition.

the ability of his friend Lewis to grasp life. Lewis seems to be able to call
on primitive energies: he believes in madness, for one thing, and he is always
conscious, both in society and in individuals, of "unpredictable violence, still
only lightly papered over with urban civility."[4] Lewis represents to Ed the
human power to determine and re-create life: "He /Lewis/ was the only man I
knew determined to get something out of life who had both the means and the will
to do it" (p. 10). Lewis is physically and mentally capable of conquering,
or accomplishing his ambitions in a manner that is strictly his own. Ed admires
this ability but is, at this time, unable to achieve it himself. Consequently he
is somewhat envious of the perfect form Lewis shows in whatever he does.

Ed Gentry, at the beginning of the novel, seems incapable of redefining
and remolding his life. The first hint that the appearance is deceptive occurs
in the scene with the owl. Ed identifies with the bird as he lies in his tent
dreaming of what has been and what is yet to come. The bird sits perched on the
tent "in its own silence and equilibrium" (p. 78), hunting and finding the food that
sustains its life. Like Lewis, the bird is capable of reaching its own goals, or
(if it fails) at least of making the attempt on its own. Like Lewis, the bird
is active and assertive. Thinking about the owl, Ed "begins the process of
recognizing his bestial side,"[5] but it is only a beginning. Ed is hunting, but
hunting for the answers that will make his life meaningful: "I hunted with him
as well as I could, there in my weightlessness" (p. 79, my underlining). Ed,
by making the daring trip down the Cahulawassee, is secretly groping for something
that can explain and determine his life.

---

[4] L. E. Sissman, "Poet Into Novelist," The New Yorker (2 May 1970). P. 125.

[5] Donald J. Greiner, "The Harmony of Bestiality in James Dickey's Deliverance,"
South Carolina Review, 5 (December 1972). P. 45.

Fonville 3

Ed's consent to the trip has been his first step toward pursuing experience actively, but that step places him outside his familiar habitat. He therefore has no natural standards to base his evaluations on. "What I thought about mainly was that I was in a place where none--or almost none--of my daily ways of living my life would work; there was no habit I could call on" (p. 83). The moral code of Atlanta will not apply in this wilderness. Breaking away from the routine of his life, he finds he must use his judgment to survive on the river.

At first Ed is not physically or emotionally prepared to attempt survival in nature. It is Lewis who takes action in a crisis. Lewis is the one who so assuredly murders Bobby's abuser. When conventional morals collapse, Lewis is the one who decides the plan for burial. And Lewis alone, of all the men, is "the one who claims to believe in madness."[6] After the boats capsize, however, and Lewis is injured, Ed must take the position of leadership. Then Ed must face not only a conflict with nature and other men, but also a conflict within himself. He must prove to himself that he can conquer and survive.

Throughout the novel, Ed is continually conscious of the absurdity of an adventure that is sinister and horrifying beyond his ability to believe. After the first murder, he is unable to rationally comprehend what has happened:

It was not believable. I had never done anything like it even in my mind. To say that it was like a game would not describe exactly how it felt. I knew that it was not a game, and yet, whenever I could, I glanced at the corpse to see if it would come out of the phony trance it was in, stand up and shake hands all around (pp. 113-14).

For Ed, the ordeal is not the game Lewis tries to make it, but it is "something to be acted out" (p. 129). Even when Ed is preparing to kill his enemy, the

---

[6] Greiner, p. 45.

Fonville 4

reality of the moment is somewhat remote: "These were worthy motions I was going through, but only motions, and it was shocking to remind myself that if I came on him with the rifle I would have to carry them through or he would kill me" (p. 150).

Though Ed finds it difficult to grasp the reality of the whole adventure, he does discover the reality of savagery in the world. He had never before been aware that brutality could exist so blatantly in man. When the mountaineer tests the sharpness of a knife against Ed's chest, Ed is more concerned with the indifference of the act than with the pain it causes:

> I had never felt such brutality and carelessness of touch, or such
>
> disregard for another person's body. It was not the steel or the
>
> edge of the steel that was frightening; the man's fingernail, used
>
> in any gesture of his, would have been just as brutal; the knife
>
> only magnified his unconcern (p. 98).

As the story progresses, Ed's own brutality becomes apparent. He is fully able to plan and carry through the assassination of a fellow human being. When the man is dead, Ed feels an animal savagery similar to the one that the mountaineer showed: "I took the knife in my fist. . . . It is not ever going to be known; you can do what you want to; nothing is too terrible. . . . I can do anything I have a wish to do" (p. 170). Through Ed's thoughts we make the same discovery he does; we find out "that each of us harbors in the deepest recesses of himself an unknown part which we are afraid to face because we might be forced to acknowledge our own brutality."[7]

Ed sees his own bestiality, but perhaps part of the reason he retains our sympathy is this: he does <u>not</u> do "anything /he has⧸ a wish to do," but only those things he is compelled to do. He is locked in a situation not of

---

[7]Greiner, p. 44.

Fonville 5

his own making. Dickey himself made this point about the novel in an
interview: "There are men in those remote parts that'd just as soon kill
you as look at you. And you could turn into a counter-monster yourself,
doing whatever you felt compelled to do to survive."[8]

   The steps Ed takes to survive, no matter how brutal or unbelievable
they seem to him, all lead to some alteration in his character. Ed's climb
up the cliff sharply demonstrates the gradual change that has taken place.
He crawls painfully and intimately up the bluff, groping wildly for each
handhold, but when he finally reaches the top, he is able to look back over
the river and see the beauty and meaning of his battle. He has measured
himself against a violent and demanding world, and come out ahead. As Calvin
Bedient points out, referring specifically to the climb, Ed is "only so
much as he fights against for his life. . . . The gift of danger is thus the
sudden empowerment of the soul."[9] He has climbed from his old way of looking
at things into a new realm of understanding. Afterwards, this new vision of
life is prominent in almost everything he does. "The river underlies, in
one way or another, everything I do. It is always finding a way to serve me,
from my archery to some of my recent ads and to the collages I have been
attempting for my friends" (p. 235). Ed is no longer the same person. Now
his life holds meaning and purpose.

   Ed's experience redefines the relationship he has with other people.
He no longer feels inferior to Lewis. He learns from confrontation that he
too has the power to conquer. Ironically, it is Ed who actually lives
Lewis' dreams of survival. As Lewis had put it before the trip, "survival

---

[8]Quoted in Paul Edward Gray, "New Books in Review," Yale Review, 60
(Autumn 1970). P. 105.

[9]"Gold-Glowing Mote," Nation (6 April 1970). P. 408.

depends--well, it depends on _having_ to survive. The kind of life I'm

talking about depends on its being the last chance. The very last of all"

(p. 42). For Ed, stalking and finally murdering the mountaineer is the last

chance at survival, to be sure, but it is a chance at something more.

When Ed first had agreed to make the trip, he had seen that it held

the possibility of something more than just Lewis' kind of survival. It

held "the promise . . . that promised other things, another life, deliverance"

(p. 30). By taking part in Lewis' dream and carrying it beyond mere physical

endurance, Ed finds a new kind of freedom.[10] As Hawthorne says in _The Marble_

Faun, the "result of a broken law is ever an ecstatic sense of freedom."[11]

Ed, by strategically planning and executing the murder of his enemy, has

escaped from many things into a special freedom that changes his life. He

has escaped from the captivity he felt in his job, from his envy of Lewis,

from the murderous mountaineer. Finally, in eluding death itself, he has

escaped, "through courage and cunning, from the most violent, indifferent,

lustful, relentless, and incomprehensible redneck of them all."[12]

---

[10]Ed's feeling of freedom is the strongest argument against the

interpretation of Peter G. Beidler, "'The Pride of Thine Heart Hath

Deceived Thee': Narrative Distortion in Dickey's _Deliverance_," _South

Carolina Review_, 5 (December 1972). Pp. 29-40.

[11]_The Portable Hawthorne_, ed. Malcolm Cowley. New York: Viking Press,

1948. P. 587.

[12]Bedient, p. 408.

Fonville 7

Bibliography

Bedient, Calvin, "Gold-Glowing Mote," <u>Nation</u> (6 April 1970). Pp. 407-08.

Beidler, Peter G., "'The Pride of Thine Heart Hath Deceived Thee':

   Narrative Distortion in Dickey's <u>Deliverance</u>," <u>South Carolina Review</u>,

   5 (December 1972). Pp. 29-40.

DeMott, Benjamin, "Book Reviews," <u>Saturday Review</u> (28 March 1970). P. 25.

Dickey, James, <u>Deliverance</u>. New York: Dell, 1970.

Eyster, Warren, "Two Regional Novels," <u>Sewanee Review</u>, 89 (Summer 1971). Pp. 469-72.

Gray, Paul Edward, "New Books in Review," <u>Yale Review</u>, 60 (Autumn 1970). Pp. 101-08.

Greiner, Donald J., "The Harmony of Bestiality in James Dickey's <u>Deliverance</u>,"

   <u>South Carolina Review</u>, 5 (December 1972). Pp. 43-49.

Hawthorne, Nathaniel, <u>The Marble Faun</u>, in <u>The Portable Hawthorne</u>, ed.

   Malcolm Cowley. New York: Viking Press, 1948.

Sissman, L. E., "Poet Into Novelist," <u>The New Yorker</u> (2 May 1970).

   Pp. 123-26.

Noise Pollution: More Than a Nuisance

Asa M. Manning

English 112H, Section 11

Professor Carol Berkowitz

May 23, 1973

Manning 1

Noise Pollution: More Than a Nuisance

Man has not always lived in a noisy environment. In fact, only in the past three decades has noise become a major concern in our lives. In 1950, our cities were 35 times noisier than they were in 1850 (Sickle, p. 262). The tremendous increase in urban population is partly responsible for the increase in noise, but noise in our cities still climbs steadily at an alarming rate. Yet man has never liked even small amounts of noise. Its undesirability was realized when the word was coined: noise is from the Latin nausea, meaning "sickness." Noise can be defined as any unwanted sound, and whether it be static on a radio or the roar of a truck, noise is far more dangerous than most people believe.

Sounds, wanted or unwanted, travel in waves of various cycles and frequencies. The human ear can sense frequencies from 20 cycles per second to about 20,000 cps (Denes, p. 103). Sounds below and above these frequencies are known as infrasound and ultrasound, respectively. The unit of measurement of intensity of sound is the decibel (dB), defined as the smallest sound the human ear can hear. As examples, we can measure the decibel levels of some familiar sounds as follows:

Barely perceptible sound	0 dB
Average whisper at four feet	20 dB
Night noises in a city	40 dB
Normal conversation at three feet	60-70 dB
Pneumatic drill at ten feet	90 dB
Hammering on a steel plate at two feet	115 dB

(Denes, pp. 103-04)

Manning 2

Noise affects both our emotional and our physiological health. The emotional effects are partly the result of man's evolution; we have learned through millions of years to treat noise as a warning of impending danger. Noise acts, therefore, as a "powerful stimulant bringing us to an extraordinary level of alertness" (Sickle, p. 261). This stimulation causes stress, and when the environment is constantly noisy, we are constantly under stress.

A survey of London residents in 1961 and 1962 revealed that 97 percent of the people questioned noticed noise while at home, and, of these people, 56 percent were disturbed by the noise (Burns, p. 103). Stress from noise cannot cause a well-adjusted person to have abnormal reactions, but noise can act as a trigger for people already under stress from everyday worries. The trauma that can result is often extreme enough to force a person into irrational acts. The London survey seems significant if we consider that a fair portion of those disturbed by noise stands a chance of being under other pressures.

A more common result of noise is the reduction in efficiency of workers distracted by it. For example, when the Aetna Life Insurance Company installed acoustical wallboard in its offices, lowering the noise level by 14.5 percent, typists' errors went down 29 percent, machine operators' errors went down 52 percent, employee turnover decreased 47 percent, and absenteeism decreased 27 percent (Time, p. 29). The typical "tired mother syndrome"--irritability, depression, fatigue, and tension--is thought to be associated with kitchen noises (Sickle, p. 265). Of the many appliances there, most operate at or above 70 dB.

And noise can get you between work and home: Dr. Joseph Buckley developed a "stress vault," in which rats were jiggled, subjected to bright flashes of light, and exposed to sudden loud noises, to simulate a subway train. After a while, the rats became irritable and even dangerous to handle. "The irritability of New York subway riders is well-known" (Sickle, p. 264).

The worst emotional effect of noise may be what it does to us as we sleep. It has been shown that noise not loud enough to awaken the subject causes changes in the brain waves. Noises that do awaken a sleeper often make him too irritable to resume his sleep. Both these kinds of noise disrupt the sleep- and dream-cycles necessary for mental health. One can even awaken in the morning tired from the struggle to overcome noise (Bailey, p. 46). A quiet night's sleep is getting harder to find, although, with our increasing problems, we need it more.

The effects noise has on our physiological health are more direct. In the early 1960s, Dr. Gerd Jansen of Dortmund, Germany, studied factory workers over a two-year period and exposed them to "bursts of sudden, unpredictable noise at varying sound levels for periods of from one-half second to ninety minutes" (Gordon, p. 188). He found that the autonomic nervous system began to react at 70 dB. These reactions included constricted blood vessels, shrinking lymph nodes, pale skin, dilated pupils, increased heartbeat, wincing, suspension of breath, tensing of muscles, and spasms in the esophagus, stomach, and intestines. The reactions often lasted five times as long as the noise (Sickle, p. 264), were directly related to the volume of noise, and were unaffected by the subject's health, by whether the noise annoyed him, or by whether he had become accustomed to it (Gordon, p. 188).

The effect of noise on the heart can be long lasting, and compounded by continuous exposure to noise. Rabbits exposed to noises of 102 dB for ten weeks had a higher level of cholesterol than the control subjects, and clogging and hardening of the aorta had increased (Still, p. 192). These effects also occur in humans, and all lead to heart attacks.

Noise is associated with other illnesses and diseases. It is believed that noise alters the hormonal balance of the nervous system, disrupting the body's metabolism and increasing susceptibility to disease. This hypothesis is confirmed by the observation that airline mechanics are plagued with diarrhea, nausea, and the presence of air in the bags containing the lungs (Sickle, p. 264). Noise is also linked to hypertension, hallucinations, stomach ulcers, allergies, loss of equilibrium, and impaired vision. Research on animals has shown that rats become infertile, homosexual, and cannibalistic after continuous exposure to noise. High-level sound--165 dB--kills cats (Sickle, p. 265).

In a unique experiment on fetuses, Dr. Lester W. Sonntag investigated their sensitivity to noise. He found that in the final three months of pregnancy, any sudden noise (such as a clap) caused the fetus to stir. A sonic boom caused convulsions (Sickle, p. 265).

The most devastating effect of loud noises is the damage they inflict on our ears. The increasing noise level seems to have caught even nature off guard, for she has given man no way to adapt to excessive noise. The only "protection" we have is the destruction of parts of the ear and gradual deafness. Dr. Jansen and Dr. Samuel Rosen tested tribesmen of the Sudan, who live in one of the quietest places on earth, and found no signs of "hypertension, heart disease, or hearing loss even in the elderly" (Gordon, p. 188). Yet when exposed to taped noises of a German factory, the Sudanese had reactions no greater than those of the Germans who lived with the noise daily.

Continuous loud noise damages the cochlear cells of the ear, which function in transmitting sound impulses to the brain. In an environment simulating a discotheque, Dr. David Lipscomb exposed guinea pigs to 88 hours of 120 dB sound. The cochlear cells shriveled like peas (Sickle, p. 263). Similar damage in humans begins at sounds above 90 dB. A noise of 100 dB can be tolerated for only 20 minutes before panic begins (Sickle, p. 263). Actual pain begins at 120 dB, and death occurs at 180 dB. The most dangerous noise is "loud, meaningless, irregular, and unpredictable" (Gordon, p. 188). The intensity of the noise, the length of exposure, and the susceptibility of the subject are directly related to the damage inflicted.

Damage to our ears is already present in the form of partial deafness. At present, 18 million Americans suffer from hearing loss. Another 34 million are exposed to dangerous noise levels daily. Of these people, 50 percent will experience irreversible hearing loss (Gordon, p. 188). Yet noise-induced deafness is not limited to industry. The younger generation is deafening itself with loud music. Some discotheques have been measured at 122 dB, demonstrating why many musicians have periods of temporary deafness. In an investigation of schoolchildren in Knoxville, Tennessee, 11 percent of the high school seniors had permanent hearing loss. The problem was summed up by the director of the investigation this way: "Essentially the aging process accelerates so that twenty year olds have sixty year old ears" (Still, p. 49).

The damage inflicted by ultrasound and infrasound is harder to pinpoint because the sources cannot be detected by the human ear. Infrasound at 7 dB causes lack of straight thinking; stronger infrasound causes "body tissues such as eyes and internal organs to vibrate with it; turning it

up even more leads to headaches, nausea, internal hemorrhaging, and death"
(Sickle, p. 266). Damage to the inner ear can be extensive. Ultrasound
causes virtually the same damage. In an English factory, the workers
complained of nausea, fatigue, and headaches. The noise level was measured
at an acceptable 76 dB. But when the machinery was studied further, intense
ultrasound was detected. When the problem was corrected, the symptoms
ceased (Gordon, p. 192).

The solutions to noise pollution are available. The engineering
ability that produced all the noisy machinery can, if required, make it
quiet. Many pieces of equipment, from quiet garbage trucks to quiet outboard
motors, are already available. Yet the American public must be willing
to pay for quiet. We need a change of attitude, too: housewives,
teenagers, and industrialists must stop associating noise with power--
we should associate it with pain, disease, and deafness.

One science-fiction writer tells of a future time when only his
central character can hear; he describes the conditions that made him flee
to the country:

> The roar of the spacebound rockets, the incessant chatter of
> the helicars; the grinding, crunching, exploding din of earthshifting
> equipment, the whining ultrasonics of the turbine-borne traffic.
>
> You can't imagine it, I know.
>
> Back in the twentieth century they would have known what I was
> talking about, before the coming of telepathy, which rendered the
> sense of hearing unnecessary. A now obsolete sense which was
> nevertheless a constant source of pain, because of the unbearable
> clangor of everyday life. Until gradually, mercifully, that
> sense was lost (Coney, p. 196).

Manning 7

But we cannot depend on developing telepathic abilities. We must
take action now to let people know that noise is more than a nuisance,
and we must be willing to sacrifice some prestige in order to achieve
our ends. As a well-informed noise-hater once said, "Ironically, all
that is needed to put the new noise controls into effect is a scream--
from well-placed individuals and the public" (Bailey, p. 132). But
it should be added that the time to scream is now, or there might be no one
who can hear you.

Manning 8

Bibliography

Bailey, Anthony. 1969. "'Noise Is a Slow Agent of Death,'" The New York

   Times Magazine. 23November: 46-47, 131-32.

Burns, William. 1968. Noise and Man. London: William Clowes and Sons.

Coney, Michael G. 1970. "Sixth Sense," World's Best Science Fiction: 1970, ed.

   Donald A. Wollheim and Terry Carr. New York: Ace Publishing.

Denes, Peter B., and Elliot N. Pinson. 1963. The Speech Chain.

   Garden City, N.Y.: Doubleday Anchor Books.

Gordon, James S. 1970. "We're Poisoning Ourselves with Noise," Reader's

   Digest. February:187-94.

Sickle, Dirck V. 1971. The Ecological Citizen. New York: Harper & Row.

Still, Henry. 1970. In Quest of Quiet. Harrisburg, Pa.: Stackpole Books.

Time. 1961. "Noise Haters." 2January: 29. Cited in this paper as Time.

Index

B

C

D

G

H

J

K

L

M

N

O

P

U

Y

A 4
B 5
C 6
D 7
E 8
F 9
G 0
H 1
I 2
J 3

A Grammar of English

Applications to Writing